# はじめに

　本書は，発行累計20万部超の大ベストセラー『はじめての新TOEIC®テスト本番模試』（模試2回分）の改訂版です。2016年5月29日実施の公開テストからTOEIC（Test of English for International Communication）の出題形式が一部変更されました。主な新形式の問題は，Part 3と4の「図表を使った問題」や「表現の意図を問う問題」，Part 6の「適する文を選ぶ問題」，Part 7の「テキストメッセージなどのやり取り」，「表現の意図を問う問題」，「文が入る適切な位置を選ぶ問題」，そして「トリプル・パッセージ（3つの関連する文書）」です。問題形式以外では，例えばPart 3では，3名による会話や，やり取りの多い会話が加わり，Haven't you heard? — Heard what? のような，短い応答が含まれるようになったことが特徴です。これはとてもよい変化です。より実践的な会話を学ぶことで，TOEIC®で高スコアを取るだけが目的ではなく，英語学習自体が楽しくなることが期待されます。本書は，これらの変更点を含め，最新のTOEIC®の傾向に合うよう，問題の差し替えや全体的な見直しを行いました。また，著者が実際に新傾向の公開テストを受験した際の印象や問題傾向も随所に反映しています。

　本書は，好評既刊の『TOEIC®テスト予想模試 新形式問題対応』（模試1回分）と『スコアが上がる新TOEIC®テスト本番模試600問』（模試3回分）との3本立ての模試シリーズとして生まれ変わりました。他書2冊と同等のクオリティーを維持すべく，念入りに設問を練り，端的でわかりやすい解説を施しました。問題を解き終わったら，不正解だった問題だけでなく正解した問題の解説もていねいに読んでください。というのも，①「自信があって正解」②「あまり自信はなかったが正解」③「当てずっぽうで答えて正解」では状況が全く異なるからです。それぞれの問題に「自信ランク」をつけて，日本語訳や解説を読んだり何度も解いたりして，1冊を徹底的に使いこなしましょう。また，模試2回分を有効に使って，自分のレベルを確かめたり，苦手なパートや分野を見極めたり，各パートの問題を解く時間配分を決めるなど，いろいろな方法で活用していただければと思います。さらに，とじ込みの「特別冊子」には，確実に点を稼げるテクニックが満載の「即効！スコアアップ虎の巻」と，TOEIC初級者の壁となるビジネス用語のうち最頻出のものを網羅した「重要ビジネスワード200」を掲載しています。特に「虎の巻」は新傾向の問題に関する情報が満載です。取り外しができますので，重要ポイントや苦手な文法，覚えにくい単語・表現などを自由に書き込み，試験直前に携帯したり当日持参したりして，最大限にご活用ください。

　最後になりましたが，いつもTOEIC®の模試本で貴重な執筆の機会をくださる関西外国語大学短期大学部の宮野智靖教授，そして株式会社旺文社の編集部の皆様に，この場を借りて心より感謝いたします。

2016年9月

著者　入江　泉

※本書中のTOEIC®テストは，TOEIC® LISTENING AND READINGテストを指します。
※本書は2009年9月に刊行された『はじめての新TOEIC®テスト本番模試』に，2016年5月から導入された新形式問題への対策を加え，加筆・修正したものです。

# CONTENTS

## もくじ

| | |
|---|---|
| はじめに …………………… 1 | Directions の日本語訳 …… 9 |
| 本書の構成と特長 ………… 3 | 予想スコア換算表 ………… 10 |
| TOEIC® テストについて … 4 | 付属 CD について ………… 12 |
| TOEIC® テストインフォメーション‥ 6 | |

### 第1回　模擬試験

| | |
|---|---|
| PART 1 | 14 |
| PART 2 | 18 |
| PART 3 | 19 |
| PART 4 | 23 |
| PART 5 | 26 |
| PART 6 | 29 |
| PART 7 | 33 |

### 第2回　模擬試験

| | |
|---|---|
| PART 1 | 56 |
| PART 2 | 60 |
| PART 3 | 61 |
| PART 4 | 65 |
| PART 5 | 68 |
| PART 6 | 71 |
| PART 7 | 75 |

| 別冊<br>（解答・解説編）<br>のもくじ | 第1回　模擬試験　解答一覧 …………… 3 |
|---|---|
| | 第1回　模擬試験　解答・解説 …………… 4 |
| | 第2回　模擬試験　解答一覧 ………… 71 |
| | 第2回　模擬試験　解答・解説 ……… 72 |

編集協力：株式会社シー・レップス，株式会社鷗来堂，斉藤　敦
問題作成協力：株式会社 CPI Japan, Joel Rian, Kumiko Nishiguchi
英文校閲：Nadia McKechnie, Kaori Naito Church
装丁デザイン：牧野剛士　本文デザイン：アチワデザイン室（前田由美子），尾引美代
写真：© iStockphoto.com　録音：ユニバ合同会社

# 本書の構成と特長

本書は以下の要素で構成されています。

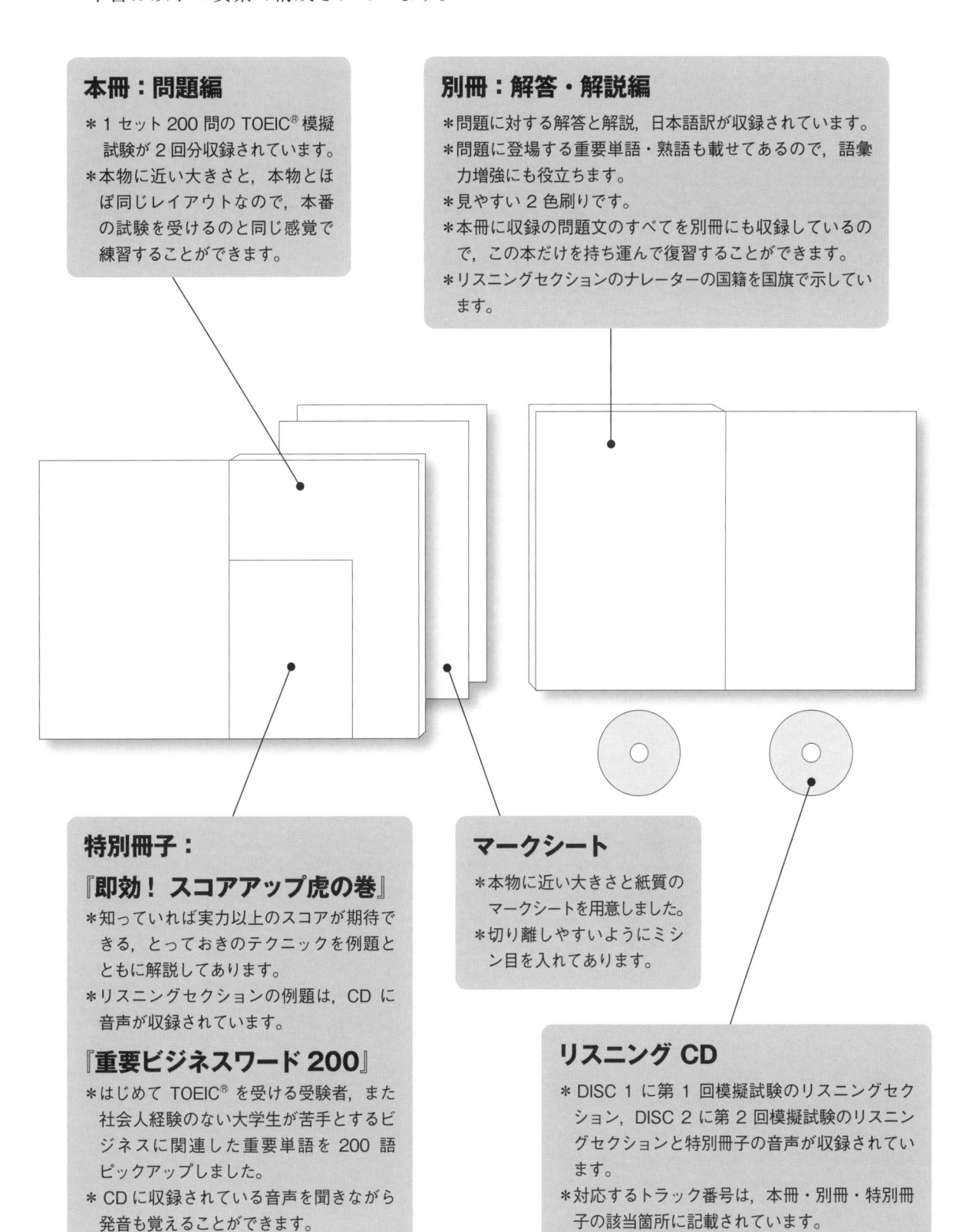

### 本冊：問題編
* 1セット200問のTOEIC®模擬試験が2回分収録されています。
* 本物に近い大きさと，本物とほぼ同じレイアウトなので，本番の試験を受けるのと同じ感覚で練習することができます。

### 別冊：解答・解説編
* 問題に対する解答と解説，日本語訳が収録されています。
* 問題に登場する重要単語・熟語も載せてあるので，語彙力増強にも役立ちます。
* 見やすい2色刷りです。
* 本冊に収録の問題文のすべてを別冊にも収録しているので，この本だけを持ち運んで復習することができます。
* リスニングセクションのナレーターの国籍を国旗で示しています。

### 特別冊子：
### 『即効！スコアアップ虎の巻』
* 知っていれば実力以上のスコアが期待できる，とっておきのテクニックを例題とともに解説してあります。
* リスニングセクションの例題は，CDに音声が収録されています。

### 『重要ビジネスワード200』
* はじめてTOEIC®を受ける受験者，また社会人経験のない大学生が苦手とするビジネスに関連した重要単語を200語ピックアップしました。
* CDに収録されている音声を聞きながら発音も覚えることができます。

### マークシート
* 本物に近い大きさと紙質のマークシートを用意しました。
* 切り離しやすいようにミシン目を入れてあります。

### リスニングCD
* DISC 1に第1回模擬試験のリスニングセクション，DISC 2に第2回模擬試験のリスニングセクションと特別冊子の音声が収録されています。
* 対応するトラック番号は，本冊・別冊・特別冊子の該当箇所に記載されています。
* また，12ページの「付属CDについて」でも内容を確認できます。

# TOEIC® テストについて

※ 2016 年 9 月現在の情報です。

## TOEIC® テストとは？

　TOEIC とは，Test of English for International Communication の略で，アメリカにあるテスト開発機関 ETS（Educational Testing Service）により開発された，英語によるコミュニケーション能力を幅広く評価する世界共通のテストです。世界各国の学校・企業・団体で，さまざまな目的で活用されており，日本でも大学の単位認定や推薦入試の基準，企業での昇進・昇格の要件などとして採用されています。

　受験者の能力は合格・不合格ではなく，10 ～ 990 点のスコアで評価するのが特徴で，解答はすべてマークシートに記入する客観方式をとっています。試験は指示文を含めてすべて英語で行われます。

## TOEIC® テストの構成

　TOEIC は以下のパートで構成されています。（合計 2 時間／ 200 問）

|  | Part | 内容 | 問題数 |
| --- | --- | --- | --- |
| リスニングセクション（約 45 分間／ 100 問） | 1 | 写真描写問題 | 6 |
|  | 2 | 応答問題 | 25 |
|  | 3 | 会話問題 | 39（13 会話× 3 設問） |
|  | 4 | 説明文問題 | 30（10 トーク× 3 設問） |
| リーディングセクション（75 分間／ 100 問） | 5 | 短文穴埋め問題 | 30 |
|  | 6 | 長文穴埋め問題 | 16（4 長文× 4 設問） |
|  | 7 | 読解問題<br>・1 つの文書<br>・複数の文書 | 29<br>25 |

# 各 Part のくわしい内容は？

| | |
|---|---|
| **Part 1**<br>**写真描写問題** | 4つの短い説明文を聞き，その中から，問題用紙に印刷された写真を最も的確に描写しているものを選ぶ問題です。説明文は1度だけ放送され，問題用紙には印刷されていません。 |
| **Part 2**<br>**応答問題** | 1つの質問または文に対し，3つの応答が1度だけ放送されます。質問または文に対し最もふさわしい応答をその中から選びます。質問または文も応答も問題用紙には印刷されていません。 |
| **Part 3**<br>**会話問題** | 2人もしくは3人の会話文を聞き，その内容に関する3つの設問に答える問題です。設問の質問文と答えの選択肢は問題用紙に印刷されており，質問文は会話文の後に放送されます。会話文も設問の質問文も1度しか放送されません。 |
| **Part 4**<br>**説明文問題** | アナウンスやナレーションといった説明文（トーク）を聞いて，その内容に関する3つの設問に答える問題です。Part 3と同様，設問の質問文も放送されます。説明文も設問の質問文も1度しか放送されません。 |
| **Part 5**<br>**短文穴埋め問題** | 不完全な文を完成させるのに最もふさわしいものを，4つの選択肢の中から選ぶ問題です。1問につき1カ所の不完全な部分（空所）があります。 |
| **Part 6**<br>**長文穴埋め問題** | 不完全な文書を完成させるのに最もふさわしいものを，4つの選択肢の中から選ぶ問題です。1つの文書につき4カ所の不完全な部分（空所）があります。 |
| **Part 7**<br>**読解問題** | さまざまな文書を読み，その内容に関する設問に答える問題です。1つの文書を読んで解答する問題，2つの文書を読んで解答する問題，3つの文書を読んで解答する問題の3つのパターンがあります。 |

# TOEIC® テストインフォメーション

## 受験料

公式サイトをご覧ください。

## 受験の流れ

約1週間前　　受験票到着

【当日】
受付
試験の説明・音テスト
試験開始～試験終了
問題用紙・解答用紙の回収
解散

【当日の持ち物】
☐受験票
☐証明写真1枚（受験票に貼付）
　規定のもの。サイズは縦4cm×横3cm。
☐公的に自己を証明する写真付の本人確認書類（有効期限内のもの）
　運転免許証・学生証・パスポート・マイナンバーカード・住民基本台帳カードなど
☐筆記用具
　鉛筆（またはシャープペンシル），消しゴム
☐腕時計
　腕時計以外のもの（携帯電話・置時計・ストップウォッチなど）は時計として使用できません。

【禁止事項】
・問題用紙やその他資材への書き込みは禁止されています。
・試験教室からの問題用紙や解答用紙の持ち出し，また問題内容を漏えいする行為は禁止されています。
・リスニングテスト中にリーディングセクションの問題文を見ること，またその逆も禁止されています。

## テスト結果の通知

受験者には試験終了後 30 日以内に，スコアなどが記載された Official Score Certificate（公式認定証）が送付されます。また，公式認定証の海外への発送や再発行も可能です。

[お問い合わせ先]
(一財) 国際ビジネスコミュニケーション協会
● IIBC 試験運営センター
電話：03-5521-6033
● 公式サイト
https://www.iibc-global.org

※このページの情報は 2024 年 6 月現在のものです。詳細や変更は実施団体の公式サイトなどでご確認ください。

# TOEIC® のスコアと能力レベルの関係は？

## PROFICIENCY SCALE
― TOEIC® スコアとコミュニケーション能力レベルとの相関表 ―

| レベル | TOEIC® スコア | 評価（ガイドライン） |
|---|---|---|
| A | 860〜 | **Non-Native として十分なコミュニケーションができる。**<br>自己の経験の範囲内では，専門外の分野の話題に対しても十分な理解とふさわしい表現ができる。<br>Native Speaker の域には一歩隔たりがあるとはいえ，語彙・文法・構文のいずれをも正確に把握し，流暢に駆使する力を持っている。 |
| B | 730〜 | **どんな状況でも適切なコミュニケーションができる素地を備えている。**<br>通常会話は完全に理解でき，応答もはやい。話題が特定分野にわたっても，対応できる力を持っている。業務上も大きな支障はない。<br>正確さと流暢さに個人差があり，文法・構文上の誤りが見受けられる場合もあるが，意思疎通を妨げるほどではない。 |
| C | 470〜 | **日常生活のニーズを充足し，限定された範囲内では業務上のコミュニケーションができる。**<br>通常会話であれば，要点を理解し，応答にも支障はない。複雑な場面における的確な対応や意思疎通になると，巧拙の差が見られる。<br>基本的な文法・構文は身についており，表現力の不足はあっても，ともかく自己の意思を伝える語彙を備えている。 |
| D | 220〜 | **通常会話で最低限のコミュニケーションができる。**<br>ゆっくり話してもらうか，繰り返しや言い換えをしてもらえば，簡単な会話は理解できる。身近な話題であれば応答も可能である。<br>語彙・文法・構文ともに不十分なところは多いが，相手が Non-Native に特別な配慮をしてくれる場合には，意思疎通をはかることができる。 |
| E | 〜220 | **コミュニケーションができるまでに至っていない。**<br>単純な会話をゆっくり話してもらっても，部分的にしか理解できない。<br>断片的に単語を並べる程度で，実質的な意思疎通の役には立たない。 |

資料提供：（一財）国際ビジネスコミュニケーション協会

# SPEAKING AND WRITING テスト／IP テストとは？

　TOEIC® にはスピーキングとライティングのテストもあります。リスニング／リーディングとは別に実施されます。申し込み方法や試験日程などは，公式サイトを参照してください。また，個人受験ではなく，企業・団体で申し込み，試験会場と日程を任意に設定できる IP テスト（団体特別受験制度）もあります。

# Directions の日本語訳

TOEIC®では各 PART についての指示（Directions）はすべて英語で行われます。以下にそれぞれの Directions の日本語訳を掲載しますので，事前に内容を把握しておきましょう。（訳は旺文社作成）

## リスニングテスト

リスニングテストでは，話される英語をどの程度理解できるかを示すよう求められます。リスニングテスト全体の時間はおよそ 45 分 です。4 つの Part があり，各 Part で指示が与えられます。解答は別紙の解答用紙に記入しなければなりません。問題用紙に解答を書いてはいけません。

### ■ PART 1 の指示文

この Part では各設問で，問題用紙にある写真についての 4 つの説明文を聞きます。説明文が聞こえたら，写真に見えているものを最もよく描写している説明文を 1 つ選んでください。そして解答用紙の該当する設問番号のところに解答をマークしてください。説明文は問題用紙には印刷されておらず，一度しか読まれません。

下の例題を見てください。
次に 4 つの説明文を聞いてください。
　(A) 彼女たちは家具を動かしています。
　(B) 彼女たちは会議室に入ろうとしています。
　(C) 彼女たちはテーブルの所に座っています。
　(D) 彼女たちはカーペットを掃除しています。
説明文 (C)「彼女たちはテーブルの所に座っています」が写真を最もよく描写しているので，(C) を選び解答用紙にマークします。

では，Part 1 を始めます。

### ■ PART 2 の指示文

英語で話されている質問または文と，3 つの応答を聞きます。質問または文と応答は問題用紙には印刷されておらず，一度しか読まれません。質問または文に最もふさわしい応答を選び，解答用紙の (A), (B), (C) のうち 1 つをマークしてください。

### ■ PART 3 の指示文

2 人以上の人物の間で交わされる会話を聞きます。それぞれの会話で話し手が話す内容に関する 3 つの設問に答えてください。それぞれの設問に最もふさわしい解答を選び，解答用紙の (A), (B), (C), (D) のうち 1 つをマークしてください。会話は問題用紙には印刷されておらず，一度しか読まれません。

### ■ PART 4 の指示文

1 人の話し手によるトークを聞きます。それぞれのトークで話し手が話す内容に関する 3 つの設問に答えてください。それぞれの設問に最もふさわしい解答を選び，解答用紙の (A), (B), (C), (D) のうち 1 つをマークしてください。トークは問題用紙には印刷されておらず，一度しか読まれません。

## リーディングテスト

リーディングテストではさまざまな種類の文を読んで，読解力を測るいろいろな質問に答えます。リーディングテスト全体の時間は 75 分です。3 つの Part があり，各 Part で指示が与えられます。与えられた時間の中でできるだけたくさんの質問に答えてください。
解答は別紙の解答用紙に記入しなければなりません。問題用紙に解答を書いてはいけません。

### ■ PART 5 の指示文

以下のそれぞれの文には，語（句）が抜けています。それぞれの文の下に，4 つの選択肢が与えられています。文を完成させるのに最もふさわしい解答を選び，解答用紙の (A), (B), (C), (D) のうち 1 つをマークしてください。

### ■ PART 6 の指示文

以下の文書を読んでください。各文書の中で，語（句）または 1 文が抜けています。その文書の下にそれぞれの空所に対する 4 つの選択肢が与えられています。文書を完成させるのに最もふさわしい解答を選び，解答用紙の (A), (B), (C), (D) のうち 1 つをマークしてください。

### ■ PART 7 の指示文

この Part では，雑誌や新聞の記事，E メール，インスタントメッセージなどの文書を読みます。それぞれの文書あるいは一連の文書の後にいくつかの設問が続きます。それぞれの設問に最もふさわしい解答を選び，解答用紙の (A), (B), (C), (D) のうち 1 つをマークしてください。

Copyright © 2015 Educational Testing Service. www.ets.org *Updated Listening and Reading Directions for the TOEIC® Test* are reprinted by permission of Educational Testing Service, the copyright owner. All other information contained within this publication is provided by Obunsha Co., Ltd. and no endorsement of any kind by Educational Testing Service should be inferred.

# 予想スコア換算表

　模擬試験の答え合わせを終えたら，下の表を参考に，正解数をスコアに換算して，予想スコアを出してみましょう。

　この表は，旺文社が独自に作成したものであり，実際の TOEIC® テストのスコア算出方法とは異なりますので，あくまで現在の実力を推し量る目安としてください。

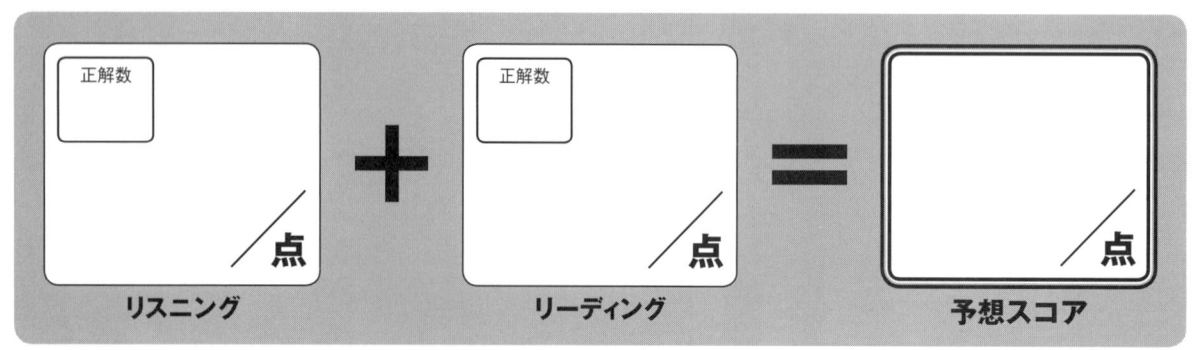

## 第1回模擬試験

### リスニング

| 正解数 | 予想スコア | 正解数 | 予想スコア | 正解数 | 予想スコア |
|---|---|---|---|---|---|
| 100 | 495 | 69 | 390 | 38 | 235 |
| 99 | 495 | 68 | 385 | 37 | 230 |
| 98 | 495 | 67 | 380 | 36 | 225 |
| 97 | 495 | 66 | 375 | 35 | 220 |
| 96 | 495 | 65 | 370 | 34 | 215 |
| 95 | 490 | 64 | 365 | 33 | 210 |
| 94 | 490 | 63 | 360 | 32 | 205 |
| 93 | 490 | 62 | 355 | 31 | 200 |
| 92 | 485 | 61 | 350 | 30 | 195 |
| 91 | 485 | 60 | 345 | 29 | 190 |
| 90 | 480 | 59 | 340 | 28 | 185 |
| 89 | 480 | 58 | 335 | 27 | 180 |
| 88 | 475 | 57 | 330 | 26 | 175 |
| 87 | 475 | 56 | 325 | 25 | 170 |
| 86 | 470 | 55 | 320 | 24 | 165 |
| 85 | 470 | 54 | 315 | 23 | 160 |
| 84 | 465 | 53 | 310 | 22 | 155 |
| 83 | 460 | 52 | 305 | 21 | 150 |
| 82 | 455 | 51 | 300 | 20 | 145 |
| 81 | 450 | 50 | 295 | 19 | 140 |
| 80 | 445 | 49 | 290 | 18 | 135 |
| 79 | 440 | 48 | 285 | 17 | 130 |
| 78 | 435 | 47 | 280 | 16 | 125 |
| 77 | 430 | 46 | 275 | 15 | 120 |
| 76 | 425 | 45 | 270 | 14 | 115 |
| 75 | 420 | 44 | 265 | 13 | 110 |
| 74 | 415 | 43 | 260 | 12 | 105 |
| 73 | 410 | 42 | 255 | 11 | 100 |
| 72 | 405 | 41 | 250 | 〜10 | 測定不能 |
| 71 | 400 | 40 | 245 | | |
| 70 | 395 | 39 | 240 | | |

### リーディング

| 正解数 | 予想スコア | 正解数 | 予想スコア | 正解数 | 予想スコア |
|---|---|---|---|---|---|
| 100 | 495 | 69 | 385 | 38 | 230 |
| 99 | 495 | 68 | 380 | 37 | 225 |
| 98 | 490 | 67 | 375 | 36 | 220 |
| 97 | 490 | 66 | 370 | 35 | 215 |
| 96 | 485 | 65 | 365 | 34 | 210 |
| 95 | 485 | 64 | 360 | 33 | 205 |
| 94 | 485 | 63 | 355 | 32 | 200 |
| 93 | 480 | 62 | 350 | 31 | 195 |
| 92 | 480 | 61 | 345 | 30 | 190 |
| 91 | 480 | 60 | 340 | 29 | 185 |
| 90 | 475 | 59 | 335 | 28 | 180 |
| 89 | 475 | 58 | 330 | 27 | 175 |
| 88 | 470 | 57 | 325 | 26 | 170 |
| 87 | 470 | 56 | 320 | 25 | 165 |
| 86 | 465 | 55 | 315 | 24 | 160 |
| 85 | 465 | 54 | 310 | 23 | 155 |
| 84 | 460 | 53 | 305 | 22 | 150 |
| 83 | 455 | 52 | 300 | 21 | 145 |
| 82 | 450 | 51 | 295 | 20 | 140 |
| 81 | 445 | 50 | 290 | 19 | 135 |
| 80 | 440 | 49 | 285 | 18 | 130 |
| 79 | 435 | 48 | 280 | 17 | 125 |
| 78 | 430 | 47 | 275 | 16 | 120 |
| 77 | 425 | 46 | 270 | 15 | 115 |
| 76 | 420 | 45 | 265 | 14 | 110 |
| 75 | 415 | 44 | 260 | 13 | 105 |
| 74 | 410 | 43 | 255 | 12 | 100 |
| 73 | 405 | 42 | 250 | 〜11 | 測定不能 |
| 72 | 400 | 41 | 245 | | |
| 71 | 395 | 40 | 240 | | |
| 70 | 390 | 39 | 235 | | |

正解数 ／点 リスニング ＋ 正解数 ／点 リーディング ＝ ／点 予想スコア

## 第2回模擬試験

### リスニング

| 正解数 | 予想スコア | 正解数 | 予想スコア | 正解数 | 予想スコア |
|---|---|---|---|---|---|
| 100 | 495 | 69 | 395 | 38 | 240 |
| 99 | 495 | 68 | 390 | 37 | 235 |
| 98 | 495 | 67 | 385 | 36 | 230 |
| 97 | 495 | 66 | 380 | 35 | 225 |
| 96 | 495 | 65 | 375 | 34 | 220 |
| 95 | 490 | 64 | 370 | 33 | 215 |
| 94 | 490 | 63 | 365 | 32 | 210 |
| 93 | 490 | 62 | 360 | 31 | 205 |
| 92 | 485 | 61 | 355 | 30 | 200 |
| 91 | 485 | 60 | 350 | 29 | 195 |
| 90 | 485 | 59 | 345 | 28 | 190 |
| 89 | 480 | 58 | 340 | 27 | 185 |
| 88 | 480 | 57 | 335 | 26 | 180 |
| 87 | 475 | 56 | 330 | 25 | 175 |
| 86 | 475 | 55 | 325 | 24 | 170 |
| 85 | 470 | 54 | 320 | 23 | 165 |
| 84 | 470 | 53 | 315 | 22 | 160 |
| 83 | 465 | 52 | 310 | 21 | 155 |
| 82 | 460 | 51 | 305 | 20 | 150 |
| 81 | 455 | 50 | 300 | 19 | 145 |
| 80 | 450 | 49 | 295 | 18 | 140 |
| 79 | 445 | 48 | 290 | 17 | 135 |
| 78 | 440 | 47 | 285 | 16 | 130 |
| 77 | 435 | 46 | 280 | 15 | 125 |
| 76 | 430 | 45 | 275 | 14 | 120 |
| 75 | 425 | 44 | 270 | 13 | 115 |
| 74 | 420 | 43 | 265 | 12 | 110 |
| 73 | 415 | 42 | 260 | 11 | 105 |
| 72 | 410 | 41 | 255 | 10 | 100 |
| 71 | 405 | 40 | 250 | 〜9 | 測定不能 |
| 70 | 400 | 39 | 245 | | |

### リーディング

| 正解数 | 予想スコア | 正解数 | 予想スコア | 正解数 | 予想スコア |
|---|---|---|---|---|---|
| 100 | 495 | 69 | 390 | 38 | 235 |
| 99 | 495 | 68 | 385 | 37 | 230 |
| 98 | 495 | 67 | 380 | 36 | 225 |
| 97 | 490 | 66 | 375 | 35 | 220 |
| 96 | 490 | 65 | 370 | 34 | 215 |
| 95 | 485 | 64 | 365 | 33 | 210 |
| 94 | 485 | 63 | 360 | 32 | 205 |
| 93 | 485 | 62 | 355 | 31 | 200 |
| 92 | 480 | 61 | 350 | 30 | 195 |
| 91 | 480 | 60 | 345 | 29 | 190 |
| 90 | 480 | 59 | 340 | 28 | 185 |
| 89 | 475 | 58 | 335 | 27 | 180 |
| 88 | 475 | 57 | 330 | 26 | 175 |
| 87 | 470 | 56 | 325 | 25 | 170 |
| 86 | 470 | 55 | 320 | 24 | 165 |
| 85 | 465 | 54 | 315 | 23 | 160 |
| 84 | 465 | 53 | 310 | 22 | 155 |
| 83 | 460 | 52 | 305 | 21 | 150 |
| 82 | 455 | 51 | 300 | 20 | 145 |
| 81 | 450 | 50 | 295 | 19 | 140 |
| 80 | 445 | 49 | 290 | 18 | 135 |
| 79 | 440 | 48 | 285 | 17 | 130 |
| 78 | 435 | 47 | 280 | 16 | 125 |
| 77 | 430 | 46 | 275 | 15 | 120 |
| 76 | 425 | 45 | 270 | 14 | 115 |
| 75 | 420 | 44 | 265 | 13 | 110 |
| 74 | 415 | 43 | 260 | 12 | 105 |
| 73 | 410 | 42 | 255 | 11 | 100 |
| 72 | 405 | 41 | 250 | 〜10 | 測定不能 |
| 71 | 400 | 40 | 245 | | |
| 70 | 395 | 39 | 240 | | |

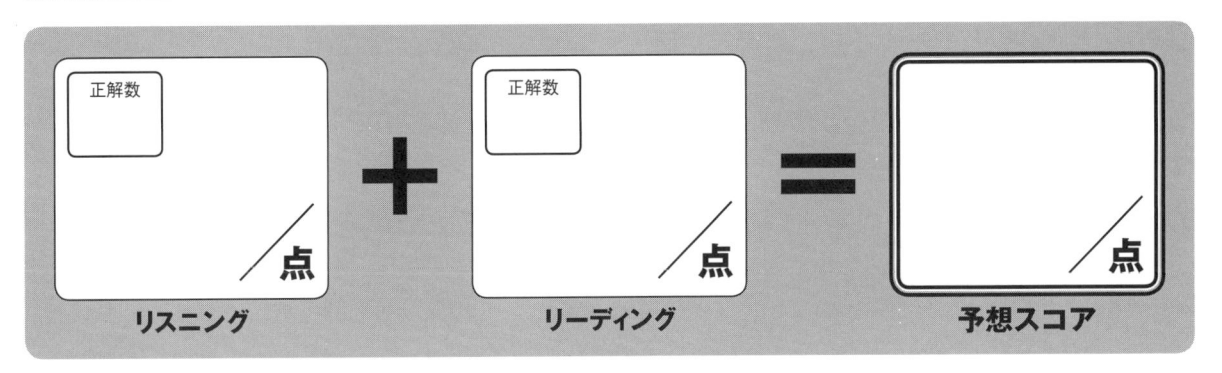

正解数 /点 リスニング ＋ 正解数 /点 リーディング ＝ /点 予想スコア

# 付属 CD について

付属 CD の，DISC 1 に第 1 回模擬試験のリスニングセクションの音声が，DISC 2 に第 2 回模擬試験のリスニングセクションの音声と特別冊子の音声がそれぞれ収録されています。本文の該当箇所には (CD 1) (1-7) のようにDISC 番号とトラック番号を表示してあります。利便性を考えてトラックを細かく区切ってありますので，下の一覧表を参考に，復習時などにお役立てください。

**DISC 1**（第1回模擬試験）収録時間約 48 分

| トラック | 内容 | トラック | 内容 |
|---|---|---|---|
| 1 | Part 1 Directions | 43 | No.56-58 |
| 2 | No.1 | 44 | No.59-61 |
| 3 | No.2 | 45 | No.62-64 |
| 4 | No.3 | 46 | No.65-67 |
| 5 | No.4 | 47 | No.68-70 |
| 6 | No.5 | 48 | Part 4 Directions |
| 7 | No.6 | 49 | No.71-73 |
| 8 | Part 2 Directions | 50 | No.74-76 |
| 9 | No.7 | 51 | No.77-79 |
| 10 | No.8 | 52 | No.80-82 |
| 11 | No.9 | 53 | No.83-85 |
| 12 | No.10 | 54 | No.86-88 |
| 13 | No.11 | 55 | No.89-91 |
| 14 | No.12 | 56 | No.92-94 |
| 15 | No.13 | 57 | No.95-97 |
| 16 | No.14 | 58 | No.98-100 |
| 17 | No.15 | | |
| 18 | No.16 | | |
| 19 | No.17 | | |
| 20 | No.18 | | |
| 21 | No.19 | | |
| 22 | No.20 | | |
| 23 | No.21 | | |
| 24 | No.22 | | |
| 25 | No.23 | | |
| 26 | No.24 | | |
| 27 | No.25 | | |
| 28 | No.26 | | |
| 29 | No.27 | | |
| 30 | No.28 | | |
| 31 | No.29 | | |
| 32 | No.30 | | |
| 33 | No.31 | | |
| 34 | Part 3 Directions | | |
| 35 | No.32-34 | | |
| 36 | No.35-37 | | |
| 37 | No.38-40 | | |
| 38 | No.41-43 | | |
| 39 | No.44-46 | | |
| 40 | No.47-49 | | |
| 41 | No.50-52 | | |
| 42 | No.53-55 | | |

**DISC 2**（第2回模擬試験／特別冊子）収録時間約 62 分

| トラック | 内容 | トラック | 内容 |
|---|---|---|---|
| 1 | Part 1 Directions | 43 | No.56-58 |
| 2 | No.1 | 44 | No.59-61 |
| 3 | No.2 | 45 | No.62-64 |
| 4 | No.3 | 46 | No.65-67 |
| 5 | No.4 | 47 | No.68-70 |
| 6 | No.5 | 48 | Part 4 Directions |
| 7 | No.6 | 49 | No.71-73 |
| 8 | Part 2 Directions | 50 | No.74-76 |
| 9 | No.7 | 51 | No.77-79 |
| 10 | No.8 | 52 | No.80-82 |
| 11 | No.9 | 53 | No.83-85 |
| 12 | No.10 | 54 | No.86-88 |
| 13 | No.11 | 55 | No.89-91 |
| 14 | No.12 | 56 | No.92-94 |
| 15 | No.13 | 57 | No.95-97 |
| 16 | No.14 | 58 | No.98-100 |
| 17 | No.15 | 59 | 虎の巻　Part 1 例題 1 |
| 18 | No.16 | 60 | 虎の巻　Part 1 例題 2 |
| 19 | No.17 | 61 | 虎の巻　Part 1 例題 3 |
| 20 | No.18 | 62 | 虎の巻　Part 2 例題 1 |
| 21 | No.19 | 63 | 虎の巻　Part 2 例題 2 |
| 22 | No.20 | 64 | 虎の巻　Part 2 例題 3 |
| 23 | No.21 | 65 | 虎の巻　Part 3 例題 |
| 24 | No.22 | 66 | 虎の巻　Part 4 例題 |
| 25 | No.23 | 67 | 重要ビジネスワード 1 |
| 26 | No.24 | 68 | 重要ビジネスワード 2 |
| 27 | No.25 | 69 | 重要ビジネスワード 3 |
| 28 | No.26 | 70 | 重要ビジネスワード 4 |
| 29 | No.27 | 71 | 重要ビジネスワード 5 |
| 30 | No.28 | 72 | 重要ビジネスワード 6 |
| 31 | No.29 | 73 | 重要ビジネスワード 7 |
| 32 | No.30 | 74 | 重要ビジネスワード 8 |
| 33 | No.31 | | |
| 34 | Part 3 Directions | | |
| 35 | No.32-34 | | |
| 36 | No.35-37 | | |
| 37 | No.38-40 | | |
| 38 | No.41-43 | | |
| 39 | No.44-46 | | |
| 40 | No.47-49 | | |
| 41 | No.50-52 | | |
| 42 | No.53-55 | | |

※ 付属 CD を取り出す際にシールの粘着面が CD に付着しないようにご注意ください。
※ 付属 CD は，音楽 CD プレーヤーで再生することを前提としておりますので，パソコンなどでの再生時には不具合が生じる可能性がございますことをご予めご了承ください。

※ リスニングセクションは付属 CD の DISC 1 を再生してください。

# 第1回 模擬試験

# LISTENING TEST

In the Listening test, you will be asked to demonstrate how well you understand spoken English. The entire Listening test will last approximately 45 minutes. There are four parts, and directions are given for each part. You must mark your answers on the separate answer sheet.
Do not write your answers in your test book.

## PART 1

**Directions:** For each question in this part, you will hear four statements about a picture in your test book. When you hear the statements, you must select the one statement that best describes what you see in the picture. Then find the number of the question on your answer sheet and mark your answer. The statements will not be printed in your test book and will be spoken only one time.

Statement (C), "They're sitting at a table," is the best description of the picture, so you should select answer (C) and mark it on your answer sheet.

1.

2.

*GO ON TO THE NEXT PAGE*

3.

4.

5.

6.

## PART 2

**Directions:** You will hear a question or statement and three responses spoken in English. They will not be printed in your test book and will be spoken only one time. Select the best response to the question or statement and mark the letter (A), (B), or (C) on your answer sheet.

7. Mark your answer on your answer sheet.
8. Mark your answer on your answer sheet.
9. Mark your answer on your answer sheet.
10. Mark your answer on your answer sheet.
11. Mark your answer on your answer sheet.
12. Mark your answer on your answer sheet.
13. Mark your answer on your answer sheet.
14. Mark your answer on your answer sheet.
15. Mark your answer on your answer sheet.
16. Mark your answer on your answer sheet.
17. Mark your answer on your answer sheet.
18. Mark your answer on your answer sheet.
19. Mark your answer on your answer sheet.
20. Mark your answer on your answer sheet.
21. Mark your answer on your answer sheet.
22. Mark your answer on your answer sheet.
23. Mark your answer on your answer sheet.
24. Mark your answer on your answer sheet.
25. Mark your answer on your answer sheet.
26. Mark your answer on your answer sheet.
27. Mark your answer on your answer sheet.
28. Mark your answer on your answer sheet.
29. Mark your answer on your answer sheet.
30. Mark your answer on your answer sheet.
31. Mark your answer on your answer sheet.

## PART 3

**Directions:** You will hear some conversations between two or more people. You will be asked to answer three questions about what the speakers say in each conversation. Select the best response to each question and mark the letter (A), (B), (C), or (D) on your answer sheet. The conversations will not be printed in your test book and will be spoken only one time.

32. What is the woman's problem?
    (A) Her document is missing.
    (B) Her computer is not functioning.
    (C) An e-mail address is incorrect.
    (D) A file is not complete.

33. When should the files be sent?
    (A) By 2:00 P.M.
    (B) By 3:00 P.M.
    (C) By 4:00 P.M.
    (D) By 5:00 P.M.

34. What does the man suggest the woman do?
    (A) Call the design engineer
    (B) Revise the file
    (C) Log onto a different computer
    (D) Use a delivery service

35. What does the woman ask the man to do?
    (A) Send her a refund
    (B) Give her a new purse
    (C) Repair her purse
    (D) Offer her a discount

36. What does the woman like about her purse?
    (A) Its design
    (B) Its size
    (C) Its price
    (D) Its texture

37. What will the man probably do next?
    (A) Make a telephone call
    (B) Choose a different purse
    (C) Visit another branch
    (D) Pay by check

38. Why is the woman calling?
    (A) To ask for her account balance
    (B) To make a payment
    (C) To renew a contract
    (D) To apply for a card

39. What condition does the man mention?
    (A) The minimum balance for an account
    (B) Credit scores to open an account
    (C) Qualifications to be new members
    (D) The time limit of the interest rate

40. What does the woman ask the man to do?
    (A) Review a charge
    (B) Send her a document
    (C) Increase her credit limit
    (D) Confirm receipt of her e-mail

41. Who most likely is the man?
    (A) A customer
    (B) A technician
    (C) A salesperson
    (D) A receptionist

42. What does the man want to talk to Ms. Shen about?
    (A) Late documents
    (B) Office equipment
    (C) Computer repairs
    (D) Brochure design

43. What is Ms. Shen's plan for today?
    (A) Meeting customers
    (B) Dealing with shareholders
    (C) Reorganizing schedules
    (D) Talking with staff

GO ON TO THE NEXT PAGE

44. What is the purpose of the man's call?
    (A) To submit a progress report
    (B) To confirm a delivery time
    (C) To revise technical information
    (D) To prepare a presentation

45. Where is Mr. Adjani now?
    (A) At a building site
    (B) At his desk
    (C) In his apartment
    (D) In a meeting

46. What will the woman do next?
    (A) Start a meeting
    (B) Phone Mr. Adjani
    (C) Get contact information
    (D) Read a text message

---

47. Where most likely is the man?
    (A) In a printer factory
    (B) In a product warehouse
    (C) In an engineering office
    (D) In a customer service center

48. What does the woman prefer about TZ inkjet cartridges?
    (A) Availability
    (B) Functionality
    (C) Quality
    (D) Familiarity

49. What does the woman decide to do?
    (A) Track a delivery online
    (B) Look at a different Web site
    (C) Accept the man's suggestion
    (D) Sell the office supplies

---

50. Where most likely are the speakers?
    (A) At an airport
    (B) At a hotel
    (C) At a travel agency
    (D) At a restaurant

51. What problem does the woman mention?
    (A) Attitude of staff
    (B) High prices
    (C) Long waiting lines
    (D) Lack of room service

52. What does the man recommend the woman do?
    (A) Settle her bill online
    (B) Line up early
    (C) Change rooms
    (D) Wait a few minutes

---

53. What are the speakers discussing?
    (A) A recruiting program
    (B) An upcoming event
    (C) Employee benefits
    (D) Office schedules

54. What does the woman mean when she says, "You've got to be kidding"?
    (A) She is surprised by what the man said.
    (B) She disagrees with the man's opinion.
    (C) She sympathizes with Margaret's situation.
    (D) She appreciates the man's humor.

55. What is mentioned about Ms. Kang?
    (A) She commonly assisted colleagues.
    (B) She frequently went to Chicago.
    (C) She usually provided funding for projects.
    (D) She often helped at parties.

56. What does the woman ask the man to do?
    (A) Inform Mr. Howell of her schedule
    (B) Give Mr. Howell her phone number
    (C) Confirm her schedule
    (D) Get hold of some documents

57. What does the woman mean when she says, "by all means"?
    (A) She needs to buy a new file for the trip.
    (B) She cannot be contacted if there is an emergency.
    (C) She will be able to receive telephone calls.
    (D) She has to think carefully before making a decision.

58. When does the woman prefer to be contacted?
    (A) At noon
    (B) In the afternoon
    (C) At any time
    (D) In the evening

59. What are the speakers talking about?
    (A) Upcoming promotions
    (B) Hiring strategies
    (C) Overseas expansion
    (D) Regional markets

60. What is a stated goal of Marcel and Vicki?
    (A) Getting local experience
    (B) Recruiting more staff
    (C) Enrolling in a university
    (D) Learning a language

61. How is the man using his lunch hours nowadays?
    (A) To prepare for a trip
    (B) To improve his skills
    (C) To contact universities
    (D) To do research on South America

**Coupon**

**Axton Foods Co.**

Wake up Feeling Fresh!

Take **$5 Off** coffee, any brand in store

Valid through October 31.

62. Why is the man looking for a certain product?
    (A) He wants to try healthy foods.
    (B) He read about it in a publication.
    (C) He has tried it out before a few times.
    (D) He needs to rate it for his blog.

63. Look at the graphic. How much will the man pay?
    (A) 5 dollars
    (B) 10 dollars
    (C) 15 dollars
    (D) 20 dollars

64. What does the woman encourage the man to do?
    (A) Purchase an additional bag
    (B) Go to a Web site
    (C) Fill out a membership card
    (D) Apply for a new account

GO ON TO THE NEXT PAGE

| Floor | Tenants |
|---|---|
| 5 | Bilo Investments / Jowon Media, Inc. |
| 4 | Wannable Textiles / Deni Biomedical |
| 3 | Aril Publishing / Somtio Engineering |
| 2 | Cimin Lighting, Inc. / Rea Catering |
| 1 | Gillo Realty, Inc. / Ashik Software Co. |

**65.** Why did the woman come to the building?

(A) To visit an apartment
(B) To retrieve a lost item
(C) To go to an interview
(D) To rent an office

**66.** Look at the graphic. What floor does the woman have to go to?

(A) Floor 2
(B) Floor 3
(C) Floor 4
(D) Floor 5

**67.** What does the man recommend the woman do?

(A) Take an elevator
(B) Change a nameplate
(C) Check the information displays again
(D) Update her online profile

**Halon Technologies Inc.**

Nancy Katz

Campus Access Level C

**68.** What is the woman asking about?

(A) How to obtain an ID
(B) How to pay a bill
(C) How to get to a branch office
(D) How to apply for a job

**69.** Look at the graphic. What area does the woman work in?

(A) Operations
(B) IT
(C) Administration
(D) Research

**70.** According to the man, what should the woman do after she gets an employee card?

(A) Take another photo
(B) Deactivate her old card
(C) Carry it with her at all times
(D) Report to the marketing department

## PART 4

**Directions:** You will hear some talks given by a single speaker. You will be asked to answer three questions about what the speaker says in each talk. Select the best response to each question and mark the letter (A), (B), (C), or (D) on your answer sheet. The talks will not be printed in your test book and will be spoken only one time.

71. What is the speaker calling about?
    (A) A job interview
    (B) An interview result
    (C) A schedule change
    (D) A job description

72. What did the speaker do a few days ago?
    (A) Talked with Michael on the phone
    (B) Left a message about an interview
    (C) Sent a letter with an application
    (D) Transferred to the personnel department

73. How long does Michael have to respond?
    (A) One day
    (B) Two days
    (C) Three days
    (D) Four days

74. What has delayed the aircraft?
    (A) Planes ahead of it
    (B) Obstacles on the runway
    (C) Mechanical safety check
    (D) Bad weather

75. How much longer will the plane have to wait?
    (A) 10 minutes
    (B) 20 minutes
    (C) 40 minutes
    (D) 45 minutes

76. What are passengers traveling to Mexico City advised to do?
    (A) Follow previously stated information
    (B) Get a travel update at their destination
    (C) Board from a different gate
    (D) Contact airline staff upon disembarkation

77. What is the report mainly about?
    (A) Luxury markets
    (B) Corporate performance
    (C) Economic trends
    (D) Business investments

78. How much do analysts expect profits to rise for the year?
    (A) 4 percent
    (B) 6 percent
    (C) 12 percent
    (D) 16 percent

79. What does the report imply?
    (A) Shopping trends are changing.
    (B) CEO policies are failing.
    (C) More customers are coming into stores.
    (D) Online sales are decreasing.

80. What is the speaker doing?
    (A) Introducing a product
    (B) Cleaning a house
    (C) Helping a customer
    (D) Arranging a program

81. What does the man imply when he says, "it'll be spotless in seconds"?
    (A) The cloth will dry fast.
    (B) The surface will be clean quickly.
    (C) The chemicals need time to mix.
    (D) The cleaner cannot remove all dirt.

82. What are some listeners invited to do?
    (A) Ask the speaker questions
    (B) Participate in a demonstration
    (C) Talk about their experiences
    (D) Receive product samples

GO ON TO THE NEXT PAGE

83. What is the main purpose of the talk?

(A) To develop a curriculum
(B) To explain the existing service
(C) To ask for donations
(D) To inform parents about a new facility

84. What is a feature of the center?

(A) Child computers
(B) Protective enclosures
(C) Special teachers
(D) Expanded curriculums

85. What will Aaron Cummings talk about?

(A) The history of the center
(B) Future plans
(C) The details of activities
(D) Ways to sign up

86. Who is the talk most likely intended for?

(A) Corporate shareholders
(B) Financial reporters
(C) Company employees
(D) Market researchers

87. What success is mentioned by the speaker?

(A) A reduction in production costs
(B) An increase in stock prices
(C) An increase in revenue
(D) A reduction in working hours

88. What does the speaker mean when she says, "I believe you should get credit"?

(A) She considers sales to be adequate.
(B) She hopes higher goals will be achieved.
(C) She owes money to her staff.
(D) She thinks her employees deserve a reward.

89. Which department does Richard Slater normally work in?

(A) Accounting
(B) IT
(C) Consumer Finance
(D) Planning

90. What does the man mean when he says, "I know this is an added burden for us"?

(A) He wants to have more staff.
(B) There will be another position available.
(C) A department will be divided into two.
(D) The company will face some hardship.

91. What will the listeners do next?

(A) Offer opinions
(B) View a presentation
(C) Ask questions
(D) Write monthly reports

92. Who most likely is the speaker?

(A) A business expert
(B) A company president
(C) A news reporter
(D) A communication specialist

93. According to the speaker, what does the report say is necessary for a good presentation?

(A) Practice while in university
(B) Substantial mastery of material
(C) Thorough relaxation exercises
(D) Advanced speaking techniques

94. What is preparation particularly effective for?

(A) Making points clear
(B) Choosing a topic
(C) Facing the public
(D) Replying to inquiries

**Naden Park**

- Golf Course
- Playground
- Basto Lake
- Volleyball court
- Summer Hill
- Bicycle path

N

---

**KASIK PAINT CO.**

**Office Supplies Order Form**

Order Number: 903H2

| Item | Units ordered |
| --- | --- |
| Desk lamps | 8 |
| Photocopier ink | 6 |
| Laptops | 4 |
| Fax machine | 1 |

---

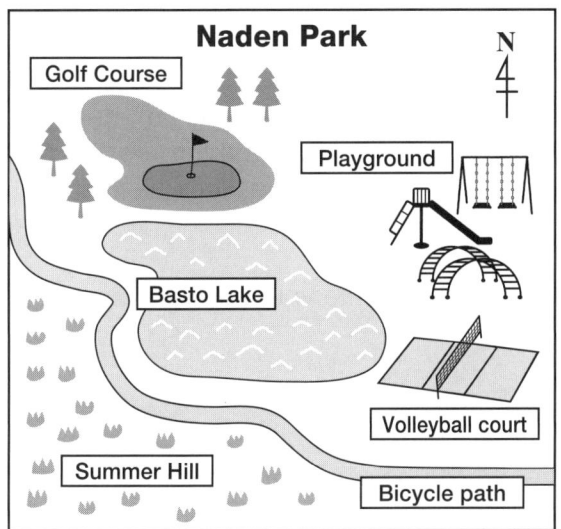

95. What type of event is being prepared?
    (A) A talent contest
    (B) A marathon
    (C) An outdoor gathering
    (D) A local tour

96. Look at the graphic. Where will the company staff meet?
    (A) At the golf course
    (B) At the volleyball court
    (C) At the playground
    (D) At Summer Hill

97. What has already been sent companywide?
    (A) Travel coupons
    (B) Public transportation passes
    (C) Directions to the venue
    (D) A list of festivities organizers

98. Look at the graphic. How many laptops does the company need in total?
    (A) 3
    (B) 5
    (C) 6
    (D) 7

99. According to the telephone message, what has the company recently done?
    (A) Improved its headquarters
    (B) Processed a claim
    (C) Hired some staff
    (D) Changed a launch date

100. What is the listener asked to do?
    (A) Train recruits
    (B) Adjust a price
    (C) Make a phone call
    (D) Wait for a text

---

This is the end of the Listening test. Turn to Part 5 in your test book.

GO ON TO THE NEXT PAGE

# READING TEST

In the Reading test, you will read a variety of texts and answer several different types of reading comprehension questions. The entire Reading test will last 75 minutes. There are three parts, and directions are given for each part. You are encouraged to answer as many questions as possible within the time allowed.

You must mark your answers on the separate answer sheet. Do not write your answers in your test book.

## PART 5

**Directions:** A word or phrase is missing in each of the sentences below. Four answer choices are given below each sentence. Select the best answer to complete the sentence. Then mark the letter (A), (B), (C), or (D) on your answer sheet.

101. Mr. Krishna informed the company of ------- plan to visit several important clients on the West Coast the following week.
    (A) its
    (B) it
    (C) he
    (D) his

102. Genetic advances at Warsaw Pharmaceuticals mean it may soon be possible to protect people from a ------- variety of diseases.
    (A) long
    (B) wide
    (C) thick
    (D) high

103. Director Rao convinced the board to begin export sales to Europe this year, ------- at least lay the groundwork for doing so.
    (A) while
    (B) since
    (C) but
    (D) or

104. Alistair Properties Co. ------- to closing most deals in dollars, but due to client demand began accepting euros and yen as well.
    (A) accustomed
    (B) had been accustomed
    (C) will accustom
    (D) will have been accustomed

105. First Harbor Pharmaceutical Inc. is one of the top private caregivers in the province and ------- is a leader in advanced medical research.
    (A) since
    (B) whichever
    (C) although
    (D) moreover

106. CEO Brian Greene stated at the meeting that an increase in sales of 13% by the end of the year was quite -------.
    (A) attains
    (B) attaining
    (C) attainable
    (D) attainably

107. *Sun Lady* bath soap is certainly ------- than any similar product in fine stores today.
    (A) fragrant
    (B) more fragrant
    (C) most fragrant
    (D) fragrance

108. Mr. Ephron wished there ------- more funds for the company picnic, but the employees seemed satisfied with the snacks and beverages provided.
    (A) is
    (B) are
    (C) would
    (D) were

109. News reports indicate that some corporations are preparing ------- an economic upturn by making large investments now.
    (A) for
    (B) and
    (C) to
    (D) but

110. Ms. Singh made it her personal ------- to track the company's profit margins in each of the major regions it operated in.
    (A) interesting
    (B) interest
    (C) interestingly
    (D) interested

111. Evertrue Media Corporation is ------- the number one firm in the entertainment industry in terms of market share.
    (A) responsively
    (B) undoubtedly
    (C) mutually
    (D) compassionately

112. Greater Vancouver, particularly during times of economic slowdowns, is ------- many Canadian IT companies locate their offices.
    (A) how
    (B) why
    (C) when
    (D) where

113. Mr. Anwar's design team was ------- on time with all its projects, causing the company to rely on it a great deal.
    (A) invariable
    (B) invariant
    (C) invariably
    (D) invariability

114. Trainor Inc. maintains a competitive bonus system ------- order to motivate staff in all of its departments.
    (A) in
    (B) by
    (C) from
    (D) at

115. Five cents of every dollar ------- on goods in the Tyler Department Store goes toward local charities that help children.
    (A) credited
    (B) cashed
    (C) paid
    (D) spent

116. Mr. M'Krumah is in ------- of the company's Lagos branch, operating all its major business activities in West Africa.
    (A) responsibility
    (B) touch
    (C) charge
    (D) engaged

117. ------- a sensation among teenagers, the *Jumping Box* online game rapidly became popular throughout East Asia.
    (A) Creates
    (B) Creating
    (C) Created
    (D) Create

118. Director Kim is an ------- fine scholar in the field of robotics, as well as being a good businessman.
    (A) intrusively
    (B) oppositely
    (C) exceptionally
    (D) affordably

119. Real estate prices in Hanoi are expected to rise by as much as 15% ------- the local business boom continues.
    (A) and
    (B) but
    (C) as
    (D) or

120. Mr. Armatelli feels that ------- is certainly the best way to resolve any problems among co-workers.
    (A) talking
    (B) has talked
    (C) talks
    (D) will talk

GO ON TO THE NEXT PAGE

121. Mr. Larson used to work for the Imperial Builders, but he found a new job with Central Constructions three years -------.
    (A) else
    (B) soon
    (C) ago
    (D) already

122. The marketing department came up with an excellent plan, but relied on local salespeople for proper ------- of it.
    (A) execute
    (B) execution
    (C) executed
    (D) executively

123. Passengers must show the boarding passes ------- were given to them in the ticketing area prior to boarding the aircraft.
    (A) what
    (B) whose
    (C) that
    (D) who

124. Umagi Corporation's new steel ------- its shape and strength even when exposed to very high temperatures or pressures.
    (A) sustenance
    (B) sustains
    (C) sustainably
    (D) sustainable

125. This MP3 player is guaranteed against breakdowns caused by the manufacturer's ------- during shipping.
    (A) warranty
    (B) mindset
    (C) default
    (D) negligence

126. Mr. Nagy always brought a keen ------- perspective to trends in global manufacturing.
    (A) analysis
    (B) analyze
    (C) analytic
    (D) analytically

127. After successfully producing 20,000 units last year, the Rabo Corporation's Brazil subsidiary was able ------- on its own as a manufacturer.
    (A) had stood
    (B) to stand
    (C) standing
    (D) stood

128. Connor Furniture Inc. has been selling top brands for over 21 ------- years in major cities across the country.
    (A) straight
    (B) direct
    (C) connected
    (D) totaled

129. Passengers ------- internationally must go to Terminal D, which houses all gates for overseas flights.
    (A) travel
    (B) to travel
    (C) traveling
    (D) traveled

130. Packages that ------- from Los Angeles may take up to five days to arrive in Cairo using Interprize Express Service.
    (A) original
    (B) originate
    (C) originally
    (D) originating

# PART 6

**Directions:** Read the texts that follow. A word, phrase, or sentence is missing in parts of each text. Four answer choices for each question are given below the text. Select the best answer to complete the text. Then mark the letter (A), (B), (C), or (D) on your answer sheet.

**Questions 131-134** refer to the following letter.

---

January 14
Marie-Therese Deneuve
34 Rue de la Croce
Marseilles

Dear Ms. Deneuve,

We are pleased to present you with a business loan of up to € 250,000. We are offering this ------- because you are one of our most valued customers with an excellent credit history.
**131.**

-------. You only have to pay an interest rate of 6.7%. This is a rate you are unlikely to find
**132.**
------- else. This special rate is available ------- to a selected group of valuable customers such as
**133.** **134.**
yourself. If you would like to discuss this offer further, please call me at 008-7745-3009 ext. 19.

Sincerely,

Xavier Bayer
Senior Customer Service Representative
Bank of West Marseilles
The Bank to France, the Bank to Europe, the Bank to the World

---

131. (A) requirement
 (B) inquiry
 (C) request
 (D) opportunity

132. (A) Your loan application is incomplete as it is.
 (B) We would also like to inform you of another positive aspect.
 (C) We cannot help you any further at this point.
 (D) Interest rates are not favorable in today's economy.

133. (A) somewhere
 (B) anywhere
 (C) everywhere
 (D) nowhere

134. (A) according
 (B) close
 (C) thanks
 (D) only

*GO ON TO THE NEXT PAGE*

**Questions 135-138** refer to the following e-mail.

To: Michael Chen <michael.chen@goldcrestbanking.ca>
From: Orianne Durand <orianne.Durand@tzdesign.com>
Subject: Update
Date: Wednesday, February 23

Dear Mr. Chen,

We ------- the revised visuals for the design of your company's new gym shoe, *Street Tiger*.
    **135.**
Please see the PDF files attached ------- the composition of the materials and the internal structure.
                                **136.**
Our apologies for the extra time necessary to complete the revisions.

Our art directors are still ------- your suggestions from last week's meeting into the logo you want as
                         **137.**
well. -------.
    **138.**

Thanks again for choosing us to create this very important new product for you.

Sincerely,

Orianne Durand
Chief Designer
TZ Design Ltd.

---

**135.** (A) will complete
(B) would have completed
(C) have completed
(D) have been completing

**136.** (A) show
(B) shows
(C) shown
(D) showing

**137.** (A) integrating
(B) articulating
(C) evaluating
(D) asserting

**138.** (A) Please make sure to keep it in a safe place.
(B) We hope to show you the selections during Monday's presentation.
(C) You might already have noticed some necessary changes.
(D) Apart from that, they were considered acceptable.

30

**Questions 139-142** refer to the following article.

According to the latest research, more and more employees are suffering from stress in the workplace. -------. In one study, 43% of employees ------- as being under heavy stress had weak concentration and poor work performance. Corporations operating in highly competitive environments commonly prefer to extend current employee work hours ------- hire new staff, but such long hours invariably lower employee productivity.

Women combining motherhood with careers were found to be at particular risk; -------, reports from workplaces imply that working mothers may experience exhaustion from the responsibility of balancing both homes and jobs. Experts recommend corporations expand the number of daycare centers to reduce their burdens.

139. (A) Reports suggest it is a serious problem among all levels of workers.
 (B) It has become of great importance to a successful job search.
 (C) Both men and women have been found to be unaffected by such difficulties.
 (D) Research shows that many employees are confused by this concept.

140. (A) are described
 (B) will describe
 (C) described
 (D) to describe

141. (A) more than
 (B) less than
 (C) than not
 (D) rather than

142. (A) specific
 (B) specifically
 (C) specify
 (D) specification

GO ON TO THE NEXT PAGE

**Questions 143-146** refer to the following notice.

---

**Travel and Weather Update**
**EuroLine Bus Corporation**

************** Update for the Eastern European Region **************

Bus service on the Prague to Sofia route is currently experiencing severe delays due to sudden and heavy rainstorms. The ------- flooding has affected many places. Roads in such areas have
**143.**
become impassable because of these high waters, ------- have closed them to vehicle travel of any
**144.**
kind.

Travelers are advised to check the main terminal board for the latest information on arrival and departure times. Passengers preparing ------- on any buses at the gates are advised to wait. Buses
**145.**
there will leave only when the weather clears enough for them to do so.

-------.
**146.**

---

143. (A) innocuous
(B) anticipated
(C) interrupted
(D) consequent

144. (A) what
(B) that
(C) which
(D) those

145. (A) departing
(B) will depart
(C) to depart
(D) departed

146. (A) Finally, the scheduled departure times have now been posted.
(B) Please continue to watch this board for further updates.
(C) Thank you to all who have participated in our bus tour.
(D) We hope you will continue to enjoy the weather during your trip.

# PART 7

**Directions:** In this part you will read a selection of texts, such as magazine and newspaper articles, e-mails, and instant messages. Each text or set of texts is followed by several questions. Select the best answer for each question and mark the letter (A), (B), (C), or (D) on your answer sheet.

**Questions 147-148** refer to the following table.

### Travel information for The Irish Princess

| Destinations (from Cork) | Gibraltar | Tenerife | Antigua | Aruba |
|---|---|---|---|---|
| Estimated arrival date | 17th | 20th | 22nd | 24th |
| Present Travel Status | Arrival on Schedule | Updating | Updating | Two days late |
| Medical Certificate required | No | Yes | No | No |
| Visa Requirements | Not required for EU residents | Necessary for stays over 30 days | See Passenger Service for Updates | Not required for EU residents |

IRELAND-CARIBBEAN CRUISE LINES INC.

**147.** On what date will passengers on The Irish Princess most likely arrive in Aruba?

(A) 20th
(B) 22nd
(C) 24th
(D) 26th

**148.** Which destination requires a visa for stays over a month?

(A) Gibraltar
(B) Tenerife
(C) Antigua
(D) Aruba

GO ON TO THE NEXT PAGE

**Questions 149-150** refer to the following text message chain.

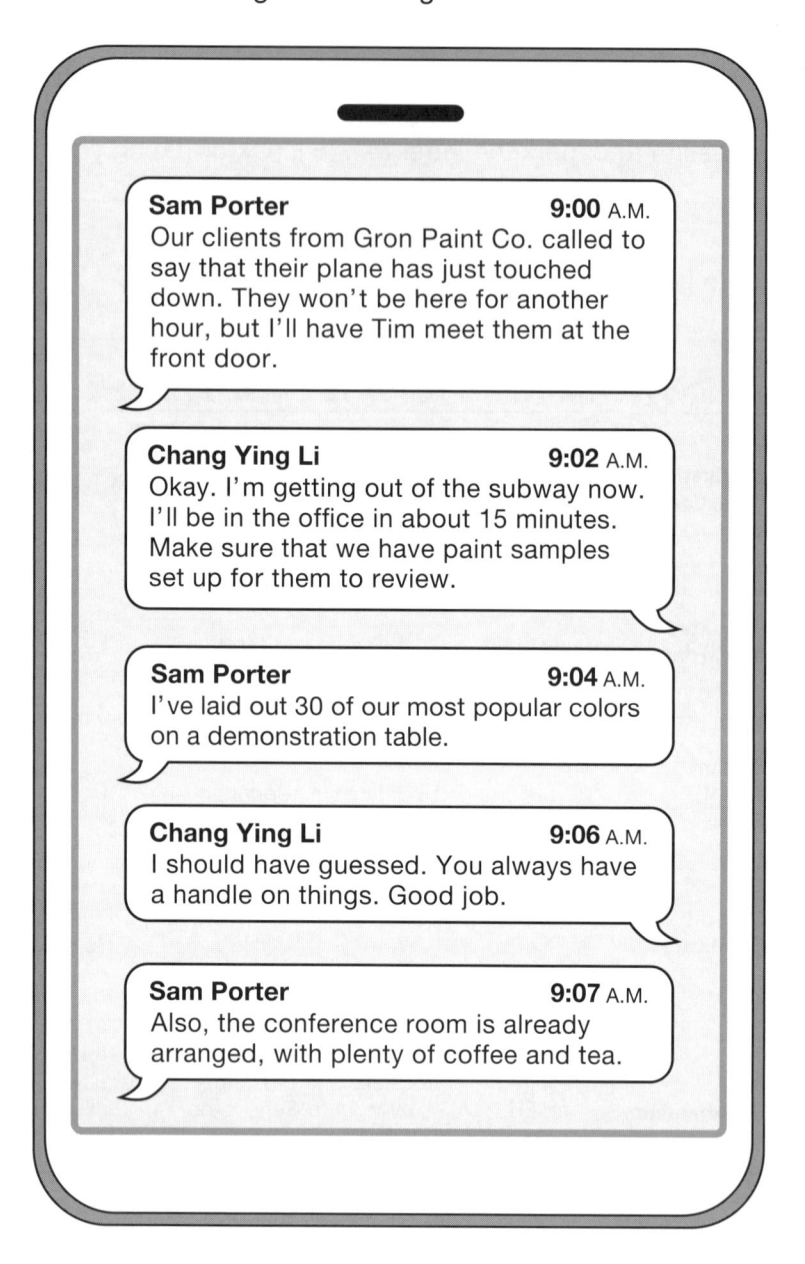

**Sam Porter** — 9:00 A.M.
Our clients from Gron Paint Co. called to say that their plane has just touched down. They won't be here for another hour, but I'll have Tim meet them at the front door.

**Chang Ying Li** — 9:02 A.M.
Okay. I'm getting out of the subway now. I'll be in the office in about 15 minutes. Make sure that we have paint samples set up for them to review.

**Sam Porter** — 9:04 A.M.
I've laid out 30 of our most popular colors on a demonstration table.

**Chang Ying Li** — 9:06 A.M.
I should have guessed. You always have a handle on things. Good job.

**Sam Porter** — 9:07 A.M.
Also, the conference room is already arranged, with plenty of coffee and tea.

149. At 9:06 A.M., what does Chang Ying Li mean when she writes, "I should have guessed"?

(A) Mr. Porter often anticipates needs.
(B) Mr. Porter must make a decision.
(C) Mr. Porter requires further advice.
(D) Mr. Porter usually follows instructions.

150. What does Mr. Porter indicate that he will do?

(A) Call some clients
(B) Have someone meet a group
(C) Wait by a door
(D) Get some samples tested

**Questions 151-152** refer to the following memo.

# MEMORANDUM

To: All Staff
From: Sven Bjorg
Time: 10:45 A.M., Wednesday
RE: Christian Jonson

Dear Staff,

As you already know, Christian is leaving us this Friday after more than 30 years with the firm. Before taking his present job as head of Research, he worked in various areas, including Production—both here and in Oslo—Design, and IT. Over the last 18 months, he has been overseeing the highly successful Z45-t drug trials in Zurich.

He has been an invaluable member of Lind Technologies and I know he will be sorely missed by his colleagues and friends. However, I am happy to say he has agreed to stay with us for the next four weeks in a part-time capacity so we will benefit from his expertise.

I hope you will join me and the rest of the Board of Directors for a Bread and Cheese Reception in the Premier Boardroom this Friday afternoon from 4:30 P.M. to formally congratulate Christian on his retirement and wish him every success in his new life!

Thank you,

Sven Bjorg
Managing Director
Lind Technologies

---

**151.** Which department is Mr. Jonson working in now?

(A) Research
(B) Production
(C) Design
(D) IT

**152.** What will Mr. Jonson do over the coming month?

(A) Contribute personal knowledge
(B) Conduct a job search
(C) Hire part-time workers
(D) Attend a board meeting

GO ON TO THE NEXT PAGE

**Questions 153-154** refer to the following label.

## Installation Guide for your Sparkle White Dishwasher
**Wonder Electronics Co.**

Install the appliance in accordance with the instructions below.

- Ensure that the appliance is not connected to any power outlets during installation.

- Do not remove any of the metal plates covering electronic components or wiring inside.

- Confirm the power supply of the residence is compatible with this appliance. If it is not, a converter will be necessary (sold separately).

- Install this appliance on a flat surface. Failure to do so could severely affect its stability.

- Connect the appliance's water tubes to the main pipes beneath your sink. Check the diagram on the back of the appliance for the correct procedure.

- Following installation, please dispose of the packaging in an environmentally friendly way.

For more information on this and other fine appliances made by Wonder Electronics Co., go to www.wonderelectronicsonthenet.com.

153. What is NOT listed as an installation step for the appliance?
   (A) Checking that the electrical supply is suitable
   (B) Contacting company technicians
   (C) Ensuring positioning is on a surface that is level
   (D) Referring to graphs on the device

154. What are users suggested to do?
   (A) Test the appliance when installation is complete
   (B) Replace the water pipes beneath the sink if necessary
   (C) Disconnect the power supply when not in use
   (D) Consider the environment when discarding items

**Questions 155-157** refer to the following e-mail.

---

* E-mail *

**From:** Thiago de Silva <tdesilva@ozatmail.net>
**To:** Lucia Morais <lucia.morais@olivehotel.fr> Manager, Olive Hotel
**Date:** Wednesday, October 7
**Subject:** My room

Dear Ms. Morais,

Two weeks ago I e-mailed you to reserve accommodations, along with an online deposit to secure them. — [1] —. I was scheduled to check in tomorrow, so that I can attend the European Manufacturing Conference there in Lyons.

However, I have recently been accepted into a 1-week international management development course in Switzerland, so I would like to cancel my reservation. — [2] —. One of the original team members has had to drop out for health reasons and I have been offered his spot. — [3] —. I realize this is extremely short notice, but considering these circumstances I am hoping I can still get my money back.

Please e-mail as soon as possible to let me know. — [4] —. I hope to hear from you before then.

Kind regards,
Thiago de Silva

---

**155.** What is the purpose of the e-mail?

(A) To schedule an arrival
(B) To confirm a transaction
(C) To state a change
(D) To make a payment

**156.** What is a stated concern of Mr. de Silva?

(A) Room availability
(B) Hotel amenities
(C) Refund policy
(D) Cancellation deadlines

**157.** In which of the positions marked [1], [2], [3] and [4] does the following sentence best belong?

"I have to leave for the training program within the next 12 hours."

(A) [1]
(B) [2]
(C) [3]
(D) [4]

GO ON TO THE NEXT PAGE

**Questions 158-160** refer to the following instructions.

### How to use Eazee Breeze in your washing machine

Measure out Eazee Breeze Detergent concentrate (1 scoop per medium load of clothes) into a cup of lukewarm water and allow it to dissolve completely for about 5-10 minutes or until it can no longer be seen. Turn on your washing machine, choosing the shortest cycle and making sure your soiled clothes are fully immersed in water. Next, pour the Eazee Breeze mixture onto the clothes. Let clothes soak for at least 15 minutes to allow Eazee Breeze's fast-penetrating formula to work on grime, stains and odors.* Next, close the lid and continue the cycle. With Eazee Breeze you can say goodbye to scrubbing, cut down on wash time and save on electricity.

* Eazee Breeze is safe for all types of fabrics, but as a precaution do not soak dark clothes and whites together.

158. What is the first step in using Eazee Breeze?

   (A) Letting the substance melt
   (B) Soaking clothes in water
   (C) Letting water sit for 15 minutes
   (D) Washing clothes for 5 minutes

159. The word "soiled" in line 5 is closest in meaning to

   (A) rough
   (B) shabby
   (C) dirty
   (D) old

160. What are people using Eazee Breeze advised NOT to do?

   (A) Add extra concentrate
   (B) Scrub items before washing
   (C) Use together with other products
   (D) Combine colors and whites

**Questions 161-164** refer to the following online chat discussion.

---

**Alvarez, Hector** [11:05 A.M.]
Hi everyone. I went over the last report on our sales. They are still too low. Give me your thoughts.

**Terao, Katsuya** [11:06 A.M.]
Our sales staff needs more training in how to approach customers—especially because many of them are new.

**Dean, Andrew** [11:10 A.M.]
We could focus more on online sales. With big upgrades to our Web site, we could generate more revenue online. Elisa Smythe has shown me several revenue projections that seem to indicate that.

**Alvarez, Hector** [11:13 A.M.]
I can see that. We're not getting the level of sales online that our competitors are.

**Rao, Manisha** [11:15 A.M.]
I have to caution you that changes to our Web site wouldn't be cheap. It would impact my teams the most, because we'd have to devote a lot of IT resources to that.

**Baldwin, Veronica** [11:17 A.M.]
We might also have to adjust our product line. Rick Jones has plenty of data showing that online shoppers and in-store shoppers sometimes have different preferences.

**Alvarez, Hector** [11:20 A.M.]
Nevertheless, I'd like to explore that option. Have Elisa share her information with Rick. Then I want both of them—and all of you—to join me in my office tomorrow at 2:00 P.M.

---

**161.** At 11:05 A.M., what does Mr. Alvarez mean when he writes, "Give me your thoughts"?

(A) He has to meet a deadline.
(B) He needs to update an account.
(C) He hopes to persuade a supervisor.
(D) He wants to gather some opinions.

**162.** For what type of company do these people most likely work?

(A) A retail outlet
(B) A consulting agency
(C) A cyber security firm
(D) An event planning company

**163.** According to the discussion, whose department would be most affected by Mr. Dean's suggestion?

(A) Mr. Terao's department
(B) Ms. Rao's department
(C) Ms. Baldwin's department
(D) Mr. Jones' department

**164.** What information will Ms. Smythe most likely share with Mr. Jones?

(A) Training methods
(B) Customer profiles
(C) Financial statistics
(D) Team organization

GO ON TO THE NEXT PAGE

**Questions 165-168** refer to the following advertisement.

# Shanghai Romance

## MUSICAL LOVERS WILL LOVE THIS NEW PRODUCTION FROM THE RED BALLOON PERFORMANCE COMPANY.

◆

### Chosen Best Musical by the Evening Star Monthly!

Set in China in the 1920s, this lavish extravaganza will thrill and excite you!

Read what people are saying about it:

> "I'm not much of a theatergoer, but I loved it!"
> –Amy Winters, university student, Edinburgh

> "If you want lighthearted entertainment for the whole family, this show is for you. We and the kids had a grand time seeing it."
> –Frank Coswell, business owner, London

Don't miss out on Helen McTavish's performance as Eleanor Gantry. Also starring Richard Mace as Ewan Lockhart.

Tickets are available at the box office from May 18, with online sales starting the day before. Reserve yours anytime until June 20. Seats can otherwise be obtained at the door. The final performance will be on June 27 unless extended.

Discounted matinee performances are held at 2:00 P.M. every Saturday and Wednesday for £35-£40. These cannot be purchased online or used in combination with group discounts or season passes.
For more details, call the Box Office (9:30 A.M. – 11:00 P.M., Monday through Saturday), at 0845-671-1200 or visit us online at www.thamestheater.co.uk.

*Refunds available up to half an hour before each performance begins, less fees.

**165.** What is indicated about Shanghai Romance?

(A) It has an international cast.
(B) It is a show for adults.
(C) It is a long running show.
(D) It has received favorable reviews.

**166.** Who has praised Shanghai Romance?

(A) The theater owner
(B) Audience members
(C) Play writers
(D) Stage actors

**167.** When can the earliest tickets be purchased?

(A) May 17
(B) May 18
(C) June 20
(D) June 27

**168.** How can guests get lower prices?

(A) By attending afternoon performances
(B) By purchasing tickets online
(C) By seeing the performance twice
(D) By contacting the performers

*GO ON TO THE NEXT PAGE*

**Questions 169-171** refer to the following e-mail.

---

**E-mail**

**From:** Joseph Mooresville <joseph@gentryparts.au>  President & CEO  Gentry Car Parts Inc.
**To:** Emiko Takeda <emiko.takeda@ichigoauto.co.jp>  Purchasing Director  Ichigo Automobile Corporation
**Date:** September 4
**Subject:** Your visit

---

Dear Ms. Takeda,

Here are the directions you requested. They should bring you directly to our main factory outside Melbourne.

As you drive out of the airport, get onto Highway Nine going west. Take that for about 15 kilometers, until you reach the Pettigrew Overpass. Continue on for an additional 3 kilometers to Exit 3. Take that exit and it will lead you to Coldicote Road. Turn right there, and head north for about 4 more kilometers.

After you pass the Herald Hotel on your right, you'll only be a minute or two away from us. If you see Blake Stadium, you'll know you've gone too far, so make a U-turn at Carlton Park or East Pacific Bank and come back toward us.

Guest parking inside the facility is free, but please be sure to enter one of the spaces marked for visitors. My assistants, Marsha Jensen and William Marsden, will meet you at the gate and see you through security. You'll be able to see them as soon as you pull up.

If you have any questions at any time, please e-mail me at the address above. Or you are welcome to contact me by phone. I look forward to seeing you soon.

Sincerely,

Joseph Mooresville

*World Specialists in Car Parts Design*

---

**169.** How far is Ms. Takeda instructed to drive down Highway Nine?
(A) Three kilometers
(B) Four kilometers
(C) Fifteen kilometers
(D) Eighteen kilometers

**170.** What landmark will Ms. Takeda see before she reaches the Melbourne factory?
(A) Herald Hotel
(B) Blake Stadium
(C) Carlton Park
(D) East Pacific Bank

**171.** What should Ms. Takeda do upon arriving?
(A) Park outside the facility
(B) Show her guest pass
(C) Contact security
(D) Look for Mr. Mooresville's staff

**Questions 172-175** refer to the following newspaper article.

# Big Changes at Diaz Motors

Diaz Motors yesterday announced substantial changes at the company's assembly plants in Guadalajara, where it employs 3,200 people, and Veracruz, where it employs 1,200. From April 1, staff will work four-day weeks and take 20% reductions in base salaries. — [1] —. This policy will be subject to a 12-month review, at which time it will be decided whether to continue it.

CEO Felipe Kahlo said the move was designed to secure the long-term competitiveness of the company. — [2] —. Earlier this month, Diaz introduced a voluntary layoff program and eliminated 300 part-time jobs at its subsidiary component plant just outside of Mexico City. Diaz's board of directors has also reportedly discussed outsourcing some processes to lower-cost Guatemala.

— [3] —. According to the latest statistics, car purchases from Diaz and other South American automakers have fallen by 63% over the past three months. This decline is despite a $US 200 million investment the company made recently in advanced production technologies. Diaz stock held steady in light trading on the announcement.

Union officials are reported to be in negotiations with company representatives over ways to avoid further layoffs or outsourcing. — [4] —. Senior union director Miguel Hayek said he was willing to work with management to safeguard jobs in the face of current uncertainty in the market.

172. What is the article mainly about?

(A) Economic trends in South America
(B) Labor relations at auto companies
(C) Productivity changes in car factories
(D) Ongoing corporate reorganizations

173. The word "subsidiary" in paragraph 2, line 7, is closest in meaning to

(A) divisional
(B) remaining
(C) partial
(D) sequential

174. What problem is Diaz Motors facing?

(A) A lack of competitive technologies
(B) Sharp decreases in stock prices
(C) A reduction of market share
(D) A slump in consumer demand

175. In which of the positions marked [1], [2], [3] and [4] does the following sentence best belong?

"The news comes as the Mexican car manufacturer battles a regional recession."

(A) [1]
(B) [2]
(C) [3]
(D) [4]

GO ON TO THE NEXT PAGE

**Questions 176-180** refer to the following survey and e-mail.

---

### Car4U Inc.

# Customer Survey

Customer Name: (Mr.)/Ms.)  _Ibrahim Rafsanjani_

Address: _17 Rue De Mons, Lyons, France 90A-E7K_

E-mail: _Rafsanjani2947@francotel.com_

Date of Car Rental: From _8 June_ to _15 June_

Applicable rules, fees or other information regarding your rental: _N/A_

Please indicate your level of service satisfaction with Car4U Inc. by rating us in each of the categories below, from 1 to 5.   1= Very unsatisfied   5 = Very satisfied

| Category | Condition of car at time of rental | Cost per day | Service Staff Helpfulness | Car Model Options | Drop-off and Pick-up convenience |
|---|---|---|---|---|---|
| Rating | 4 | 3 | 3 | 1 | 3 |

Comments: _I think my responses above show my opinion about renting from you. I have also rented from Falcon Rental Co., and frankly I believe they do a better job. It's easy to see why they're the number one car rental agency in Europe. I would recommend that you work to improve your service if you want to compete with them._

Thank you for taking the time to fill out our survey. Fully completed surveys earn 200 Frequent Flier Miles on World Wings Airlines. Let World Wings fly you across the globe—and choose Car4U when you land.

---

* E-mail *

**From:** eva.veblen@car4u.net
**To:** robert.heller@car4u.net
**Date:** 18 July
**Subject:** Survey

Dear Mr. Heller,

We completed a survey of customer satisfaction last month: over 3,000 respondents were included. I have a broad statistical analysis of the results I will send later. However, I have attached this particular response because the scores are representative of many of the surveys we collected. Furthermore, the respondent offered a succinct written summary of what other customers might also feel.

As you can see, it indicates that we have varying levels of performance in different areas. I spoke with some analysts in the company who said it is "impossible" to perform well in all areas.

However, I don't accept this as necessarily true. Instead, I would like to suggest that we try to make improvements in our worst area of performance, clearly shown in the survey, by expanding our budget in that area. I know that it's not easy to increase expenses, but in my opinion it would be a very positive move that would result in the long-term success of our company.

Yours truly,

Eva Veblen
Director of Operations

**176.** What is Mr. Rafsanjani most satisfied with?

(A) The state of the cars
(B) Rental fees
(C) The quality of customer service
(D) Car models available

**177.** Why does Mr. Rafsanjani mention Falcon Rental Co.?

(A) To provide a comparison
(B) To comment on a car he rented
(C) To support his comments on price
(D) To complain about the company's service

**178.** What do people who answer the survey get?

(A) Lower rental prices
(B) Complimentary airline upgrades
(C) Frequent flier miles
(D) Discounted accommodations

**179.** Why did Ms. Veblen attach the single response?

(A) It answers her boss' request.
(B) It is a good example of the overall survey results.
(C) It corrects a previous statistical error.
(D) It solicits approval for more responses.

**180.** What does Ms. Veblen suggest doing to improve the company's performance?

(A) Conducting market research
(B) Cutting down on labor expenses
(C) Increasing the variety of cars
(D) Analyzing the results of the survey

*GO ON TO THE NEXT PAGE*

**Questions 181-185** refer to the following Web page and e-mail.

---

www.cheshirefoods.com/raspberryleaftea/

Thank you for visiting Cheshire Foods. See our main Internet homepage for exciting links to other great Cheshire products.

**Recommended! Raspberry Leaf Tea**

A delicate blend of raspberry leaf, natural flavor and real pieces of apple comes together to make this deliciously fragrant tea.
Completely organic, without artificial flavorings, colors or preservatives.

### What's inside?

Raspberry Leaves, Hibiscus, Blackberry Leaves, Natural Raspberry Flavor, Tartaric Acid, Rosehips, Raspberries, Apple pieces.
**CAFFEINE-FREE**

### How to enjoy it?

Place the teabag in a cup or teapot of boiled water (one bag per person). Immerse for 3-5 minutes to bring out the full flavor. Best drunk without adding milk, cream or any other liquids or condiments.

**Unfortunately, we are unable to make direct sales.
Please pick up some at your local grocery store.**

---

*E-mail*

**To:** CustomerService@Cheshirefoods.com
**From:** gloria7902@laketel.com
**Date:** Wednesday, May 3
**Subject:** Ordering raspberry tea

Dear Cheshire Foods,

I have enjoyed your Raspberry Leaf Tea for many years. I usually take mine with a bit of Korean or Chinese ginseng, and find it delicious. I even check for product updates regularly on your Web site.

Indeed, I think it would be ideal if I were able to buy it there directly. That's because I sometimes forget to pick it up when I'm out shopping. At other times, your tea may not be available at a particular store I go to. In such cases, I purchase other products, though they are not as enjoyable as yours.

Is there any way that I could order directly from your company—perhaps by catalog or phone? If you have no way for customers to do so at this time, I suggest you consider making such an option available. You would certainly benefit through increased sales, and customers like me would benefit through the convenience of the product being brought right to our doors. I should tell you that Longfellow Grey Tea does provide such a service already.

Sincerely,

Gloria Han

181. What is a stated feature of Cheshire Foods Raspberry Leaf Tea?

    (A) Low price
    (B) New flavors
    (C) Natural ingredients
    (D) Wide popularity

182. What suggestion does the Web site offer?

    (A) To add apple pieces to the tea
    (B) To allow to cool before consuming
    (C) To use the appropriate type of teapot
    (D) To avoid adding any dairy products

183. What is indicated about Ms. Han?

    (A) She enjoys tea in a different way from the producer's instructions.
    (B) She prefers ginseng to raspberry leaf tea.
    (C) She purchases tea in large quantities.
    (D) She goes shopping for tea at a certain store.

184. What does Ms. Han ask Cheshire Foods to do?

    (A) Post product updates on their Web site
    (B) Provide product details
    (C) Use larger tea boxes
    (D) Increase their products' availability

185. How does Ms. Han try to persuade Cheshire Foods to consider her suggestion?

    (A) By mentioning a competitor
    (B) By threatening to shop elsewhere
    (C) By illustrating a business mistake
    (D) By showing past losses

GO ON TO THE NEXT PAGE

**Questions 186-190** refer to the following list, schedule, and memo.

---

**Starden Foods, Inc.**

Created by Consumer Research Department
June 29

**Comparison of marketing expenses on food categories with sales changes**

Study covered all 637 stores in the European Union. A comparison next quarter will focus on stores in the Americas and the Asia Pacific.

| Department | Amount spent on marketing (in millions) | Change in unit sales from last year |
|---|---|---|
| Fruits and Vegetables | €4.3 | +4.2% |
| Breads | €12.8 | +3.8% |
| Dry Goods | €26.6 | -1.9% |
| Meats | €18.2 | +0.5% |
| Dairy | €31.4 | -2.2% |
| Seafood | €12.6 | +0.1% |

Note: Scheduled for discussion at the Marketing Plans Meeting on July 25. There will be an updated schedule soon.

---

**Starden Foods, Inc.**

**Division Manager Committee Meetings for the Month of July**

Final agendas for each meeting will be issued at least 3 days ahead of time. Attendance at all meetings is mandatory, unless urgent client-related or other business arises.

| Date | Topic |
|---|---|
| July 4 | Supplier Review |
| July 11 | Marketing Plans |
| July 18 | Store Maintenance Issues |
| July 25 | Quality Control |
| July 31 | Human Resources |

Board directors may attend any meeting with little or no advance notice.

To: Division Managers
From: Brenda Phan, COO
Date: July 12
Subject: Business Report

**MEMO**

Colleagues,

In yesterday's meeting, we discussed whether there is a correlation between the amount of money spent on marketing certain products and the revenue generated from those products. Currently, we can say that the connection is not very clear. We reviewed the list that compares shopper spending traits, and found some surprises. Helen Smith had to miss the meeting, but we talked afterwards. She pointed out products that experienced high sales growth.

You might intuitively feel that we have to spend more money on our products experiencing the lowest sales. However, I think it would be better instead to increase marketing support for our products experiencing the highest sales.

If a product category is experiencing weak sales, I do not think that more advertising alone can improve the situation. Instead, we have to look at other factors, such as quality or price. That is what I tried to stress to Evan Lee, who unexpectedly but fortunately was able to join the meeting. He seemed to agree with my analysis. In any event, I have attached a report detailing this idea, which I'd like to discuss at our next meeting. I don't think that we should put it off until the last gathering of the month.

Thank you,

Brenda Phan

---

**186.** According to the list, what is true about the research?
(A) It compares different shopper categories.
(B) It spans several quarters.
(C) It includes many Asian stores.
(D) It covers a single region.

**187.** What is suggested about the list?
(A) It was created by an outside firm.
(B) It will be distributed at a meeting.
(C) A meeting about it was rescheduled.
(D) A report about it has been written.

**188.** What is indicated about the July 11 meeting?
(A) A member had urgent business.
(B) A rule was revised.
(C) A maintenance issue was solved.
(D) An important client was invited.

**189.** In the memo, the word "connection" in paragraph 1, line 3, is closest in meaning to
(A) termination
(B) wire
(C) relationship
(D) payment

**190.** Who most likely is Evan Lee?
(A) A marketing expert
(B) A senior executive
(C) A consumer analyst
(D) A dairy manufacturer

GO ON TO THE NEXT PAGE

**Questions 191-195** refer to the following product information, online review, and response.

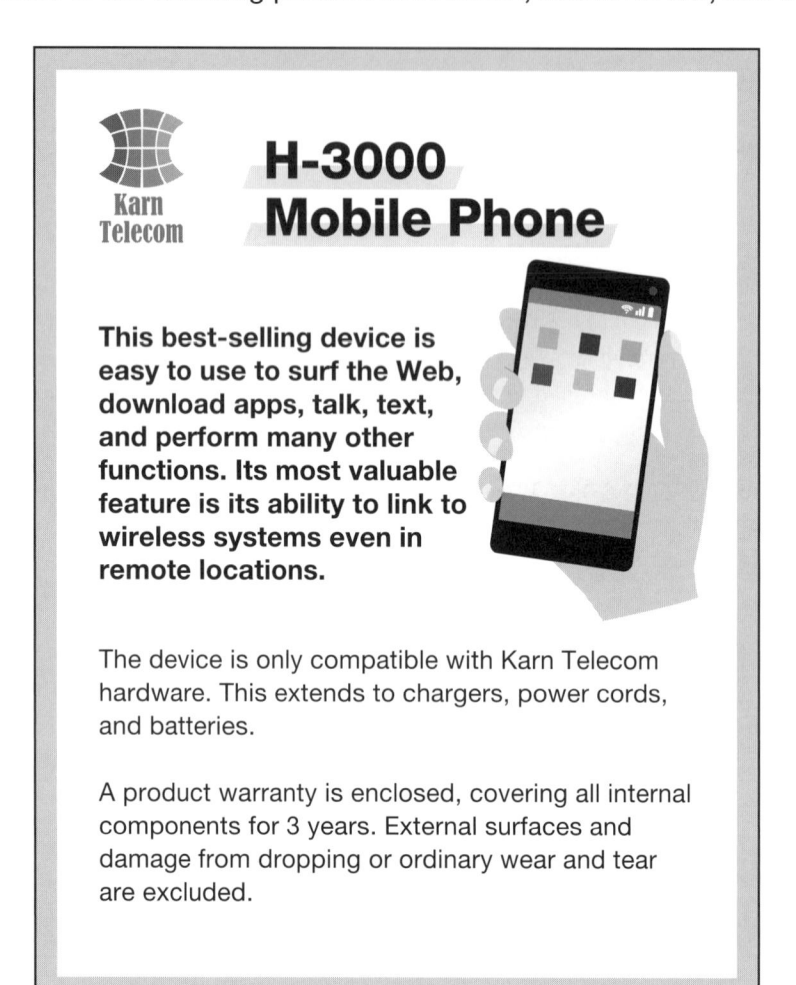

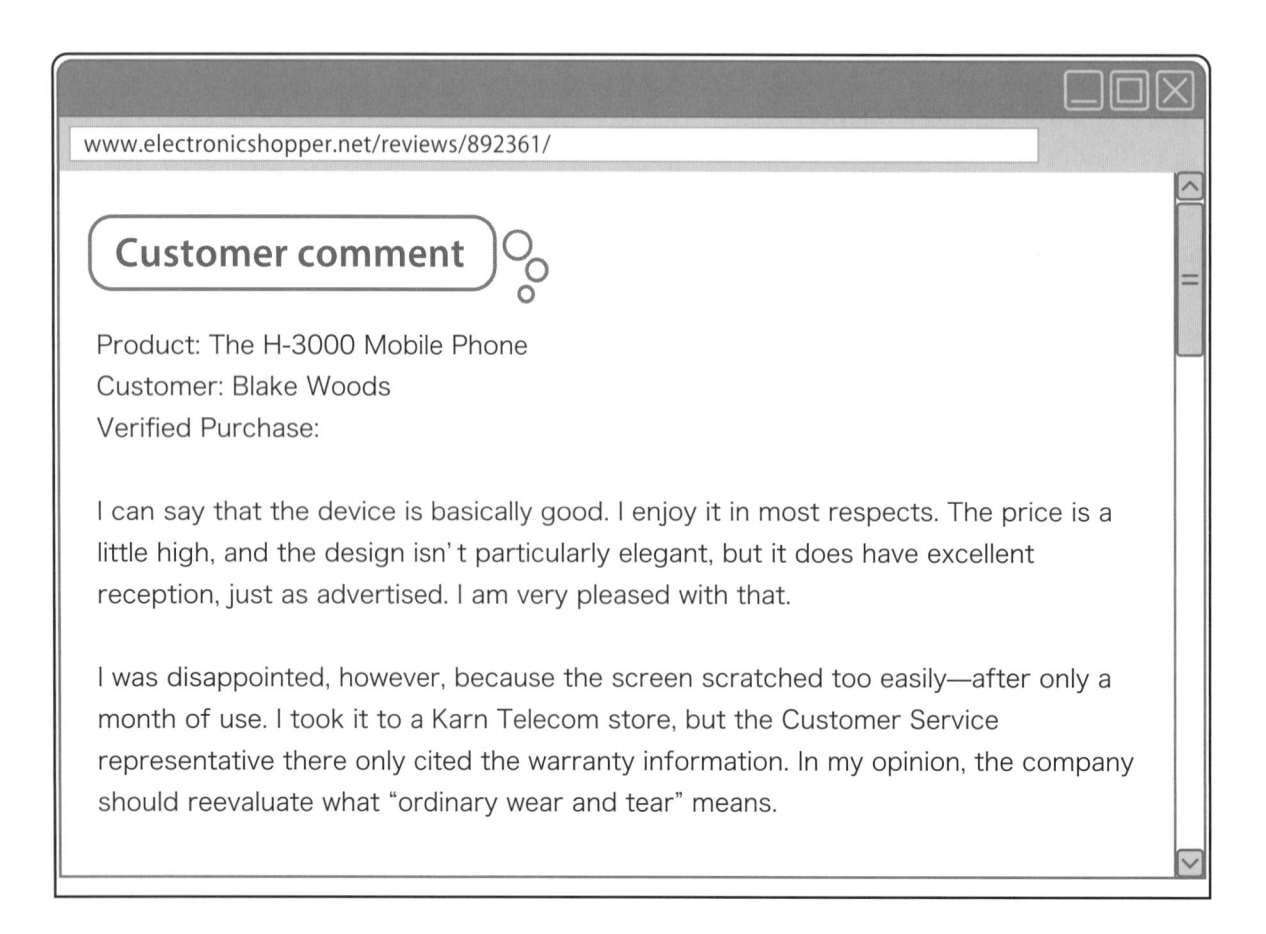

### Karn Telecom
# H-3000 Mobile Phone

This best-selling device is easy to use to surf the Web, download apps, talk, text, and perform many other functions. Its most valuable feature is its ability to link to wireless systems even in remote locations.

The device is only compatible with Karn Telecom hardware. This extends to chargers, power cords, and batteries.

A product warranty is enclosed, covering all internal components for 3 years. External surfaces and damage from dropping or ordinary wear and tear are excluded.

---

www.electronicshopper.net/reviews/892361/

**Customer comment**

Product: The H-3000 Mobile Phone
Customer: Blake Woods
Verified Purchase:

I can say that the device is basically good. I enjoy it in most respects. The price is a little high, and the design isn't particularly elegant, but it does have excellent reception, just as advertised. I am very pleased with that.

I was disappointed, however, because the screen scratched too easily—after only a month of use. I took it to a Karn Telecom store, but the Customer Service representative there only cited the warranty information. In my opinion, the company should reevaluate what "ordinary wear and tear" means.

www.electronicshopper.net/reviews/892361/

**Customer comment**

Product: The H-3000 Mobile Phone
Customer: Blake Woods
Response from: Karn Telecom Customer Service

Thank you very much for your review. Your feedback is very important to us. Unfortunately, our 3-year warranty is explicit on the subject of surface wear, and the response given to you by the Customer Service representative you spoke with is consistent with that. However, if you do opt for a replacement, we recommend our Z-1X model, which has a stronger screen and is more scratch-resistant. Additionally, we would suggest enrolling in our Extended Care Program. This will warranty your internal components for 2 additional years. The cost for this program is only $175. We want to make sure that you receive the very best support for your product, and we look forward to your continued patronage and feedback.

191. What is NOT mentioned in the product information?

   (A) Internet use
   (B) Access security
   (C) Battery components
   (D) Sales ranking

192. In the online review, the word "respects" in paragraph 1, line 1, is closest in meaning to

   (A) predictions
   (B) transmissions
   (C) aspects
   (D) patterns

193. What is Mr. Woods particularly pleased with about the mobile phone?

   (A) Its connectivity
   (B) Its compatibility
   (C) Its design
   (D) Its price

194. What is the total warranty length Karn Telecom can offer?

   (A) 1 year
   (B) 3 years
   (C) 4 years
   (D) 5 years

195. What was the Customer Service representative correct about?

   (A) The method to avoid scratches
   (B) The need for program enrollment
   (C) The coverage for a device
   (D) The best kind of mobile phone screen

GO ON TO THE NEXT PAGE

**Questions 196-200** refer to the following notice, e-mail, and article.

# Jowel Community Center
17 Lakeland Street
www.jowelcenter.org

**Special Event: Building Your Wealth — Tips for Ordinary People**
Speaker: Joseph Steinz, Personal Financial Consultant
April 23

<u>Free and open to the public</u>

**Learn:** Home budget management skills
Choosing the right bank or financial institution
The basics of stocks, bonds, and other investing or reinvesting options

30-Minute Question and Answer Session to follow the talk
Tea, coffee and snacks provided

While the event is free and open to the public, space is limited, and guaranteed seating can be assured only to the first 75 people who register. Please visit the Web site above to register. For more information, contact Bozena Kovac, special event organizer: bozena@jowelccenter.org.

---

* E-mail *

| To: | bozena@jowelccenter.org |
| From: | joseph.steinz@zoneumail.net |
| Date: | April 11 |
| Subject: | Second Reminder: Certification |

Dear Ms. Kovac,

I regret to inform you that I will not be able to speak at your April 23 Community Center event on finance management. I have an urgent business matter that I have to attend to on that day. I do not want to let down your attendees, so I have arranged a colleague of mine to take my place. I can guarantee that he is more than qualified to do so as he has both taught and written extensively on this topic. Details are in the attachment.

I apologize for this situation, and trust the event will work out well. If I can help in any other way, please do not hesitate to let me know.

Yours sincerely,

Joseph Steinz

# NEWS DAILY

## Special Event at Jowel Community Center

By Eve Sanders, Special Correspondent

It was a pleasure to hear Wazir Sanjrani speak at the April 23 financial planning event at the Jowel Community Center. This highly accomplished investor took complex topics such as stocks, bonds, and mutual funds, and simplified them so that everyone could understand. He did this repeatedly and in a friendly way, making the talk not only informative but pleasant.

He also explained clearly how people could slowly grow their money starting with just a low sum. This was encouraging, since most of the attendees were simple working men and women. I think all of the attendees also appreciated the fact that Mr. Sanjrani allowed a full one-hour question and answer session.

However, I believe the audiovisual system of the center could benefit from renovation. Several times, it faded out and it was difficult to understand what the speaker was saying.

---

**196.** What information is NOT mentioned in the notice?

(A) Photo IDs
(B) Participant registration
(C) Refreshment items
(D) Event location

**197.** What is indicated about Wazir Sanjrani?

(A) He updated a Web site.
(B) He earned speaker fees.
(C) He works at a bank.
(D) He replaced a presenter.

**198.** What is indicated about the event?

(A) The main topic of the session was changed.
(B) The payment to sign up was increased.
(C) Entrance to the location was unrestricted.
(D) The question and answer time was extended.

**199.** In the article, what does Ms. Sanders say the speaker did well?

(A) He summarized his financial accomplishments.
(B) He reviewed the best financial markets.
(C) He put difficult topics into plain terms.
(D) He made individual investment portfolios.

**200.** What problem is mentioned in the article?

(A) Attendees were fewer than expected.
(B) Some equipment was defective.
(C) Some topics were omitted.
(D) Financial analyses were unclear.

---

**Stop! This is the end of the test. If you finish before time is called, you may go back to Parts 5, 6, and 7 and check your work.**

※ リスニングセクションは付属 CD の DISC 2 を再生してください。

# 第2回 模擬試験

※ リスニングセクションは付属 CD の DISC 2 を再生してください。

## LISTENING TEST

In the Listening test, you will be asked to demonstrate how well you understand spoken English. The entire Listening test will last approximately 45 minutes. There are four parts, and directions are given for each part. You must mark your answers on the separate answer sheet.
Do not write your answers in your test book.

### PART 1

**Directions:** For each question in this part, you will hear four statements about a picture in your test book. When you hear the statements, you must select the one statement that best describes what you see in the picture. Then find the number of the question on your answer sheet and mark your answer. The statements will not be printed in your test book and will be spoken only one time.

Statement (C), "They're sitting at a table," is the best description of the picture, so you should select answer (C) and mark it on your answer sheet.

1.

2.

*GO ON TO THE NEXT PAGE*

3.

4.

5.

6.

GO ON TO THE NEXT PAGE

## PART 2

**Directions:** You will hear a question or statement and three responses spoken in English. They will not be printed in your test book and will be spoken only one time. Select the best response to the question or statement and mark the letter (A), (B), or (C) on your answer sheet.

7. Mark your answer on your answer sheet.
8. Mark your answer on your answer sheet.
9. Mark your answer on your answer sheet.
10. Mark your answer on your answer sheet.
11. Mark your answer on your answer sheet.
12. Mark your answer on your answer sheet.
13. Mark your answer on your answer sheet.
14. Mark your answer on your answer sheet.
15. Mark your answer on your answer sheet.
16. Mark your answer on your answer sheet.
17. Mark your answer on your answer sheet.
18. Mark your answer on your answer sheet.
19. Mark your answer on your answer sheet.
20. Mark your answer on your answer sheet.
21. Mark your answer on your answer sheet.
22. Mark your answer on your answer sheet.
23. Mark your answer on your answer sheet.
24. Mark your answer on your answer sheet.
25. Mark your answer on your answer sheet.
26. Mark your answer on your answer sheet.
27. Mark your answer on your answer sheet.
28. Mark your answer on your answer sheet.
29. Mark your answer on your answer sheet.
30. Mark your answer on your answer sheet.
31. Mark your answer on your answer sheet.

## PART 3

**Directions:** You will hear some conversations between two or more people. You will be asked to answer three questions about what the speakers say in each conversation. Select the best response to each question and mark the letter (A), (B), (C), or (D) on your answer sheet. The conversations will not be printed in your test book and will be spoken only one time.

32. Where are the speakers?
    (A) In Dublin
    (B) In London
    (C) In Brussels
    (D) In Paris

33. What does the woman want Michelle to do?
    (A) Send her an e-mail
    (B) Call her directly
    (C) Fax her some files
    (D) Come to see her

34. What does one of the men say will happen in a few minutes?
    (A) A conference will end.
    (B) A train will leave.
    (C) A deadline will arrive.
    (D) A project will be launched.

35. Who most likely is the woman?
    (A) A tour agent
    (B) An airline clerk
    (C) A bank representative
    (D) An insurance salesperson

36. What would the man prefer to take on his trip?
    (A) A debit card
    (B) A credit card
    (C) Cash
    (D) Traveler's checks

37. What does the SunCrest logo on ATMs and buildings indicate?
    (A) The brand is popular.
    (B) The usage fee is low.
    (C) Debit cards can be used.
    (D) The machine is new.

38. Where most likely are the speakers?
    (A) On an airplane
    (B) On a bus
    (C) On a ship
    (D) On a train

39. What is the final destination?
    (A) Philadelphia
    (B) Boston
    (C) New York
    (D) Washington, D.C.

40. When is the woman likely to reach her destination?
    (A) In about two hours
    (B) In about three hours
    (C) In about four hours
    (D) In about five hours

41. Where most likely are the speakers?
    (A) At a conference
    (B) At a presentation
    (C) At a workplace
    (D) At a library

42. What will happen on June 25?
    (A) New employees will start work.
    (B) A department will relocate.
    (C) Presentations will end.
    (D) Training will begin.

43. What must the speakers do today?
    (A) Alter the program schedule
    (B) Verify attendance
    (C) Hand in their brochures
    (D) Go to a conference

*GO ON TO THE NEXT PAGE*

44. What is the woman doing?
    (A) Returning goods
    (B) Concluding a transaction
    (C) Applying for credit
    (D) Explaining about products

45. How much did the woman save?
    (A) 10 percent
    (B) 20 percent
    (C) 25 percent
    (D) 30 percent

46. What did the woman misunderstand?
    (A) The credit card limit
    (B) The item price
    (C) The location of the store
    (D) The refund policy

47. What are the speakers mainly discussing?
    (A) Expanding their market share
    (B) Offering a discount
    (C) Lowering expenses
    (D) Selling new products

48. Why does the man think that they need to change their supplier?
    (A) To access better materials
    (B) To remain competitive
    (C) To order online
    (D) To raise product prices

49. What did Ricardo do?
    (A) Transferred to eastern Europe
    (B) Simplified operations
    (C) Saved money
    (D) Reviewed the data

50. What most likely is the Red Wolf?
    (A) A radio
    (B) A mobile phone
    (C) A Web site
    (D) A television set

51. What does the man offer to do for the woman?
    (A) Exchange a model
    (B) Upgrade a component
    (C) Show her some products
    (D) Order a product

52. Why does the woman say, "the simpler, the better"?
    (A) She does not need a lot of extra functions.
    (B) She wants to acquire the product promptly.
    (C) She values unique design features.
    (D) She strongly believes in quality over quantity.

53. Where most likely are the speakers?
    (A) At an amusement park
    (B) At a bus terminal
    (C) At a movie theater
    (D) At a bookstore

54. What is the woman's preferred time?
    (A) 1:00
    (B) 3:00
    (C) 7:00
    (D) 10:00

55. What does the man suggest the woman do?
    (A) Wait for two hours
    (B) Check another area
    (C) Get a refund
    (D) Accept an alternative

56. What are the speakers doing?
    (A) Touring a site
    (B) Preparing for an event
    (C) Taking a break
    (D) Making a presentation

57. What does the woman mean when she says, "I think I'd rather not"?
    (A) She is not interested in the exhibition.
    (B) She hopes that she will quit her job soon.
    (C) She wants to stay and work in the office.
    (D) She might be able to accompany the man.

58. What will the attendees receive?
    (A) Presents
    (B) Complimentary tickets
    (C) Gift certificates
    (D) Conference brochures

59. What happened last night?
    (A) A door was installed.
    (B) A system was changed.
    (C) An entrance was closed.
    (D) A code was updated.

60. What does the man say about the woman's ID card?
    (A) It needs a new magnetic strip.
    (B) It needs to be replaced.
    (C) It works when slid through a reader.
    (D) It works at another entrance.

61. Why does the man recommend seeing Susan?
    (A) She supervises human resources.
    (B) She manages IT.
    (C) She makes repairs.
    (D) She has more details.

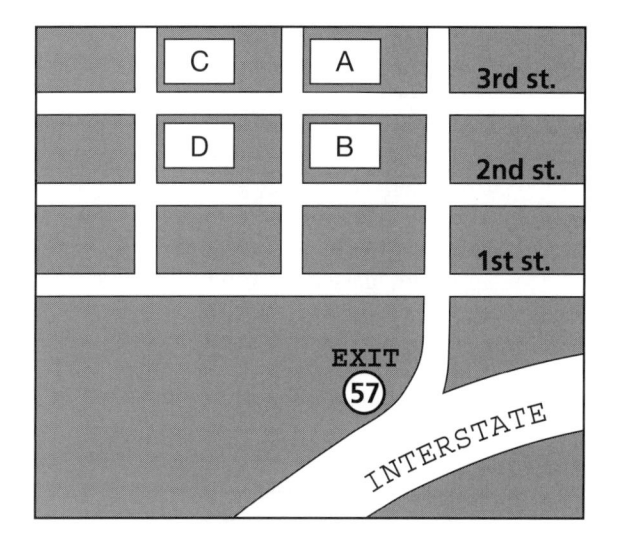

62. What is probably the woman's problem?
    (A) She has lost some documents.
    (B) She cannot find a location.
    (C) She has to change plans quickly.
    (D) She does not have a car.

63. What is the man being asked to do?
    (A) Attend a meeting
    (B) Travel downtown
    (C) Clean an office
    (D) Sign some papers

64. Look at the graphic. Where is the downtown branch office located?
    (A) Building A
    (B) Building B
    (C) Building C
    (D) Building D

GO ON TO THE NEXT PAGE

**STYLE** #55xl-navy

100% COTTON

Dry clean or machine wash cold. Inside out with like colors. Tumble dry low. Non-chlorine bleach only.

Made in U.S.A.

L

$16.99

---

**Candie's Candleworks**

**$4 Jar Candles**
**Buy One, Get One FREE**

Present this coupon to receive one jar candle of equal or lesser value with the purchase of one at regular price.
Must be presented at time of purchase.
Limit one coupon per customer.

---

65. What is the conversation mainly about?

    (A) An incorrect purchase
    (B) Overpayment for an item
    (C) A problem with an item
    (D) An item being out of stock

66. Look at the graphic. How could the problem have been avoided?

    (A) By using cold water
    (B) By using hot water
    (C) By using bleach
    (D) By drying the item

67. What does the woman suggest the man do?

    (A) Buy a different size
    (B) Wash the item again
    (C) Get a refund for the item
    (D) Purchase another item

68. What is the woman's problem?

    (A) She cannot use a coupon.
    (B) She does not have enough money.
    (C) She cannot find an item.
    (D) She cannot get a refund.

69. Look at the graphic. How many free candles will the woman get?

    (A) Two
    (B) Three
    (C) Four
    (D) Six

70. What will the man most likely do next?

    (A) Contact another store
    (B) Wrap some items
    (C) Take a customer's order
    (D) Look for another candle

## PART 4

**Directions:** You will hear some talks given by a single speaker. You will be asked to answer three questions about what the speaker says in each talk. Select the best response to each question and mark the letter (A), (B), (C), or (D) on your answer sheet. The talks will not be printed in your test book and will be spoken only one time.

71. According to the speaker, what can be found in the training materials?
    (A) Locations of all the divisions
    (B) Names of their competitors
    (C) Information about the company's expertise
    (D) Advice on investments

72. What is implied about Leighton?
    (A) It has gained a large market share.
    (B) It has existed for a long time.
    (C) It has used complex strategies.
    (D) It has recruited new managers.

73. What will the listeners do next?
    (A) Take off their ID badges
    (B) Retrieve their mobile phones
    (C) Go up to the second floor
    (D) Tour the trading area

74. What is the advertisement mainly about?
    (A) A product demonstration
    (B) A travel opportunity
    (C) A local competition
    (D) A sales campaign

75. What feature of Lemon Gold One Gel is mentioned?
    (A) Size
    (B) Popularity
    (C) Usefulness
    (D) Price

76. What does the speaker imply when he says, "Seats will be given on a first come, first served basis"?
    (A) There are no more seats left.
    (B) People should come to the place early.
    (C) The show will start earlier than planned.
    (D) A light meal will be given during the show.

77. What is the report mainly about?
    (A) An upcoming takeover
    (B) An appointment of a new CEO
    (C) An upturn in consumer spending
    (D) New markets in China

78. What will the companies achieve as a result of the deal?
    (A) Higher revenue
    (B) Better products
    (C) Reduced costs
    (D) Improved technologies

79. According to the report, what has been Mr. Rice's policy at Astar Pharmaceuticals?
    (A) Increasing size
    (B) Upgrading services
    (C) Raising share prices
    (D) Production in mainland China

80. What does the speaker imply when she says, "I can barely hear music on it, no matter which direction I turn the dial"?
    (A) There is something wrong with the volume dial.
    (B) The directions are too complicated for her.
    (C) She cannot find the dial to turn.
    (D) She wants to know what music is on.

81. What does the speaker want to do?
    (A) Find a manual
    (B) Extend a warranty
    (C) Locate a repair shop
    (D) Receive a new product

82. What does the speaker say about herself?
    (A) She has had the same problem before.
    (B) She has made partial repairs.
    (C) She has called previously.
    (D) She has received a replacement.

*GO ON TO THE NEXT PAGE*

83. What is the main purpose of the talk?
    (A) To announce a schedule
    (B) To perform a new opera
    (C) To outline a goal
    (D) To discuss problems

84. According to the speaker, how many euros have been donated so far?
    (A) 2.0 million
    (B) 2.1 million
    (C) 2.2 million
    (D) 2.3 million

85. What is an advantage of being a sponsor?
    (A) Music previews
    (B) Backstage passes
    (C) Free champagne
    (D) Exclusive events

86. Who most likely are the listeners?
    (A) Corporate staff
    (B) Business journalists
    (C) Media analysts
    (D) Market regulators

87. What is Richard Kashumbe's current occupation?
    (A) Marketing manager
    (B) Film director
    (C) Communication expert
    (D) Journalist

88. What will happen next?
    (A) Refreshments will be served.
    (B) A different speaker will talk.
    (C) A press conference will begin.
    (D) Questions will be taken.

89. Why does the woman say, "Yes, you heard right"?
    (A) To agree with an opinion
    (B) To emphasize what she says
    (C) To ask for permission
    (D) To show her gratitude

90. What is true of the goods in Aisle 3?
    (A) They are from major companies.
    (B) They are unique to Victoria Supermarket.
    (C) They are all edible.
    (D) They are sold only in the morning.

91. What are customers using Aisle 3 unable to do?
    (A) Pay by credit cards
    (B) Buy leading brands
    (C) Receive shopping points
    (D) Shop in other aisles

92. What is the broadcast mainly about?
    (A) Financial results
    (B) Leadership changes
    (C) Brand development
    (D) Market trends

93. What is Bob Heller expected to do next?
    (A) Leave the company
    (B) Hire a rival
    (C) Transfer to Toronto
    (D) Oversee investments

94. What has Jason Yu said he will do?
    (A) Increase net income
    (B) Raise staffing levels
    (C) Lower manufacturing costs
    (D) Launch new products

## Johnson Corp.

### Maintenance Request Form

Submitted by: __Royce Brown__
Supervisor: __Michael Halvorsen__
Location: __Meeting Room 4__

### Room Setup

- 70 chairs, 7 rows of 10
- Set up projector screen on west side of room

### Top Products
(in $ thousands)

95. Why is the woman calling?
    (A) To cancel an order
    (B) To amend a request
    (C) To make an appointment
    (D) To schedule a meeting

96. Look at the graphic. What does the woman want Mike to do before the meeting?
    (A) Put the screen on the east side of the room
    (B) Move some tables to the other room
    (C) Reduce the number of chairs
    (D) Change the type of projector

97. When will Mike most likely return the call?
    (A) This morning
    (B) This afternoon
    (C) Tomorrow morning
    (D) Tomorrow afternoon

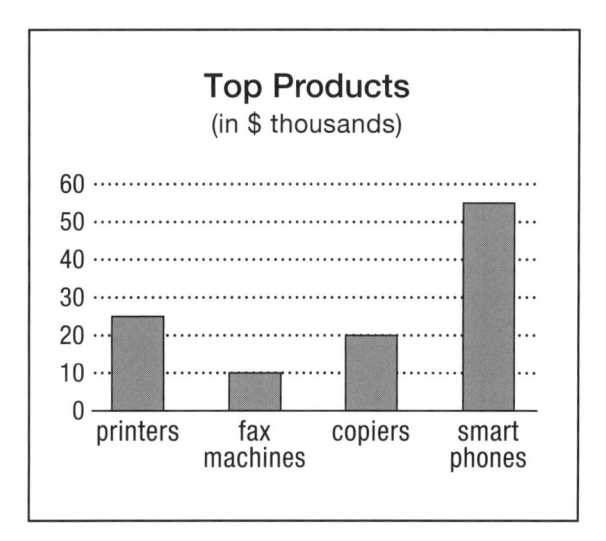

98. Where most likely does the man work?
    (A) At a printing company
    (B) At an office supply retailer
    (C) At a research firm
    (D) At a telecommunications center

99. Look at the graphic. What figure does the man predict as a result of the campaign?
    (A) $20,000
    (B) $30,000
    (C) $40,000
    (D) $50,000

100. What will the man do after the meeting?
    (A) Help with a campaign
    (B) Put together a report
    (C) Make a presentation
    (D) Consult with a department

This is the end of the Listening test. Turn to Part 5 in your test book.

GO ON TO THE NEXT PAGE

## READING TEST

In the Reading test, you will read a variety of texts and answer several different types of reading comprehension questions. The entire Reading test will last 75 minutes. There are three parts, and directions are given for each part. You are encouraged to answer as many questions as possible within the time allowed.

You must mark your answers on the separate answer sheet. Do not write your answers in your test book.

## PART 5

**Directions:** A word or phrase is missing in each of the sentences below. Four answer choices are given below each sentence. Select the best answer to complete the sentence. Then mark the letter (A), (B), (C), or (D) on your answer sheet.

101. Heart Life Corporation's new medicine will be distributed in pharmacies after ------- over a period of 18 months certifies that it is safe.
    (A) test
    (B) testing
    (C) tested
    (D) have tested

102. The entire downtown business area was filled ------- 12 hours with shoppers enjoying holiday discounts.
    (A) as
    (B) in
    (C) on
    (D) for

103. Analysts report that shopping online for groceries has ------- changed the entire supermarket experience.
    (A) dramatically
    (B) accusingly
    (C) impenetrably
    (D) combatively

104. Chinese retailer Zin Mart predicted no ------- in profits for the year, despite a slowdown in consumer spending.
    (A) deteriorate
    (B) deteriorated
    (C) deteriorating
    (D) deterioration

105. In case this event is canceled, ticket holders will each ------- the full face value of their purchase.
    (A) entitle
    (B) receive
    (C) remove
    (D) object

106. Trascki Automobile Company has gone from strength ------- strength since entering the North American market.
    (A) on
    (B) in
    (C) and
    (D) to

107. Millions of consumers are rushing to buy the game software, leaving storeowners ------- to meet demand.
    (A) conflicting
    (B) contesting
    (C) targeting
    (D) struggling

108. The ------- merit of Mr. Rysbecki's financial model comes from its ability to predict demand for the company's products.
    (A) relative
    (B) relation
    (C) relate
    (D) relatively

109. Mr. Kim said he would prefer ------- in the Seoul office rather than transfer to the smaller branch in Incheon.
    (A) remains
    (B) to remain
    (C) remained
    (D) had remained

110. CEO Gawande of IndoOne Tech was known for his honest and ------- approach to business negotiations.
    (A) opening
    (B) openly
    (C) open
    (D) opened

111. The client ------- us make several revisions to the advertising campaign literature, such as putting the logo in a more prominent position.
    (A) had
    (B) did
    (C) permitted
    (D) got

112. Harris Corporation acted ------- in recruiting the very best personnel for all of its divisions.
    (A) assertion
    (B) asserting
    (C) asserts
    (D) assertively

113. Green World Foods emerged as the most ------- brand in a survey, with 93% of respondents feeling positive about the company.
    (A) imported
    (B) trusted
    (C) reviewed
    (D) assumed

114. The emergence of satellite TV is generating a crucial ------- that even local entertainment companies can market globally.
    (A) understands
    (B) understandably
    (C) understanding
    (D) understandable

115. The board of directors at Dragon Robotics Co. reacted ------- to the idea of merging with a rival corporation.
    (A) positively
    (B) positive
    (C) positiveness
    (D) positivity

116. Professor Shah's expertise in industrial engineering earned him an ------- reputation in his field.
    (A) insurable
    (B) unwarranted
    (C) unintentional
    (D) enviable

117. Director Khan said the senior managers of the company had made a number of ------- comments regarding its reorganization.
    (A) construction
    (B) constructive
    (C) construct
    (D) constructively

118. The expansion of Titan Corporation's factories in Indonesia ------- as part of its goal of increasing output from its facilities in the region.
    (A) will see
    (B) is seeing
    (C) was seen
    (D) being seen

119. Global Footwear Inc. is ------- larger than its domestic rivals, which gives it a much larger marketing budget.
    (A) consecutively
    (B) considerably
    (C) consequently
    (D) confusingly

120. Following months of -------, Joshua Technologies publicly announced its takeover of Carpon Digital Design for £375.5 million.
    (A) education
    (B) speculation
    (C) performance
    (D) regulation

GO ON TO THE NEXT PAGE

69

121. Lopez Telecom Co. won a contract to build a telecommunication network in Eastern Europe, ------- in a 14% rise in profits.
    (A) result
    (B) to result
    (C) resulting
    (D) will result

122. The success of the Crystal Mountain Resort Hotel ------- by its low vacancy rate of only about 3% almost year-round.
    (A) could determine
    (B) can be determined
    (C) to be determined
    (D) is determining

123. One of the main strengths of Ms. Chou's company lies in ------- ability to uncover previously undeveloped markets.
    (A) it
    (B) herself
    (C) hers
    (D) its

124. Attendees at the One Globe Financial Seminar will have a chance to learn ------- corporations should carefully manage their internal cash reserves at all times.
    (A) they
    (B) why
    (C) them
    (D) what

125. Organic foods at Happy Face Restaurants are becoming ------- popular, as people realize the benefits of making healthy food choices.
    (A) increasing
    (B) increase
    (C) increasingly
    (D) increment

126. Although White Sky Airlines has lost some of its market share in recent years, it is still ------- than its rivals.
    (A) establishing
    (B) establishes
    (C) more established
    (D) most established

127. The *Dancing Baby* doll created a great ------- among consumers, and sold in very large numbers upon its initial release.
    (A) sensation
    (B) compensation
    (C) determination
    (D) promotion

128. The communications department ------- the company's media coverage, both at home and abroad.
    (A) monitors
    (B) renovates
    (C) contacts
    (D) invests

129. PetCare1.com is a corporation ------- has been able to tap into the multibillion dollar pet market by shipping a variety of dog and cat-related products directly to owners.
    (A) who
    (B) whose
    (C) which
    (D) what

130. Caris Coffee has ------- its commitment to donate 5% of its annual profits to charities in Eastern Kenya.
    (A) confirmed
    (B) contributed
    (C) contacted
    (D) concerned

# PART 6

**Directions:** Read the texts that follow. A word, phrase, or sentence is missing in parts of each text. Four answer choices for each question are given below the text. Select the best answer to complete the text. Then mark the letter (A), (B), (C), or (D) on your answer sheet.

**Questions 131-134** refer to the following e-mail.

To: Francesco Milletti
From: Masoud Akbar
Date: 31 August
Subject: Replacement request

Dear Mr. Milletti,

I received your e-mail yesterday. In it, you ------- the shipment of the construction materials from Milan. I have pasted information from that e-mail below.
**131.**

| | |
|---|---|
| Steel beams | 200 |
| Wood beams | 175 |
| Concrete mix | 500 kilograms |
| Glass Panes | 600 |
| Tools | 34 pieces |

We have checked the shipment, and most of the goods that arrived are fine. There is one issue, however: ------- the number of glass panes noted above totaled what we had ordered, there were
**132.**
variances in quality. Some of the panes were quite thick, for example, while others were thin.

-------. We would therefore like to have 100 replacement panes ------- to us.
**133.**                                                                   **134.**

If you are able to do this before 7 September, that would be ideal, as that would mean minimum disruption to our construction schedule. Please let me know when we can expect the replacement units.

Regards,
Masoud Akbar

---

**131.** (A) confirmed
(B) negotiated
(C) permitted
(D) accepted

**132.** (A) yet
(B) despite
(C) unless
(D) although

**133.** (A) We really like these high-quality products.
(B) We really need all the items to be of a similar quality.
(C) These panes are normally either too thick or thin.
(D) There are no complaints whatsoever about the price.

**134.** (A) send
(B) sent
(C) sending
(D) to send

*GO ON TO THE NEXT PAGE*

71

**Questions 135-138** refer to the following letter.

Ajit Rahman
22 Ackley Road
Nashville, TN
December 3

Dear Mr. Rahman,

Please find a recent summary of the ------- on your account below.
                                          **135.**

    Amount in account at start of period: $500,000
    Withdrawal, November 13 ................. $6,000
    Deposit, November 15 ....................... $5,320
    Withdrawal, November 30 ................. $4,200
    Ending Balance: .............................. $495,120

We'd also like to remind you that ------- for overdraft protection is highly recommended. Such
                                   **136.**
protection guards you against fees which would otherwise be incurred.

You are currently eligible for up to $5,000 in overdraft protection. Many of our customers feel
that this provides them with -------, as they know they will not be penalized if they write checks for
                              **137.**
amounts temporarily not in their accounts. -------.
                                            **138.**

Sincerely,

Renee Zuiller
Account Manager
r.zuiller@d-bank.com

---

**135.** (A) upgrades
(B) purchases
(C) transactions
(D) investments

**136.** (A) applies
(B) applicable
(C) applications
(D) applying

**137.** (A) secure
(B) secured
(C) more security
(D) more securely

**138.** (A) Please e-mail me if you are interested in this program.
(B) Please let me know if this is possible at your earliest convenience.
(C) If you have any recommendations, I would like to hear them.
(D) I look forward to receiving your next report soon.

**Questions 139-142** refer to the following notice.

The management at Lysell Corporation ------- staff to take care of their bodies as well as their careers.
139.

Apart from our company fitness center and health plan, we have recently launched a Healthy Living campaign, ------- by the Human Resources Department. -------. More precisely, the campaign
140.                                                                 141.
is designed to get our staff to exercise, eat right, and watch their weight. Already, 210 employees have signed up for it.

Elisabeth Choi from the Human Resources Department, who leads the campaign, recommended the staff could get in ------- in various ways, such as cycling to work instead of driving, or taking the
142.
stairs instead of the elevators.

139. (A) encouraging
(B) encouragement
(C) encouragingly
(D) encourages

140. (A) contacted
(B) converted
(C) developed
(D) declared

141. (A) However, the campaign has been running quite smoothly.
(B) The aim of the campaign is to help our staff improve their well-being.
(C) The communication plan would boost the campaign's impact.
(D) Therefore, we would appreciate your contribution to this cause.

142. (A) position
(B) place
(C) touch
(D) shape

GO ON TO THE NEXT PAGE

**Questions 143-146** refer to the following e-mail.

From: David Martin, Operations Director
To: Luiz Rodriguez, Carmel Falls Manager
Subject: Georgetown Branch Opening
Date: Monday, May 5

Luiz,

As you know, the Georgetown Branch of PizzaMan Inc. is due to open this fall. As a result, we now need to ------- staff in the local area.
                  143.

The Carmel Falls Branch is only 10 miles away, so we would like to offer some of your staff the opportunity to join ------- there. We feel that their previous experience of working for PizzaMan
                          144.
could be extremely important in ------- the new branch a success.
                                145.

Please let your employees know about this great new career option as soon as possible. -------.
                                                                                         146.

Sincerely,

David Martin

---

**143.** (A) reorganize
(B) recruit
(C) outsource
(D) survey

**144.** (A) theirs
(B) us
(C) our
(D) their

**145.** (A) causing
(B) going
(C) letting
(D) making

**146.** (A) We will give priority to those who have been with us the longest.
(B) We look forward to serving you at our new Carmel Falls branch.
(C) This is the very first time we have treated you like this.
(D) All staff members should report to work on time each day.

## PART 7

**Directions:** In this part you will read a selection of texts, such as magazine and newspaper articles, e-mails, and instant messages. Each text or set of texts is followed by several questions. Select the best answer for each question and mark the letter (A), (B), (C), or (D) on your answer sheet.

**Questions 147-148** refer to the following ticket.

ADMIT ONE ADULT
# Summer of Strings
*An evening of classical music with the Singapore National Symphony Orchestra*

Kwan Teok Hall
Doors Open: 7:30 P.M.
Performance First Half: 8:15 P.M.
Intermission: 10:00 P.M.
Performance Second Half: 10:30 P.M.

No cameras, videos or other recording devices allowed. No admittance after 10 minutes before the show starts. Please turn off all phones prior to entering. Except in the event of a performance cancellation, all ticket sales are final.

**147.** When is the latest that ticketed guests may enter to see the performance?

(A) 7:30 P.M.
(B) 8:05 P.M.
(C) 8:15 P.M.
(D) 10:00 P.M.

**148.** What is stated on the ticket?

(A) Seating may be unreserved.
(B) Refunds are not usually available.
(C) No cancellations are allowed.
(D) Performance dates are limited.

GO ON TO THE NEXT PAGE

**Questions 149-150** refer to the following text message chain.

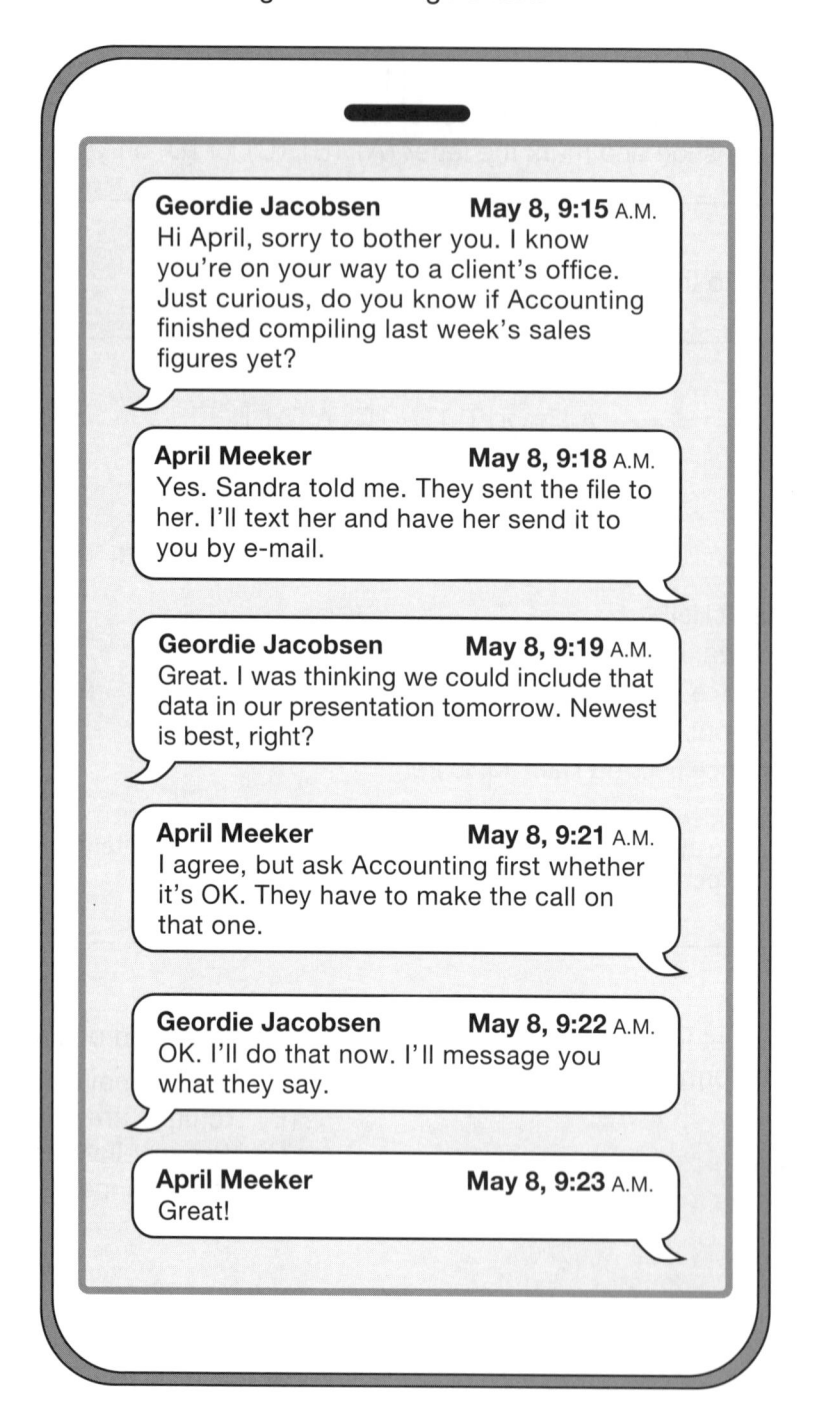

**Geordie Jacobsen**      May 8, 9:15 A.M.
Hi April, sorry to bother you. I know you're on your way to a client's office. Just curious, do you know if Accounting finished compiling last week's sales figures yet?

**April Meeker**      May 8, 9:18 A.M.
Yes. Sandra told me. They sent the file to her. I'll text her and have her send it to you by e-mail.

**Geordie Jacobsen**      May 8, 9:19 A.M.
Great. I was thinking we could include that data in our presentation tomorrow. Newest is best, right?

**April Meeker**      May 8, 9:21 A.M.
I agree, but ask Accounting first whether it's OK. They have to make the call on that one.

**Geordie Jacobsen**      May 8, 9:22 A.M.
OK. I'll do that now. I'll message you what they say.

**April Meeker**      May 8, 9:23 A.M.
Great!

**149.** What is Ms. Meeker doing now?

(A) Gathering some data
(B) Preparing for a presentation
(C) Writing an e-mail to Accounting
(D) Going to a client's office

**150.** At 9:21 A.M., what does Ms. Meeker most likely mean when she writes, "They have to make the call on that one"?

(A) Accounting has to give permission to use data.
(B) Accounting has to give a presentation.
(C) She has to make a phone call to Accounting.
(D) She has to forward the data to Mr. Jacobsen.

Questions 151-152 refer to the following information.

## Annual Pan-Pacific Telecom Association Meeting

Macau Lotus Hotel
Pandora Room
July 7

The Association is pleased to announce that during this year's meeting, a keynote lecture will be given by Mr. Sun Liu Fan, widely regarded as the world's leading authority on global telecommunications. His research has led to the development of new insights on emerging advances in the industry. This has enabled both corporations and government regulators to maximize the benefits of this dynamic field.

Following the release of his latest book, *A World Connected*, Mr. Sun will share his most recent findings on telecommunications in emerging markets.

All those wishing to attend the lecture can get more information at www.panpacifictelecomassoc.net/lectures/.

*Fees for attending the annual meeting are not inclusive of the lecture. Those should be covered in advance through the online address noted above.

151. According to the information, what is Mr. Sun renowned for?

(A) His regulatory authority over markets
(B) His financial investments into industry
(C) His many years of experience in different corporations
(D) His expertise and research in a specific field

152. What will attendees who want to hear the lecture have to do?

(A) Join the Association
(B) E-mail Mr. Sun
(C) Pay an extra charge
(D) Download a pass

GO ON TO THE NEXT PAGE

**Questions 153-154** refer to the following instructions.

## The Revlar Microwave Oven User Guide

**P**osition your oven away from sources of heat or moisture, for optimum efficiency.

**D**o not operate it when empty.

**U**se appropriate, heat-resistant cookware, including knives, forks or spoons, at all times. Keep bowls partially covered while cooking, but never seal them completely.

**Y**ou may see moisture collecting on the inner walls or the door when the oven is in use. This is normal.

**C**ooking time varies according to quantity, as well as the fat or water content of the food. Monitor cooking progress to prevent food from drying out, burning or catching fire.

**F**ood with skins or membranes – like whole apples, potatoes or tomatoes – must be pierced before cooking.

**C**lean the insides of the oven and its door after each use so that it remains perfectly dry. This will prevent corrosion.

153. What is stated about the cookware?
  (A) It should be kept away from moisture.
  (B) It should not be used in an operating oven.
  (C) It should be able to withstand heat.
  (D) It should be sealed inside bowls.

154. What is recommended in the instructions?
  (A) The oven should be operated when empty.
  (B) The food should be dry before cooking.
  (C) Airtight containers should be used.
  (D) Holes should be poked into some food before cooking.

**Questions 155-157** refer to the following e-mail.

```
* E-mail *                                                                                              ×
From:     Kim Su-mi, Director, Han Kang Construction Corp.    KOREA
To:       Fara Suleiman, President, Malaya One Real Estate    MALAYSIA
Subject:  Consort Building
Date:     1 August
```

Dear Ms. Suleiman,

Following our videoconference of 29 July with our architects Franklin & Josephs, we feel it is necessary to visit your office to discuss the ongoing progress of the Consort Building project. We hope 4 August might be acceptable to you.

In your last e-mail, you also mentioned needing our assistance with some of your interior work. As you are aware, our agreement covers only the exterior of the building. Beyond that, we can recommend Maxima Space Co., headquartered in Rome. They have extensive experience with interiors, and have worked with us on buildings like yours in the past. Maxima Vice-president Ron Fascenelli has told me his corporation is quite capable of installing carpeting, furnishings, and handling painting for each of the 273 offices within the office building, in addition to other decorating needs as may be required.

I have taken the liberty of asking Mr. Fascenelli to send you a brochure package about his company by post. You can also learn more about them through their Web site www.maximaspaceitalia.com or simply e-mailing Mr. Fascenelli at ron.f@maximaspace.com.

We hope this helps you in your situation.

Yours sincerely,

Kim Su-mi

---

**155.** What is the purpose of Ms. Kim's upcoming meeting with Ms. Suleiman?

(A) To meet construction architects
(B) To propose an additional project outlines
(C) To provide updates on construction work
(D) To inspect building specifications

**156.** Why does Ms. Kim recommend Maxima Space Co.?

(A) They have developed many building exteriors.
(B) They dominate the market in Rome.
(C) They have done a lot of work in interior projects.
(D) They offer the lowest prices.

**157.** What does Ms. Suleiman expect to receive soon?

(A) An e-mail from the vice-president
(B) Some reading material from overseas
(C) A phone call regarding construction deadlines
(D) A Web site service agreement

GO ON TO THE NEXT PAGE

**Questions 158-160** refer to the following advertisement.

### Come Join the Team at Symington Company
### We Animate the World!

**Symington Company, headquartered in New Zealand, announces openings in its Riga, Latvia office.**

**About us:** We are one of the largest companies in the Asia-Pacific region, known for our cutting-edge animation technologies. Our employees are dedicated, hard-working, and generally long-term. Our compensation packages are in most cases well above industry averages. We were chosen "Best Company to Work For" this year by the business news Web site, 21CTrade.com.
**Our recent moves:** We are now entering the European market. The Riga office is intended to serve as the company's base for the Eastern Europe-Russia region.

We are looking for staff in the following areas:

- **Computer Graphics & Animation**
- **Print Illustration**
- **Information Technologies**
- **Management**

All applicants must have at least 3 years of experience in their respective fields. Managerial applicants must have at least 4 additional years. Medium fluency in English required; medium or advanced fluency in Russian, German or French is preferred.

Those interested in one of the positions listed above may apply online at www.symingtonanimation.com/jobs/animation/latvia/. Callers to Personnel about this position will be directed back to this site. Faxed résumés will receive no response. Interviews will take place from October 5 to October 12 at our Riga headquarters, and those who are selected for positions will be notified by October 20. Most positions will start October 23.

**158.** What is indicated about Symington Company?

(A) It is well known in the European region.
(B) It is respected for its Web site technologies.
(C) It is famous for its award-winning products.
(D) It is noted for its generosity to its staff.

**159.** How much experience is required for applicants for managerial positions?

(A) Three years
(B) Four years
(C) Five years
(D) Seven years

**160.** When will Symington Corporation inform successful candidates?

(A) By October 5
(B) By October 12
(C) By October 20
(D) By October 23

GO ON TO THE NEXT PAGE

**Questions 161-163** refer to the following article.

## Accounting for the New Century —in the Right Way

If your company commonly has errors in its financial reports, the accounting computer network, not the staff, is usually more to blame. — [1] —. The errors themselves are only a symptom of that underlying problem.

Consulting companies can advise you on which accounting computers to purchase. These computers are able to manage very large amounts of data, and are linked to a central network. — [2] —. Best of all, they commonly have easy-to-follow operation instructions. Consulting companies can offer advice on using these computers and teach staff to increase productivity through them.

These consulting companies also maintain industry-wide benchmarks for your accounting department. — [3] —. Their Ax Blue reports published each year provide an overview of how corporations and corporate departments in over 200 areas stay world-class. Meeting benchmarks like these ensures that your company is rising to the best practices within your industry. — [4] —.

161. According to the article, why do most accounting errors occur?

 (A) Reports are done too quickly.
 (B) Companies have insufficient data.
 (C) Computer systems are inadequate.
 (D) Supervisors lack management skills.

162. How are the Ax Blue reports helpful to corporations?

 (A) They list the largest corporations in each field.
 (B) They show how to maintain top standards in different sectors.
 (C) They showcase the best managers at major businesses.
 (D) They provide an overview of important markets.

163. In which of the positions marked [1], [2], [3] and [4] does the following sentence best belong?

 "AxTor Consulting Group is a good example of this."

 (A) [1]
 (B) [2]
 (C) [3]
 (D) [4]

**Questions 164-167** refer to the following notice.

## BLIGO TRADING SERVICES
Friday, July 28

Following the senior directors' meeting last week, it has been decided that structural changes at the Bligo Hong Kong branch are necessary. The following measures are to be implemented to make operations more cost-efficient. These changes will be implemented in stages.

### August 1
All help desk issues will be handled by our Bangalore, India global consumer service center. Help desk facilities in Hong Kong, including both human operators and the automated answering system, will cease.

### August 20
The human resources department will utilize Web technologies for recruiting, staff management, employee benefits and other staff services to the maximum extent to decrease current costs in the department.

### August 31
Personnel from the sales and marketing divisions will merge into one group, with expected staffing reductions of 42%.

While it is regrettable that some of these steps will result in job losses for the departments concerned, we are pleased to announce that several new positions have been created in our Mainland China division. Staff who are interested in applying are urged to contact Lisa Vu at lisa.vu@bligo.net for an application form.

---

**164.** What is the purpose of the changes being made by Bligo Trading?
(A) To improve facilities
(B) To reduce operating costs
(C) To reward performance
(D) To upgrade services

**165.** What change is being planned for the human resources department?
(A) Fewer people will be recruited.
(B) Regular work hours will be reduced.
(C) Employee benefits will decrease.
(D) Online systems will be used.

**166.** What will happen on August 31?
(A) Sales will be emphasized over marketing.
(B) A company merger will occur.
(C) Two departments will be combined.
(D) The size of a group will be increased.

**167.** The word "concerned" in paragraph 5, line 2, is closest in meaning to
(A) worried
(B) controlled
(C) related
(D) detailed

**Questions 168-171** refer to the following online chat discussion.

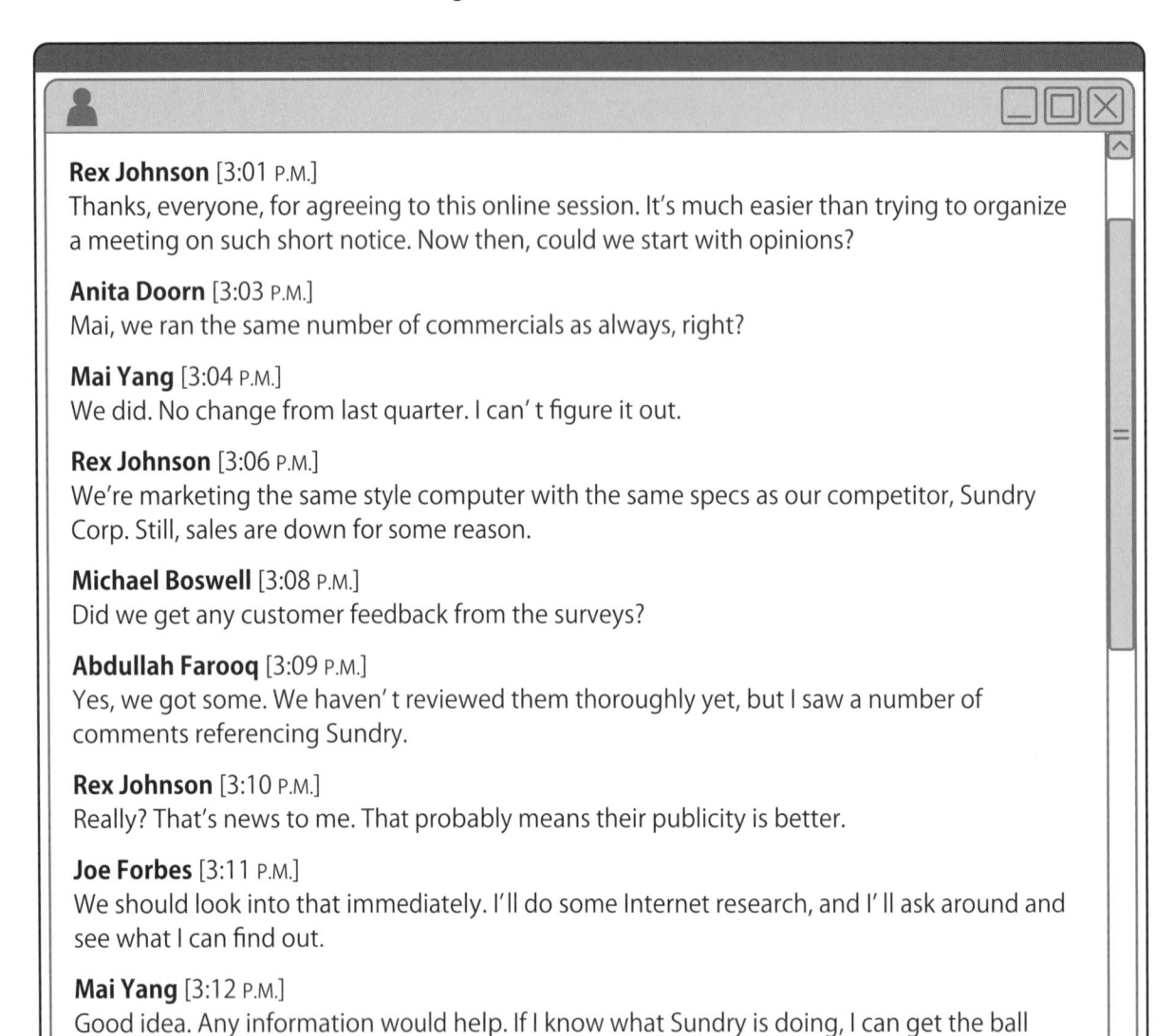

---

**Rex Johnson** [3:01 P.M.]
Thanks, everyone, for agreeing to this online session. It's much easier than trying to organize a meeting on such short notice. Now then, could we start with opinions?

**Anita Doorn** [3:03 P.M.]
Mai, we ran the same number of commercials as always, right?

**Mai Yang** [3:04 P.M.]
We did. No change from last quarter. I can't figure it out.

**Rex Johnson** [3:06 P.M.]
We're marketing the same style computer with the same specs as our competitor, Sundry Corp. Still, sales are down for some reason.

**Michael Boswell** [3:08 P.M.]
Did we get any customer feedback from the surveys?

**Abdullah Farooq** [3:09 P.M.]
Yes, we got some. We haven't reviewed them thoroughly yet, but I saw a number of comments referencing Sundry.

**Rex Johnson** [3:10 P.M.]
Really? That's news to me. That probably means their publicity is better.

**Joe Forbes** [3:11 P.M.]
We should look into that immediately. I'll do some Internet research, and I'll ask around and see what I can find out.

**Mai Yang** [3:12 P.M.]
Good idea. Any information would help. If I know what Sundry is doing, I can get the ball rolling on production of a new commercial.

---

**168.** What is the reason for the discussion?

(A) To discuss a commercial
(B) To review sales figures
(C) To analyze a customer survey
(D) To solicit input from staff

**169.** What most likely is Ms. Yang's job in the company?

(A) She oversees advertisements.
(B) She builds computer applications.
(C) She designs Web pages.
(D) She manages sales.

**170.** At 3:10 P.M., what does Mr. Johnson most likely mean when he writes, "That's news to me"?

(A) He was unaware.
(B) He was misinformed.
(C) He wants to tell more people.
(D) He wants to contact the media.

**171.** According to the discussion, what most likely will happen next?

(A) Customer feedback will be received.
(B) Sales will go up.
(C) A new commercial will be reviewed.
(D) A company will be researched.

**Questions 172-175** refer to the following information.

## ～ Science-M Contest ～
### Sponsored by Suvar Corporation
### Islamabad, Pakistan

Are you the next great scientist to come out of Pakistan?

Suvar Corporation is sponsoring a nationwide campaign to find the next generation of young geniuses from our country.

**Top Prize:** A full 4-year scholarship to the university of your choice anywhere within the nation. — [1] —.

**Second Place:** A set of 10 software educational packages from Suvar Corporation.

**Third Place:** Gift certificates for use at department stores in Lahore, Islamabad, Karachi and other major cities.

Here is how you can compete against the best young minds in Pakistan.

To enter the contest, you must be over 12 and under 20.* — [2] —. Entrants may submit any original creation within the following areas:

- Robotics
- Software
- Biotech
- Hardware
- Pharmaceuticals

All submissions must be entirely the work of the entrant, without any assistance from teachers, parents or other adults. — [3] —. If an entrant wishes to work with classmates on a submission, it must then be clearly labeled as teamwork.

The deadline for registering submissions is June 15. — [4] —. Entry inspections by a panel of judges will begin June 18, with a final winner chosen June 21.

*While anyone within this age group can compete, most top prizes in past years have usually gone to those aged between 17 and 19.

---

**172.** What is the stated purpose of the Science-M Contest?

(A) To find marketable technical products
(B) To improve business research capabilities
(C) To help fund educational programs
(D) To discover talented people

**173.** Which is NOT listed as a gift for prize winners?

(A) Coupons for goods
(B) Educational materials
(C) Fees for tuition
(D) Travel tickets

**174.** What rule is mentioned about the contest?

(A) Group work must be specified.
(B) Adult assistance is encouraged.
(C) Registration fees are required.
(D) Submissions require teacher approval.

**175.** In which of the positions marked [1], [2], [3] and [4] does the following sentence best belong?

"While not necessary, a strong background in science is preferred."

(A) [1]
(B) [2]
(C) [3]
(D) [4]

**Questions 176-180** refer to the following notice and e-mail.

---

June 17

# Project Coordinator
Orange Tech Co.

Orange Tech is the largest telecom company in our regional markets. Recently, we were awarded a contract for the construction of satellite broadcasting systems throughout the Republic of South Africa.

To cope with this increased workload, we are searching for a reliable project coordinator to assist the operations manager in charge of this task.

Candidates must have a minimum of a BA degree, with a graduate degree preferred. They must have at least three years' experience in the field, and be able to demonstrate excellent interpersonal skills.

Knowledge of the following software applications is required:
- **TX25**
- **InfoScoop**
- **Arcana**
- **IsoFin**

Regular duties will include database management, compilation of weekly reports, installation schedule development, and resolution of any outstanding technical issues.

Please submit credentials by July 9 to Adam De Groot at the following address, adam.degroot@orangetech.za

---

**E-mail**

**To:** adam.degroot@orangetech.za
**From:** darren.zimbele@africatel.com
**Date:** Wednesday, June 20
**Subject:** Open Position

Attachments: References.doc
CV.doc

Dear Mr. De Groot,

I am writing about your project coordinator position.

I graduated from Keele University, with an MSc in computer engineering two years ago. Since then, I have worked in Kampala Tech Co. as a software analyst, first in their Kimberly and Pretoria branches and now here in Johannesburg. There, I gained extensive experience working with TX25, InfoScoop, Arcana, IsoFin, and many other software packages.

Beyond my technical background, I also get on well with all sorts of people. Even while under the stress of tight work deadlines, I never get angry or frustrated.

I look forward to hearing from you soon.

Sincerely,

Darren Zimbele

**176.** What will Orange Tech require their new recruit to do?

(A) Manage a new project
(B) Get a new contract
(C) Expand into a new market
(D) Acquire a new company

**177.** In the notice, the word "interpersonal" in paragraph 3, line 3, is closest in meaning to

(A) profitable
(B) communicative
(C) academic
(D) linguistic

**178.** Where does Mr. Zimbele currently work?

(A) Cape Town
(B) Kimberly
(C) Pretoria
(D) Johannesburg

**179.** What can be inferred about Mr. Zimbele from his application?

(A) He does not have enough work experience.
(B) He does not have the required academic background.
(C) He does not have sufficient references.
(D) He does not have adequate software skills.

**180.** Why does Mr. Zimbele mention deadlines?

(A) To emphasize his attention to details
(B) To highlight his computer skills
(C) To show his leadership background
(D) To demonstrate his patience

*GO ON TO THE NEXT PAGE*

**Questions 181-185** refer to the following advertisement and e-mail.

# Branson Lawn & Garden Co.
## We make the exterior of every home a lovely one.

- Lawn care
- Garden care
- Bush, tree and hedge trimming
- Special services as required

Deposits accepted but not required.
Handling both commercial and residential projects. Our clients include:
- *XSoft Computer Corporation*
- *Briar City Park*
- *Leviston Apartment Complex*
- *And homes all over the city*

Our Management Team:
**Linda Wu** — President
linda.wu@bransononline.com
**Armando Benitez** — Personnel manager
armando.b@bransononline.com
**Mary Listz** — Client Project manager
mary.l@bransononline.com
**Frank Cole** — Equipment manager
frank.cole@bransononline.com

*Voted Number 1 Landscaping Service by City Life Magazine*

Drop by our office at 302 Beckridge Way or contact us at: info@bransononline.com.
You'll be glad you did!

*On the job seven days a week, through all four seasons. All work done from November 1 through April 1 requires additional fees.

---

**E-mail**

**From:** michelle017@northtel.com
**To:** linda.wu@bransononline.com
**Date:** Monday, May 25
**Subject:** Your Company

Dear Ms. Wu,

Thank you for taking the time to talk with me on the phone earlier today. After doing so, I think I might be interested in hiring your company for some landscaping projects around my home. Ordinarily, I enjoy taking care of my yard and garden on weekends, but I'm so busy at the office nowadays it's hard for me to devote as much time to it as I used to.

I think that if you carried out the work we discussed for me every fourteen days, I could keep the greenery around my home looking good. So I'd like to start with that sort of schedule. However, weekly visits might be required during spring, when everything grows very fast. If your company also does snow removal, I might also have monthly work for you in winter, or more frequently according to the snowfall.

I understand you will be sending out one of your managers tomorrow who is responsible for customer cost estimates. During that meeting I would like to discuss the service contract, including all labor, equipment and other factors. I would prefer a complete total of that in your estimate, rather than being surprised later by unanticipated prices.

Best regards,

Michelle Walker

**181.** What is implied about Branson Lawn & Garden Co.?

(A) It accepts online payments.
(B) It offers big discounts.
(C) It has a good reputation.
(D) It does interiors as well as exteriors.

**182.** What is stated about Branson Lawn & Garden Co.?

(A) It serves only corporate clients.
(B) It requires a deposit before beginning work.
(C) It limits projects during some seasons.
(D) It charges more during certain periods.

**183.** How often does Ms. Walker want initial service?

(A) Every week
(B) Every other week
(C) Every month
(D) Every other month

**184.** Who will Ms. Walker meet tomorrow?

(A) Linda Wu
(B) Armando Benitez
(C) Mary Listz
(D) Frank Cole

**185.** What is one request made by Ms. Walker?

(A) Getting a comprehensive quote
(B) Receiving fast performance
(C) Confirming top equipment
(D) Understanding project details

GO ON TO THE NEXT PAGE

**Questions 186-190** refer to the following letter, voucher, and Web page.

October 27

Richard Yeoh
Laxfield Office Supplies Corporation
7861 Clayton Plaza
Denver, CO 98775

Dear Mr. Yeoh,

I was sorry to hear that your stay at our hotel in Portland, Oregon, was less than satisfactory. You should not have had your seminars exposed to the noise from work crews renovating our lobby and main entrance. I understand that at many points your presenters struggled to be heard because of that.

Unfortunately, when taking your reservation for the Premier Gold Room, our receptionist made a mistake by overlooking the fact that it was adjacent to the areas under renovation. As a Sunshine Hotels Card member, you are entitled to nothing less than top-class service.

To make up for your inconvenience in some small way, I hope that you will accept the voucher enclosed.

With very best regards,

*Josef Loos*

Josef Loos
Vice President
Sunshine Hotels, Inc.

---

## Sunshine Hotels Inc.
Taking care of you 365 days a year!

### Guest Voucher

This voucher entitles the bearer to a 50% discount on our hotels anywhere in the United States or Canada, including our Royal Suite or Deluxe Suite rooms.

Voucher No. A982JQRV08

Expires December 27
Non-transferable, single-use only

Sunshine Hotels Card members receive an additional 10% off. Valid only for online reservations at www.sunshinehotels/vouchers/. Please enter voucher number noted above.

https://www.sunshinehotels/vouchers/

Today's Date: December 20

# Sunshine Hotels Inc.
*Online Reservations*

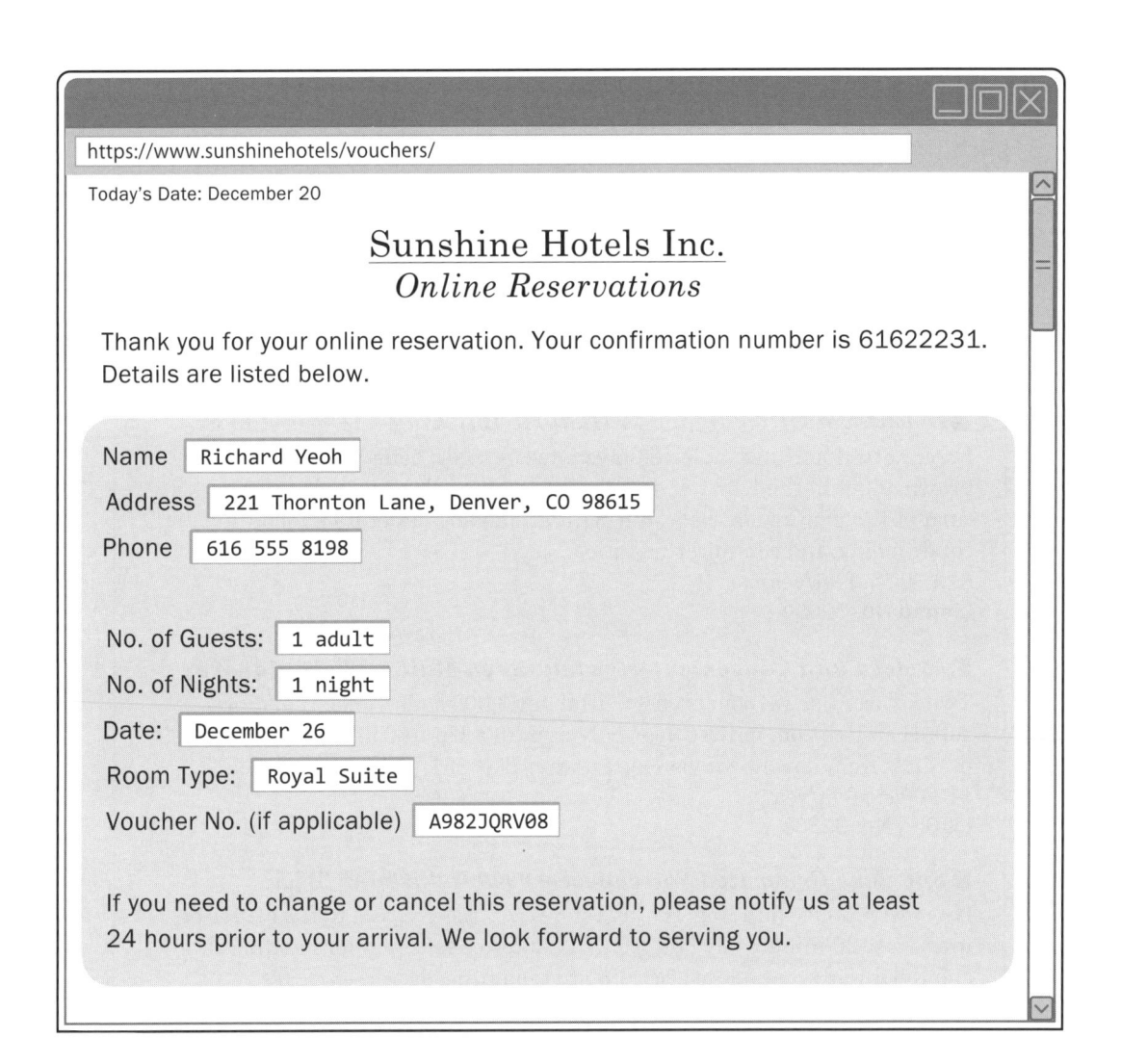

Thank you for your online reservation. Your confirmation number is 61622231. Details are listed below.

Name: Richard Yeoh
Address: 221 Thornton Lane, Denver, CO 98615
Phone: 616 555 8198

No. of Guests: 1 adult
No. of Nights: 1 night
Date: December 26
Room Type: Royal Suite
Voucher No. (if applicable): A982JQRV08

If you need to change or cancel this reservation, please notify us at least 24 hours prior to your arrival. We look forward to serving you.

**186.** What is the purpose of the letter?
(A) To confirm a reservation
(B) To explain facilities
(C) To reply to an inquiry
(D) To make an apology

**187.** What problem occurred at the seminars?
(A) Baggage was not delivered.
(B) Speakers could not be heard.
(C) Locations were changed.
(D) Presentations were rescheduled.

**188.** In the letter, the word "way" in paragraph 3, line 1, is closest in meaning to
(A) manner
(B) condition
(C) payment
(D) portion

**189.** What is the maximum discount available to Mr. Yeoh?
(A) 10%
(B) 50%
(C) 60%
(D) 70%

**190.** What is indicated about Mr. Yeoh?
(A) He had seminars at a hotel near his office.
(B) He reserved the wrong room for the seminars.
(C) He will stay at a Sunshine Hotel on December 20.
(D) He was given a voucher valid for two months.

*GO ON TO THE NEXT PAGE*

**Questions 191-195** refer to the following advertisement, form, and e-mail.

## Thorren Industries

### This Week's Top Properties!

Philadelphia, Pennsylvania

■ *Downtown Office Space in Historic Building—18 Winston St.*
Entire 3rd floor (just under 8,000 sq. feet) in gorgeous historic brownstone, in the heart of downtown. Beautifully restored turn-of-the-century interior, but with all modern amenities including air conditioning and computer facilities.
$13.00/sq. feet/year
**Listing No. 32330**

■ *Modern and Convenient—Portmandieu Mall, 4325 Poplar Way*
Two adjacent showroom properties (about 3,000 sq. feet each) in quiet suburban location, in first-floor-only building. Up-to-date facilities. Just 30 minutes from downtown via expressway, Exit 351.
$13.00/sq. feet/year
**Listing No. 32338**

■ *Spacious Renovated Warehouse—2000 Industrial Drive*
Huge warehouse building, totally renovated. Easy access to the center of town, just 20 minutes by bus. Total 41,000 sq. feet. Landlord willing to subdivide, will rent space according to tenant needs.
$15.00/sq. feet/year
**Listing No. 41323**

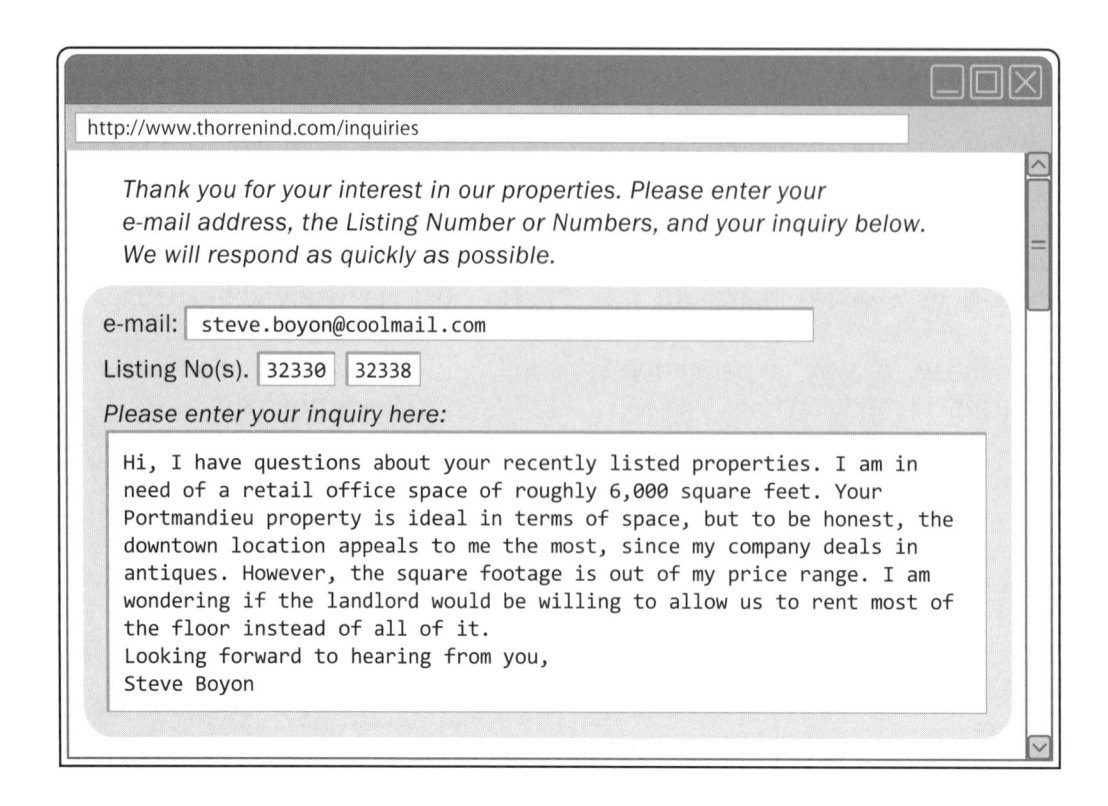

For inquiries regarding the above properties, please visit our Web site at www.thorrenind.com/inquiries.

---

http://www.thorrenind.com/inquiries

*Thank you for your interest in our properties. Please enter your e-mail address, the Listing Number or Numbers, and your inquiry below. We will respond as quickly as possible.*

e-mail: steve.boyon@coolmail.com
Listing No(s). 32330  32338

*Please enter your inquiry here:*

```
Hi, I have questions about your recently listed properties. I am in
need of a retail office space of roughly 6,000 square feet. Your
Portmandieu property is ideal in terms of space, but to be honest, the
downtown location appeals to me the most, since my company deals in
antiques. However, the square footage is out of my price range. I am
wondering if the landlord would be willing to allow us to rent most of
the floor instead of all of it.
Looking forward to hearing from you,
Steve Boyon
```

**E-mail**

**To:** steve.boyon@coolmail.com
**From:** anetta.fasiq@thorrenreal.com
**Date:** May 12
**Subject:** Listing No. 32330

Dear Mr. Boyon,

Thank you for your interest in this property. We have contacted the landlord, Mr. John Fedder. Unfortunately, he has informed us that the property cannot be subdivided. However, he commented that he has spent a lot of time and money having the building restored, and seemed delighted by the nature of your business. He has graciously offered to negotiate a better price per square foot. If this is of interest to you, please contact me via e-mail, or by phone at (612) 555-8181. I will contact him immediately and arrange for you to meet as soon as possible.

Regards,

Anetta Fasiq

---

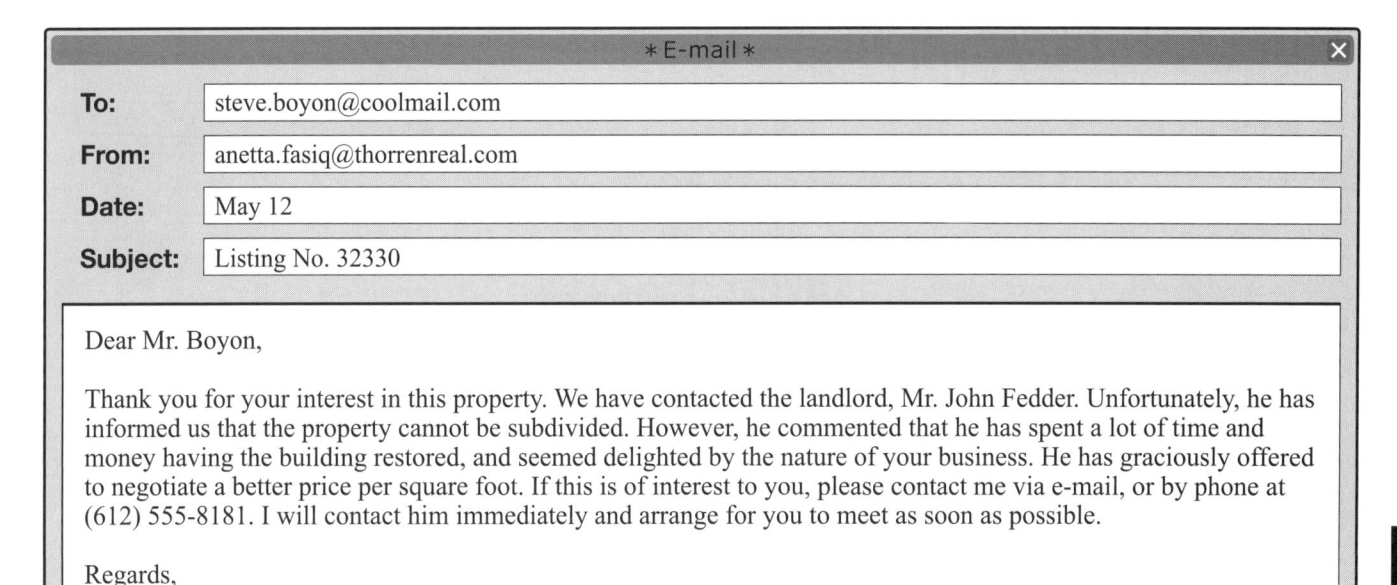

**191.** What most likely does Thorren Industries specialize in?
(A) Retail merchandising
(B) Real estate
(C) Building renovation
(D) Construction

**192.** What is the purpose of Mr. Boyon's inquiry?
(A) To negotiate a lower price
(B) To complete a lease
(C) To ask about rental terms
(D) To give feedback on a property listing

**193.** What does Mr. Boyon imply about the property on Poplar Way?
(A) The space is ideal.
(B) It is too expensive for him.
(C) It is not conveniently located.
(D) It does not have adequate facilities.

**194.** What is implied about Mr. Fedder?
(A) He is fond of antiques.
(B) He specializes in renovation.
(C) He can rent out parts of his property.
(D) He has contacted Mr. Boyon.

**195.** In the e-mail, what does Ms. Fasiq say she can do for Mr. Boyon?
(A) Help reduce the rental price
(B) Accelerate the rental process
(C) Recommend a different property
(D) Renovate some facilities

GO ON TO THE NEXT PAGE

**Questions 196-200** refer to the following draft slide and e-mails.

---

**X-Cola Consumers: Survey Responses by Age Group** (DRAFT 1)

| Age Group | Number of Responses |
|---|---|
| 20-29 | 705 |
| 30-39 | 142 |
| 40-49 | 117 |
| 50+ | 51 |

Hansen Food & Beverage Corporation
X-Cola Market Research Team
Julia Arbenz, Team Leader

---

Note to Eric: Here's the first draft of the slide for the presentation on Wednesday, for your review. Please e-mail me as soon as possible with any feedback. Thanks! — Julia

---

**\*E-mail\***

**To:** Julia Arbenz <j.arbenz@x-cola.com>
**From:** Eric Bradshaw <eric.b@x-cola.com>
**Date:** January 14, 11:56 A.M.
**Subject:** Consumer data, first draft

Hi Julia,

Thanks for your hard work. At a glance, the data doesn't look that different from last year's. First, it might be good to make the table into a chart. Also, this year, could we add data for consumers between the ages of 13 and 19? In other words, teenagers, but we can label this group "young adults."

The reason I ask is, our senior staff have already proposed diverting more money to ad campaigns for people 30 and over, but personally I'm a little hesitant to concur with that idea.

If you have any survey data on young adults, would you send it to me, as well as your thoughts? I'd appreciate both.

Thanks,

Eric Bradshaw
Marketing Director, Hansen Food & Beverage

* E-mail *

**To:** Eric Bradshaw <eric.b@x-cola.com>
**From:** Julia Arbenz <j.arbenz@x-cola.com>
**Date:** January 14, 1:02 P.M.
**Subject:** Re: Consumer data, first draft

Hi Eric,

I just checked the data you requested. Surprisingly, the number of responses was even lower than the 50+ age group in the survey results I sent in the first draft.

However, that might be because teenagers simply don't bother to return as many surveys as people in older age brackets. So, in actuality, the number of teenage consumers might be greater.

In any event, from a research perspective, I am inclined to side with your opinion. If you would like me to convey that to the senior staff, please let me know. I'll be sending you an updated slide momentarily.

Best wishes,

Julia

---

**196.** What most likely is Julia's job position?

(A) Team assistant
(B) Senior manager
(C) IT specialist
(D) Marketing analyst

**197.** What is indicated about the number of teenage consumer responses?

(A) It is significantly small.
(B) It has increased proportionally.
(C) It is the same as last year.
(D) It is as was expected.

**198.** What does Julia imply about ad campaign money?

(A) It should be spent on ads for younger people.
(B) It has already been raised by her team.
(C) It is sufficient for more ads to be made.
(D) More funding is needed for further research.

**199.** In the second e-mail, the word "brackets" in paragraph 2, line 2, is closest in meaning to

(A) lengths
(B) ranges
(C) differences
(D) targets

**200.** What does Julia say she will do next?

(A) Reexamine the data
(B) Contact senior staff
(C) Call Eric
(D) Provide a new slide

---

**Stop! This is the end of the test. If you finish before time is called, you may go back to Parts 5, 6, and 7 and check your work.**

# スコアアップのテクニック

**攻略手順**

**❶ ディレクションの時間に最初の2枚の写真に目を通す**
ディレクションが流れている間に，1ページ目の No. 1 と No. 2 の2枚の写真を観察してみよう。写っている物や人物の位置，人物の動作など，どんな単語が読まれるかを推測する。No. 1 は He's [She's] 〜のパターンが定番で，動作（動詞や目的語）が決め手になる。

**❷ 素早く解答し，問題間のポーズを無駄にしない**
正解がわかったらすぐにマークし，次の写真を見て問題に備えよう。答えがわからない問題があっても引きずらず，次の問題の音声が流れる前に気持ちを切り替えて集中しよう。

**問題攻略テクニック**

**テクニック 1　似た発音の単語に注意**
work と walk，coffee と copy，fold と hold など，発音の似た単語を用いた引っ掛けに注意しよう。

**テクニック 2　位置関係を表す前置詞や熟語を覚える**
写真描写では，位置関係を表す語句が頻繁に使われる。on the wall「壁に掛かって」や side by side「並んで」などがその例である。また前置詞はイメージを持つことが重要だ。例えば，into だと「人や物がある場所に入っていく」という動きのイメージがある。

**テクニック 3　「人物」が主語のときの動詞と目的語をしっかり捉える**
主語が「人物」の場合，その人物の動作は多くの場合，現在進行形（be ＋動詞の ing 形）で表される。ただし，動詞は正しい描写でも目的語が正しくない場合もあるので，動詞の ing 形と目的語をしっかり聞き取ることがポイント。

**テクニック 4　「物」が主語のときは受動態が多い**
主語が「物」の場合，動詞は受動態の場合が多い。〈is [are] being ＋過去分詞〉または〈have [has] been ＋過去分詞〉の2種類あり，過去分詞の聞き取りがポイントになる。

**テクニック 5　写っていない物や人，曖昧な物や人に関する描写に注意**
人物が写っていない写真で人を表す語が出てきたら誤答だ。写真にはっきりと写っている人や物，客観的事実のみが正解になり，見えにくい物や判断しにくい動作を含む選択肢はたいてい誤答だ。ただし，曖昧な物や人を something, someone と表す場合もある。

# PART 1 例題 CD2 59-61

**1**

(A) He's making some coffee.
(B) He's walking into a room.
(C) He's looking at a computer screen.
(D) He's putting on a pair of glasses.

訳 (A) 彼はコーヒーを入れている。　　(B) 彼は部屋に歩いて入っていくところである。
(C) 彼はコンピューターの画面を見ている。　　(D) 彼は眼鏡をつけているところである。

## 正解：(C)

コンピューターの画面を見ている様子を適切に表した (C) が正解。(A) は，男性はコーヒーを飲んでいる可能性はあるが，making で誤答と判断できる。(B) は，working と walking という似た音の語を用いた引っ掛け。(D) の be putting on は眼鏡をつけている最中を表すので誤り。He's wearing some glasses.「眼鏡を身につけている」という状態を表す描写なら正解となる。

**2**

(A) The woman is talking on the phone.
(B) The woman is holding something.
(C) One of the men is waving his hands.
(D) The men are seated across from each other.

訳 (A) 女性は電話で話している。　　(B) 女性は何かを持っている。
(C) 男性の 1 人は両手を振っている。　　(D) 2 人の男性は向かい合って座っている。

## 正解：(B)

女性が左手に何かを持っている様子を適切に表した (B) が正解。(A) は，talking on the phone という動作が誤り。(C) は waving という動作が誤り。hands を使うなら，The two men are shaking hands.「2 人の男性は握手をしている」などがふさわしい。同性が 2 人以上写っているときの One of ~「~のうちの 1 人は」という表現も確認しよう。(D) は 2 人の男性は向かい合っているが，何かに座っている状態ではないので seated が不適。この are seated のように，主語「人」に対して現在進行形を使わないパターンも確認しておこう。

# PART 1

**3**
(A) An entrance floor is being cleaned. テクニック 2
(B) A man is watering some plants. テクニック 4
(C) Some pots have been placed around the pond. テクニック 5
(D) The fountain is surrounded by plants.

訳 (A) 玄関の床が清掃されているところである。　(B) 男性が植物に水をやっている。
(C) いくつかの鉢が池の周りに並べられている。　(D) 噴水が植物に囲まれている。

### 正解：(D)

写真中央の噴水に焦点を当てた (D) が正解。(A) は，床は掃除されていないので誤り。floor は地面ではなく屋内の「床」を指す。また，〈is being ＋過去分詞〉の受動態では「誰かがその動作を行っている最中」を表すので，人物が写っていない写真で〈is being ＋過去分詞〉が使われている選択肢は誤答だ。(B) は，man が聞こえただけで消去しよう。water「～に水をやる」は PART 1 で頻出の動詞。(C) は，〈have been ＋過去分詞〉の受動態を用いているが，池は写っていないので誤り。have been placed「配置された」や be surrounded by ～「～に囲まれている」など，「物」の位置や状態を表す表現をたくさん知っておこう。

# PART 2 スコアアップのテクニック

**攻略手順**

### 音声に集中し，リズムよく解答する

PART 2 は 30 問から 25 問に減り，やや難化傾向にある。このパートは問題用紙を見る必要がなく，ひたすら音声だけを聞いて答えるため，集中力の持続が要求される。集中力が切れて冒頭の疑問詞を聞き逃しただけで答えが選べなくなる可能性もある。たとえ問題を聞き逃しても焦ったり落ち込んだりせず，どれかにマークをして気を取り直して次の問題に取り組もう。

**問題攻略テクニック**

### テクニック 1　冒頭の疑問詞を聞き取るだけで正解できるパターン

疑問詞で始まる疑問文では，その疑問詞を聞き取るだけで正解が決まる問題がある。また，疑問詞の疑問文には Yes / No で答えないので，Yes / No で始まる選択肢は聞き飛ばそう。

### テクニック 2　質問文に出た単語と同じ単語や似た発音の単語を利用した選択肢に注意

質問文に出てきた単語と同じ単語を利用した選択肢，また lunch と launch，riding と writing のような似た発音の単語を利用した選択肢に注意しよう。

### テクニック 3　質問文から連想される語(句)を利用した選択肢に注意

restaurant → reservation / meal や meeting → schedule / agenda といった，質問文に出てきた単語から連想される語句を利用した選択肢に引っ掛からないようにしよう。

### テクニック 4　Why 〜 ? と聞かれても，理由を答えないパターン

Why don't you 〜 ? は「〜してはどうですか」という提案表現で，理由を尋ねているわけではないので注意。また，Why 〜 ? で「理由」を尋ねる質問に対して Because 〜 . で答える代わりに，センテンスや〈To ＋動詞の原形…〉(目的) で答える場合もある。

### テクニック 5　はっきりとした答えではない選択肢が正解となるパターン

質問に対して，「わかりません」「〜に聞いてください」「あなたに任せます」のような，自分の意思をはっきりと述べないパターンが正解となる場合が多い。

### テクニック 6　付加疑問文や否定疑問文では Yes / No に執着しない

You 〜 , don't you? や Hasn't Jane sent 〜 ? といった付加疑問文や否定疑問文に対して，Yes / No で答えている応答があるが，重要なのはその後に続く部分である。

# 例題 PART 2

**1**
Where do you usually get your hair cut?
(A) Yes, once a month or so.
(B) At a barbershop near here.
(C) On Sunday afternoon.

訳 いつもどこで散髪しますか。
(A) はい，1 か月に 1 回かそこらです。　(B) この近くの理髪店で。　(C) 日曜の午後に。

## 正解：(B)

疑問詞 Where で尋ねられて，具体的な「場所」を答えている (B) が正解。(A) は疑問詞の疑問文に対して Yes で答えているので，Yes が聞こえた時点で誤答と判断できる。(C) は「時」を答えているので誤り。

**2**
Mr. Wilson looks tired, doesn't he?
(A) He's been busy recently.
(B) No, I've got a flat tire.
(C) We saw him last week.

訳 Wilson さんは疲れているようですね。
(A) 彼は最近忙しいです。　(B) いいえ，タイヤがパンクしたのです。　(C) 私たちは先週彼に会いました。

## 正解：(A)

Wilson さんが疲れている理由を答えている (A) が正解。(B) は，tired と似た音の tire を使った引っ掛け。付加疑問文では Yes/No にとらわれずに，以降の内容の聞き取りに集中する。

**3**
Why don't you come to the party tonight?
(A) Because I have a cold.
(B) Let me think about it.
(C) The dinner was great.

訳 今夜，パーティーに来てはどうですか。
(A) 風邪をひいているからです。　(B) 考えさせてください。　(C) 夕食はとても良かったです。

## 正解：(B)

Why don't you 〜?「〜してはどうですか」という提案に対して，「行く・行かない」の意思を伝えずに「考えさせて」と保留している (B) が正解。理由を尋ねられているのではないので，(A) は Because が聞こえた時点で消去しよう。(C) は質問文の party から連想される dinner を用いた引っ掛け。

# PART 3 & 4 スコアアップのテクニック

## 攻略手順

### ❶ 放送を聞く前に設問（質問文と選択肢）を把握する

ディレクションの時間や，各問題の会話やトークの放送が始まる前に，次の問題の設問を見て何が問われているかを把握すると効果的に解ける。会話やトークを聞く際に，該当する箇所やキーワードを拾うのに集中（スキャニング）できるし，事前に設問をチェックすることで，会話やトークの内容をある程度予測できるというメリットもある。

### ❷ PART 4 は問題指示文を聞く

トークの前に Questions 1 through 3 refer ... telephone message. のように，トークの種類が読み上げられるので，内容が予測できる。

## 問題攻略テクニック

### テクニック 1 「言い換え」に慣れよう

選択肢の多くは本文の表現を言い換えて（パラフレーズ）おり，この言い換えに気づくことがポイントである。これはリーディングの PART 7 にも言える。

### テクニック 2 言い淀みや不完全な表現に慣れよう

リスニングの新傾向として，PART 2, 3, 4 において，Hmm ... や Uh ... などの言い淀みが用いられるようになったが，特に対策の必要はない。実際の会話では当たり前のことなので，リラックスして聞こう。また，PART 3 では 3 人の会話ややり取りの長い会話が加わり，Could you? といった短く不完全な応答も含まれるようになった。前後の文脈から，どんな文の省略かを考えてみよう。

### テクニック 3 文中の表現の意図を問う問題は先読みが効果的

PART 3, 4 で，会話やトークの中の表現の意図を問う問題（例 What does the man mean when he says, "..."?）が加わった。先にこの「...」の文言を押さえてから，会話やトークではその部分を集中して聞こう。パターンは大きく分けて 2 つ。1 つは，Why not? → 「同意している」のような，その表現自体の知識を問うパターン，もう 1 つは，比較的長めの引用で，前後の文脈の理解を問うパターンだ。

### テクニック 4 図表を使った問題は事前に内容をチェック

PART 3, 4 で図表（graphic）を用いた問題が加わった。これも事前に図表の内容をざっと確認しておきたい。すべての文字を読む必要はない。「何に関する図表か」に焦点を絞って確認し，会話やトークの主題・目的を予測しよう。

# 例題 PART 3

Questions 1 through 3 refer to the following conversation.

M: Good afternoon. My name is Gabriel Sanchez. Can I speak with Mr. Joel Matthews, please?
W: I'm sorry, but he's out of the country on business this week. This is his assistant, Janice Taylor. Can I give him a message?
M: <u>Oh, would you mind?</u> I'm interested in the position of head chef that was advertised in last Friday's paper and I was wondering if he had received my résumé yet. I sent it last Saturday.
W: Hmm. Well, he left on… uhh, Tuesday — Tuesday afternoon, so he probably hasn't seen it yet.
M: Ah, I see.
W: But he should be back in the restaurant the day after tomorrow. I'll let him know then.

訳 問題 1-3 は次の会話に関するものです。

M: こんにちは。Gabriel Sanchez と申します。Joel Matthews さんとお話しできますか。
W: 申し訳ありませんが，彼は今週出張のため国内にはおりません。私は彼のアシスタントの Janice Taylor と申します。メッセージをお伝えしましょうか。
M: ああ，そうしていただけますか。先週金曜日の新聞に求人広告が出ていた料理長の職に興味があるのですが，Matthews さんがもう私の履歴書を受け取っただろうかと思いまして。先週の土曜日にお送りしたのですが。
W: そうですか。彼が出発したのは，ええと…火曜日，火曜日の午後ですので，たぶんまだ見ていないと思います。
M: ああ，そうなんですか。
W: でも彼は明後日にはレストランに戻ってくるはずです。そのときに彼に伝えますね。

**1** Where does the woman most likely work?
(A) At a restaurant
(B) At a travel company
(C) At an advertising company
(D) At a newspaper

訳 女性はどこで働いていると考えられますか。
(A) レストラン  (B) 旅行会社  (C) 広告会社  (D) 新聞社

**正解：(A)**
基本事項の質問は会話全体からキーワードを拾おう。男性が，I'm interested in the position of <u>head chef</u> 〜と言って料理長の職に応募していること，また，女性が he should be back in the <u>restaurant</u> 〜と言っていることから，正解は (A) と判断できる。

# PART 3

**2**
What did the man do last week?
(A) He advertised a job.
(B) He applied for a job.
(C) He went on a business trip.
(D) He met with Mr. Matthews.

訳 先週男性は何をしましたか。
(A) 求人広告を出した。　(B) 仕事に応募した。
(C) 出張に行った。　(D) Matthews さんと会った。

### 正解：(B)
設問を先読みすると，男性の発言内で先週に関することに注意して聞ける。男性は，I sent it last Saturday. と言っているが，この it は直前の my résumé のこと。「履歴書を送った」を「仕事に応募した」と言い換えた (B) が正解。

**3**
Why does the man say, "Oh, would you mind"?
(A) To decline a request
(B) To make a complaint
(C) To accept an offer
(D) To consider a question

訳 男性はなぜ"Oh, would you mind"と言っていますか。
(A) 要望を断るため　(B) 苦情を言うため
(C) 申し出を承諾するため　(D) 問題を熟考するため

### 正解：(C)
Would you mind ～ing? は「～していただけませんか」という依頼表現である。直前の Can I give him a message? という申し出を受けた Would you mind giving him a message? の省略形で，「そうしていただけますか，そうしてもらえるとありがたいです」という意味合いである。よって，(C) が正解。なお，新傾向の PART 3 では，この例題のようにやり取りが長めの会話が扱われ，また，Hmm や uhh, Tuesday — Tuesday afternoon などの言い淀みや，Ah, I see. のような短い応答だけで次の話し手が話すといったパターンも含まれるので，慣れておこう。

# 例題　CD2 66　PART 4

Questions 1 through 3 refer to the following telephone message and schedule.

Hi John, it's Carly. Listen, it's around noon, and I'm here at the conference venue. I just got a call from the office. It looks like we'll have to cut out of the conference early. We've been asked to go meet a client this afternoon at the downtown convention center at five. It takes a little under an hour to get there from here by taxi. Could you meet me in the lobby after Stephanie Almarro's seminar? It's too bad we have to leave early, but at least we'll get to hear Kenji Endo. I hear he's really good. Thanks John, see you soon.

| Conference Schedule ||
| --- | --- |
| Session Time | Speakers |
| 1:00 – 1:50 | Kenji Endo |
| 2:00 – 2:50 | Jack Winters |
| 3:00 – 3:50 | Stephanie Almarro |
| 4:00 – 4:50 | Kareem Singh |

訳　問題 1-3 は次の電話のメッセージと予定表に関するものです。こんにちは，John，Carly よ。聞いて。今は正午頃で，私は会議の開催場所にいるんだけど，たった今，事務所から電話をもらって，どうやら私たちは会議から早めに引き上げなければいけないみたいなの。今日の午後 5 時に，ダウンタウンのコンベンションセンターで顧客に会うように言われたの。ここからタクシーでそこに行くには 1 時間弱かかるわ。Stephanie Almarro のセミナーの後，ロビーで落ち合いましょう。早めに出なければならないのは残念だけど，せめて Kenji Endo の話を聞けるのはいいわね。彼は本当にいいって聞いているわ。よろしく John，じゃあね。

| 会議予定表 ||
| --- | --- |
| セッション時間 | 講演者 |
| 1:00 – 1:50 | Kenji Endo |
| 2:00 – 2:50 | Jack Winters |
| 3:00 – 3:50 | Stephanie Almarro |
| 4:00 – 4:50 | Kareem Singh |

**1**　Where is the woman now?
(A) At a conference venue
(B) At her company
(C) At a convention center
(D) In a taxi

訳　女性は今どこにいますか。
(A) 会議の開催場所
(B) 自分の会社
(C) コンベンションセンター
(D) タクシーの中

**正解：(A)**

話し手が今どこにいるかを問う問題。第 2 文の I'm here at the conference venue から，(A) が正解。「話し手は誰か」「誰に向けて話しているか」「話し手はどこにいるか」などの基本情報はたいてい最初の方にヒントがある。

# PART 4

**2**
Why is the woman calling?
(A) A meeting has been canceled.
(B) A conference has been rescheduled.
(C) Plans have been changed.
(D) Travel plans have been delayed.

訳 女性はなぜ電話をしていますか。
(A) 会議が取りやめになった。　(B) 会議の予定が変更になった。
(C) 計画が変更された。　　　 (D) 旅行の計画が先延ばしされた。

### 正解：(C)
電話の目的を問う問題。~ we'll have to cut out of the conference early. We've been asked ~ at five. の部分から，話し手の女性と聞き手の John は 2 人とも会議に出席することになっているが，5 時に顧客と会うために予定より早く出なければならないことがわかる。これを Plans have been changed. と簡潔に表した (C) が正解。

**3**
Look at the graphic. What time will the man meet the woman in the lobby?
(A) Around 1:00 P.M.
(B) Around 2:00 P.M.
(C) Around 3:00 P.M.
(D) Around 4:00 P.M.

訳 図を見てください。何時に男性は女性とロビーで会いますか。
(A) 午後 1 時頃　(B) 午後 2 時頃　(C) 午後 3 時頃　(D) 午後 4 時頃

### 正解：(D)
図表問題は，先に何に関する図表かをチェックすると効率よく解ける。ここでは，会議の予定表で，誰が何時に講演を行うかが書かれていることさえ押さえれば十分だ。女性は Could you meet me in the lobby after Stephanie Almarro's seminar? と言っており，予定表を見ると，Stephanie Almarro の講演は 3:00 – 3:50 なので，2 人が会う時間として最も適切なのは (D) の「午後 4 時頃」である。図表問題は，会話やトークと図表の情報を組み合わせて答える（クロスリファレンス）問題である。

# スコアアップのテクニック

**攻略手順**

### ❶ 選択肢と空所の前後を見て，全文を読まずに解ける問題かどうかを判断する

英文を読むときは常に主語と述語動詞を意識すること。ただし，空所の前後を読むだけで解けるものは，全文を読まずに素早くマークしよう。

### ❷ PART 5 は 1 問 20 秒，PART 6 は 1 文書 2 分を目標にリズムよく解こう

PART 7 で読む分量が増えたことで，見直しの時間を十分に取ることはあまり期待できない。PART 5 は，1 問を約 20 秒以内，全体で 10 分，PART 6 は 1 文書（4 問）を約 2 分，全体で 8 分を目標とし，PART 7 を解くのに 57 分を確保したい。

**問題攻略テクニック**

### テクニック1 文構造を見極める

「品詞問題」は空所の前後を見ただけで解答できるものが多い。例えば「冠詞と名詞の間には形容詞が入る」などのタイプだ。この手の「文構造ルール」をたくさん覚えよう。他には，① 前置詞の後には名詞相当句が続く（SV は続かない），② 文頭に空所がある場合，直後がコンマで区切られていたら入るのは副詞，直後が〈節 , 節〉なら従位接続詞，などだ。

### テクニック2 複数の品詞を持つ語に注意

複数の品詞を持つ語が文中でどんな意味・用法なのかを見極めることがポイントになることがある。例えば，① to は不定詞の to なのか前置詞なのか？ ② that は代名詞・形容詞（指示語）なのか接続詞なのか関係代名詞なのか？ などだ。

### テクニック3 文全体を読んで適切な語彙を選ぶ

選択肢を見て語彙問題とわかったら，素早く文脈をつかもう。

### テクニック4 慣用句・熟語を見極める

空所が慣用句・熟語の一部であることに素早く気づこう。

### テクニック5 PART 6 の文挿入問題は文脈が大事

新傾向では PART 6 に文を挿入する問題が 1 問増えた。ただし，従来の文脈で判断するパターンの問題が文になっただけで，難しく考える必要はない。this などの指示語や they などの代名詞が指すもの，前後の文をつなぐには補足内容が適切か，逆接関係か，具体例か，話はポジティブイメージかネガティブか…といった文脈の流れの理解がポイントとなる。

# PART 5　例題

**1**
After the company's losses were announced last Tuesday, the ------- of its stock fell dramatically.
(A) valued
(B) value
(C) valuate
(D) valuable

訳　先週の火曜日に会社の損失が発表されて以後，その会社の株価は劇的に下落した。

**正解：(B)**
問題文を読む前に選択肢を見ると，品詞の問題だとわかる。そこでまず空所の前後に目をやると，〈the ------- of〉の形にふさわしいのは名詞だ。よって，value「価値；価格」が正解と決まる。なお，the の後は必ず名詞が続くが，〈the ------- 名詞〉だと空所にはたいていの場合形容詞が入るので，前だけでなく後ろもしっかりと見よう。他の選択肢の意味は，(A) は動詞 value「～を評価する」の過去形・過去分詞，(C) は動詞「～を評価する」，(D) は形容詞「貴重な」。

**2**
Speaking ------- behalf of all the employees, Alan Lee thanked the departing CEO for all he had done for the company.
(A) on
(B) at
(C) for
(D) by

訳　全従業員を代表して，Alan Lee は，去っていく最高経営責任者に対して彼が会社にしてくれたことのすべてに感謝の辞を述べた。

**正解：(A)**
Speaking ～ employees の部分は分詞構文である。しかし，この問題では分詞構文の知識はあまり必要なく，熟語の on behalf of ～「～を代表して」を知っているかどうかがポイントだ。上の 1 番の問題と同様，ここでも on behalf of に気づけば文全体を読む必要はない。すぐに (A) をマークして次の問題に進もう。

# PART 5

**3**   We have no option but to ------- halt production of our new sport utility model due to a downturn in global markets and lack of consumer demand.

(A) temporarily
(B) formerly
(C) initially
(D) consecutively

訳 世界市場の景気の下降と消費者需要の不足により，われわれにはわが社の新しいスポーツ用多目的車の生産を一時的に中止する以外に選択肢がない。

## 正解：(A)

選択肢には副詞が並んでおり，文全体を読んで文脈上で適切な意味の語を選ぶ「語彙問題」だとわかる。「景気の下降と消費者需要の不足により，これから生産を一時的に中止する」という文脈が適切なので，(A) が正解。他の選択肢の意味は，(B)「以前は」，(C)「最初のうちは」，(D)「連続的に」。

13

# PART 6 例題

**Questions 1-4** refer to the following letter.

Mr. Timothy Mann
116, Bay Drive
San Francisco
California 94106
January 15

Dear Mr. Mann,

We'd like to remind you that your subscription to *Best Car* is due to ------- at the end of March. We would also like to make you a special
1.
offer, if you renew by the end of February: ------- two free copies, we'll
2.
also send you a Best Car family card. This card entitles you to many benefits, ------- discounts on car rentals nationwide.
3.

All you need to do is fill out the enclosed renewal card, and drop it in the nearest mailbox. Postage has been prepaid. -------.
4.

We look forward to hearing from you.

Sincerely,

The Customer Service Team
Dominic Boules, Manager

1. (A) expires
   (B) expire
   (C) expiring
   (D) expiration

2. (A) In order to
   (B) As for
   (C) In addition to
   (D) As long as

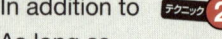

14

# PART 6

3. (A) including
   (B) inclusive
   (C) included
   (D) includes

4. (A) Please send this letter back to us as soon as possible.
   (B) Your subscription will then be discontinued.
   (C) Please include necessary postage with this card.
   (D) We sincerely hope you will take full advantage of this offer.

訳 問題 1-4 は次の手紙に関するものです。

Timothy Mann 様
Bay 通り 116
サンフランシスコ
カリフォルニア 94106
1 月 15 日


Mann 様

3月末で「ベストカー」のご購読期限が切れることをお知らせしたいと思います。また、もし2月末までに更新されましたら、特別な提供がございます。2か月分のご購読無料に加え、ベストカー・ファミリーカードもお送りします。このカードがあれば、全国で利用できるレンタカーの割引を含め、たくさんの特典が受けられます。
お客様にしていただくのは、同封した更新カードに記入して、お近くのポストに投函していただくだけです。郵便料金は前納済みです。この特別提供をフルにご活用していただけることを願っています。
お返事をお待ちしております。


敬具
顧客サービス部
Dominic Boules 部長

15

# PART 6

### 1  正解：(B)

動詞 expire の変化形の問題。前にある that は接続詞で，節内の主語は your subscription，動詞は is である。be due to do で「～することになっている」という意味であることに気づくかがポイント。この to は不定詞の to で，空所には動詞の原形である (B) が入る。混同しやすいのは due to ～「～が原因で」で，この to は前置詞なので後には名詞相当句が続く。例：The accident was due to their carelessness.「その事故は彼らの不注意が原因だった」

### 2  正解：(C)

文頭に適する表現を入れる問題。two free copies は名詞句なので，空所には前置詞の役割をする語句が入る。空所の後にある also に着目して，「2 か月分の購読無料に加えて～も送る」という文脈がふさわしい。よって，(C) の「～に加えて」が正解。この to は前置詞だが，(A) の in order to ～「～するために」の to は不定詞の to なので後には動詞の原形が続く。他の選択肢の意味は，(B) は「～に関しては」，(D) は「～する限り」で後にはSV が続く。

### 3  正解：(A)

品詞問題。直前の benefits までで文が完結しており，空所直後は（文ではなく）語句なので，空所には前置詞を入れるのが適切。よって，(A) including「～を含めて」が正解。文書全体の内容を理解せずとも，空所を含む 1 文を見ただけで解ける問題である。

### 4  正解：(D)

空所に適する文を選ぶ問題。文章の最後の締めとして適するものはどれかを文脈から考える。この手紙の主旨は，雑誌の購読期限がもうすぐ切れることを知らせた後，特典について説明すること。よって，(D) が最も文脈に合う。this offer は前で説明した特典のことである。郵送料金は前納済みなので (C) は不適。他の選択肢の意味は，(A)「できるだけ早急にこの手紙を返送してください」，(B)「そうすれば，お客様の購読は中止されます」，(C)「このカードと一緒に必要な送料を含めてください」。

# PART 7 スコアアップのテクニック

## 攻略手順

### ❶ 難しい問題や苦手な問題は捨ててもよい
SP（1文書）の記事や長い手紙よりもDP（2文書）やTP（3文書）の方が易しいと感じる人も中にはいるだろう。自分にとって易しい問題や得意な文書形式の問題を優先して解く手もある。

### ❷ 時間切れになる前にすべてにマークする
終了時刻が近づき，解く時間がない問題にも必ずどれかにマークをしよう。

## 問題攻略テクニック

### テクニック 1 「言い換え」に素早く反応しよう
PART 3&4 と同様，本文と選択肢の言い換えを見極めよう。

### テクニック 2 スキミングとスキャニングを利用しよう
読む分量が多いが，すべてを精読する時間はない。文書を読んで設問を解くときは，スキミング（素早く全体を読んで大意をつかむ方法）とスキャニング（質問内容を把握してから該当する箇所を本文から探す方法）のテクニックを活用しよう。特に，具体的な人名に関する質問や，リストやフォームといった文書形式では，スキャニングが有効だ。

### テクニック 3 テキストメッセージやオンラインチャットは形式に慣れる
新傾向で導入されたテキストメッセージやオンラインチャット形式の文書では，硬い表現よりむしろカジュアルな口調が見られる。くだけた英文を「読む」ことに慣れよう。

### テクニック 4 文書中の表現の意図を問う問題は，先に設問をチェック
文書中の表現の意図を問う問題が新たに加わった。先に設問を確認して，その表現がある箇所を探しながら文書を読み（スキャニング），見つけたらその前後をしっかり理解しよう。

### テクニック 5 文挿入問題は前後の流れが悪い箇所を探す
設問で与えられた1文が文書中のどこに入るかを選ぶ問題も新傾向だ。まずは挿入される文を確認し，その後，文書でスキミングを行い，流れが悪い箇所を突き止めよう。

### テクニック 6 TP の解き方は DP と同じ
新しく加わった TP の問題は，DP に文書が1つ増えただけで，複数の文書をまたいで情報を組み合わせて解答する問題など，設問の傾向や対策は DP と同じだ。

# PART 7　例題（シングルパッセージ）

**Questions 1-2** refer to the following text message chain.

---

**Abdul Jazareh　5:56** P.M.
Donna, could you e-mail me a copy of the Donworth Inc. portfolio?

**Donna Hastings　5:58** P.M.
Donworth? I don't think it's been digitized yet. We only have a printed version.

**Abdul Jazareh　5:59** P.M.
Do you know where it is?

**Donna Hastings　6:01** P.M.
You mean it's not at the Lexington branch?

**Abdul Jazareh　6:02** P.M.
Nope, I've been looking all over for it.

**Donna Hastings　6:05** P.M.
Then it's got to be at the downtown office. <u>Hang on, OK?</u>

**Abdul Jazareh　6:07** P.M.
Don't they close at 6:00?

**Donna Hastings　6:12** P.M.
I just talked to Cynthia Stride. She says it's there. She just locked up, but she said she will drop back in, scan it, and send it to you. I gave her your e-mail address.

**Abdul Jazareh　6:14** P.M.
Oh, thanks so much, Donna!

---

訳　問題 1-2 は次のテキストメッセージのやり取りに関するものです。

**Abdul Jazareh　　午後 5:56**
Donna，Donworth 社のポートフォリオをメールしてくれない？

**Donna Hastings　　午後 5:58**
Donworth ？　まだデジタル化されていないと思うけど。印刷版しかないわよ。

**Abdul Jazareh　　午後 5:59**
どこにあるかわかる？

**Donna Hastings　　午後 6:01**
Lexington 支社にないということ？

**Abdul Jazareh　　午後 6:02**
うん，そこら中探し回っているんだけど。

**Donna Hastings　　午後 6:05**
ではきっとダウンタウンの事務所にあるのね。<u>少し待ってて，いいかしら？</u>

**Abdul Jazareh　　午後 6:07**
あそこは 6 時に閉まるんじゃなかった？

# PART 7

**Donna Hastings**　午後 6:12
今 Cynthia Stride と話したけど，あそこにあるって言っていたわ。ちょうど戸締りしたばかりだけど，戻ってスキャンしてあなたに送ってくれるって。あなたのメールアドレスを教えておいたわ。

**Abdul Jazareh**　午後 6:14
ああ，本当にありがとう Donna！

---

**1** Where most likely does Ms. Stride work?
(A) At Donworth Inc.
(B) At the Lexington branch
(C) At the downtown office
(D) At a printing company

訳　Stride さんはどこで働いていると考えられますか。
(A) Donworth 社　(B) Lexington 支社　(C) ダウンタウンの事務所　(D) 印刷会社

## 正解：(C)

通常，テキストメッセージのやり取りは 2 名，オンラインチャット形式のやり取りは 3 名以上である。Ms. Stride に関する設問なので本文から Ms. Stride という人物名をスキャニングすると，6:12 に Hastings さんが I just talked to Cynthia Stride. と書いている。その前で，「それ（＝デジタル化された Donworth 社のポートフォリオ）はきっとダウンタウンの事務所にある」と書いた後，Ms. Stride と話をしたことから，Ms. Stride はダウンタウンの事務所の人だと推測できる。よって，(C) が正解。

---

**2** At 6:05 P.M., what does Ms. Hastings most likely mean when she writes, "Hang on, OK"?
(A) She wants to get a printed portfolio.
(B) She intends to visit the downtown office.
(C) She is too busy to call Mr. Jazareh.
(D) She needs a short amount of time.

訳　午後 6 時 5 分に，Hastings さんが書いている "Hang on, OK" は何を意味していると考えられますか。
(A) 印刷されたポートフォリオを入手したい。　(B) ダウンタウンの事務所を訪問するつもりである。
(C) 忙しすぎて Jazareh さんに電話できない。　(D) 少々時間が必要である。

## 正解：(D)

文中の表現の意図を問う問題。先に設問を確認して，Hang on, OK と書かれている箇所を本文でスキャニングする。hang on には「（返事を）待つ」という意味があるので，これを知っていれば (D) が選べそうだが，念のため文脈を見よう。Hastings さんは Hang on, OK? と書いた 7 分後に「Cynthia Stride と話したけど〜」と続けていることから，Cynthia Stride に連絡を取る間，Jazareh さんに待つよう言っていることがわかる。

19

# PART 7

**Questions 1-3** refer to the following letter.

Mr. Patrick Slater
President
Garden International
394 Selby Ave.
St. Paul, MN 55104

Dear Mr. Slater,

I am writing with regard to the industrial grade lawnmower model X900 that we purchased from your company half a year ago. —[1]—.

As you may recall, at the time of purchase, I spoke with you at length about our requirements. I explained that our country club is located in a highly wooded area and that we needed a model that can cope with this. —[2]—.

However, in the last two months, I have had to contact your maintenance department a total of six times due to twigs and other small pieces of wood becoming jammed in the blades, causing the machine to short circuit. —[3]—. On his last visit Andy Hart confirmed there is nothing wrong with the machine itself but that it is simply not up to the task required.

I would appreciate it if you would either replace the lawnmower with a more dependable model or refund the full purchase price. —[4]—.

As ours is a high-class establishment and the upkeep of our estate is of the greatest importance to us, we are keen to sort this matter out as soon as possible.

An early reply in regard to this matter would be appreciated.

Sincerely yours,

Brian Beatty
Maintenance Manager
Mountain View Country Club

# PART 7

訳 問題 1-3 は次の手紙に関するものです。

Patrick Slater 社長
Garden International
Selby 通り 394 番地
セントポール，ミネソタ州 55104


Slater 様

弊社が御社から半年前に購入した工業用の芝刈り機モデル X900 に関してお便り申し上げます。− [1] −

覚えていらっしゃると思いますが，購入時，私は弊社の必要条件を詳細にお話ししました。弊社のカントリークラブは非常に樹木の茂った地域に位置しており，このことに対処できるモデルが必要であることをご説明しました。そのときに御社はこの特別なモデルこそが作業に申し分のないものと全面的に保証してくださいました。

しかしながら，ここ 2 か月の間，小枝や他の小さな木片が刃に詰まった状態になって機械をショートさせるため，御社のメンテナンス部門に合計 6 回も連絡しなければなりませんでした。− [3] − Andy Hart さんが最後に来たときに，彼は機械本体には何も問題がないが，単に要求された仕事には向かないものであるということを確認しました。

御社が芝刈り機をもっと頼りになるモデルと交換してくださるか，購入金額を全額払い戻してくださったら大変ありがたく思います。− [4] −

弊社のクラブは高級な施設で，弊社の地所を維持することは弊社にとって最も重要なことでありますので，この問題をできるだけ早く解決することを切望しております。

この件に関し早めにお返事をいただければ幸いです。


敬具
Brian Beatty
メンテナンス・マネージャー
Mountain View カントリークラブ

# PART 7

**1**
Who is Andy Hart?
(A) An employee of Garden International
(B) A colleague of Brian Beatty
(C) A gardener at Mountain View Country Club
(D) A machine salesman

訳 Andy Hart とは誰ですか。
(A) Garden International の社員　　(B) Brian Beatty の同僚
(C) Mountain View カントリークラブの庭師　(D) 機械のセールスマン

**正解：(A)**

設問を先読みして，Andy Hart という人物名をスキャニングする。第 3 段落中ほどの On his last visit Andy Hart confirmed there is nothing wrong with the machine itself 〜の部分から，Beatty さんが Garden International のメンテナンス部門に連絡した結果，Andy Hart が Beatty さんのところへ機械のチェックをしに来たことがわかる。よって，Andy Hart は Garden International の修理担当社員だと推測できる。

**2**
What does Mr. Beatty ask Mr. Slater to do?
(A) Repair the lawnmower
(B) Replace the broken parts
(C) Provide them with a more reliable machine
(D) Pay for the cost of repairs

訳 Beatty さんは Slater さんに何をするように頼んでいますか。
(A) 芝刈り機を修理する　　(B) 故障した部品を交換する
(C) もっと確実な機械を自分たちに提供する　(D) 修理費を支払う

**正解：(C)**

設問を先読みして，「Beatty さんの Slater さんへの依頼」に焦点を絞って本文を読む（スキャニング）。第 4 段落の 〜 replace the lawnmower with a more dependable model or refund the full purchase price から，Beatty さんは「もっと頼りになるモデルと交換するか，購入金額を全額払い戻しすること」を頼んでいるので，正解は (C)。文中の dependable を選択肢では reliable と言い換えている。

# PART 7

**3** In which of the positions marked [1], [2], [3] and [4] does the following sentence best belong?

テクニック ②
テクニック ⑤

"At that time you gave me every assurance that this particular model was the right one for the job."

(A) [1]
(B) [2]
(C) [3]
(D) [4]

訳 [1], [2], [3], [4] と記載された箇所のうち，次の文が入るのに最もふさわしいのはどれですか。
「そのときに御社はこの特別なモデルこそが作業に申し分のないものと全面的に保証してくださいました」
(A) [1]　　(B) [2]　　(C) [3]　　(D) [4]

## 正解 (B)

文を挿入する適切な位置を問う問題。まずは，設問で与えられた 1 文を確認する。At that time がヒントで，「そのときに，御社（＝ Garden International）はこの（芝刈り機の）モデルが申し分のないものと保証してくれた」とはつまり，Beatty さんが芝刈り機を購入したときの話だと推測がつく。そこで本文を冒頭からスキミングしていくと，第 2 段落は購入したときの様子，第 3 段落は使用後の様子について書かれているので，空所 [2] に入れると流れに合う。

# PART 7 例題（ダブルパッセージ）

**Questions 1-5** refer to the following advertisement and e-mail.

---

**Junior Advertising Executive Wanted For Prominent Fashion Publication Aimed At Young Women.**

A college degree in a related subject is required as is familiarity with publishing. At least two years' comparable work experience is essential. Successful applicants will also be able to demonstrate a knowledge of current trends in fashion. Those interested should e-mail a résumé with a cover letter to arrive no later than April 21 to Melanie Marshall at the following address: Mmarshall@stargroup.com

---

From: abigailFNY@hotmail.com
To: Mmarshall@stargroup.com
Date: April 15th
Subject: Application for Junior Advertising Executive position

Dear Ms. Marshall,

I would like to apply for the position advertised in last week's edition of *The Evening Herald*. I have attached my résumé for your consideration. I believe I have the experience and skills that you are looking for and that I am the right person for the job.

I was born in England, where I studied Communications and Media at the University of East Anglia. After leaving college, I worked for a department store in London, as a trainee fashion buyer for a year, before relocating to New York two years ago. Since last September, I have been working on a temporary basis as an advertising assistant for a trade publication *Trends In Fashion Today*. I feel that my unique background could add value to your Advertising Executive position.

Thank you very much for your time and consideration.

Sincerely,

Abigail Fraser

# PART 7

訳 問題1-5は次の広告とEメールに関するものです。
若い女性向けの有名ファッション誌のための広告宣伝幹部補佐を求む。
出版に精通していると同時に，関連した科目の大学学位が必要とされます。少なくとも2年の同様の仕事の経験が必須です。また，ファッションの最新流行の知識を実証できる応募者がこの職に就くことができるでしょう。興味がある人はカバーレターと一緒に履歴書を Melanie Marshall 宛てに4月21日必着で以下のアドレスにEメールしてください。Mmarshall@stargroup.com

---

送信者：abigailFNY@hotmail.com
宛先：Mmarshall@stargroup.com
日付：4月15日
件名：広告宣伝幹部補佐職への応募

Marshall 様

先週の Evening Herald 紙に広告が出されていた職に応募させていただきたいと思います。履歴書を添付いたしましたので，ご検討ください。私には御社が求めておられる経験とスキルがあり，私こそがこの職に最もふさわしい人材であると信じています。

私はイングランドで生まれ，コミュニケーションとメディアをイースト・アングリア大学で学びました。大学を出てから，2年前にニューヨークに転居するまで，ロンドンの百貨店で1年間ファッションバイヤーの訓練生として働きました。昨年の9月からは，期限付きで業界紙 *Trends In Fashion Today* の広告宣伝アシスタントとして働いています。私の独特の経歴は，御社の広告宣伝幹部職に価値をもたらすと思います。

ご検討の程よろしくお願いします。

敬具
Abigail Fraser

25

# PART 7

> **1** Where does Melanie Marshall most likely work?
> (A) For a magazine
> (B) For an advertising agency
> (C) For a fashion store
> (D) For a design office

訳 Melanie Marshall はどこで働いていると考えられますか。
(A) 雑誌　(B) 広告代理店　(C) ファッションストア　(D) デザインオフィス

### 正解：(A)
Melanie Marshall という人物名をスキャニングすると，広告の最後にある。募集されている職に興味がある人が連絡する人物である。広告のタイトルの Wanted For Prominent Fashion Publication から，ファッション誌の求人とわかる。よって，Melanie Marshall の職種として適切なのは (A) で，Publication を magazine と言い換えている。

> **2** Where did Abigail Fraser attend college?
> (A) London
> (B) East Anglia
> (C) New York
> (D) Northern England

訳 Abigail Fraser はどこの大学に行きましたか。
(A) ロンドン　(B) イースト・アングリア　(C) ニューヨーク　(D) イングランド北部

### 正解：(B)
Abigail Fraser という人物をスキャニングすると，Eメールを書いた人物である。さらに E メールから大学について書かれている箇所をスキャニングすると，第 2 段落に I studied 〜 at the University of East Anglia「イースト・アングリア大学で〜を学んだ」とあるので，正解は (B)。本文の study を質問文では attend と言い換えている。

# PART 7

**3** What requirement does Abigail Fraser most likely NOT meet?
(A) Knowledge of publishing
(B) A relevant college degree
(C) Amount of similar work experience
(D) Familiarity with current trends in advertising

訳 Abigail Fraser が満たしていない可能性のある必須要件は何ですか。
(A) 出版の知識
(B) 関連性のある大学の学位
(C) 似たような職務の経験量
(D) 広告における最新の流行への精通

### 正解：(C)

応募の必須要件は広告で述べられており、選択肢では (A), (B), (C) が該当する。そこで E メールを見ると、I worked for a department store in London, as a trainee fashion buyer for a year から、デパートの勤務経験は 1 年、また、Since last September, I have been working ～より、昨年の 9 月から業界紙のアシスタントをしていることがわかるが、E メールの日付は 4 月なので 1 年未満である。よって、E メールの情報では職歴は合計 2 年未満と考えられ、広告にある At least two years' comparable work experience is essential. という必須要件に満たない。よって、(C) が正解。このように、DP と TP では、複数の文書にわたって情報を探し、その情報を結びつけて解答する問題が特徴的である。

**4** What is indicated about Abigail Fraser?
(A) Her present job is not permanent.
(B) She graduated from university two years ago.
(C) She is currently out of the country.
(D) Her present job is not challenging enough.

訳 Abigail Fraser についてどんなことが示されていますか。
(A) 彼女の現在の職は常勤ではない。
(B) 彼女は 2 年前に大学を卒業した。
(C) 彼女は現在国外にいる。
(D) 彼女の現在の職は十分にやりがいのあるものではない。

### 正解：(A)

「どんなことが示されているか」というピンポイント情報ではないタイプの問題は、文書全体から判断する必要がある。E メールをスキミングしていくと、第 2 段落の後半に I have been working on a temporary basis as an advertising assistant ～「期限付きで広告宣伝アシスタントとして働いている」とある。on a temporary basis は「臨時で、期限付きで」という意味で、これを not permanent と言い換えた (A) が正解。

# PART 7

**5** In the e-mail, the word "unique" in paragraph 2, line 6, is closest in meaning to
(A) special
(B) single
(C) affluent
(D) strange

訳　Eメールの第2段落・6行目の "unique" に最も意味が近いのは
(A) 特別な　(B) ただ1つの　(C) 裕福な　(D) 奇妙な

**正解：(A)**

unique には「唯一の；素晴らしい；独特の；無類の」などの意味があり，選択肢では (A)，(B)，(D) が類義語になる。Abigail Fraser が自分の経歴をアピールしている場面なので，unique は (A) special「特別な」と同じ意味で使われているとわかる。PART 7 の語彙問題では，多義語に焦点があたり，文脈上どの語義で使われているかを問うパターンが多い。

# 8 電話・インターネット・Eメール・手紙

## 電話

- **mobile phone** 携帯電話　　注意 phone のみで「携帯電話」を意味することも多い。
- **text message** （携帯電話同士の）テキストメッセージ　関連 text （携帯電話で）メールを送る
- **leave a message** 伝言を残す　　対 take a message 伝言を受ける
- **disconnect** 動 〜の接続を断つ　　用例 disconnect the line 電話を切る
- **hang up** 電話を切る
- **answering machine** 留守番電話
- **extension** 名 内線　　用例 extension number 内線番号
- **line** 名 電話回線　　用例 hold the line 電話を切らずに待つ
- **area code** 市外局番
- **customer service** 顧客サービス

## インターネット

- **online** 形 オンライン（式）の；インターネット上の　副 オンラインで　用例 online chat オンラインチャット
- **install** 動 〜をインストールする
- **Web site** ウェブサイト　　類 Web page ウェブページ，ホームページ
- **access** 〜にアクセス[接続]する

## Eメール・手紙

- **sender** 名 送り主，差出人，（Eメールの）送信者
- **recipient** 名 受領者
- **subject** 名 件名
- **attach** 動 〜を添付する　　名 attachment 添付物，添付ファイル
- **enclose** 動 〜を同封する
- **forward** 動 〜を転送する；〜を送信する
- **reply** 名 返事　動 返事をする　　用例 reply to an inquiry 問い合わせに返答する
- **regarding** 前 〜に関して
- **including** 〜を含めて　　対 excluding 〜を除いて
- **hear from 〜** 〜から連絡をもらう
- **look forward to 〜** 〜を楽しみに待つ

29

# 7 金融・収支・投資・景気

## 金融・収支

- □ **market** 名 市場, マーケット
- □ **tax** 名 税金 — 用例 tax included 税込みで
- □ **debt** 名 負債；借金
- □ **profit** 名 利益
- □ **loss** 名 損失
- □ **revenue** 名 歳入；収益
- □ **earnings** 名 (投資による) 収益；(稼いだ) 所得
- □ **sales** 名 <複数形で>売り上げ(高)
- □ **turnover** 名 (一定期間の) 売上高；総売上高
- □ **expenses** 名 <複数形で>経費 — 用例 travel expenses 旅費

## 投資

- □ **shareholder** 名 株主 — 用例 shareholders' meeting 株主総会
- □ **stock** 名 株 — 関連 stockholder 株主
- □ **investment** 名 投資 — 動 invest ～を投資する
- □ **dividend** 名 配当
- □ **interest rate** 利率 — 注意 名詞 interest には「利息」という意味がある。
- □ **statement** 名 報告書；取引明細書 — 用例 bank statement 銀行取引報告書
- □ **merger** 名 合併 — 動 merge 合併する
- □ **take over ～** ～を買収する, 乗っ取る — 類 acquire

## 景気

- □ **economy** 名 経済, 景気 — 注意 economic は「経済(上)の」, economical は「節約する」, economics は「経済学」。
- □ **recession** 名 景気後退；(一時的な) 不景気
- □ **depression** 名 不況；経済不振
- □ **slowdown** 名 (景気の) 後退
- □ **sluggish** 形 不況の；停滞した
- □ **bankruptcy** 名 倒産；破産 — 動 bankrupt ～を破産させる
- □ **turnaround** 名 業績の好転；経営の黒字化

# 6 商品・生産・物流

## 商品・生産

- □ **product** 图 生産品；製品 　関連 produce ～を生産する，生み出す　production 生産
- □ **item** 图 項目；品目 　用例 damaged item 損傷品
- □ **goods** 图 商品；品物
- □ **defective** 形 欠陥のある
- □ **replacement** 图 交換(品) 　動 replace A with B　A を B と取り替える
- □ **factory** 图 工場，製造所
- □ **plant** 图 (製造)工場；装置，設備
- □ **warehouse** 图 倉庫；商品保管所 　関連 storeroom 貯蔵室；物置
- □ **stock** 图 貯蔵；たくわえ 　用例 out of stock 在庫切れで　in stock 在庫して
- □ **shortage** 图 不足 　関連 be short of ～　～が不足している　run out of ～　～を使い果たす
- □ **facility** 图 ＜しばしば複数形で＞(病院・図書館などの)施設 　用例 medical facilities 医療施設
- □ **equipment** 图 設備，装置，用品 　用例 electrical equipment 電気設備
- □ **supplies** 图 ＜複数形で＞生活必需品 　用例 office supplies 事務用品
- □ **appliance** 图 電化製品，電気器具 　用例 home appliances 家電製品
- □ **device** 图 機器，装置，道具 　関連 tool (職人が使う)道具，工具
- □ **supply** 動 ～を供給する　图 供給 　反 demand 需要　图 supplier 供給業者

## 物流

- □ **package** 图 小包
- □ **envelope** 图 封筒
- □ **delivery** 图 配達 　用例 delivery charge 配達料　動 deliver ～を配達する
- □ **shipment** 图 発送；出荷 　動 ship ～を運送する
- □ **distribute** 動 (郵便物)を配達する；～に割り当てる　图 distribution 配給，配達
- □ **loading** 图 積み込み；船積み 　動 load (運搬物など)を積む
- □ **cargo** 图 積荷；貨物 　用例 unload cargo 積み荷を降ろす
- □ **courier** 图 宅配便業者
- □ **invoice** 图 送り状 　関連 bill 請求書

# 5 給与・手当・異動

## 給与

- □ **salary** 图（通常月ごとに支払われる固定の）給料
- □ **income** 图（定期的に入る）収入；（特に年間の）収益, 所得
- □ **fee** 图（専門職業者へ支払われる1回ごとの）報酬, 謝礼
- □ **wage** 图（特に肉体労働などの通常日給・時給・週給の）賃金；給料
- □ **payment** 图 支払い, 支払金
- □ **payroll** 图（会社の）給料支払い名簿；（従業員の）支払い給与総額
- □ **paycheck** 图 給料；給料支払小切手
- □ **remuneration** 图（労働に対する）報酬；給料
- □ **compensation** 图 賠償；報酬
- □ **raise** 图 昇給, 賃上げ

## 手当

- □ **welfare** 图 福利厚生；福祉
- □ **benefit** 图 給付金；手当
- □ **allowance** 图（一定の）手当；支給額　　用例 family allowance 家族手当
- □ **pension** 图 年金
- □ **health insurance** 健康保険
- □ **paid holiday** 有給休暇
- □ **vacation** 图 休暇；休日
- □ **incentive** 图 奨励金
- □ **award** 图 賞金；賞品
- □ **commission** 图 手数料；歩合

## 異動

- □ **promotion** 图 昇進　　動 promote ～を昇進させる
- □ **appoint A as [to be] B** A を B に任命する　图 appointment 任命, 指名
- □ **allocate A to B** A を B に割り当てる
- □ **transfer** 图 異動, 転勤　動 ～を異動させる, 転勤させる　用例 transfer him to Tokyo office 彼を東京支店に転勤させる
- □ **relocate A to B** A を B に移転させる

# 4 就職・資格・退職

## 就職・資格

- **apply for 〜** 〜に応募する 　　用例 apply for a position 職に応募する
- **hire** 動 〜を雇う
- **résumé** 名 履歴書 　　関 CV 履歴書　cover letter カバーレター，添え状
- **job opening** 仕事の空き；就職口
- **recruit** 動 〜を募集する　名 新入社員
- **trainee** 名 研修生 　　動 train 〜を養成する　名 trainer 訓練者
- **orientation** 名 オリエンテーション
- **part time** 非常勤で，パートタイムで 　　対 full time 常勤で
- **employment** 名 雇用 　　対 unemployment 失業
- **temporary** 形 一時的な 　　副 temporarily 一時的に / 対 permanent 永久的な
- **shift** 名 交替勤務；シフト制
- **requirement** 名 (職の)必須要件
- **condition** 名 (合意・契約などの)条件
- **terms** 名 <複数形で>（支払い・契約などの）条件
- **certificate** 動 〜を認証する　名 証明書；免許状　名 certification 証明(書)
- **qualification** 名 資格 　　関連 be qualified for 〜 〜の資格がある
- **skill** 名 技術；スキル
- **knowledge** 名 知識
- **background** 名 経歴
- **degree** 名 学位 　　用例 graduate degree 大学院の学位

## 退職

- **retire** 動 (定年・病気などで)退職する 　　名 retirement 退職
- **resign** 動 (自ら告げて正式に)辞職する 　　類 quit, leave
- **reorganization** 名 再編成，再組織化
- **layoff** 名 一時解雇
- **fire** 動 〜を解雇する 　　類 dismiss (fire よりも堅い語)

# 3 会議・出張

## 会議

- **conference** 图 会議；会談
- **board meeting** 取締役会議　　用例 executive board meeting 常任理事会
- **committee** 图 委員会
- **attend** 動 〜に出席する
- **venue** 图 開催地
- **exhibition** 图 展示；展示会；博覧会
- **agenda** 图 協議事項，議事日程(表)
- **discussion** 图 討論　　動 discuss 〜について話し合う（≒ talk about）
- **handout** 图 配布資料；(会議などで配る) プリント
- **projector** 图 プロジェクター
- **minutes** 图 ＜複数形で＞議事録　　用例 take the minutes 議事録を取る
- **chairperson** 图 議長；委員長
- **representative** 图 代表者，代理人

## 出張

- **passenger** 图 乗客
- **departure** 图 出発　　動 depart 出発する　　反 arrival 到着
- **bound for 〜** 〜行きの
- **round-trip ticket** 往復切符　　反 one-way ticket 片道切符
- **boarding** 图 搭乗；乗船　　用例 boarding pass 搭乗券
- **aisle seat** 通路側の席　　反 window seat 窓側の席
- **destination** 图 目的地　　用例 final destination 最終目的地
- **take off** 離陸する　　反 land 着陸する
- **delay** 图 遅延　　動 〜を遅らせる
- **itinerary** 图 旅程表
- **fare** 图 運賃
- **accommodations** 图 ＜複数形で＞宿泊設備

34

# 2 顧客・業種・業務

**顧客・業種**

- client 图 顧客
- contract 图 契約(書) — 関連 agreement 合意, 契約
- manufacturer 图 製造業者 — 動 manufacture ～を製造する
- retailer 图 小売業者
- agency 图 代理店, 仲介 — 関連 agent 代理人　travel agency 旅行代理店　real estate agency 不動産業者
- publisher 图 出版社 — 類 publishing company
- architect 图 建築家
- secretary 图 秘書
- editor 图 編集者
- accountant 图 会計士
- lawyer 图 法律家；弁護士 — 関連 attorney 弁護士；法定代理人
- salesclerk 图 店員 — 類 shop assistant
- professor 图 (大学)教授 — 関連 instructor (スポーツや大学の)講師

**業務**

- duties 图 <複数形で>職務, 責務
- operation 图 事業, 経営；操作, 運転 — 動 operate ～を経営する, 操作する
- performance 图 (業務の)実績 — 類 achievement, accomplishment　用例 sales performance 販売実績
- campaign 图 キャンペーン
- strategy 图 戦略
- publicity 图 広報, 宣伝
- proposal 图 提案(書)
- submit 動 ～を提出する — 類 hand in ～　图 submission 提出
- expire 動 有効期限が切れる — 関連 due 期限が来て (形容詞)
- deadline 图 締め切り, 期限 — 用例 meet the deadline 期限に間に合わせる
- schedule 動 ～の予定を決める — 関連 reschedule ～の予定を変更する
- be in charge of ～ ～を担当している — 関連 be responsible for ～ ～に責任がある

35

# 1 会社・組織・役職

## 会社・組織

- **company** 图 会社，企業 　関 corporation 法人，有限[株式]会社
- **firm** 图 商会，商店，会社 　用例 law firm 法律事務所
- **organization** 图 団体，組織 　動 organize ～を組織化する
- **institute** 图 協会，研究所，専門学校
- **establish** 動 ～を設立する 　用例 establish a company 会社を設立する
- **head office** 本店；本社
- **headquarters** 图 本社；本部
- **branch** 图 支社；支店 　用例 overseas branch 海外支店
- **department** 图 (会社などの) 部門，…部[課]；(行政組織の) 省；(学校機構の) 学部，科
- **division** 图 (会社などの) 部，局，課；(学校機構の) 学部
- **human resources [HR] department** 人事部 　関 personnel department
- **research and development [R&D] department** 研究開発部

## 役職

- **CEO** 图 最高経営責任者 (chief executive officer の略)
- **president** 图 社長；会長 　関 director 重役，取締役
- **vice president** 副社長；副会長
- **employer** 图 雇用者；雇い主 　対 employee 被雇用者；従業員
- **board** 图 重役会；委員会 　用例 board of directors 取締役会
- **executive** 图 経営幹部；重役
- **administration** 图 管理；運営 　用例 the administration 執行部；経営陣
- **manager** 图 マネージャー，部長，課長 　動 manage ～を経営[運営]する　图 management 管理；経営(陣)
- **staff** 图 従業員，スタッフ 　関 worker 労働者
- **boss** 图 上司；社長
- **supervisor** 图 監督者；上司
- **subordinate** 图 部下；従属者
- **colleague** 图 同僚 　類 co-worker (職場の)同僚；仕事仲間

# 第1回 模擬試験 解答用紙

REGISTRATION No. 受験番号

フリガナ

NAME 氏名

## LISTENING SECTION

### Part 1

| No. | ANSWER A B C D |
|---|---|
| 1 | Ⓐ Ⓑ Ⓒ Ⓓ |
| 2 | Ⓐ Ⓑ Ⓒ Ⓓ |
| 3 | Ⓐ Ⓑ Ⓒ Ⓓ |
| 4 | Ⓐ Ⓑ Ⓒ Ⓓ |
| 5 | Ⓐ Ⓑ Ⓒ Ⓓ |
| 6 | Ⓐ Ⓑ Ⓒ Ⓓ |
| 7 | Ⓐ Ⓑ Ⓒ |
| 8 | Ⓐ Ⓑ Ⓒ |
| 9 | Ⓐ Ⓑ Ⓒ |
| 10 | Ⓐ Ⓑ Ⓒ |

### Part 2

| No. | ANSWER A B C |
|---|---|
| 11 | Ⓐ Ⓑ Ⓒ |
| 12 | Ⓐ Ⓑ Ⓒ |
| 13 | Ⓐ Ⓑ Ⓒ |
| 14 | Ⓐ Ⓑ Ⓒ |
| 15 | Ⓐ Ⓑ Ⓒ |
| 16 | Ⓐ Ⓑ Ⓒ |
| 17 | Ⓐ Ⓑ Ⓒ Ⓓ |
| 18 | Ⓐ Ⓑ Ⓒ Ⓓ |
| 19 | Ⓐ Ⓑ Ⓒ Ⓓ |
| 20 | Ⓐ Ⓑ Ⓒ Ⓓ |

| No. | ANSWER A B C |
|---|---|
| 21 | Ⓐ Ⓑ Ⓒ |
| 22 | Ⓐ Ⓑ Ⓒ |
| 23 | Ⓐ Ⓑ Ⓒ |
| 24 | Ⓐ Ⓑ Ⓒ |
| 25 | Ⓐ Ⓑ Ⓒ |
| 26 | Ⓐ Ⓑ Ⓒ |
| 27 | Ⓐ Ⓑ Ⓒ |
| 28 | Ⓐ Ⓑ Ⓒ |
| 29 | Ⓐ Ⓑ Ⓒ |
| 30 | Ⓐ Ⓑ Ⓒ |

### Part 3

| No. | ANSWER A B C D |
|---|---|
| 31 | Ⓐ Ⓑ Ⓒ |
| 32 | Ⓐ Ⓑ Ⓒ Ⓓ |
| 33 | Ⓐ Ⓑ Ⓒ Ⓓ |
| 34 | Ⓐ Ⓑ Ⓒ Ⓓ |
| 35 | Ⓐ Ⓑ Ⓒ Ⓓ |
| 36 | Ⓐ Ⓑ Ⓒ Ⓓ |
| 37 | Ⓐ Ⓑ Ⓒ Ⓓ |
| 38 | Ⓐ Ⓑ Ⓒ Ⓓ |
| 39 | Ⓐ Ⓑ Ⓒ Ⓓ |
| 40 | Ⓐ Ⓑ Ⓒ Ⓓ |

| No. | ANSWER A B C D |
|---|---|
| 41 | Ⓐ Ⓑ Ⓒ Ⓓ |
| 42 | Ⓐ Ⓑ Ⓒ Ⓓ |
| 43 | Ⓐ Ⓑ Ⓒ Ⓓ |
| 44 | Ⓐ Ⓑ Ⓒ Ⓓ |
| 45 | Ⓐ Ⓑ Ⓒ Ⓓ |
| 46 | Ⓐ Ⓑ Ⓒ Ⓓ |
| 47 | Ⓐ Ⓑ Ⓒ Ⓓ |
| 48 | Ⓐ Ⓑ Ⓒ Ⓓ |
| 49 | Ⓐ Ⓑ Ⓒ Ⓓ |
| 50 | Ⓐ Ⓑ Ⓒ Ⓓ |

| No. | ANSWER A B C D |
|---|---|
| 51 | Ⓐ Ⓑ Ⓒ Ⓓ |
| 52 | Ⓐ Ⓑ Ⓒ Ⓓ |
| 53 | Ⓐ Ⓑ Ⓒ Ⓓ |
| 54 | Ⓐ Ⓑ Ⓒ Ⓓ |
| 55 | Ⓐ Ⓑ Ⓒ Ⓓ |
| 56 | Ⓐ Ⓑ Ⓒ Ⓓ |
| 57 | Ⓐ Ⓑ Ⓒ Ⓓ |
| 58 | Ⓐ Ⓑ Ⓒ Ⓓ |
| 59 | Ⓐ Ⓑ Ⓒ Ⓓ |
| 60 | Ⓐ Ⓑ Ⓒ Ⓓ |

| No. | ANSWER A B C D |
|---|---|
| 61 | Ⓐ Ⓑ Ⓒ Ⓓ |
| 62 | Ⓐ Ⓑ Ⓒ Ⓓ |
| 63 | Ⓐ Ⓑ Ⓒ Ⓓ |
| 64 | Ⓐ Ⓑ Ⓒ Ⓓ |
| 65 | Ⓐ Ⓑ Ⓒ Ⓓ |
| 66 | Ⓐ Ⓑ Ⓒ Ⓓ |
| 67 | Ⓐ Ⓑ Ⓒ Ⓓ |
| 68 | Ⓐ Ⓑ Ⓒ Ⓓ |
| 69 | Ⓐ Ⓑ Ⓒ Ⓓ |
| 70 | Ⓐ Ⓑ Ⓒ Ⓓ |

### Part 4

| No. | ANSWER A B C D |
|---|---|
| 71 | Ⓐ Ⓑ Ⓒ Ⓓ |
| 72 | Ⓐ Ⓑ Ⓒ Ⓓ |
| 73 | Ⓐ Ⓑ Ⓒ Ⓓ |
| 74 | Ⓐ Ⓑ Ⓒ Ⓓ |
| 75 | Ⓐ Ⓑ Ⓒ Ⓓ |
| 76 | Ⓐ Ⓑ Ⓒ Ⓓ |
| 77 | Ⓐ Ⓑ Ⓒ Ⓓ |
| 78 | Ⓐ Ⓑ Ⓒ Ⓓ |
| 79 | Ⓐ Ⓑ Ⓒ Ⓓ |
| 80 | Ⓐ Ⓑ Ⓒ Ⓓ |

| No. | ANSWER A B C D |
|---|---|
| 81 | Ⓐ Ⓑ Ⓒ Ⓓ |
| 82 | Ⓐ Ⓑ Ⓒ Ⓓ |
| 83 | Ⓐ Ⓑ Ⓒ Ⓓ |
| 84 | Ⓐ Ⓑ Ⓒ Ⓓ |
| 85 | Ⓐ Ⓑ Ⓒ Ⓓ |
| 86 | Ⓐ Ⓑ Ⓒ Ⓓ |
| 87 | Ⓐ Ⓑ Ⓒ Ⓓ |
| 88 | Ⓐ Ⓑ Ⓒ Ⓓ |
| 89 | Ⓐ Ⓑ Ⓒ Ⓓ |
| 90 | Ⓐ Ⓑ Ⓒ Ⓓ |

| No. | ANSWER A B C D |
|---|---|
| 91 | Ⓐ Ⓑ Ⓒ Ⓓ |
| 92 | Ⓐ Ⓑ Ⓒ Ⓓ |
| 93 | Ⓐ Ⓑ Ⓒ Ⓓ |
| 94 | Ⓐ Ⓑ Ⓒ Ⓓ |
| 95 | Ⓐ Ⓑ Ⓒ Ⓓ |
| 96 | Ⓐ Ⓑ Ⓒ Ⓓ |
| 97 | Ⓐ Ⓑ Ⓒ Ⓓ |
| 98 | Ⓐ Ⓑ Ⓒ Ⓓ |
| 99 | Ⓐ Ⓑ Ⓒ Ⓓ |
| 100 | Ⓐ Ⓑ Ⓒ Ⓓ |

## READING SECTION

### Part 5

| No. | ANSWER A B C D |
|---|---|
| 101 | Ⓐ Ⓑ Ⓒ Ⓓ |
| 102 | Ⓐ Ⓑ Ⓒ Ⓓ |
| 103 | Ⓐ Ⓑ Ⓒ Ⓓ |
| 104 | Ⓐ Ⓑ Ⓒ Ⓓ |
| 105 | Ⓐ Ⓑ Ⓒ Ⓓ |
| 106 | Ⓐ Ⓑ Ⓒ Ⓓ |
| 107 | Ⓐ Ⓑ Ⓒ Ⓓ |
| 108 | Ⓐ Ⓑ Ⓒ Ⓓ |
| 109 | Ⓐ Ⓑ Ⓒ Ⓓ |
| 110 | Ⓐ Ⓑ Ⓒ Ⓓ |

| No. | ANSWER A B C D |
|---|---|
| 111 | Ⓐ Ⓑ Ⓒ Ⓓ |
| 112 | Ⓐ Ⓑ Ⓒ Ⓓ |
| 113 | Ⓐ Ⓑ Ⓒ Ⓓ |
| 114 | Ⓐ Ⓑ Ⓒ Ⓓ |
| 115 | Ⓐ Ⓑ Ⓒ Ⓓ |
| 116 | Ⓐ Ⓑ Ⓒ Ⓓ |
| 117 | Ⓐ Ⓑ Ⓒ Ⓓ |
| 118 | Ⓐ Ⓑ Ⓒ Ⓓ |
| 119 | Ⓐ Ⓑ Ⓒ Ⓓ |
| 120 | Ⓐ Ⓑ Ⓒ Ⓓ |

| No. | ANSWER A B C D |
|---|---|
| 121 | Ⓐ Ⓑ Ⓒ Ⓓ |
| 122 | Ⓐ Ⓑ Ⓒ Ⓓ |
| 123 | Ⓐ Ⓑ Ⓒ Ⓓ |
| 124 | Ⓐ Ⓑ Ⓒ Ⓓ |
| 125 | Ⓐ Ⓑ Ⓒ Ⓓ |
| 126 | Ⓐ Ⓑ Ⓒ Ⓓ |
| 127 | Ⓐ Ⓑ Ⓒ Ⓓ |
| 128 | Ⓐ Ⓑ Ⓒ Ⓓ |
| 129 | Ⓐ Ⓑ Ⓒ Ⓓ |
| 130 | Ⓐ Ⓑ Ⓒ Ⓓ |

### Part 6

| No. | ANSWER A B C D |
|---|---|
| 131 | Ⓐ Ⓑ Ⓒ Ⓓ |
| 132 | Ⓐ Ⓑ Ⓒ Ⓓ |
| 133 | Ⓐ Ⓑ Ⓒ Ⓓ |
| 134 | Ⓐ Ⓑ Ⓒ Ⓓ |
| 135 | Ⓐ Ⓑ Ⓒ Ⓓ |
| 136 | Ⓐ Ⓑ Ⓒ Ⓓ |
| 137 | Ⓐ Ⓑ Ⓒ Ⓓ |
| 138 | Ⓐ Ⓑ Ⓒ Ⓓ |
| 139 | Ⓐ Ⓑ Ⓒ Ⓓ |
| 140 | Ⓐ Ⓑ Ⓒ Ⓓ |

| No. | ANSWER A B C D |
|---|---|
| 141 | Ⓐ Ⓑ Ⓒ Ⓓ |
| 142 | Ⓐ Ⓑ Ⓒ Ⓓ |
| 143 | Ⓐ Ⓑ Ⓒ Ⓓ |
| 144 | Ⓐ Ⓑ Ⓒ Ⓓ |
| 145 | Ⓐ Ⓑ Ⓒ Ⓓ |
| 146 | Ⓐ Ⓑ Ⓒ Ⓓ |
| 147 | Ⓐ Ⓑ Ⓒ Ⓓ |
| 148 | Ⓐ Ⓑ Ⓒ Ⓓ |
| 149 | Ⓐ Ⓑ Ⓒ Ⓓ |
| 150 | Ⓐ Ⓑ Ⓒ Ⓓ |

### Part 7

| No. | ANSWER A B C D |
|---|---|
| 151 | Ⓐ Ⓑ Ⓒ Ⓓ |
| 152 | Ⓐ Ⓑ Ⓒ Ⓓ |
| 153 | Ⓐ Ⓑ Ⓒ Ⓓ |
| 154 | Ⓐ Ⓑ Ⓒ Ⓓ |
| 155 | Ⓐ Ⓑ Ⓒ Ⓓ |
| 156 | Ⓐ Ⓑ Ⓒ Ⓓ |
| 157 | Ⓐ Ⓑ Ⓒ Ⓓ |
| 158 | Ⓐ Ⓑ Ⓒ Ⓓ |
| 159 | Ⓐ Ⓑ Ⓒ Ⓓ |
| 160 | Ⓐ Ⓑ Ⓒ Ⓓ |

| No. | ANSWER A B C D |
|---|---|
| 161 | Ⓐ Ⓑ Ⓒ Ⓓ |
| 162 | Ⓐ Ⓑ Ⓒ Ⓓ |
| 163 | Ⓐ Ⓑ Ⓒ Ⓓ |
| 164 | Ⓐ Ⓑ Ⓒ Ⓓ |
| 165 | Ⓐ Ⓑ Ⓒ Ⓓ |
| 166 | Ⓐ Ⓑ Ⓒ Ⓓ |
| 167 | Ⓐ Ⓑ Ⓒ Ⓓ |
| 168 | Ⓐ Ⓑ Ⓒ Ⓓ |
| 169 | Ⓐ Ⓑ Ⓒ Ⓓ |
| 170 | Ⓐ Ⓑ Ⓒ Ⓓ |

| No. | ANSWER A B C D |
|---|---|
| 171 | Ⓐ Ⓑ Ⓒ Ⓓ |
| 172 | Ⓐ Ⓑ Ⓒ Ⓓ |
| 173 | Ⓐ Ⓑ Ⓒ Ⓓ |
| 174 | Ⓐ Ⓑ Ⓒ Ⓓ |
| 175 | Ⓐ Ⓑ Ⓒ Ⓓ |
| 176 | Ⓐ Ⓑ Ⓒ Ⓓ |
| 177 | Ⓐ Ⓑ Ⓒ Ⓓ |
| 178 | Ⓐ Ⓑ Ⓒ Ⓓ |
| 179 | Ⓐ Ⓑ Ⓒ Ⓓ |
| 180 | Ⓐ Ⓑ Ⓒ Ⓓ |

| No. | ANSWER A B C D |
|---|---|
| 181 | Ⓐ Ⓑ Ⓒ Ⓓ |
| 182 | Ⓐ Ⓑ Ⓒ Ⓓ |
| 183 | Ⓐ Ⓑ Ⓒ Ⓓ |
| 184 | Ⓐ Ⓑ Ⓒ Ⓓ |
| 185 | Ⓐ Ⓑ Ⓒ Ⓓ |
| 186 | Ⓐ Ⓑ Ⓒ Ⓓ |
| 187 | Ⓐ Ⓑ Ⓒ Ⓓ |
| 188 | Ⓐ Ⓑ Ⓒ Ⓓ |
| 189 | Ⓐ Ⓑ Ⓒ Ⓓ |
| 190 | Ⓐ Ⓑ Ⓒ Ⓓ |

| No. | ANSWER A B C D |
|---|---|
| 191 | Ⓐ Ⓑ Ⓒ Ⓓ |
| 192 | Ⓐ Ⓑ Ⓒ Ⓓ |
| 193 | Ⓐ Ⓑ Ⓒ Ⓓ |
| 194 | Ⓐ Ⓑ Ⓒ Ⓓ |
| 195 | Ⓐ Ⓑ Ⓒ Ⓓ |
| 196 | Ⓐ Ⓑ Ⓒ Ⓓ |
| 197 | Ⓐ Ⓑ Ⓒ Ⓓ |
| 198 | Ⓐ Ⓑ Ⓒ Ⓓ |
| 199 | Ⓐ Ⓑ Ⓒ Ⓓ |
| 200 | Ⓐ Ⓑ Ⓒ Ⓓ |

# 第2回 模擬試験 解答用紙

REGISTRATION No. 受験番号

フリガナ

NAME 氏名

## LISTENING SECTION

### Part 1
| No. | ANSWER A B C D |
|---|---|
| 1 | Ⓐ Ⓑ Ⓒ Ⓓ |
| 2 | Ⓐ Ⓑ Ⓒ Ⓓ |
| 3 | Ⓐ Ⓑ Ⓒ Ⓓ |
| 4 | Ⓐ Ⓑ Ⓒ Ⓓ |
| 5 | Ⓐ Ⓑ Ⓒ Ⓓ |
| 6 | Ⓐ Ⓑ Ⓒ Ⓓ |
| 7 | Ⓐ Ⓑ Ⓒ |
| 8 | Ⓐ Ⓑ Ⓒ |
| 9 | Ⓐ Ⓑ Ⓒ |
| 10 | Ⓐ Ⓑ Ⓒ |

### Part 2
| No. | ANSWER A B C |
|---|---|
| 11 | Ⓐ Ⓑ Ⓒ |
| 12 | Ⓐ Ⓑ Ⓒ |
| 13 | Ⓐ Ⓑ Ⓒ |
| 14 | Ⓐ Ⓑ Ⓒ |
| 15 | Ⓐ Ⓑ Ⓒ |
| 16 | Ⓐ Ⓑ Ⓒ |
| 17 | Ⓐ Ⓑ Ⓒ |
| 18 | Ⓐ Ⓑ Ⓒ |
| 19 | Ⓐ Ⓑ Ⓒ |
| 20 | Ⓐ Ⓑ Ⓒ |

| No. | ANSWER A B C |
|---|---|
| 21 | Ⓐ Ⓑ Ⓒ |
| 22 | Ⓐ Ⓑ Ⓒ |
| 23 | Ⓐ Ⓑ Ⓒ |
| 24 | Ⓐ Ⓑ Ⓒ |
| 25 | Ⓐ Ⓑ Ⓒ |
| 26 | Ⓐ Ⓑ Ⓒ |
| 27 | Ⓐ Ⓑ Ⓒ |
| 28 | Ⓐ Ⓑ Ⓒ |
| 29 | Ⓐ Ⓑ Ⓒ |
| 30 | Ⓐ Ⓑ Ⓒ |

| No. | ANSWER A B C D |
|---|---|
| 31 | Ⓐ Ⓑ Ⓒ Ⓓ |
| 32 | Ⓐ Ⓑ Ⓒ Ⓓ |
| 33 | Ⓐ Ⓑ Ⓒ Ⓓ |
| 34 | Ⓐ Ⓑ Ⓒ Ⓓ |
| 35 | Ⓐ Ⓑ Ⓒ Ⓓ |
| 36 | Ⓐ Ⓑ Ⓒ Ⓓ |
| 37 | Ⓐ Ⓑ Ⓒ Ⓓ |
| 38 | Ⓐ Ⓑ Ⓒ Ⓓ |
| 39 | Ⓐ Ⓑ Ⓒ Ⓓ |
| 40 | Ⓐ Ⓑ Ⓒ Ⓓ |

### Part 3
| No. | ANSWER A B C D |
|---|---|
| 41 | Ⓐ Ⓑ Ⓒ Ⓓ |
| 42 | Ⓐ Ⓑ Ⓒ Ⓓ |
| 43 | Ⓐ Ⓑ Ⓒ Ⓓ |
| 44 | Ⓐ Ⓑ Ⓒ Ⓓ |
| 45 | Ⓐ Ⓑ Ⓒ Ⓓ |
| 46 | Ⓐ Ⓑ Ⓒ Ⓓ |
| 47 | Ⓐ Ⓑ Ⓒ Ⓓ |
| 48 | Ⓐ Ⓑ Ⓒ Ⓓ |
| 49 | Ⓐ Ⓑ Ⓒ Ⓓ |
| 50 | Ⓐ Ⓑ Ⓒ Ⓓ |

| No. | ANSWER A B C D |
|---|---|
| 51 | Ⓐ Ⓑ Ⓒ Ⓓ |
| 52 | Ⓐ Ⓑ Ⓒ Ⓓ |
| 53 | Ⓐ Ⓑ Ⓒ Ⓓ |
| 54 | Ⓐ Ⓑ Ⓒ Ⓓ |
| 55 | Ⓐ Ⓑ Ⓒ Ⓓ |
| 56 | Ⓐ Ⓑ Ⓒ Ⓓ |
| 57 | Ⓐ Ⓑ Ⓒ Ⓓ |
| 58 | Ⓐ Ⓑ Ⓒ Ⓓ |
| 59 | Ⓐ Ⓑ Ⓒ Ⓓ |
| 60 | Ⓐ Ⓑ Ⓒ Ⓓ |

| No. | ANSWER A B C D |
|---|---|
| 61 | Ⓐ Ⓑ Ⓒ Ⓓ |
| 62 | Ⓐ Ⓑ Ⓒ Ⓓ |
| 63 | Ⓐ Ⓑ Ⓒ Ⓓ |
| 64 | Ⓐ Ⓑ Ⓒ Ⓓ |
| 65 | Ⓐ Ⓑ Ⓒ Ⓓ |
| 66 | Ⓐ Ⓑ Ⓒ Ⓓ |
| 67 | Ⓐ Ⓑ Ⓒ Ⓓ |
| 68 | Ⓐ Ⓑ Ⓒ Ⓓ |
| 69 | Ⓐ Ⓑ Ⓒ Ⓓ |
| 70 | Ⓐ Ⓑ Ⓒ Ⓓ |

### Part 4
| No. | ANSWER A B C D |
|---|---|
| 71 | Ⓐ Ⓑ Ⓒ Ⓓ |
| 72 | Ⓐ Ⓑ Ⓒ Ⓓ |
| 73 | Ⓐ Ⓑ Ⓒ Ⓓ |
| 74 | Ⓐ Ⓑ Ⓒ Ⓓ |
| 75 | Ⓐ Ⓑ Ⓒ Ⓓ |
| 76 | Ⓐ Ⓑ Ⓒ Ⓓ |
| 77 | Ⓐ Ⓑ Ⓒ Ⓓ |
| 78 | Ⓐ Ⓑ Ⓒ Ⓓ |
| 79 | Ⓐ Ⓑ Ⓒ Ⓓ |
| 80 | Ⓐ Ⓑ Ⓒ Ⓓ |

| No. | ANSWER A B C D |
|---|---|
| 81 | Ⓐ Ⓑ Ⓒ Ⓓ |
| 82 | Ⓐ Ⓑ Ⓒ Ⓓ |
| 83 | Ⓐ Ⓑ Ⓒ Ⓓ |
| 84 | Ⓐ Ⓑ Ⓒ Ⓓ |
| 85 | Ⓐ Ⓑ Ⓒ Ⓓ |
| 86 | Ⓐ Ⓑ Ⓒ Ⓓ |
| 87 | Ⓐ Ⓑ Ⓒ Ⓓ |
| 88 | Ⓐ Ⓑ Ⓒ Ⓓ |
| 89 | Ⓐ Ⓑ Ⓒ Ⓓ |
| 90 | Ⓐ Ⓑ Ⓒ Ⓓ |

| No. | ANSWER A B C D |
|---|---|
| 91 | Ⓐ Ⓑ Ⓒ Ⓓ |
| 92 | Ⓐ Ⓑ Ⓒ Ⓓ |
| 93 | Ⓐ Ⓑ Ⓒ Ⓓ |
| 94 | Ⓐ Ⓑ Ⓒ Ⓓ |
| 95 | Ⓐ Ⓑ Ⓒ Ⓓ |
| 96 | Ⓐ Ⓑ Ⓒ Ⓓ |
| 97 | Ⓐ Ⓑ Ⓒ Ⓓ |
| 98 | Ⓐ Ⓑ Ⓒ Ⓓ |
| 99 | Ⓐ Ⓑ Ⓒ Ⓓ |
| 100 | Ⓐ Ⓑ Ⓒ Ⓓ |

## READING SECTION

### Part 5
| No. | ANSWER A B C D |
|---|---|
| 101 | Ⓐ Ⓑ Ⓒ Ⓓ |
| 102 | Ⓐ Ⓑ Ⓒ Ⓓ |
| 103 | Ⓐ Ⓑ Ⓒ Ⓓ |
| 104 | Ⓐ Ⓑ Ⓒ Ⓓ |
| 105 | Ⓐ Ⓑ Ⓒ Ⓓ |
| 106 | Ⓐ Ⓑ Ⓒ Ⓓ |
| 107 | Ⓐ Ⓑ Ⓒ Ⓓ |
| 108 | Ⓐ Ⓑ Ⓒ Ⓓ |
| 109 | Ⓐ Ⓑ Ⓒ Ⓓ |
| 110 | Ⓐ Ⓑ Ⓒ Ⓓ |

| No. | ANSWER A B C D |
|---|---|
| 111 | Ⓐ Ⓑ Ⓒ Ⓓ |
| 112 | Ⓐ Ⓑ Ⓒ Ⓓ |
| 113 | Ⓐ Ⓑ Ⓒ Ⓓ |
| 114 | Ⓐ Ⓑ Ⓒ Ⓓ |
| 115 | Ⓐ Ⓑ Ⓒ Ⓓ |
| 116 | Ⓐ Ⓑ Ⓒ Ⓓ |
| 117 | Ⓐ Ⓑ Ⓒ Ⓓ |
| 118 | Ⓐ Ⓑ Ⓒ Ⓓ |
| 119 | Ⓐ Ⓑ Ⓒ Ⓓ |
| 120 | Ⓐ Ⓑ Ⓒ Ⓓ |

| No. | ANSWER A B C D |
|---|---|
| 121 | Ⓐ Ⓑ Ⓒ Ⓓ |
| 122 | Ⓐ Ⓑ Ⓒ Ⓓ |
| 123 | Ⓐ Ⓑ Ⓒ Ⓓ |
| 124 | Ⓐ Ⓑ Ⓒ Ⓓ |
| 125 | Ⓐ Ⓑ Ⓒ Ⓓ |
| 126 | Ⓐ Ⓑ Ⓒ Ⓓ |
| 127 | Ⓐ Ⓑ Ⓒ Ⓓ |
| 128 | Ⓐ Ⓑ Ⓒ Ⓓ |
| 129 | Ⓐ Ⓑ Ⓒ Ⓓ |
| 130 | Ⓐ Ⓑ Ⓒ Ⓓ |

### Part 6
| No. | ANSWER A B C D |
|---|---|
| 131 | Ⓐ Ⓑ Ⓒ Ⓓ |
| 132 | Ⓐ Ⓑ Ⓒ Ⓓ |
| 133 | Ⓐ Ⓑ Ⓒ Ⓓ |
| 134 | Ⓐ Ⓑ Ⓒ Ⓓ |
| 135 | Ⓐ Ⓑ Ⓒ Ⓓ |
| 136 | Ⓐ Ⓑ Ⓒ Ⓓ |
| 137 | Ⓐ Ⓑ Ⓒ Ⓓ |
| 138 | Ⓐ Ⓑ Ⓒ Ⓓ |
| 139 | Ⓐ Ⓑ Ⓒ Ⓓ |
| 140 | Ⓐ Ⓑ Ⓒ Ⓓ |

### Part 7
| No. | ANSWER A B C D |
|---|---|
| 141 | Ⓐ Ⓑ Ⓒ Ⓓ |
| 142 | Ⓐ Ⓑ Ⓒ Ⓓ |
| 143 | Ⓐ Ⓑ Ⓒ Ⓓ |
| 144 | Ⓐ Ⓑ Ⓒ Ⓓ |
| 145 | Ⓐ Ⓑ Ⓒ Ⓓ |
| 146 | Ⓐ Ⓑ Ⓒ Ⓓ |
| 147 | Ⓐ Ⓑ Ⓒ Ⓓ |
| 148 | Ⓐ Ⓑ Ⓒ Ⓓ |
| 149 | Ⓐ Ⓑ Ⓒ Ⓓ |
| 150 | Ⓐ Ⓑ Ⓒ Ⓓ |

| No. | ANSWER A B C D |
|---|---|
| 151 | Ⓐ Ⓑ Ⓒ Ⓓ |
| 152 | Ⓐ Ⓑ Ⓒ Ⓓ |
| 153 | Ⓐ Ⓑ Ⓒ Ⓓ |
| 154 | Ⓐ Ⓑ Ⓒ Ⓓ |
| 155 | Ⓐ Ⓑ Ⓒ Ⓓ |
| 156 | Ⓐ Ⓑ Ⓒ Ⓓ |
| 157 | Ⓐ Ⓑ Ⓒ Ⓓ |
| 158 | Ⓐ Ⓑ Ⓒ Ⓓ |
| 159 | Ⓐ Ⓑ Ⓒ Ⓓ |
| 160 | Ⓐ Ⓑ Ⓒ Ⓓ |

| No. | ANSWER A B C D |
|---|---|
| 161 | Ⓐ Ⓑ Ⓒ Ⓓ |
| 162 | Ⓐ Ⓑ Ⓒ Ⓓ |
| 163 | Ⓐ Ⓑ Ⓒ Ⓓ |
| 164 | Ⓐ Ⓑ Ⓒ Ⓓ |
| 165 | Ⓐ Ⓑ Ⓒ Ⓓ |
| 166 | Ⓐ Ⓑ Ⓒ Ⓓ |
| 167 | Ⓐ Ⓑ Ⓒ Ⓓ |
| 168 | Ⓐ Ⓑ Ⓒ Ⓓ |
| 169 | Ⓐ Ⓑ Ⓒ Ⓓ |
| 170 | Ⓐ Ⓑ Ⓒ Ⓓ |

| No. | ANSWER A B C D |
|---|---|
| 171 | Ⓐ Ⓑ Ⓒ Ⓓ |
| 172 | Ⓐ Ⓑ Ⓒ Ⓓ |
| 173 | Ⓐ Ⓑ Ⓒ Ⓓ |
| 174 | Ⓐ Ⓑ Ⓒ Ⓓ |
| 175 | Ⓐ Ⓑ Ⓒ Ⓓ |
| 176 | Ⓐ Ⓑ Ⓒ Ⓓ |
| 177 | Ⓐ Ⓑ Ⓒ Ⓓ |
| 178 | Ⓐ Ⓑ Ⓒ Ⓓ |
| 179 | Ⓐ Ⓑ Ⓒ Ⓓ |
| 180 | Ⓐ Ⓑ Ⓒ Ⓓ |

| No. | ANSWER A B C D |
|---|---|
| 181 | Ⓐ Ⓑ Ⓒ Ⓓ |
| 182 | Ⓐ Ⓑ Ⓒ Ⓓ |
| 183 | Ⓐ Ⓑ Ⓒ Ⓓ |
| 184 | Ⓐ Ⓑ Ⓒ Ⓓ |
| 185 | Ⓐ Ⓑ Ⓒ Ⓓ |
| 186 | Ⓐ Ⓑ Ⓒ Ⓓ |
| 187 | Ⓐ Ⓑ Ⓒ Ⓓ |
| 188 | Ⓐ Ⓑ Ⓒ Ⓓ |
| 189 | Ⓐ Ⓑ Ⓒ Ⓓ |
| 190 | Ⓐ Ⓑ Ⓒ Ⓓ |

| No. | ANSWER A B C D |
|---|---|
| 191 | Ⓐ Ⓑ Ⓒ Ⓓ |
| 192 | Ⓐ Ⓑ Ⓒ Ⓓ |
| 193 | Ⓐ Ⓑ Ⓒ Ⓓ |
| 194 | Ⓐ Ⓑ Ⓒ Ⓓ |
| 195 | Ⓐ Ⓑ Ⓒ Ⓓ |
| 196 | Ⓐ Ⓑ Ⓒ Ⓓ |
| 197 | Ⓐ Ⓑ Ⓒ Ⓓ |
| 198 | Ⓐ Ⓑ Ⓒ Ⓓ |
| 199 | Ⓐ Ⓑ Ⓒ Ⓓ |
| 200 | Ⓐ Ⓑ Ⓒ Ⓓ |

# CONTENTS

## 第1回　模擬試験　解答・解説

PART 1 ……………………………………………………… 4
PART 2 ……………………………………………………… 6
PART 3 ………………………………………………………11
PART 4 ………………………………………………………24
PART 5 ………………………………………………………34
PART 6 ………………………………………………………40
PART 7 ………………………………………………………44

## 第2回　模擬試験　解答・解説

PART 1 ………………………………………………………72
PART 2 ………………………………………………………74
PART 3 ………………………………………………………79
PART 4 ………………………………………………………92
PART 5 …………………………………………………… 102
PART 6 …………………………………………………… 108
PART 7 …………………………………………………… 112

| 本冊（問題編）のもくじ | 第1回　模擬試験 | ……………… 13 |
|---|---|---|
| | 第2回　模擬試験 | ……………… 55 |

# 第1回 模擬試験 解答・解説

**解答一覧**

| 設問番号 | 正解 | 設問番号 | 正解 | 設問番号 | 正解 | 設問番号 | 正解 | 設問番号 | 正解 |
|---|---|---|---|---|---|---|---|---|---|
| 1 | B | 41 | C | 81 | B | 121 | C | 161 | D |
| 2 | B | 42 | B | 82 | B | 122 | B | 162 | A |
| 3 | A | 43 | D | 83 | D | 123 | C | 163 | B |
| 4 | A | 44 | B | 84 | B | 124 | B | 164 | C |
| 5 | D | 45 | A | 85 | B | 125 | D | 165 | D |
| 6 | B | 46 | C | 86 | C | 126 | C | 166 | B |
| 7 | A | 47 | D | 87 | C | 127 | B | 167 | A |
| 8 | C | 48 | D | 88 | D | 128 | A | 168 | A |
| 9 | B | 49 | C | 89 | B | 129 | C | 169 | D |
| 10 | C | 50 | B | 90 | D | 130 | B | 170 | A |
| 11 | A | 51 | C | 91 | B | 131 | D | 171 | D |
| 12 | B | 52 | A | 92 | C | 132 | B | 172 | D |
| 13 | A | 53 | B | 93 | B | 133 | B | 173 | A |
| 14 | B | 54 | A | 94 | D | 134 | D | 174 | D |
| 15 | A | 55 | A | 95 | C | 135 | C | 175 | C |
| 16 | A | 56 | A | 96 | D | 136 | D | 176 | A |
| 17 | B | 57 | C | 97 | C | 137 | A | 177 | A |
| 18 | C | 58 | D | 98 | D | 138 | B | 178 | C |
| 19 | A | 59 | A | 99 | C | 139 | A | 179 | B |
| 20 | B | 60 | D | 100 | C | 140 | C | 180 | C |
| 21 | A | 61 | B | 101 | D | 141 | D | 181 | C |
| 22 | C | 62 | B | 102 | B | 142 | B | 182 | D |
| 23 | A | 63 | C | 103 | D | 143 | D | 183 | A |
| 24 | B | 64 | B | 104 | B | 144 | C | 184 | D |
| 25 | B | 65 | C | 105 | D | 145 | C | 185 | A |
| 26 | A | 66 | D | 106 | C | 146 | B | 186 | D |
| 27 | C | 67 | A | 107 | B | 147 | D | 187 | C |
| 28 | A | 68 | A | 108 | D | 148 | B | 188 | A |
| 29 | B | 69 | C | 109 | A | 149 | A | 189 | C |
| 30 | A | 70 | C | 110 | B | 150 | B | 190 | B |
| 31 | A | 71 | A | 111 | B | 151 | A | 191 | B |
| 32 | B | 72 | B | 112 | D | 152 | A | 192 | C |
| 33 | D | 73 | A | 113 | C | 153 | B | 193 | A |
| 34 | C | 74 | C | 114 | A | 154 | D | 194 | D |
| 35 | B | 75 | B | 115 | D | 155 | C | 195 | C |
| 36 | A | 76 | C | 116 | C | 156 | C | 196 | A |
| 37 | A | 77 | B | 117 | B | 157 | D | 197 | D |
| 38 | D | 78 | B | 118 | C | 158 | A | 198 | D |
| 39 | D | 79 | A | 119 | C | 159 | C | 199 | C |
| 40 | B | 80 | A | 120 | A | 160 | D | 200 | B |

# PART 1

## 放送文と訳

**1** 🍁

(A) They're looking out the window.
(B) They're examining the documents.
(C) They're polishing the table.
(D) They're writing on the paper.

(A) 彼女たちは窓の外を見ている。
(B) 彼女たちは書類を吟味している。
(C) 彼女たちはテーブルを磨いている。
(D) 彼女たちは紙に書いている。

## 正解と解説

### 正解 (B)

2人の女性が書類を見て何かを話し合っている様子である。選択肢の中で正解にふさわしいのは、(B) である。写真に写っている window, table, paper に惑わされないようにしよう。「動作」が写真と一致しないので他の選択肢は不適切。

examine [igzǽmin] ～を調べる；～を吟味する
polish [páliʃ] ～を磨く

---

**2** 🇬🇧

(A) He's pointing at himself.
(B) He's wearing a tie.
(C) He's moving the computer.
(D) He's taking off his glasses.

(A) 彼は自分自身を指さしている。
(B) 彼はネクタイを着けている。
(C) 彼はコンピューターを移動させている。
(D) 彼は眼鏡を外しているところである。

### 正解 (B)

男性が宙を指さしているが、自分自身を指さしていないので、(A) は不適切。右手でマウスを触ってはいるがコンピューターを移動させてはいないし、眼鏡を外しているところでもないので、(C), (D) も不適切。「ネクタイを着けている」という (B) が正解である。

point at ～  ～を指さす
take off ～  （体から服・帽子など）を外す

---

**3** 🍁

(A) The wheels are on the pavement.
(B) The cart is tipped over.
(C) The store window is broken.
(D) The shopping bag is empty.

(A) 車輪が舗道に接触している。
(B) カートがひっくり返っている。
(C) 店の窓が割れている。
(D) 買い物袋が空である。

### 正解 (A)

ショッピングカートが1台路上にある。これを言い表している (A) が正解。カートはひっくり返っていないし、窓は割れていないので、(B), (C) は不適切。(D) は bag をきちんと聞き取れないと正解と勘違いしてしまう可能性があるので、細部にわたってきちんと聞き取ろう。

wheel [hwiːl] 車輪
pavement [péivmənt] 舗道
tip over ～  ～をひっくり返す

## 放送文と訳

**4** 🇨🇦

(A) She's viewing the screen.
(B) She's touching the monitor.
(C) She's holding the handset.
(D) She's typing on the keyboard.

(A) 彼女はスクリーンを眺めている。
(B) 彼女はモニターを触っている。
(C) 彼女は受話器を握っている。
(D) 彼女はキーボードで打ち込んでいる。

## 正解と解説

### 正解 (A)

1人の女性がコンピューターのスクリーンを見ているので正解は (A)。彼女は右手にマウスを持っているが，他には何も触っていないので他の選択肢は誤答である。

view [vjuː] 〜を眺める
handset [hǽndsèt]（電話の）送受話器

---

**5** 🇬🇧

(A) Some buildings are being built.
(B) Some employees are working in the office.
(C) Some shops are being cleaned.
(D) Some people are walking along the avenue.

(A) いくつかの建物が建築中である。
(B) 何人かの社員がオフィスで働いている。
(C) いくつかの店が清掃中である。
(D) 何人かの人々が通りを歩いている。

### 正解 (D)

建物に挟まれた通りを歩いている人々を適切に表した (D) が正解。写真に写っている buildings や shops に引っ掛からないようにして，現在進行形で表されている「動作」部分をしっかりと聞き取ろう。

---

**6** 🇦🇺

(A) The woman is at a table.
(B) The woman is in a corner.
(C) The woman is behind the screen.
(D) The woman is under the window.

(A) 女性はテーブルに着いている。
(B) 女性は隅にいる。
(C) 女性はスクリーンの後ろにいる。
(D) 女性は窓の下にいる。

### 正解 (B)

女性は部屋の隅にいるので，正解は (B)。このように人物の位置関係を示す前置詞の at や behind, under をしっかりと理解しておこう。写真を見たら素早く人物の位置関係を把握し，正しい表現のものを選ぼう。

in a corner 隅に
behind [bəháind] 〜の後ろに

# PART 2

## 放送文と訳

### 7  M🇦🇺 W🇬🇧

**M**: Could you review these figures for me?
**W**: (A) I've already done that twice.
　　 (B) From the accounting office.
　　 (C) Yes, these figs are tasty.

**M**: これらの計算を見直してくださいませんか。
**W**: (A) もうすでに2回やりました。
　　 (B) 会計事務所からです。
　　 (C) はい，これらのイチジクは味が良いです。

### 正解 (A)

Could you ~? は「~してくださいませんか」とていねいに依頼する疑問文。I've already done that twice.「もうすでに2回やった」と「見直し」を拒否している (A) が正解。(B) は figures から連想される accounting office で引っ掛けようとしている。(C) は figures と figs で音の混乱をねらっている。

review [rivjúː] ~を見直す
figure [fígjər]（複数形で）計算
accounting office 会計事務所　fig [fig] イチジク

### 8  W🇺🇸 M🇨🇦

**W**: How many weeks are left in this quarter?
**M**: (A) Two dimes and a nickel.
　　 (B) Yes, our main headquarters.
　　 (C) Only one.

**W**: この四半期はあと何週間残っていますか。
**M**: (A) 10セント硬貨2枚と5セント硬貨1枚です。
　　 (B) はい，私たちの本社です。
　　 (C) 1週間だけです。

### 正解 (C)

How many ~? で「数」を尋ねている。(A) は「硬貨の枚数」を答えているため不適切。(B) は quarter と headquarters で混乱させようとしているが，疑問詞の疑問文に Yes で答えているので，不正解とすぐに気づいてほしい。「1週間」と明確に答えている (C) が正解。

quarter [kwɔ́ːrtər] 四半期
dime [daim]（米国・カナダの）10セント硬貨
nickel [níkl]（米国・カナダの）5セント硬貨
headquarters [hédkwɔ̀ːrtərz] 本社

### 9  W🇺🇸 M🇨🇦

**W**: Where is Mr. Chen going on vacation?
**M**: (A) Two weeks.
　　 (B) No one knows.
　　 (C) He went to Peru last year.

**W**: Chen さんはどこに休暇に行くのですか。
**M**: (A) 2週間です。
　　 (B) 誰も知りません。
　　 (C) 彼は昨年ペルーに行きました。

### 正解 (B)

Where ~? で「場所」について尋ねている。(A) は「期間」を答えているので不適切。(C) には「場所」が出てくるが，質問文が is ~ going と「未来」について聞いているのに対して，「過去」のことを答えており時制が合わないので正解ではない。「誰も知らない」と答えている (B) が正解。

### 10  M🇨🇦 W🇬🇧

**M**: Why are you leaving so early?
**W**: (A) I love autumn leaves.
　　 (B) About 2:00 P.M.
　　 (C) I'm not feeling well.

**M**: なぜこんなに早く退社するのですか。
**W**: (A) 紅葉が大好きです。
　　 (B) 午後2時頃です。
　　 (C) 気分が良くないのです。

### 正解 (C)

Why ~? で「理由」について尋ねている。「なぜこんなに早く退社するのか」と聞かれているので，「早退」の理由を述べたものが正解になる。(A) は質問文の leaving と leaves で音の混乱をねらっている。(B) は「時」を答えているので正解ではない。「気分が良くない」という返答が「早退」の理由としてふさわしいので，(C) が正解。

autumn leaves 紅葉（leaves は leaf の複数形）
feel well 気分が良い

### 11  W🇬🇧 W🇺🇸

**W**: Did Ms. Shibata ask Tom about his new client?
**W**: (A) Yes, in an e-mail.
　　 (B) They're called West Pacific Industries.
　　 (C) I'll ask her for advice.

**W**: Shibata さんは Tom に彼の新しい顧客について尋ねましたか。
**W**: (A) はい，E メールで。
　　 (B) 彼らは West Pacific Industries と呼ばれています。
　　 (C) 彼女に助言を求めてみます。

### 正解 (A)

Did Ms. Shibata ask Tom about ~?「Shibata さんは Tom に~について尋ねたか」の質問に対して，Yes, in an e-mail.「はい，E メールで」と答えている (A) が正解。「会社の名前」を聞いてはいないので，(B) は不適切。(C) は質問文と同じ ask を用いた引っ掛け。

client [kláiənt] 顧客
ask A for B　A に B を求める

| 放送文と訳 | 正解と解説 |
|---|---|

## 12  W 🇬🇧  M 🇦🇺

**W**: You haven't resigned from your position, have you?
**M**: (A) I have read the sign, in fact.
　　(B) No, that's just a rumor.
　　(C) For personal reasons.

W：役職を辞任なさってはいませんよね？
M：(A) 私は実際に標識を読みました。
　　(B) はい，ただのうわさですよ。
　　(C) 個人的な理由です。

### 正解 (B)

「～していませんよね」と念押しや確認をする付加疑問文である。No, that's just a rumor.「はい（辞めていません），ただのうわさですよ」と答えている (B) が正解。(A) は resigned と read the sign で音の混乱をねらっている。「辞職の理由」を聞かれてはいないので (C) は不適切。

resign [rizáin] 辞職する　　position [pəzíʃən] 職
in fact 実は　　rumor [rúːmər] うわさ
personal reason 個人的な理由

## 13  M 🇨🇦  W 🇺🇸

**M**: How much do I have to pay for express bus tickets?
**W**: (A) Check the board.
　　(B) I bought them online.
　　(C) For two adults, please.

M：急行バスのチケットにいくら払わなければなりませんか。
W：(A) 掲示板を確認してください。
　　(B) 私はそれらをオンラインで買いました。
　　(C) 大人を2枚お願いします。

### 正解 (A)

How much ～? で「値段」を尋ねている。「手段」を聞く How ではないので，(B) は正解ではない。(C) には数字が含まれているが，「チケットの枚数」を答えており，「値段」を答えてはいない。「（案内）掲示板を確認するように」と言っている (A) が正解。

express [ikspres] 急行の
board [bɔːrd] 掲示板

## 14  M 🇨🇦  W 🇺🇸

**M**: What ideas are you bringing to the morning meeting?
**W**: (A) After breakfast.
　　(B) I haven't given it a thought.
　　(C) Of course I'll be there.

M：朝の会議でどんな考えを持ち出すつもりですか。
W：(A) 朝食後に。
　　(B) そのことについて考えていませんでした。
　　(C) もちろん行きます。

### 正解 (B)

What ～? で「何」かを尋ねている。「時」を答えている (A) は不適切。morning から連想される breakfast に注意。持ち出す考えについて I haven't given it a thought.「少しも考えていなかった」と答えている (B) が正解。

bring [briŋ]（話題など）を持ち出す
give ～ a thought　～について考える

## 15  W 🇬🇧  M 🇦🇺

**W**: I think you should resend that scan.
**M**: (A) Didn't it go through?
　　(B) Yes, they can send it then.
　　(C) I'll buy butter and raisins.

W：あの画像を再送した方がいいと思いますよ。
M：(A) 送られなかったのですか。
　　(B) はい，彼らはそのときにそれを送ることができます。
　　(C) 私はバターとレーズンを買います。

### 正解 (A)

「あの画像を再送した方がいいと思う」という平叙文に対して，Didn't it go through?「送られなかったのか」と聞いている (A) が正解。(B) は質問文の resend と send, scan と can で音の混乱をねらっている。

resend [riːsénd] ～を再送する
scan [skæn]（読み込み）画像
go through つながる，届く
raisin [réizn] レーズン

## 16  M 🇦🇺  W 🇺🇸

**M**: When's the presentation due to start?
**W**: (A) I've no idea.
　　(B) Yes, it's a beautiful present.
　　(C) Jenna will be speaking.

M：プレゼンテーションはいつ始まる予定ですか。
W：(A) わかりません。
　　(B) はい，すてきなプレゼントですね。
　　(C) Jenna が話します。

### 正解 (A)

When ～? で「時」について尋ねている。「人」を答えている (C) は不適切。presentation につられて present を含む (B) を選ばないように注意しよう。「いつ始まる予定か」という質問に対して，I've no idea.「わからない」と答えている (A) が正解である。

presentation [prèzəntéiʃən] プレゼンテーション
be due to do　～する予定である

| 放送文と訳 | 正解と解説 |
|---|---|
| **17** M🇦🇺 W🇬🇧<br><br>M: How are negotiations proceeding to date on the merger with that overseas company?<br>W: (A) I'll accompany you to the sea.<br>　　(B) Could be better.<br>　　(C) The due date is July 19.<br><br>M: あの海外の会社との合併に向けて交渉はこれまでどのように進んでいますか。<br>W: (A) 海までご一緒します。　　**(B) あまりよくありません。**<br>　　(C) 期限は7月19日です。 | **正解 (B)**<br><br>How 〜？で「状態」を尋ねている。(A) は質問文の company と accompany, overseas と sea で音の混乱をねらっている。(C) は date で引っ掛けようとしている。「交渉の進み具合」を答えている (B) Could be better.「あまりよくない，いまいち」が正解である。<br><br>negotiation [nigòuʃiéiʃən] 交渉<br>proceed [prəsíːd] 進む　　to date 今まで<br>merger [mə́ːrdʒər] 合併<br>accompany [əkʌ́mpəni] 〜に同行する |
| **18** M🇦🇺 W🇬🇧<br><br>M: How about moving your desk over there?<br>W: (A) The movie was quite exciting.<br>　　(B) Because of the computer on it.<br>　　(C) Okay, but could you help me?<br><br>M: あなたの机を向こうに移動させてはどうですか。<br>W: (A) 映画はとても胸がわくわくするものでした。<br>　　(B) コンピューターが上に載っているからです。<br>　　**(C) わかりました。でも，手伝ってもらえますか。** | **正解 (C)**<br><br>How about 〜ing?「〜するのはどうか」と「提案」されて，Okay, but could you help me?「わかりました。でも，手伝ってもらえますか」と答えている (C) が正解。(A) は moving と movie で音の混乱をねらっている。(B) は何らかの「理由」を述べているが，質問文の内容とかみ合わない。<br><br>quite [kwait] とても<br>exciting [iksáitiŋ] (人を)わくわくさせる |
| **19** W🇺🇸 M🇦🇺<br><br>W: Would you mind leading the planning session today instead of Rick?<br>M: (A) No, if I can make time for it.<br>　　(B) That's what he said.<br>　　(C) I didn't mind at all.<br><br>W: Rick の代わりに今日，企画会議を指揮してもらって構いませんか。<br>M: **(A) 構いませんよ，もし時間が許すなら。**<br>　　(B) それが彼の言ったことです。<br>　　(C) 全く気にしませんでした。 | **正解 (A)**<br><br>Would you mind 〜ing? は「〜していただけませんか」とていねいに依頼する疑問文。No, if I can make time for it.「構いませんよ，もし時間が許すなら」と答えている (A) が正解。OK の意味のときに No と答えることに要注意。(B) は質問文と内容がかみ合わない。(C) は，「今，構わないか」を聞いているのに「過去形」で答えているので不適切。<br><br>lead [liːd] 〜を指揮する　　instead of 〜 〜の代わりに　　make time 時間を作る |
| **20** W🇺🇸 M🇨🇦<br><br>W: Where is the building maintenance being carried out?<br>M: (A) Jack's team is doing it.<br>　　(B) On the third floor.<br>　　(C) No, it will carry on.<br><br>W: ビルのメンテナンスはどこで実施されていますか。<br>M: (A) Jack のチームが行っています。<br>　　**(B) 3階です。**<br>　　(C) いいえ，それは続きます。 | **正解 (B)**<br><br>Where 〜？で「場所」について尋ねている。On the third floor.「3階です」と答えている (B) が正解。(C) は being carried out と carry on で混乱させようとしている。<br><br>maintenance [méintənəns] メンテナンス<br>carry out 〜 〜を行う<br>carry on 続く |
| **21** W🇺🇸 M🇦🇺<br><br>W: Why don't you ask for a raise?<br>M: (A) It would be of no use.<br>　　(B) Sorry, I can't give you one.<br>　　(C) It's 15 percent higher.<br><br>W: 昇給を頼んではどうですか。<br>M: **(A) 無駄ですよ。**<br>　　(B) すみません，お渡しできません。<br>　　(C) 15%高いです。 | **正解 (A)**<br><br>Why don't you ask for a raise?「昇給を頼んではどうですか」という「提案」の疑問文に対して，It would be of no use.「無駄ですよ」と答えている (A) が正解。(B) は答えている内容が質問文とかみ合わない。(C) は昇給率を聞いているわけではないので不適切。<br><br>raise [reiz] 昇給 |

## 放送文と訳

### 22  W 🇬🇧  M 🇨🇦

**W**: Isn't this package supposed to go to Mike?
**M**: (A) Four stamps, please.
　　 (B) He won't oppose you.
　　 (C) Not as far as I know.

W: この小包は Mike 宛ではないのですか。
M: (A) 切手を 4 枚お願いします。
　 (B) 彼はあなたに反対しませんよ。
　 **(C) 私が知る限りでは違います。**

### 23  W 🇺🇸  M 🇦🇺

**W**: Are you going to the fitness center, or straight home?
**M**: (A) I guess I'll work out.
　　 (B) Thanks, I've been exercising.
　　 (C) Running machines and weights.

W: フィットネスセンターに行くつもりですか，それとも家に真っすぐ帰りますか。
M: **(A) 運動しようかと思います。**
　 (B) ありがとう，ずっと運動しています。
　 (C) ランニングマシーンとウェイトです。

### 24  W 🇬🇧  W 🇺🇸

**W**: Would you like to apply for a store membership?
**W**: (A) I can't remember it.
　　 (B) Sure, why not?
　　 (C) Place it in storage.

W: お店の会員に申し込まれますか。
W: (A) 思い出せません。
　 **(B) はい，ぜひ。**
　 (C) 倉庫の中に置いてください。

### 25  M 🇨🇦  M 🇦🇺

**M**: Who's that talking to Mr. Wong?
**M**: (A) They've been talking for 20 minutes.
　　 (B) Our in-house lawyer.
　　 (C) No, I missed his talk.

M: Wong さんと話しているあの人は誰ですか。
M: (A) 彼らは 20 分間話し続けています。
　 **(B) 社内弁護士です。**
　 (C) いいえ，彼の話を聞き逃しました。

### 26  M 🇨🇦  W 🇬🇧

**M**: Isn't that your briefcase sitting in the corner there?
**W**: (A) Looks like it.
　　 (B) At Watson Office Supplies.
　　 (C) No, leave it at the office.

M: そこの隅に置いてあるのはあなたの書類かばんではないですか。
W: **(A) そのようです。**
　 (B) Watson 事務用品店で。
　 (C) いいえ，オフィスに置いておいてください。

## 正解と解説

### 22 正解 (C)

Isn't ～? 「～ではないのですか」と相手に確認する否定疑問文。Not as far as I know. 「私が知る限りでは違います」と答えている (C) が正解。(A) は package から連想される stamps で引っ掛けようとしている。(B) は supposed と oppose で音の混乱をねらっている。

**be supposed to** *do*　～することになっている
**oppose** [əpóuz] ～に反対する
**as far as I know** 私が知る限りでは

### 23 正解 (A)

TOEIC に頻出する「A or B ?」の二者択一問題。go to the fitness center を言い換えて，work out という表現で答えている (A) が正解。(B) は fitness center で連想される exercising で，同様に (C) も Running machines や weights で引っ掛けようとしている。

**work out**（ジムなどで）運動する
**weight** [weit] ウェイト

### 24 正解 (B)

Would you like to *do*? は「～しませんか」とていねいに勧誘する疑問文。Sure, why not? 「はい，ぜひ」と答えている (B) が正解。(A) は membership と remember, (C) は store と storage で混乱をねらっている。

**apply for ～**　～に申し込む
**membership** [mémbərʃip] 会員（権）
**storage** [stɔ́:ridʒ] 倉庫

### 25 正解 (B)

Who ～? で「人」について尋ねている。(A) は質問文に出てくる talking で引っ掛けようとしている。疑問詞の疑問文には Yes/No では答えられないので，(C) は不適切だとすぐにわかる。「人名」ではないが，「社内弁護士」と「誰か」を答えている (B) が正解。

**in-house lawyer** 社内弁護士
**miss** [mis] ～を逃す

### 26 正解 (A)

Isn't ～? 「～ではないのですか」と相手に確認する否定疑問文。Looks like it. 「そのようです」と答えている (A) が正解。「場所」を聞いてはいないので，(B) は不適切。(C) は内容が質問とかみ合わないので正解ではない。

**briefcase** [brí:fkèis] 書類かばん
**sit** [sit]（物が使われずに）置いてある
**office supplies** 事務用品

## 放送文と訳

### 27  M🇦🇺 W🇺🇸

**M**: Are you ready for the product launch?
**W**: (A) It's a new type of mobile phone.
　　(B) Thanks, but I've had lunch.
　　(C) We need another week.

M：新製品の売り出しの準備はできていますか。
W：(A) 新型の携帯電話です。
　　(B) ありがとう，でももう昼食を食べました。
　　(C) もう1週間かかります。

### 28  W🇬🇧 M🇨🇦

**W**: Do you want to speak first, or should I?
**M**: (A) After you.
　　(B) Miranda is the speaker.
　　(C) We both spoke well, I think.

W：先にお話しになりたいですか，それとも私が話しましょうか。
M：(A) お先にどうぞ。
　　(B) Miranda が演説者です。
　　(C) 私たちは2人ともうまく話せたと思いますよ。

### 29  W🇺🇸 W🇬🇧

**W**: What do I need to enter the convention?
**W**: (A) Indeed, it's quite conventional.
　　(B) Any piece of photo ID will do.
　　(C) This year in Shanghai, last year Singapore.

W：代表者会議に参加するには何が必要でしょうか。
W：(A) それは実にとてもありきたりです。
　　(B) 写真入り身分証明書であればどんなものでも結構です。
　　(C) 今年は上海で，昨年はシンガポールです。

### 30  M🇨🇦 M🇦🇺

**M**: I heard the 8:00 train will be delayed.
**M**: (A) No, here it comes now.
　　(B) Yes, it will arrive at 7:00.
　　(C) Yes, an eight-layer cake.

M：8時発の列車が遅れると聞きました。
M：(A) いいえ，ほら，今来ましたよ。
　　(B) はい，7時に着きます。
　　(C) はい，8層のケーキです。

### 31  W🇺🇸 M🇨🇦

**W**: Could you tell me how to get to Denby Street?
**M**: (A) You're on it.
　　(B) Yes, for 5 or 6 blocks.
　　(C) She took a different route.

W：Denby 通りへの行き方を教えていただけませんか。
M：(A) あなたはそこにいますよ。
　　(B) はい，5か6ブロックです。
　　(C) 彼女は違うルートを取りました。

## 正解と解説

### 正解 (C)
Are you ready for 〜?「〜の準備はできているか」に対して，We need another week.「もう1週間かかる」と答えている (C) が正解にふさわしい。(A) は product launch から連想される new type of mobile phone で引っ掛けようとしている。(B) は launch と lunch で音の混乱をねらっている。

be ready for 〜　〜の準備ができている
launch [lɔːntʃ]（新製品などの）売り出し

### 正解 (A)
A or B ?の二者択一で質問しているので，どちらかを明確に答えているものが正解にふさわしい。After you.「お先にどうぞ」と相手に先に話すように言っている (A) が正解。(B) は speaker で，(C) は spoke で引っ掛けようとしている。

both [bouθ] 両方とも

### 正解 (B)
「何が必要か」を尋ねているので，「写真入り身分証明書」と答えている (B) が正解。(A) は convention と conventional で混乱させようとしている。(C) は「場所」を答えているので不適切。

enter [éntər] 〜に参加する
convention [kənvénʃən] 代表者会議，大会
indeed [indíːd] 実に
conventional [kənvénʃnəl] ありきたりの
will do（主語が）目的を果たす，役に立つ

### 正解 (A)
「8時発の列車が遅れると聞いた」という平叙文に対して，No, here it comes now.「いいえ，ほら，今来ましたよ」と言っている (A) が正解。(B) は，未来形で答えているのに時刻が8時よりも早い7時なので内容がかみ合わない。(C) は eight で音の混乱をねらっている。

delay [diléi] 〜を遅らせる
eight-layer 8層の

### 正解 (A)
Could you tell me how to 〜? は「〜の仕方を教えてくださいませんか」とていねいに依頼する疑問文。You're on it.「あなたは今まさにその通りにいますよ」と答えている (A) が正解。(B) は「距離」を答えており，「行き方」を答えていないので不適切。(C) は street から連想される route で引っ掛けようとしている。

block [blɑk] ブロック（1街区）
route [ruːt] ルート，経路

# PART 3

## 放送文

Questions 32 through 34 refer to the following conversation.

**M**: What's wrong, Cindy? You look worried.
**W**: I need to e-mail these files to the design engineer at Durant Piper Corporation by 5:00 P.M. and my computer isn't working!
**M**: Don't worry. It's only 3:00 now. You still have two hours left. I'm sure IT will be able to fix it soon. Just to be sure, though, why don't you send the files from my computer?
**W**: Oh yes, I hadn't thought of that. Thanks, Randy!

## 放送文の訳

問題 32-34 は次の会話に関するものです。

M：どうしたの，Cindy？ 心配そうだけど。
W：Durant Piper 社のデザイン・エンジニアに，このファイルを午後 5 時までにメールしないといけないんだけど，私のコンピューターが動かないの！
M：心配しないで。今，まだ 3 時だよ。まだ 2 時間もある。IT 部がきっとすぐに直せると思うよ。でも，念のために，君のファイルを僕のコンピューターから送ったらどうだい？
W：あら，そうね。考えつかなかったわ。ありがとう，Randy！

## Vocabulary

- □ be able to *do* ～できる
- □ fix [fiks] 動 ～を修理する
- □ just to be sure 念のために
- □ think of ～ ～を考えつく

---

### 32

**設問**
What is the woman's problem?

(A) Her document is missing.
(B) Her computer is not functioning.
(C) An e-mail address is incorrect.
(D) A file is not complete.

**設問の訳**
女性の問題は何ですか。

(A) 書類が見当たらない。
(B) コンピューターが作動していない。
(C) E メールアドレスが正しくない。
(D) ファイルが完成していない。

**正解と解説**
**正解 (B)**

女性の最初の発言に I need to e-mail these files ～ and my computer isn't working! とあり，コンピューターが動かないことが問題であるとわかる。よって，この working を functioning で言い換えた (B) が正解。

incorrect [inkərékt] 間違った

---

### 33

**設問**
When should the files be sent?

(A) By 2:00 P.M.
(B) By 3:00 P.M.
(C) By 4:00 P.M.
(D) By 5:00 P.M.

**設問の訳**
ファイルはいつ送られるべきですか。

(A) 午後 2 時までに
(B) 午後 3 時までに
(C) 午後 4 時までに
(D) 午後 5 時までに

**正解と解説**
**正解 (D)**

女性が I need to e-mail these files to the design engineer at Durant Piper Corporation by 5:00 P.M. と言っていることから，正解は (D)。

---

### 34

**設問**
What does the man suggest the woman do?

(A) Call the design engineer
(B) Revise the file
(C) Log onto a different computer
(D) Use a delivery service

**設問の訳**
男性は女性に何をするように提案していますか。

(A) デザイン・エンジニアに電話する
(B) ファイルを修正する
(C) 違うコンピューターにログオンする
(D) 配達サービスを使う

**正解と解説**
**正解 (C)**

男性は，IT 部がすぐに直せるだろうと言いながらも，念のため，why don't you send the files from my computer? と，彼のコンピューターにログオンして送るように提案しているので，正解は (C)。

revise [riváiz] ～を修正する

| 放送文 | 放送文の訳 |
|---|---|
| Questions 35 through 37 refer to the following conversation.<br><br>W: Hello, I bought this purse here two days ago but the zipper broke yesterday. Can I exchange it for another one, please?<br>M: I'm sorry, ma'am, but I think this was the last one we had in the store. That style was very popular and sold out almost immediately.<br>W: Oh no! I love the shape and color. I've received so many compliments on it already.<br>M: Well, in that case, they may have them in our other outlet on Rushmore Street. I can give them a call to check if you like. | 問題 35-37 は次の会話に関するものです。<br><br>W：こんにちは，このハンドバッグをこちらで２日前に買ったのですが，昨日ジッパーが壊れたのです。別のものと交換していただけませんか。<br>M：お客様，申し訳ございませんが，これが当店にあった最後の１つだと思われます。その種類はとても人気があり，ほぼすぐに売り切れたのです。<br>W：えっ，そんな！　この形と色が大好きなんです。もうたくさんのほめ言葉をもらったのに。<br>M：それでしたら，Rushmore 通りの当社のもう１つの直営店に在庫があるかもしれません。もしよろしければ，確認の電話を入れられますが。 |

## Vocabulary

- purse [pəːrs] 名 ハンドバッグ
- exchange A for B　A を B と交換する
- ma'am [mæm] 名 お客様 <店員が女性に用いる呼びかけ>
- sell out 売り切れる
- immediately [imíːdiitli] 副 すぐに
- shape [ʃeip] 名 形
- compliment [kámpləmənt] 名 ほめ言葉
- outlet [áutlèt] 名 系列販売店，直営店

| 設問 | 設問の訳 | 正解と解説 |
|---|---|---|
| **35**<br>What does the woman ask the man to do?<br>(A) Send her a refund<br>(B) Give her a new purse<br>(C) Repair her purse<br>(D) Offer her a discount | 女性は男性に何をするように頼んでいますか。<br>(A) 返金を送る<br>(B) 新しいハンドバッグを渡す<br>(C) ハンドバッグを修理する<br>(D) 割引を提供する | **正解 (B)**<br>女性は最初の発言で，購入したハンドバッグのジッパーが壊れたことを男性店員に伝え，Can I exchange it for another one, please? と言って「別のハンドバッグと交換すること」を依頼している。よって，正解は (B)。<br><br>refund [ríːfʌnd] 返金 |
| **36**<br>What does the woman like about her purse?<br>(A) Its design<br>(B) Its size<br>(C) Its price<br>(D) Its texture | 女性はハンドバッグのどんな点が気に入っていますか。<br>(A) デザイン<br>(B) 大きさ<br>(C) 価格<br>(D) 生地 | **正解 (A)**<br>女性は I love the shape and color. と言っている。「形と色」つまり，「デザイン」が気に入っているので，正解は (A) Its design。texture は「素材の質感」である。 |
| **37**<br>What will the man probably do next?<br>(A) Make a telephone call<br>(B) Choose a different purse<br>(C) Visit another branch<br>(D) Pay by check | 男性はおそらく次に何をしますか。<br>(A) 電話をする<br>(B) 違うハンドバッグを選ぶ<br>(C) 別の支店を訪ねる<br>(D) 小切手で支払う | **正解 (A)**<br>男性は最後に，I can give them a call to check if you like. と言っている。女性が同じ物を欲しがっているので，今から電話して他の店の在庫の確認をすると考えられる。よって，正解は (A)。 |

## 放送文

Questions 38 through 40 refer to the following conversation.

**M**: Good morning, Goldstar Bank. How may I help you?
**W**: My daughter told me you're offering new customers 0% interest on Goldstar Credit Cards. Is that correct?
**M**: Yes, it is. But I should say that this offer only lasts for a period of 3 months. After that time, the interest rises to 18 percent.
**W**: Oh, I see. Well, yes, even so, I would be interested in getting one. If I give you my e-mail address, could you send me a form so I could sign up?

## 放送文の訳

問題 38-40 は次の会話に関するものです。

**M**: おはようございます，Goldstar 銀行です。ご用件をお伺いします。
**W**: Goldstar クレジットカードの新会員に 0% の金利を提供していると私の娘が言っていました。それは間違いないですか。
**M**: はい，そうです。しかし，このご提供は 3 か月間だけです。それ以降は，金利は 18% まで上がります。
**W**: ああ，そうですか。えっと，はい，たとえそうでも，カードを手に入れることに興味があります。私の E メールアドレスをお渡しすれば，申し込みができるように用紙を送ってくださいますか。

### Vocabulary

- interest [íntərist] 名金利，利子
- correct [kərékt] 形間違いのない，正しい
- last [læst] 動続く
- rise [raiz] 動上がる
- form [fɔːrm] 名記入用紙
- sign up 申し込む

---

### 38
Why is the woman calling?

(A) To ask for her account balance
(B) To make a payment
(C) To renew a contract
(D) To apply for a card

**設問の訳**: なぜ女性は電話しているのですか。
(A) 残高を聞くため
(B) 支払いをするため
(C) 契約を更新するため
(D) カードを申し込むため

**正解 (D)**
女性は 0% の金利について問い合わせた後で，could you send me a form so I could sign up? とクレジットカードの申込用紙を送るように依頼しているので，正解は (D)。

- account balance (預金の)残高
- renew [rinjúː] 〜を更新する
- apply for 〜 〜を申し込む

---

### 39
What condition does the man mention?

(A) The minimum balance for an account
(B) Credit scores to open an account
(C) Qualifications to be new members
(D) The time limit of the interest rate

**設問の訳**: 男性はどんな条件について述べていますか。
(A) 最低限の口座残高
(B) 口座開設のためのクレジットスコア
(C) 新会員になるための資格
(D) 利率適用期間の制限

**正解 (D)**
男性は this offer only lasts for a period of 3 months と述べており，金利 0% の適用が 3 か月という条件付きであることがわかるので，正解は (D)。

- balance [bǽləns] 差引残高
- credit score 信用度の得点，クレジットスコア
- qualification [kwɑ̀ləfəkéiʃən] 資格
- interest rate 利率

---

### 40
What does the woman ask the man to do?

(A) Review a charge
(B) Send her a document
(C) Increase her credit limit
(D) Confirm receipt of her e-mail

**設問の訳**: 女性は男性に何をするように頼んでいますか。
(A) 手数料を見直す
(B) 書類を彼女に送る
(C) 信用限度額を増やす
(D) 彼女の E メールの受領を確認する

**正解 (B)**
女性は最後の発言で could you send me a form 〜? と申込用紙を送るように頼んでいるので，正解は (B)。

- increase [inkríːs] 〜を増やす
- credit limit 信用限度額
- confirm [kənfə́ːrm] 〜を確認する

## 放送文

Questions 41 through 43 refer to the following conversation.

**M**: Hello, this is Rowan Mortimer. Could I speak to Angela Shen, please?
**W**: I'm sorry, Ms. Shen hasn't come into work yet. I'm her assistant, Jenny Franks.
**M**: Do you know when she will be in?
**W**: I'm afraid I have no idea. Would you like me to take a message for you?
**M**: Yes, please. I was wondering if I could see her today about some copiers she is interested in. I was planning on showing her some brochures about our equipment.
**W**: Oh yes, she told me she wouldn't have any time today because she has department meetings scheduled all day. She said she would probably have time tomorrow. I'll let her know you called.
**M**: That'd be great. I appreciate it. Good-bye.

## 放送文の訳

問題 41-43 は次の会話に関するものです。

M：もしもし，こちらは Rowan Mortimer です。Angela Shen さんとお話しできますか。
W：申し訳ありませんが，Shen はまだ出社しておりません。私は彼女のアシスタントの Jenny Franks です。
M：いつ出社されるかご存じですか。
W：あいにくわかりません。伝言を承りましょうか。
M：お願いします。彼女がご興味を持たれているコピー機について今日お会いできればと思ったのですが。わが社の機器についてのパンフレットをお見せするつもりでした。
W：ああ，そうでした。彼女は 1 日中部門会議が予定されているから今日は時間が持てないと私に言っていました。明日ならたぶん時間が取れるだろうと言っていました。お電話いただいたことを伝えておきます。
M：それは助かります。ありがとうございます。では。

## Vocabulary

- copier [kɑ́piər] 名 コピー機
- brochure [brouʃúər] 名 パンフレット
- equipment [ikwípmənt] 名 機器

---

### 41

Who most likely is the man?

(A) A customer
(B) A technician
(C) A salesperson
(D) A receptionist

**設問の訳**

男性は誰だと考えられますか。

(A) 顧客
(B) 技術者
(C) 外交販売員
(D) 受付係

**正解 (C)**

男性の I was wondering if I could see her today about some copiers she is interested in. I was planning on showing her some brochures about our equipment. という発言から，Shen さんにコピー機を売り込もうとしていることがわかるので，正解は (C) A salesperson。

---

### 42

What does the man want to talk to Ms. Shen about?

(A) Late documents
(B) Office equipment
(C) Computer repairs
(D) Brochure design

**設問の訳**

男性は Shen さんに何について話したいと思っていますか。

(A) 遅れた書類
(B) オフィス機器
(C) コンピューターの修理
(D) パンフレットのデザイン

**正解 (B)**

男性の 3 つ目の発言から，Shen さんは男性の会社のコピー機に興味があり，男性は自社製品のパンフレットを見せるつもりだったことがわかる。よって，男性が話したかった内容としては，some copiers や our equipment を Office equipment と表した (B) が正解。

---

### 43

What is Ms. Shen's plan for today?

(A) Meeting customers
(B) Dealing with shareholders
(C) Reorganizing schedules
(D) Talking with staff

**設問の訳**

Shen さんの今日の予定は何ですか。

(A) 顧客に会うこと
(B) 株主に対応すること
(C) スケジュールを組み直すこと
(D) スタッフと話すこと

**正解 (D)**

女性の発言に because she has department meetings scheduled all day とあり，Shen さんは今日，1 日中部門会議で忙しいことがわかる。部門会議は社内の会議と考えられるので，(D) Talking with staff が正解。

deal with ~ 　~に対応する
reorganize [riːɔ́ːrɡənàiz] ~を再編する，立て直す

## 放送文

Questions 44 through 46 refer to the following conversation.

M: Hello, it's John. Have you heard from Kareem Adjani at Monroe Development Corporation yet? I need to know when the heavy equipment for the Schreiber Apartment Complex will arrive.
W: I just received an e-mail from Mr. Adjani's secretary.
M: Oh. What did she say in it?
W: She said he's supervising progress at the construction area this afternoon.
M: Is there any way to reach him before I go into my next meeting?
W: Yes, his phone is probably in silent mode, but you can always text him. I'll get his address for you.
M: It'd be a great help if you could do that.

## 放送文の訳

問題 44-46 は次の会話に関するものです。

M：もしもし，John です。Monroe 開発社の Kareem Adjani から連絡はもうもらったかい？ Schreiber 共同住宅のための重機がいつ届くのか知る必要があるんだ。
W：Adjani さんの秘書からメールを受け取ったばかりよ。
M：そう。彼女はメールで何て書いていた？
W：彼は今日の午後，建設区域で進行状況を監督していると書いてあったわ。
M：僕が次の会議に行くまでに，彼に連絡を取る方法はある？
W：ええ，彼はおそらく携帯電話をマナーモードにしているけど，メールならいつでも送れるわ。アドレスを調べてあげるわね。
M：そうしてもらえるととても助かるよ。

### Vocabulary
- secretary [sékrətèri] 名 秘書
- supervise [súːpərvàiz] 動 ～を監督する
- progress [prágres] 名 進行，経過
- construction [kənstrʌ́kʃən] 名 建設
- reach [riːtʃ] 動 ～に連絡を取る
- text [tekst] 動 （携帯電話で）～にメールを送る

---

### 44
What is the purpose of the man's call?

(A) To submit a progress report
(B) To confirm a delivery time
(C) To revise technical information
(D) To prepare a presentation

**設問の訳**: 男性の電話の目的は何ですか。

(A) 経過報告書を提出すること
(B) 配達時間を確認すること
(C) 技術的な情報を修正すること
(D) プレゼンテーションを準備すること

**正解 (B)**

男性は最初の発言で I need to know when the heavy equipment for the Schreiber Apartment Complex will arrive. と，重機がいつ到着するのかを知りたいと思って女性に確認しているので，正解は (B)。

delivery time 配達時間

---

### 45
Where is Mr. Adjani now?

(A) At a building site
(B) At his desk
(C) In his apartment
(D) In a meeting

**設問の訳**: Adjani さんは今どこにいますか。

(A) 建設用地
(B) 自分の机
(C) 自分のアパート
(D) 会議

**正解 (A)**

女性の発言に She said he's supervising progress at the construction area this afternoon. とあり，Adjani さんは建設区域にいることがわかる。construction area を building site と言い換えた (A) が正解。

building site 建設用地

---

### 46
What will the woman do next?

(A) Start a meeting
(B) Phone Mr. Adjani
(C) Get contact information
(D) Read a text message

**設問の訳**: 女性は次に何をしますか。

(A) 会議を始める
(B) Adjani さんに電話をする
(C) 連絡先の情報を得る
(D) テキストメッセージを読む

**正解 (C)**

女性は最後の発言で I'll get his address for you. と言っており，男性に教えるために Adjani さんの携帯電話のメールアドレスという「情報」をこれから得ることがわかるので，正解は (C)。Adjani さんの携帯電話にメールで連絡を取るのであって電話をかけるのではないので，(B) は誤り。なお，会話中の his phone is ～のように，TOEIC では携帯電話を単に phone と表すことが多いので，覚えておこう。

CD1 40 W🇺🇸 M🇨🇦

## 放送文

Questions 47 through 49 refer to the following conversation.

W: I was wondering if you have any TZ inkjet cartridges in stock. I can't find any in the office supplies section of your Web site.
M: I'm afraid we don't sell those anymore.
W: Is that right? Does that mean I can't use my printer anymore?
M: Oh, not at all. We still sell the newer VX cartridges. They're just as good. Scroll over to the "printer and cartridges" part of the office supplies tab, and you'll see them.
W: Okay I'm scrolling ... I do see them. Umm ... I really wanted the TZ because I've used them for so long. But I guess I'll have to go with the VX.
M: Good. You won't be disappointed with the VX ones.

## 放送文の訳

問題 47-49 は次の会話に関するものです。

W：TZ インクジェット・カートリッジの在庫があるかと思いまして。御社のウェブサイトの事務用品セクションのどこにも見つからないのです。
M：申し訳ありませんが，それらはもう販売しておりません。
W：そうなんですか。私のプリンターはもう使えないということでしょうか。
M：いえ，そんなことはございません。新型の VX カートリッジならまだ販売しております。同じくらい良いですよ。事務用品タブの「プリンターとカートリッジ」部門までスクロールしていただければ見つかります。
W：はい，スクロールしています…確かにありました。うーん…とても長い間使っていたので本当に TZ が欲しかったんです。でも，VX にするしかなさそうですね。
M：良かったです。VX カートリッジをお使いになって損はないですよ。

## Vocabulary

- in stock 在庫があって
- not ~ anymore もはや~ない
- scroll [skroul] 動 スクロールする
- go with ~ ~を選ぶ，~に決める

## 設問 / 設問の訳 / 正解と解説

### 47
Where most likely is the man?

男性はどこにいると考えられますか。

(A) In a printer factory
(B) In a product warehouse
(C) In an engineering office
(D) In a customer service center

(A) プリンター工場
(B) 製品の倉庫
(C) 工学事務所
(D) カスタマーサービスセンター

**正解 (D)**

男女は電話で話しており，男性は自社のウェブサイトを見ながら客である女性の問い合わせに答えている場面が想像できる。よって，男性がいる場所として最も可能性が高いのは (D) In a customer service center である。

warehouse [wéərhàus] 倉庫

### 48
What does the woman prefer about TZ inkjet cartridges?

女性は TZ インクジェット・カートリッジの何が好きなのですか。

(A) Availability
(B) Functionality
(C) Quality
(D) Familiarity

(A) 役に立つこと
(B) 機能性
(C) 品質
(D) よく知っていること

**正解 (D)**

女性の最後の発言に I really wanted the TZ because I've used them for so long とある。長く愛用してきた商品のことを Familiarity「よく知っていること」と表した (D) が正解。

### 49
What does the woman decide to do?

女性は何をすることにしますか。

(A) Track a delivery online
(B) Look at a different Web site
(C) Accept the man's suggestion
(D) Sell the office supplies

(A) 配達物をオンラインで追跡する
(B) 違うウェブサイトを見る
(C) 男性の提案を受け入れる
(D) 事務用品を販売する

**正解 (C)**

女性は TZ にこだわっていたが，最後には I guess I'll have to go with the VX と男性の提案を受け入れようとしているので，正解は (C)。

track [træk] ~をたどる

16

## 放送文

Questions 50 through 52 refer to the following conversation.

W: Hi, I'll be checking out tomorrow, since my trip is just about over. I noticed there's always a line at the front desk here in the mornings. Is there any way to avoid that?
M: Yes, ma'am. You can use your room computer to check out. Just go to our Web site, enter your room number and your credit card information. You will find a list of all your charges there, including any from our room service. It only takes a few minutes.
W: Thanks, you've been very helpful.

## 放送文の訳

問題 50-52 は次の会話に関するものです。

W: こんにちは，私の旅はだいたい終わりなので，明日チェックアウトします。こちらのフロントには，朝いつも人の列ができていることに気づきました。それを避ける方法は何かありませんか。
M: はい，お客様。チェックアウトにお部屋のコンピューターをお使いいただけます。当ホテルのウェブサイトにアクセスし，お客様のお部屋番号とクレジットカード情報を入力していただくだけです。ルームサービスも含めて，全請求金額の一覧がそこにございます。たった数分かかるだけです。
W: ありがとう，とても助かりました。

## Vocabulary

- check out チェックアウトする
- just about ほとんど
- avoid [əvóid] 動 ～を避ける
- charge [tʃɑːrdʒ] 名 請求金額
- including [inklúːdiŋ] 動 ～を含めて

---

### 50

Where most likely are the speakers?

(A) At an airport
(B) At a hotel
(C) At a travel agency
(D) At a restaurant

**設問の訳**: 話し手たちはおそらくどこにいますか。

(A) 空港
(B) ホテル
(C) 旅行代理店
(D) レストラン

**正解 (B)**

全体を通して散りばめられたキーワードから場所を判断しよう。女性が最初の発言で I'll be checking out tomorrow と言っていることや front desk, room service などから正解は (B) At a hotel と考えられる。

travel agency 旅行代理店

---

### 51

What problem does the woman mention?

(A) Attitude of staff
(B) High prices
(C) Long waiting lines
(D) Lack of room service

**設問の訳**: 女性はどんな問題について述べていますか。

(A) 従業員の態度
(B) 高い料金
(C) 長い待ち行列
(D) ルームサービスがないこと

**正解 (C)**

女性は，朝いつもフロントにチェックアウトの行列ができていることに気づき，それを避ける方法を男性従業員に尋ねている。line は「行列」という意味で，正解は (C)。

attitude [ǽtətjùːd] 態度
lack [læk] 欠如

---

### 52

What does the man recommend the woman do?

(A) Settle her bill online
(B) Line up early
(C) Change rooms
(D) Wait a few minutes

**設問の訳**: 男性は女性に何をすることを勧めていますか。

(A) インターネット上で宿泊料を精算する
(B) 早く一列に並ぶ
(C) 部屋を替える
(D) 数分待つ

**正解 (A)**

男性は You can use your room computer to check out. と言って，客室のコンピューターでチェックアウトすることを勧めている。ホテルのウェブサイトに情報を入力することで全請求額（all your charges）がわかることなどからも，(A) Settle her bill online が正解。

settle (hotel) bill 宿泊料を精算する
line up 一列に並ぶ

## 放送文

Questions 53 through 55 refer to the following conversation.

M: Are you going to Margaret Kang's going-away party? It's next Friday at the Charles Lake Hotel.
W: What? You've got to be kidding! I had no idea she was quitting the company.
M: She's not, but she's transferring to the Melbourne branch. We got a memo on it last week.
W: I must have missed it. I'll certainly be there, however. It's the least I can do, considering all the help she's given us on past projects.

## 放送文の訳

問題 53-55 は次の会話に関するものです。

M：Margaret Kang の送別会に行くの？ 来週の金曜に Charles Lake ホテルであるよ。
W：なんですって？ 冗談でしょう！ 彼女が会社を辞めるなんて全く知らなかったわ。
M：そうではなくて，彼女はメルボルン支店に転勤するんだ。先週，それに関する社内連絡を受け取ったよ。
W：私は見落としたに違いないわ。だけど，必ず行くわ。彼女が今までのプロジェクトで私たちを助けてくれたことを考えたら，私にできるのはせいぜいそれくらいだからね。

## Vocabulary

- going-away party 送別会
- quit [kwit] 動 ～を辞める
- transfer [trænsfɚːr] 動 転勤する
- branch [bræntʃ] 名 支店
- memo [mémou] 名 連絡メモ，回覧
- considering [kənsídəriŋ] 前 ～を考慮すると

---

### 53

**設問**
What are the speakers discussing?

(A) A recruiting program
(B) An upcoming event
(C) Employee benefits
(D) Office schedules

**設問の訳**
話し手たちは何を話しているのですか。

(A) 新入社員採用プログラム
(B) 近く行われるイベント
(C) 従業員手当
(D) オフィスのスケジュール

**正解 (B)**

男性は最初の発言で，Are you going to Margaret Kang's going-away party? と，これから行われる予定の送別会の話題に触れている。よって，正解は (B)。

upcoming [ʌ́pkʌ̀miŋ] もうすぐやって来る，今度の
benefit [bénəfit] 手当

---

### 54

**設問**
What does the woman mean when she says, "You've got to be kidding"?
(A) She is surprised by what the man said.
(B) She disagrees with the man's opinion.
(C) She sympathizes with Margaret's situation.
(D) She appreciates the man's humor.

**設問の訳**
女性が "You've got to be kidding" と言う際，何を意図していますか。

(A) 彼女は男性が言ったことに驚いている。
(B) 彼女は男性の意見に反対である。
(C) 彼女は Margaret の状況に同情している。
(D) 彼女は男性のユーモアの良さを味わっている。

**正解 (A)**

直前の What? という反応や，直後の I had no idea she was quitting the company. から，女性は Kang さんが会社を辞めると思って驚いたことがわかるので，正解は (A)。kid は動詞で「冗談を言う」という意味で，You've got to be kidding! や You must be [You're] kidding! で「冗談でしょう，まさか」という口語表現。

---

### 55

**設問**
What is mentioned about Ms. Kang?

(A) She commonly assisted colleagues.
(B) She frequently went to Chicago.
(C) She usually provided funding for projects.
(D) She often helped at parties.

**設問の訳**
Kang さんについてどんなことが述べられていますか。

(A) 彼女はよく同僚を助けた。
(B) 彼女は頻繁にシカゴに行った。
(C) 彼女はたいていプロジェクトに資金を提供した。
(D) 彼女はよくパーティーで手伝った。

**正解 (A)**

女性の最後の発言に considering all the help she's given us on past projects とあり，Kang さんが同僚に助力を惜しまなかったことがわかるので，正解はその言い換えである (A) She commonly assisted colleagues. である。

commonly [kámənli] 一般に，よく
colleague [káliːg] 同僚
frequently [fríːkwəntli] 頻繁に
funding [fʌ́ndiŋ] 財政的支援

## 放送文

Questions 56 through 58 refer to the following conversation.

W: Hi Phil, I'm on my way out. Let Mr. Howell know I'll be in Pretoria today, then Kimberley until Monday, Johannesburg on Tuesday and back here in Cape Town by noon the following day.
M: Okay, Ms. Lind, but he'll still be able to get hold of you on your phone, right?
W: Yes, by all means. But as I'll be touring quite a few factories, it would be better if he called after 6:00 P.M. instead of in the afternoon.
M: Okay, I'll let him know.

## 放送文の訳

問題 56-58 は次の会話に関するものです。

W: もしもし、Phil、私は出かける途中なの。Howell さんに、私が今日はプレトリアに、月曜までキンバリーに、火曜にはヨハネスブルグにいて、その翌日の正午までにここケープタウンに帰ることを伝えてちょうだい。
M: わかりました、Lind さん、でも、彼はまだあなたの携帯電話に連絡を取ることができるんですよね？
W: ええ、もちろんよ。ただ、とてもたくさんの工場を見て回るから、午後ではなく午後6時以降に電話をしてくれた方がいいわ。
M: わかりました。彼に伝えておきます。

### Vocabulary
- on one's way out 出かける途中で
- the following day 翌日
- get hold of ～ (連絡相手)をつかまえる
- quite a few かなり多くの
- factory [fǽktəri] 名 工場

---

### 56
**What does the woman ask the man to do?**
(A) Inform Mr. Howell of her schedule
(B) Give Mr. Howell her phone number
(C) Confirm her schedule
(D) Get hold of some documents

女性は男性に何をするように頼んでいますか。
(A) Howell さんに自分のスケジュールを伝える
(B) Howell さんに自分の電話番号を伝える
(C) 自分のスケジュールを確認する
(D) 書類を入手する

**正解 (A)**

女性は最初の発言で、Let Mr. Howell know I'll be in Pretoria ～. と Howell さんに自分の今後の予定を伝えるように男性に頼んでいる。よって、正解は (A)。

---

### 57
**What does the woman mean when she says, "by all means"?**
(A) She needs to buy a new file for the trip.
(B) She cannot be contacted if there is an emergency.
(C) She will be able to receive telephone calls.
(D) She has to think carefully before making a decision.

女性が "by all means" と言う際、何を意図していますか。
(A) 彼女は出張用に新しいファイルを買う必要がある。
(B) 彼女は緊急時には連絡が取れない。
(C) 彼女は電話を取ることができる。
(D) 彼女は決断をする前に注意深く考えなければならない。

**正解 (C)**

by all means は相手の発言に承諾・同意して「もちろん」(certainly) という意味と、「どうしても、ぜひとも」(at any cost) という意味があり、ここでは前者である。直前の内容を受けているので、(C) が正解。Howell さんは女性の携帯電話に連絡を取ることができるかどうかという男性の質問に Yes と答えていることからも推測できるだろう。get hold of you on your phone を (C) では receive telephone calls と表している。

---

### 58
**When does the woman prefer to be contacted?**
(A) At noon
(B) In the afternoon
(C) At any time
(D) In the evening

女性はいつ連絡してもらいたいのですか。
(A) 正午に
(B) 午後に
(C) いつでも
(D) 夕方に

**正解 (D)**

女性の最後の発言に it would be better if he called after 6:00 P.M. instead of in the afternoon とあり、午後6時以降を望んでいることがわかるので、その言い換えである (D) In the evening が正解。

CD1 44　W-1 🇺🇸　M 🇦🇺　W-2 🇬🇧

## 放送文

Questions 59 through 61 refer to the following conversation with three speakers.

W-1 : Hi, Marcel and Vicki. Are you guys ready for your new responsibilities as manager and vice-manager of the Santiago branch? It's bound to be different from working here.

M : I don't know if I'm ready, to be honest. I'm getting more and more nervous.

W-2 : I feel the same way. I've never worked in South America before, and I've only just begun to learn Spanish.

W-1 : Don't worry too much about that. All the office staff there are pretty fluent in English.

W-2 : Maybe you're right. Still, I want to learn Spanish as quickly as possible.

M : That's why we've enrolled in an online university course, right? I don't know about you, Vicki, but I try to log on at work every lunch hour.

## 放送文の訳

問題 59-61 は 3 人の話し手による次の会話に関するものです。

W-1：こんにちは，Marcel, Vicki。2 人はサンティアゴ支店の部長と副部長として新たな責任を担う心構えはできている？ ここで働くのとはきっと違うわよ。

M：正直に言うと，心構えができているかどうかはわからないな。どんどん緊張が増しているよ。

W-2：私もよ。これまで南アメリカで働いたことはないし，スペイン語を習い始めたばかりなの。

W-1：それについては心配し過ぎないで。あそこのオフィスのスタッフは全員英語がとても堪能なのよ。

W-2：あなたの言う通りかもね。それでも，できるだけ早くスペイン語を習得したいわ。

M：だから僕たちは大学のオンライン講座に登録したんだよね？ Vicki, 君はどうかわからないけど，僕は昼休みはいつも仕事場でログオンするようにしているよ。

### Vocabulary

- responsibility [rispɑ̀nsəbíləti] 名責任
- be bound to do きっと~するはずだ
- to be honest 正直に言うと
- pretty [príti] 副かなり
- fluent in ~ ~に堪能な
- enroll in ~ ~に入学する，登録する
- lunch hour 昼休み，昼食時間

---

## 設問 59

What are the speakers talking about?

(A) Upcoming promotions
(B) Hiring strategies
(C) Overseas expansion
(D) Regional markets

### 設問の訳

話し手たちは何について話していますか。

(A) これから起こる昇進
(B) 雇用戦略
(C) 海外への展開
(D) 地域の市場

### 正解 (A)

女性 2 人と男性 1 人の 3 人の会話。1 人目の女性 (W-1) は冒頭で，あとの 2 人に Are you guys ready for your new responsibilities as manager and vice-manager ~? と言っている。部長・副部長という役職のことを new responsibilities「新しい責務」と言っていることからも，会話の話題は 2 人の昇進だと推測できる。よって，正解は (A)。

promotion [prəmóuʃən] 昇進
strategy [strǽtədʒi] 戦略
expansion [ikspǽnʃən] 拡大，展開

---

## 設問 60

What is a stated goal of Marcel and Vicki?

(A) Getting local experience
(B) Recruiting more staff
(C) Enrolling in a university
(D) Learning a language

### 設問の訳

Marcel と Vicki の目標は何だと述べられていますか。

(A) 地方での経験を得ること
(B) もっとスタッフを採用すること
(C) 大学に入学すること
(D) ある言語を習得すること

### 正解 (D)

Vicki (W-2) は，2 つ目の発言で I want to learn Spanish as quickly as possible と言っており，スペイン語の習得を目標としていることがわかる。また，Marcel (M) も最後の発言から，大学のオンライン講座に登録して昼休みにログオンし，積極的にスペイン語を学んでいることがわかる。よって，2 人の目標として正しいのは (D)。a language はスペイン語のこと。

recruit [rikrúːt] ~を採用する，募集する

---

## 設問 61

How is the man using his lunch hours nowadays?

(A) To prepare for a trip
(B) To improve his skills
(C) To contact universities
(D) To do research on South America

### 設問の訳

男性は最近，昼休みをどのように使っていますか。

(A) 旅行の準備をするために
(B) 技能を向上させるために
(C) 大学に連絡を取るために
(D) 南アメリカの研究をするために

### 正解 (B)

男性は最後の発言で That's why we've enrolled in an online university course, right? I don't know about you, Vicki, but I try to log on at work every lunch hour. と述べている。昼休みに大学のオンライン講座でスペイン語を学び，技能を向上させようとしていることがわかるので，正解は (B)。

do research on ~ ~を研究する，調査する

## 放送文

Questions 62 through 64 refer to the following conversation and coupon.

M: I'd like to buy these three bags of coffee. These were all highly rated in a consumer magazine, so I'd like to try them out. Here ... I've brought this coupon with me.
W: Let me take a look … uh … sorry … but you can only use that for one of the bags.
M: Oh, I see … Since that's the case ... um ... I'll just buy one bag instead of three. Let me use it for this one, Bright Hills Coffee.
W: OK, that bag is 20 dollars, minus the coupon value. Also, if you have time, please go to our Web site to fill out a customer survey. That will make you eligible for future discounts.

**Coupon**
*Axton Foods Co.*
Wake up Feeling Fresh!
Take **$5 off** coffee, any brand in store
Valid through October 31.

## 放送文の訳

問題 62-64 は次の会話とクーポンに関するものです。

M：この 3 袋のコーヒーをください。これらはすべて消費者雑誌で高く評価されていたので，試してみたいのです。はい …このクーポンを持ってきました。
W：見せてください。あー，すみません。そのうちの 1 袋にしかこれは使えません。
M：そうですか…そういうことならば，そうですね…3 袋でなく 1 袋買うことにします。これにクーポンを使います，Bright Hills コーヒー。
W：わかりました，そちらの袋は 20 ドルになりますが，クーポン分をお値引きいたします。もしお時間がございましたら，当店のウェブサイトでお客様アンケートにお答えください。それによって今後割引を受けられるようになります。

クーポン：
Axton 食品社

爽快な気分で目覚めましょう！
店内のすべてのブランドのコーヒー 5 ドル引き。

10 月 31 日まで有効

## Vocabulary

- rate [reit] 動 ～を評価する
- fill out ～ ～に記入する
- survey [sə́rvei] 名 調査
- eligible for ～ ～を受ける資格がある

---

### 62

**設問**
Why is the man looking for a certain product?
(A) He wants to try healthy foods.
(B) He read about it in a publication.
(C) He has tried it out before a few times.
(D) He needs to rate it for his blog.

**設問の訳**
男性はなぜ特定の商品を探しているのですか。
(A) 彼は健康的な食品を試したい。
(B) 彼は出版物でそれについて読んだ。
(C) 彼は以前に数回それを試している。
(D) 彼は自分のブログのためにそれを評価する必要がある。

**正解 (B)**
男性客は冒頭で 3 袋のコーヒーが欲しいことを伝えているが，その理由は続く These were all highly rated in a consumer magazine にある。この部分を「出版物で読んだ」と表した (B) が正解。質問文の a certain product はコーヒー，(B) の a publication は雑誌のこと。
publication [pʌ̀blikéiʃən] 出版物

### 63

**設問**
Look at the graphic. How much will the man pay?
(A) 5 dollars
(B) 10 dollars
(C) 15 dollars
(D) 20 dollars

**設問の訳**
図を見てください。男性はいくら支払いますか。
(A) 5 ドル
(B) 10 ドル
(C) 15 ドル
(D) 20 ドル

**正解 (C)**
男性が Bright Hills コーヒーにクーポンを使うことを伝えると，女性店員は that bag is 20 dollars, minus the coupon value と言っている。そこでクーポンを見ると，Take $5 off coffee, any brand in store とあるので，Bright Hills コーヒーに 20 ドル - 5 ドル = 15 ドル支払うことがわかる。

### 64

**設問**
What does the woman encourage the man to do?
(A) Purchase an additional bag
(B) Go to a Web site
(C) Fill out a membership card
(D) Apply for a new account

**設問の訳**
女性は男性に何をすることを勧めていますか。
(A) もう 1 袋購入する
(B) ウェブサイトを見る
(C) 会員カードに記入する
(D) 新しい口座の申し込みをする

**正解 (B)**
女性店員が男性客に勧めていることは女性の発言の最後にある。please go to our Web site to fill out a customer survey から，(B) が正解。会話中の fill out を用いた (C) に引っ掛からないように。

## 放送文

Questions 65 through 67 refer to the following conversation and sign.

W: Hi … um … I'm a bit lost. I've got a job interview at Stephens and Vale Law … um ... but when I got to their office, I saw a different company nameplate on the door.
M: That's because they've relocated to the same floor as Bilo Investments.
W: Thanks a lot. I didn't see that marked anywhere on the information displays.
M: It's not, because the move just took place. The updated location will be posted around the building soon. In the meantime, you should use Elevator 3. It'll take you to where you want to go.

| Floor | Tenants |
|---|---|
| 5 | Bilo Investments / Jowon Media, Inc. |
| 4 | Wannable Textiles / Deni Biomedical |
| 3 | Aril Publishing / Somtio Engineering |
| 2 | Cimin Lighting, Inc. / Rea Catering |
| 1 | Gillo Realty, Inc. / Ashik Software Co. |

## 放送文の訳

問題 65-67 は次の会話と表示に関するものです。

W：こんにちは。えーと，少し迷ってしまいました。Stephens and Vale 法律事務所で就職の面接があるのですが…，事務所に着いたら扉に別の会社の表札がありました。
M：それはその事務所が Bilo 投資信託と同じ階に移転したからです。
W：どうもありがとう。案内表示のどこにもそれは表示されていませんでした。
M：そうですね，移転はつい最近のことですから。最新の場所はすぐに建物のあちこちに掲示されるでしょう。ところで，エレベーター3に乗るといいですよ。あなたが行きたいところに連れていってくれます。

| 階 | テナント |
|---|---|
| 5 | ・ Bilo 投資信託 <br> ・ Jowon メディア |
| 4 | ・ Wannable 織物 <br> ・ Deni バイオメディカル |
| 3 | ・ Aril 出版 <br> ・ Somtio エンジニアリング |
| 2 | ・ Cimin 照明 <br> ・ Rea ケータリング |
| 1 | ・ Gillo 不動産 <br> ・ Ashik ソフトウェア |

## Vocabulary

- interview [íntərvjùː] 名 面接
- relocate [riːlóukeit] 動 移転する
- mark [mɑːrk] 動 ～に印を付ける
- display [displéi] 名 表示
- take place 行われる

---

### 設問 / 設問の訳 / 正解と解説

**65**
Why did the woman come to the building?
(A) To visit an apartment
(B) To retrieve a lost item
(C) To go to an interview
(D) To rent an office

女性はなぜこの建物に来ましたか。
(A) アパートを訪れるため
(B) なくした物を取り戻すため
(C) 面接に行くため
(D) 事務所を借りるため

**正解 (C)**
女性は冒頭で迷ったことを伝え，I've got a job interview at Stephens and Vale Law と言っている。女性がこの建物に来た目的は Stephens and Vale Law での就職面接と考えられるので，(C) が正解。

retrieve [ritríːv] （失った物など）を取り戻す

**66**
Look at the graphic. What floor does the woman have to go to?
(A) Floor 2
(B) Floor 3
(C) Floor 4
(D) Floor 5

図を見てください。女性は何階に行かなければなりませんか。
(A) 2 階
(B) 3 階
(C) 4 階
(D) 5 階

**正解 (D)**
男性は Stephens and Vale Law の場所について，they've relocated to the same floor as Bilo Investments と言っている。they は Stephens and Vale Law のことで，その事務所は Bilo 投資信託と同じ階にあることになる。そこで表示を見ると，Bilo Investments は 5 階なので，正解は (D)。

**67**
What does the man recommend the woman do?
(A) Take an elevator
(B) Change a nameplate
(C) Check the information displays again
(D) Update her online profile

男性は女性に何をすることを勧めていますか。
(A) エレベーターに乗る
(B) 表札を変える
(C) 案内表示を再度確認する
(D) インターネット上のプロフィールを更新する

**正解 (A)**
男性は Stephens and Vale Law の事務所への行き方について，you should use Elevator 3 と言っている。これを Take an elevator と簡潔に表した (A) が正解。

## 放送文

Questions 68 through 70 refer to the following conversation and card.

W: Hi, my name is Nancy Katz. It's my first day at the firm, but I still don't have a photo ID card. How can I get one?
M: I'll be happy to help you. It'll only take me a minute to print one out. After I do, you'll see that each card has a large capital letter printed on it. Letters A through D are for staff in Administration. The other ones are for employees in IT, Operations, Marketing or Research.
W: Got it. And, of course, I'll try not to, but what should I do if I lose it?
M: If that happens, please report it right away. We'll deactivate your old card and give you a new one. Just be sure to keep the card visible at all times.

**Halon Technologies Inc.**
Nancy Katz
Campus Access Level **C**

## 放送文の訳

問題 68-70 は次の会話とカードに関するものです。

W: こんにちは，私の名前は Nancy Katz です。今日が出社初日ですが，まだ写真付きの ID カードを持っていません。どうしたらもらえますか。
M: 喜んでお手伝いしましょう。一部印刷するのに 1 分しかかかりませんよ。印刷した後，それぞれのカードには大文字の大きな文字が印字されているのが見てとれるでしょう。A から D までの文字は総務部のスタッフを表します。その他の文字は IT 部，事業部，マーケティング部，または研究部の社員を表します。
W: 了解です。それからもちろん，気を付けますが，もしカードをなくしてしまった場合はどうしたらいいですか。
M: なくした場合は，すぐに報告してください。旧カードを停止して，新しいカードを差し上げます。ただ，常に見えるようにしておくことをお忘れなく。

Halon テクノロジーズ株式会社

Nancy Katz
構内アクセスレベル C

### Vocabulary
- print ~ out ～を印刷する
- capital letter 大文字
- Administration [ədmìnəstréiʃən] 名 総務部
- report [ripɔ́ːrt] 動 ～を報告する
- right away すぐに
- deactivate [diːǽktəvèit] 動 ～を無効にする
- be sure to do 必ず～する
- visible [vízəbl] 形 目に見える
- at all times 常に

---

### 68
What is the woman asking about?

(A) How to obtain an ID
(B) How to pay a bill
(C) How to get to a branch office
(D) How to apply for a job

**設問の訳**: 女性は何について尋ねていますか。
(A) 身分証明書の入手方法
(B) 請求書の支払い方法
(C) 支店への行き方
(D) 職の応募方法

**正解 (A)**
女性が尋ねていることは冒頭の I still don't have a photo ID card. How can I get one? にある。one は a photo ID card のことで，(A) が正解。get を obtain, a photo ID card を単に an ID と表している。

### 69
Look at the graphic. What area does the woman work in?
(A) Operations
(B) IT
(C) Administration
(D) Research

**設問の訳**: 図を見てください。女性はどんな部門で働いていますか。
(A) 事業部
(B) IT 部
(C) 総務部
(D) 研究部

**正解 (C)**
男性の説明と女性の ID カードから部署名を読み取る。ID カードに書かれた大文字のアルファベットは「C」で，男性が Letters A through D are for staff in Administration. と言っていることから，女性の配属部門は (C) Administration とわかる。

### 70
According to the man, what should the woman do after she gets an employee card?
(A) Take another photo
(B) Deactivate her old card
(C) Carry it with her at all times
(D) Report to the marketing department

**設問の訳**: 男性によると，女性は社員カードを取得した後何をすべきですか。
(A) もう 1 枚写真を撮る
(B) 旧カードを停止する
(C) 常に携帯する
(D) マーケティング部に報告する

**正解 (C)**
男性は最後に Just be sure to keep the card visible at all times. と言って，社員カードを常に見えるようにしておくよう言っていることから，(C) が正解。(B) の Deactivate her old card は社員カードをなくしたときの手続きなので注意。

# PART 4

| 放送文 | 放送文の訳 |
|---|---|
| Questions 71 through 73 refer to the following telephone message.<br><br>Hi Michael, it's Carla McIntyre from Lowlands Construction's personnel department. We received your application for Quality Controller and would like to offer you an interview on either January 11 or January 12. Please let me know which date is most convenient. After that, I'll send you confirmation of the date by express letter. I left a message two or three days ago about this, but got no response. If I don't hear from you within 24 hours, I'll assume you're no longer interested in the job. Please call me at 845-976-2389 extension 14 or on my phone 721-716-667. Or you can e-mail me at cmcintyre@lowlandsonline.co.uk. Unfortunately, our office fax machine is currently being repaired. | 問題 71-73 は次の電話のメッセージに関するものです。<br><br>こんにちは Michael, Lowlands 建設人事部の Carla McIntyre です。品質管理者への応募書類を受け取りましたので，1月11日か1月12日のどちらかに面接をさせていただければと思います。どちらの日がご都合がよろしいかをお知らせください。その後，速達で日付の確認をお送りします。このことについて2，3日前にメッセージを残しましたが，お返事をいただけませんでした。24時間以内にお返事をいただけないときは，もうこの仕事にご興味をお持ちでないと判断させていただきます。845-976-2389 内線 14 番，または私の携帯 721-716-667 までお電話ください。あるいは cmcintyre@lowlandsonline.co.uk まで E メールを送ってください。あいにく，当社のファックスは現在修理中です。 |

## Vocabulary

- personnel department 人事部
- convenient [kənvíːnjənt] 形 都合の良い
- confirmation [kùnfərméiʃən] 名 確認
- express letter 速達
- response [rispɔ́ns] 名 返答
- hear from ～  ～から連絡をもらう
- assume [əsúːm] 動 ～と見なす
- unfortunately [ʌnfɔ́ːrtʃənitli] 副 残念ながら，あいにく
- currently [kɔ́ːrəntli] 副 現在のところ

---

### 71

**設問:** What is the speaker calling about?

(A) A job interview
(B) An interview result
(C) A schedule change
(D) A job description

**設問の訳:** 話し手は何について電話していますか。

(A) 仕事の面接
(B) 面接の結果
(C) 予定の変更
(D) 仕事の説明

**正解 (A)**

話し手は We received your application for Quality Controller and would like to offer you an interview ～ と，Michael の応募書類を受け取ったことを伝えて面接を申し出ている。よって，正解は (A)。

---

### 72

**設問:** What did the speaker do a few days ago?

(A) Talked with Michael on the phone
(B) Left a message about an interview
(C) Sent a letter with an application
(D) Transferred to the personnel department

**設問の訳:** 話し手は数日前に何をしましたか。

(A) 電話で Michael と話した
(B) 面接に関するメッセージを残した
(C) 応募書類と一緒に手紙を送った
(D) 人事部へ異動した

**正解 (B)**

話し手が数日前に取った行動は，中ほどの I left a message two or three days ago about this にあり，この this の内容を理解できているかがポイント。話し手は電話の相手 (Michael) に面接の日取りの確認を求めていることから，(B) が正解。過去の行動を問う問題に対して動詞の過去形で始まる選択肢のパターンも確認しておこう。

---

### 73

**設問:** How long does Michael have to respond?

(A) One day
(B) Two days
(C) Three days
(D) Four days

**設問の訳:** Michael は返答するのにどのくらい時間がありますか。

(A) 1日
(B) 2日
(C) 3日
(D) 4日

**正解 (A)**

If I don't hear from you within 24 hours, I'll assume you're no longer interested in the job.「24時間以内に連絡がなければ，仕事に興味がないと判断する」がヒントになる。24時間の言い換えである (A) One day が正解。

## 放送文

Questions 74 through 76 refer to the following announcement.

Good afternoon ladies and gentlemen, this is flight attendant Jennifer Hollings. On behalf of the airline, I'd like to apologize for our late departure. Planes ahead of us have taken off, but we are having our wings inspected by ground crews. The procedure should take approximately 20 more minutes and is an essential mechanical safety process before we can be cleared for takeoff. We should now touch down in Toronto at 10:00 P.M., 45 minutes later than scheduled. Passengers for connecting Flight GO-899 to Mexico City should proceed directly upon disembarkation to Gate 10, not Gate 11 as previously stated. I'd like to thank you again for joining us on Scotts Airways.

## 放送文の訳

問題 74-76 は次のアナウンスに関するものです。

皆さまこんにちは，客室乗務員の Jennifer Hollings です。航空会社を代表して，出発の遅れにつきましてお詫び申し上げます。当機より前の飛行機はすでに離陸いたしましたが，当機はただ今地上整備員が翼を点検しております。この処理におよそあと 20 分かかると思われ，これは当機が離陸することが認められる前に不可欠な機械上の安全措置です。現在のところ，予定より 45 分遅い午後 10 時にトロントに着陸するでしょう。メキシコシティへの接続便 GO-899 にご搭乗予定の皆さまは，飛行機から降りられましたら，お知らせしてあります 11 番ゲートではなく，直接 10 番ゲートへお進みください。あらためまして，Scotts 航空をご利用いただきありがとうございます。

## Vocabulary

- on behalf of ~ ~を代表して
- apologize for ~ ~のことで謝罪する
- ahead of ~ ~の前に[の]
- take off 離陸する
- inspect [inspékt] 動 ~を点検する
- crew [kru:] 名 (一緒に作業をする)一団，チーム
- procedure [prəsí:dʒər] 名 処理
- approximately [əpráksəmitli] 副 およそ
- essential [isénʃəl] 形 不可欠な
- touch down 着陸する
- connecting flight 接続便
- disembarkation [dìsimbɑ:rkéiʃən] 名 降りること，下車
- previously [prí:viəsli] 副 以前に，すでに
- state [steit] 動 ~を述べる

## 74

**設問:** What has delayed the aircraft?

(A) Planes ahead of it
(B) Obstacles on the runway
(C) Mechanical safety check
(D) Bad weather

**設問の訳:** 何が航空機を遅らせましたか。

(A) 前の飛行機
(B) 滑走路上の障害物
(C) 機械上の安全確認
(D) 悪天候

**正解 (C)**

出発の遅れに関する機内アナウンス。中盤で，今地上整備員が翼を点検しており，それは不可欠な機械上の安全措置 (an essential mechanical safety process) と言っているので，正解は (C) Mechanical safety check。

obstacle [ábstəkl] 障害(物)

## 75

**設問:** How much longer will the plane have to wait?
(A) 10 minutes
(B) 20 minutes
(C) 40 minutes
(D) 45 minutes

**設問の訳:** あとどのくらいこの飛行機は待たなければなりませんか。
(A) 10 分
(B) 20 分
(C) 40 分
(D) 45 分

**正解 (B)**

同じく中盤で，The procedure should take approximately 20 more minutes ~とあるので，正解は (B)。放送文中にいくつか数字が出てくるので，質問内容を事前に把握してから聞き取るようにしたい。

## 76

**設問:** What are passengers traveling to Mexico City advised to do?
(A) Follow previously stated information
(B) Get a travel update at their destination
(C) Board from a different gate
(D) Contact airline staff upon disembarkation

**設問の訳:** メキシコシティへ行く乗客は何をするよう言われていますか。
(A) 以前に述べられた情報に従う
(B) 目的地で旅行の最新情報を得る
(C) 違うゲートから搭乗する
(D) 飛行機を降りたら航空会社スタッフに連絡する

**正解 (C)**

後半の Passengers for connecting Flight GO-899 to Mexico City should proceed ~ の部分で，メキシコシティへの接続便に搭乗予定の人は，降りたら 11 番ゲートではなく 10 番ゲートへ行くように指示している。これを Board from a different gate「違うゲートから搭乗する」と表した (C) が正解。

## 放送文

Questions 77 through 79 refer to the following report.

Global fashion corporation Orient Mist Incorporated has announced a 4 percent rise in profits as of the last fiscal quarter. Analysts predict profits for the year will rise further to 6 percent. This is in contrast to last year, when the company posted a 12 percent loss. Recently-appointed CEO Alexander Chou said he expected this trend to continue, helped by the company's new clothing line *Secret Fire*. Mr. Chou said the line has done especially well among college-aged women. He stated the company's future will be further improved by large numbers of customers switching to the Internet to make their purchases instead of going into stores. He noted the company's online sales have risen substantially following an upgrade of its Web site, with visitors up by 16 percent for the year.

## 放送文の訳

問題 77-79 は次のレポートに関するものです。

世界的なファッション企業の Orient Mist 社は、この前の四半期の決算で収益が4％増加したと発表しました。アナリストは、年間の収益はさらに6％まで増加すると予想しています。このことは、会社が12％の損失を公表した昨年とは対照的です。最近任命された最高経営責任者の Alexander Chou は、この動向は会社の新しい衣料品ラインである *Secret Fire* に促され、今後も続くと思うと述べています。Chou 氏によれば、*Secret Fire* は大学生年齢の女性の間で特に好評のようです。彼は、多くの顧客が商品の購入を店舗からインターネットに切り換えることによって、会社の将来はさらに良くなると述べています。彼は、ウェブサイトの改善の後に、年間で16％訪問者が増え、会社のオンラインでの売り上げが大幅に増加したと言及しています。

### Vocabulary
- global [glóubəl] 形 世界的な
- profit [práfit] 名 収益
- as of ～ ～現在で
- fiscal quarter 会計四半期
- predict [pridíkt] 動 ～だと予想する
- in contrast to ～ ～と対照的に
- post [poust] 動 ～を公表する
- loss [lɔːs] 名 損失
- do well うまくいく、よく売れる
- switch to ～ ～へ切り替える
- substantially [səbstǽnʃəli] 副 大幅に

---

### 77
**What is the report mainly about?**

(A) Luxury markets
(B) Corporate performance
(C) Economic trends
(D) Business investments

**設問の訳**: 主に何についてのレポートですか。

(A) ぜいたく品の市場
(B) 企業の業績
(C) 経済トレンド
(D) ビジネス投資

**正解 (B)**

放送文全体を聞いて答える問題。世界的なファッション企業の収益の増加や年間収益の予想などを述べていることから、正解は (B) Corporate performance「企業の業績」。

luxury [lʌ́kʃəri, lʌ́gʒ-] ぜいたく品
performance [pərfɔ́ːrməns] 業績

---

### 78
**How much do analysts expect profits to rise for the year?**

(A) 4 percent
(B) 6 percent
(C) 12 percent
(D) 16 percent

**設問の訳**: アナリストは年間でどのくらい収益が増加すると予想していますか。

(A) 4 パーセント
(B) 6 パーセント
(C) 12 パーセント
(D) 16 パーセント

**正解 (B)**

放送文の序盤で、Analysts predict profits for the year will rise further to 6 percent. と述べられていることから、正解は (B)。

---

### 79
**What does the report imply?**

(A) Shopping trends are changing.
(B) CEO policies are failing.
(C) More customers are coming into stores.
(D) Online sales are decreasing.

**設問の訳**: レポートは何を示唆していますか。

(A) ショッピングの傾向が変化している。
(B) 最高経営責任者の政策が失敗している。
(C) 店舗に足を運ぶ客が増えている。
(D) オンラインでの売り上げが減っている。

**正解 (A)**

終盤で、～ large numbers of customers switching to the Internet to make their purchases instead of going into stores とあり、店舗に行く代わりにインターネットでの購入に切り換える消費者が多くいることがわかる。つまり、「ショッピングの傾向が変化している」ことを示すので、(A) が正解。

## 放送文

Questions 80 through 82 refer to the following advertisement.

It's hard to clean all the different surfaces in your home, isn't it? Usually, you need one cleaner for the kitchen, one for the bathroom, and one for the furniture. *SteadyClean* is different. Its powerful yet gentle chemicals allow you to clean any area of your home. Just spray it on a wet cloth and wipe it over any surface: it'll be spotless in seconds! Now, I'm going to invite some of you from the audience to join me on stage. You're going to have the chance to use this product on some of the items I have up here with me. Then, you'll see just how great this cleaner really is!

## 放送文の訳

問題 80-82 は次の広告に関するものです。

皆さんのお宅のさまざまな異なる表面を掃除するのは大変ですよね？ たいてい，台所用に1つ，浴室用に1つ，家具用に1つ，クリーナーが必要です。SteadyClean は違います。強力なのに優しい薬品が皆さんのお宅のどんな場所でもきれいにしてくれます。湿った布にスプレーして拭くだけで，どんな表面もあっという間に汚れ1つなくなります！　さて，観客の皆さんの中から何名かをステージ上にお招きいたします。私がここに用意した品物のいくつかにこの商品をお使いいただく機会を差し上げます。そうすれば，このクリーナーがいかに素晴らしいかおわかりになることでしょう！

### Vocabulary

- surface [sə́ːrfəs] 名 表面
- chemical [kémikəl] 名 (化学)薬品
- wipe [waip] 動 〜を拭く
- spotless [spɔ́tlis] 形 汚れ[染み]のない
- in seconds あっという間に

---

### 80

What is the speaker doing?

(A) Introducing a product
(B) Cleaning a house
(C) Helping a customer
(D) Arranging a program

**設問の訳**

話し手は何をしていますか。

(A) 製品を紹介している
(B) 家を掃除している
(C) 客の手伝いをしている
(D) 計画を立てている

**正解 (A)**

放送文全体を聞いて判断する必要がある。商品の良さを説明しているくだりからもわかるが，SteadyClean という具体的な商品名を出していることもヒントになる。

---

### 81

What does the man imply when he says, "it'll be spotless in seconds"?

(A) The cloth will dry fast.
(B) The surface will be clean quickly.
(C) The chemicals need time to mix.
(D) The cleaner cannot remove all dirt.

**設問の訳**

男性が "it'll be spotless in seconds" と言う際，何を示唆していますか。

(A) 布が早く乾く。
(B) 表面がすぐにきれいになる。
(C) 薬品は混ぜるのに時間がかかる。
(D) クリーナーはあらゆる汚れを落とせるわけではない。

**正解 (B)**

主語の it は直前の surface「表面」を指す。spotless は spot「(表面についた)染み，汚点」に接尾辞 -less「〜がない」がついて，「汚れのない」という意味。in seconds は「数秒で，瞬く間に」という意味で，(A) の fast や (B) の quickly と同意。(B) が正解で，spotless を clean と言い換えている。

---

### 82

What are some listeners invited to do?

(A) Ask the speaker questions
(B) Participate in a demonstration
(C) Talk about their experiences
(D) Receive product samples

**設問の訳**

一部の聞き手は何をするように勧められていますか。

(A) 話し手に質問をする
(B) 実演に参加する
(C) 自分の体験について話す
(D) 製品のサンプルを受け取る

**正解 (B)**

終盤で話し手が，I'm going to invite some of you from the audience to join me on stage とステージに上がって実演に参加するように呼び掛けている。よって，正解は (B)。

participate in 〜　〜に参加する

## 放送文

Questions 83 through 85 refer to the following talk.

Good evening. At Centennial Tools Incorporated, we want the best for all our employees. That includes providing special benefits for those who are parents. We are therefore proud to announce the opening of our Centennial Headquarters Daycare Center. The center includes a playground, outdoor water fountain, and 3-meter fence to safeguard your children. Shortly, Jessica Langdon, head teacher at the center, will be telling us about how it will be run on a daily basis, the curriculum involved and the activities children there will be able to enjoy. After that, Aaron Cummings will talk about our plans for the long-term future of the center before Betsy Chung and Brian Masoud from human resources give you details of how you can enroll your child in the center.

## 放送文の訳

問題 83-85 は次の話に関するものです。

こんばんは。Centennial 工具社では，全社員に最高のものを提供したいと考えています。それには，親である社員への特別手当の支給も含まれます。それゆえ，Centennial 本社デイケアセンターを開設することをお知らせできて光栄に思います。センターには，遊び場，屋外の噴水，そして子供たちを保護する3メートルのフェンスがあります。すぐ後で，センターの校長である Jessica Langdon が，日常的にセンターがどのように運営されるのか，行われるカリキュラムや子供たちがそこで楽しむことのできる活動について話してくれます。その後で，Aaron Cummings が，センターの長期にわたる将来の計画についてお話しします。その後，人事部の Betsy Chung と Brian Masoud が，あなたのお子さんをどうすればセンターに入れることができるのかについての詳細をお話しいたします。

## Vocabulary

- special benefit 特別手当
- therefore [ðɛərfɔ́ːr] 副 それゆえに
- daycare center デイケアセンター，託児所
- playground [pléigràund] 名 遊び場
- water fountain 噴水
- safeguard [séifgàːrd] 動 ～を保護する
- shortly [ʃɔ́ːrtli] 副 まもなく，すぐに
- run [rʌn] 動 ～を運営する
- on a daily basis 日常的に，日々
- long-term [lɔ́ːŋtə́ːrm] 形 長期の

---

### 83

What is the main purpose of the talk?

(A) To develop a curriculum
(B) To explain the existing service
(C) To ask for donations
(D) To inform parents about a new facility

この話の主な目的は何ですか。

(A) カリキュラムを開発すること
(B) 現行のサービスについて説明すること
(C) 寄付を頼むこと
(D) 親に新しい施設について知らせること

**正解 (D)**

冒頭で，全社員，特に親である人に特別手当を支給したいと述べた上で，We are therefore proud to announce the opening of our Centennial Headquarters Daycare Center. と，託児所の開設を知らせている。(D) が正解で，Centennial Headquarters Daycare Center を抽象的に facility と表している。

---

### 84

What is a feature of the center?

(A) Child computers
(B) Protective enclosures
(C) Special teachers
(D) Expanded curriculums

このセンターの特徴は何ですか。

(A) 子供用のコンピューター
(B) 保護囲い
(C) 特別な教師
(D) 幅広いカリキュラム

**正解 (B)**

中盤にある The center includes ～, and 3-meter fence to safeguard your children. がヒントになる。fence to safeguard を言い換えた (B) Protective enclosures が正解。

protective [prətéktiv] 保護する，保護用の
enclosure [inklóuʒər]（柵・塀などの）囲い

---

### 85

What will Aaron Cummings talk about?

(A) The history of the center
(B) Future plans
(C) The details of activities
(D) Ways to sign up

Aaron Cummings は何について話しますか。

(A) センターの歴史
(B) 将来の計画
(C) 活動の詳細
(D) 登録方法

**正解 (B)**

Aaron Cummings という人物に関する情報を聞き取る。Aaron Cummings will talk about our plans for the long-term future of the center から，(B) が正解。特定の人物に関する問題では，質問文を先読みしていると，その人物名が出てくる箇所を集中して聞ける。

## 放送文

Questions 86 through 88 refer to the following excerpt from a meeting.

We have had a very successful fiscal year. Our sales rose by 14 percent and our market share by 12 percent. Many of you have worked long hours under tight deadlines and difficult conditions to achieve that, and I believe you should get credit. So, in order to show our appreciation, the company is creating a profit-sharing program. Five percent of our total net income will be distributed among all staff who have worked here for at least nine months. You can get details on this on the company Intranet. This is our small way of thanking you for all you've done.

## 放送文の訳

問題 86-88 は次の会議からの抜粋に関するものです。

わが社にとって非常に良い営業成績を収めた年度になりました。売り上げは14％, マーケットシェアは12％増加しました。皆さんの多くが, それを達成するために厳しい締め切りと困難な状況の下で長時間働いてきました。そして, 皆さんはその功績が認められるべきだと私は考えます。そこで, 感謝の意を表して, 会社は利益共有プログラムを作っています。社の総純利益の5％が, ここで少なくとも9か月間働いた全スタッフに分配されます。このことに関する詳細は会社のイントラネットで手に入ります。これはささやかではありますが, 皆さんがしてくださったことへの感謝の気持ちです。

### Vocabulary
- deadline [dédlàin] 名 締め切り
- achieve [ətʃíːv] 動 ～を達成する
- get credit 功績が認められる
- appreciation [əprìːʃiéiʃən] 名 感謝
- net income 純利益
- distribute [distríbju(ː)t] 動 ～を分配する
- intranet [íntrənèt] 名 企業内コンピューターネットワーク

---

### 86
Who is the talk most likely intended for?
(A) Corporate shareholders
(B) Financial reporters
(C) Company employees
(D) Market researchers

**設問の訳:** この話は誰に向けられていると考えられますか。
(A) 企業の株主
(B) 財務レポーター
(C) 会社の従業員
(D) 市場調査員

**正解 (C)**

話し手が話す you が誰なのかを考える。you の働きぶりについて感謝を述べ, それに対して会社が利益を共有すると述べていることから, 会社の社員に向けて話していると考えるのが自然であろう。よって, 正解は (C) Company employees。

---

### 87
What success is mentioned by the speaker?
(A) A reduction in production costs
(B) An increase in stock prices
(C) An increase in revenue
(D) A reduction in working hours

**設問の訳:** 話し手によってどんな成功が述べられていますか。
(A) 製造コストの削減
(B) 株価の上昇
(C) 収益の増加
(D) 労働時間の削減

**正解 (C)**

放送文の最初に, Our sales rose by 14 percent and our market share by 12 percent. とあり, ここから (C) An increase in revenue が正解とわかる。

stock price 株価
revenue [révənjùː] 収益

---

### 88
What does the speaker mean when she says, "I believe you should get credit"?
(A) She considers sales to be adequate.
(B) She hopes higher goals will be achieved.
(C) She owes money to her staff.
(D) She thinks her employees deserve a reward.

**設問の訳:** 話し手が "I believe you should get credit" と言う際, 何を意図していますか。
(A) 彼女は売り上げが十分だと見なしている。
(B) 彼女はより高い目標が達成されることを望んでいる。
(C) 彼女は従業員に借金をしている。
(D) 彼女は従業員が報酬金を受けるに値すると思っている。

**正解 (D)**

直前では, 従業員の功績について述べており, 直後の So, ～以下から, 話し手が従業員に感謝していることや, 利益共有プログラムによって従業員に報酬金が支払われることがわかる。credit は「(功績などがあると) 認めること」という意味で, (D) が正解。deserve「～を受けるに値する」は get credit の言い換え, a reward は利益共有プログラムによる報酬金のことである。

## 放送文

Questions 89 through 91 refer to the following excerpt from a meeting.

Before we begin, I'd like to make a short announcement. As some of you already know, Maria Lopez, the head of our Operations Department, is currently away sick and will not be returning for at least another six weeks. As a result, we have decided to move Richard Slater from IT to her position until she returns. Personnel from both Consumer Finance and Planning will also help as required during this period. I know this is an added burden for us. However, we need to make sure our service continues to be first-class—at the same level that *Corporate Review Magazine* praised us for. Now, as there seem to be no questions, I'd like to proceed with a look at the monthly report as planned. Please look at the first of these slides.

## 放送文の訳

問題 89-91 は次の会議からの抜粋に関するものです。

始める前に，短いお知らせをしたいと思います。あなた方のうちの何人かはすでにご存じの通り，業務部長の Maria Lopez さんが現在病欠していて，少なくともあと 6 週間は戻ってきません。それを受けて，彼女が戻るまで彼女のポジションに Richard Slater さんを IT 部から異動させることにしました。消費者融資部と企画部の社員もこの期間中，必要に応じて手伝ってくれます。このことが我々にとって追加負担になることは承知しています。しかしながら，わが社のサービスを一流のままで，すなわち Corporate Review 誌がわが社を称賛してくれたのと同じレベルで維持し続けるようにしなければなりません。さて，質問もないようですので，予定通りに月次報告書を見ていきたいと思います。スライドの 1 枚目を見てください。

### Vocabulary
- head [hed] 名 長
- added [ǽdid] 形 追加の
- burden [bə́ːrdn] 名 負担，重荷
- make sure (that) ~ 必ず~するようにする
- first-class [fə́ːrstklǽs] 形 最高の
- praise [preiz] 動 ~を称賛する
- monthly report 月次報告(書)

---

### 89
**設問:** Which department does Richard Slater normally work in?
(A) Accounting
(B) IT
(C) Consumer Finance
(D) Planning

**設問の訳:** Richard Slater は普段どこの部署で働いていますか。
(A) 経理部
(B) IT 部
(C) 消費者融資部
(D) 企画部

**正解 (B)**

質問文に具体的な人名があるので，その人名が出てきたら集中して聞きたい。we have decided to move Richard Slater from IT to her position until she returns から，普段は IT 部で働いている Richard Slater さんが一時的に異動するとわかるので，正解は (B) IT。

---

### 90
**設問:** What does the man mean when he says, "I know this is an added burden for us"?
(A) He wants to have more staff.
(B) There will be another position available.
(C) A department will be divided into two.
(D) The company will face some hardship.

**設問の訳:** 男性が "I know this is an added burden for us" と言う際，何を意図していますか。
(A) 彼はもっとたくさんのスタッフが欲しいと思っている。
(B) 別の職に空きが出る。
(C) ある部署が 2 つに分けられる。
(D) 会社が困難に直面する。

**正解 (D)**

burden は「負担，重荷」という意味だが，この語を知らなくても，added「追加の，余分な，さらなる」のニュアンスや前後の文脈から考えるとよい。話題は，業務部長の Maria Lopez さんが病欠の間，別の部署から Richard Slater さんがヘルプに入ること。そして続く「しかし，サービスは一流のままであるべき」という流れから，人手をやりくりしながらサービスを維持するという困難を乗り切らなければならないことがわかり，(D) が正解。

---

### 91
**設問:** What will the listeners do next?
(A) Offer opinions
(B) View a presentation
(C) Ask questions
(D) Write monthly reports

**設問の訳:** 聞き手は次に何をしますか。
(A) 意見を述べる
(B) プレゼンテーションを見る
(C) 質問をする
(D) 月次報告書を書く

**正解 (B)**

話し手は今から月次報告書を見ていくと伝えた後，Please look at the first of these slides. と言ってスライドを見るように指示している。つまり，聞き手は，これから話し手のプレゼンテーションを見ると考えられるので，正解は (B)。「次に何をするか」といった問題は放送文の終盤に答えのヒントがある場合が多い。

## 放送文

Questions 92 through 94 refer to the following broadcast.

I'm Jason Kim with all your business news. A report by expert, Kate Smith of Lake University, has found that the key to communicating effectively in front of groups is preparation. While relaxation exercises or advanced speaking techniques can help with nervousness, there is no alternative to having a thorough knowledge of a subject. In an experiment, speakers who were thoroughly prepared for a presentation were found to be 20-30% more persuasive than those who were not. The difference was particularly clear when speakers had to face audience questions at the end of their presentations. At that point, well-prepared speakers did an especially good job with their topics. Now, here's Alicia Hernandez with the weather.

## 放送文の訳

問題 92-94 は次の放送に関するものです。

ビジネスニュースの Jason Kim です。専門家である Lake 大学の Kate Smith の報告によれば、集団の前で効果的にコミュニケーションを取る鍵は準備であるとのことです。ストレス緩和のための運動や上級のスピーキング技術は緊張を和らげるものの、主題についての余すところのない知識を持つことに代わる方法はありません。ある実験では、プレゼンテーションを徹底的に準備した話者は、準備をしなかった人より 20〜30％説得力のあったことがわかりました。特にその違いは、話者がプレゼンテーションの終わりに聴衆の質問に直面しなければならないときに顕著でした。そのとき、よく準備した話者は自分の話題で特にうまくこなしていました。さて次は、Alicia Hernandez のお天気です。

## Vocabulary

- expert [ékspə:rt] 名 専門家
- effectively [iféktivli] 副 効果的に
- nervousness [nə́:rvəsnəs] 名 緊張
- alternative [ɔ:ltə́:rnətiv] 名 代わりのもの
- subject [sʌ́bdʒikt] 名 主題
- experiment [ikspérəmənt] 名 実験
- thoroughly [θə́:rouli] 副 徹底的に
- persuasive [pərswéisiv] 形 説得力のある
- particularly [pərtíkjələrli] 副 特に
- face [feis] 動 〜に直面する

---

### 92
Who most likely is the speaker?

(A) A business expert
(B) A company president
(C) A news reporter
(D) A communication specialist

**設問の訳:** 話し手は誰だと考えられますか。

(A) ビジネス専門家
(B) 会社社長
(C) ニュース記者
(D) コミュニケーションの専門家

**正解 (C)**

問題指示文の〜 following broadcast を聞き取れば本文は（テレビ・ラジオの）放送だとわかる。話し手は、冒頭で I'm Jason Kim with all your business news. と名乗った後、A report by expert, 〜以降である専門家による報告を伝えている。最後の Now, here's Alicia Hernandez with the weather. からも、話し手は (C) の A news reporter である。

---

### 93
According to the speaker, what does the report say is necessary for a good presentation?

(A) Practice while in university
(B) Substantial mastery of material
(C) Thorough relaxation exercises
(D) Advanced speaking techniques

**設問の訳:** 話し手によると、優れたプレゼンテーションに必要なものは何だとその報告は言っていますか。

(A) 大学時代の練習
(B) 題材への相当な精通
(C) ストレス緩和のための徹底的な運動
(D) 上級のスピーキング技術

**正解 (B)**

中盤に there is no alternative to having a thorough knowledge of a subject「主題について余すところのない知識を持つことに代わる方法はない」とあり、この部分の言い換え表現である (B)「題材への相当な精通」こそが優れたプレゼンテーションに不可欠なものだとわかる。

substantial [səbstǽnʃəl] かなりの、相当な

---

### 94
What is preparation particularly effective for?

(A) Making points clear
(B) Choosing a topic
(C) Facing the public
(D) Replying to inquiries

**設問の訳:** 準備は何に対して特に効果的ですか。

(A) 要点を明確にすること
(B) テーマを選ぶこと
(C) 公衆に向き合うこと
(D) 質問に返答すること

**正解 (D)**

しっかり準備をした人はしなかった人よりも説得力があり、The difference was particularly clear when speakers had to face audience questions 〜「特にその違いは、話者が聴衆の質問に直面したときに顕著であった」とあることから、正解は (D)。

| 放送文 | 放送文の訳 |
|---|---|
| Questions 95 through 97 refer to the following talk and map. | 問題 95-97 は次の話と地図に関するものです。 |
| Now that everyone's here, I'd like to say a few words about the company picnic next month. This year, it's going to be bigger than ever—partly as a reward for the record profits that we earned last fiscal year. It will be at Naden Park and organized by the Human Resources Department. It's a public space, so we can't reserve any section of the area. However, Human Resources will arrive early to find a spot for us just south of Basto Lake. There's a bicycle path that cuts that area into two sections. We'll be in the southwest section. Travel directions have already been e-mailed companywide, so all staff should know how to get there—by car or public transportation. Festivities will begin at 11:00 A.M., but our staff will begin setting up everything—including unpacking food and drinks—at around 9:00 A.M. | 全員そろったところで，来月の社内ピクニックについていくつかお伝えしたいと思います。今年は，いつもより規模が大きくなります。これは，昨年度得た記録的な利益に対する報奨の意味合いもあります。Naden 公園で行われ，人事部によって企画されます。公共スペースなので，公園内の場所はどこも予約できません。ですが，人事部が早めに到着して Basto 湖のすぐ南に場所を見つけます。自転車専用道路がそのエリアを 2 つの区画に分断していますが，私たちの場所は南西の区画になります。道順はすでにメールで全社にお知らせしていますので，そこへの行き方は，車でも，公共交通機関でも，社員全員が知っていることと思います。行事は午前 11 時に始まりますが，スタッフは午前 9 時頃から，食べ物や飲み物を出すことを含めすべての準備を始めます。 |

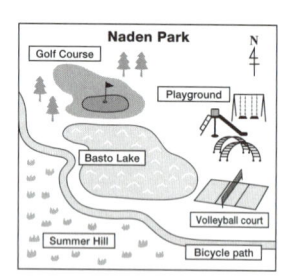

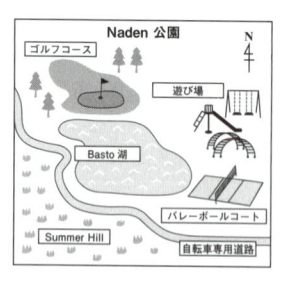

## Vocabulary

- record profit 記録的な利益
- cut ~ into ... sections ~を…区画に切り分ける
- companywide [kʌ́mpəniwàid] 副 全社的に
- festivity [festívəti] 名 祝いの行事
- unpack [ʌ̀npǽk] 動 ~の中身を出す

| 設問 | 設問の訳 | 正解と解説 |
|---|---|---|
| **95** What type of event is being prepared?<br>(A) A talent contest<br>(B) A marathon<br>(C) An outdoor gathering<br>(D) A local tour | どんな種類のイベントが準備されていますか。<br>(A) 才能のコンテスト<br>(B) マラソン<br>(C) 屋外の集まり<br>(D) 地元のツアー | **正解 (C)**<br>話し手は冒頭で I'd like to say a few words about the company picnic next month と言い，終始 company picnic について詳しく説明している。picnic を outdoor gathering と言い換えた (C) が正解。 |
| **96** Look at the graphic. Where will the company staff meet?<br>(A) At the golf course<br>(B) At the volleyball court<br>(C) At the playground<br>(D) At Summer Hill | 図を見てください。会社のスタッフはどこで落ち合いますか。<br>(A) ゴルフコース<br>(B) バレーボールコート<br>(C) 遊び場<br>(D) Summer Hill | **正解 (D)**<br>放送文中ほどの Human Resources will arrive ~ just south of Basto Lake. からまず，ピクニックをする場所は Basto Lake の南側とわかる。続く There's a bicycle path that cuts that area into two sections. We'll be in the southwest section. を踏まえて地図を見ると，自転車専用道路で分断された 2 つの区画のうち南西の区画は Summer Hill である。 |
| **97** What has already been sent companywide?<br>(A) Travel coupons<br>(B) Public transportation passes<br>(C) Directions to the venue<br>(D) A list of festivities organizers | すでに全社に送られているものは何ですか。<br>(A) 旅行の割引券<br>(B) 公共交通機関の乗車券<br>(C) 会場への行き方<br>(D) 行事主催者のリスト | **正解 (C)**<br>放送文中ほどの Travel directions have already been e-mailed companywide を参照。Travel directions を Directions to the venue と言い換えた (C) が正解。Directions to ~ は「（場所など）への道順」，venue は「開催地」という意味。<br>organizer [ɔ́ːrɡənàizər] 主催者 |

## 放送文

Questions 98 through 100 refer to the following telephone message and order form.

John, this is Stella Gomez from headquarters. I turned in an order for office supplies this morning, but I hope that you haven't processed it yet. We have to add another three laptops to our order. I was just informed that we'll be having six new employees arriving on March 21, and we need to have all the necessary office equipment set up for them before that date. The rest of the order seems fine as it is. I sent you an e-mail with this same request, but I'm not sure whether you've had a chance to read it. When you get a moment, please call me back to confirm whether you can make these adjustments. Thanks.

**KASIK PAINT CO.**
**Office Supplies Order Form**
Order Number: 903H2

| Item | Units ordered |
| --- | --- |
| Desk lamps | 8 |
| Photocopier ink | 6 |
| Laptops | 4 |
| Fax machine | 1 |

## 放送文の訳

問題 98-100 は次の電話のメッセージと注文書に関するものです。

John, 本部の Stella Gomez です。今朝, 事務用品の注文を提出したのですが, まだあなたが処理していないといいのですが。注文にさらにノートパソコンを 3 台追加しなければならなくなりました。3 月 21 日に新入社員が 6 人来るとつい先ほど知らされましたので, 当日までにすべての必要な事務機器をセットアップしておかなければなりません。その他の注文は, そのままで問題なさそうです。同じお願いをメールで送ったのですが, 読む機会があったかわからないので。時間ができたら, この調整ができるか確認のために折り返し電話をください。よろしく。

Kasik 塗料株式会社
事務用品注文用紙
注文番号：903H2

| 品物 | 注文数量 |
| --- | --- |
| デスクランプ | 8 |
| コピー機用インク | 6 |
| ノートパソコン | 4 |
| ファクシミリ | 1 |

### Vocabulary

- turn in ～ ～を提出する
- process [práses] 動 ～を処理する
- as it is そのままで
- adjustment [ədʒʌ́stmənt] 名 調整

## 設問

### 98

Look at the graphic. How many laptops does the company need in total?
(A) 3
(B) 5
(C) 6
(D) 7

### 99

According to the telephone message, what has the company recently done?
(A) Improved its headquarters
(B) Processed a claim
(C) Hired some staff
(D) Changed a launch date

### 100

What is the listener asked to do?

(A) Train recruits
(B) Adjust a price
(C) Make a phone call
(D) Wait for a text

## 設問の訳

図を見てください。会社は全部で何台のノートパソコンが必要ですか。

(A) 3 台
(B) 5 台
(C) 6 台
(D) 7 台

電話のメッセージによると, 会社は最近何を行いましたか。

(A) 本社を改善した
(B) 請求を処理した
(C) 何人か社員を雇った
(D) 開始日を変更した

聞き手は何をすることを求められていますか。

(A) 新入社員をトレーニングする
(B) 価格を調整する
(C) 電話をする
(D) 携帯電話のメールを待つ

## 正解と解説

### 正解 (D)

電話メッセージの目的は, 事務用品の注文の変更の依頼である。We have to add another three laptops to our order. から, laptops を 3 台追加する必要があることがわかる。そこで注文書を見ると, Laptops の注文数は 4 なので, 必要な数は 4＋3＝7 台である。

### 正解 (C)

会社が最近行ったことは, I was just informed that we'll be having six new employees arriving on March 21 の部分に答えがある。3 月 21 日に新入社員が 6 人来るとつまり, 新しく 6 人の社員を雇ったと言えるので, (C) が正解。

claim [kleim] 請求
launch date （活動などの）開始日,（新商品などの）発売日

### 正解 (C)

聞き手に求められていることはたいてい放送文の最後の方にある。最終文の please call me back to confirm ～から, (C) が正解。聞き手がすべきことや求められていることは, このような命令文や Could you ～? などの依頼表現で表されることが多い。

text (message) （携帯電話同士の）テキスト（メッセージ）

# PART 5

## 問題文と訳 / 正解と解説

### 101
Mr. Krishna informed the company of ------- plan to visit several important clients on the West Coast the following week.

(A) its
(B) it
(C) he
(D) his

Krishna さんは，翌週に西海岸にあるいくつかの大切な得意先を訪ねる彼の計画を，会社に知らせた。

**正解 (D)**

適切な代名詞を問う問題。空所の直後の plan は名詞なので，所有格がふさわしい。よって，この文の主語 Mr. Krishna の所有格を表す (D) his が正解となる。空所の前の the company を主語と間違えると，(A) its を選んでしまうので注意しよう。 　代名詞の所有格

inform A of B　A に B を知らせる

### 102
Genetic advances at Warsaw Pharmaceuticals mean it may soon be possible to protect people from a ------- variety of diseases.

(A) long
(B) wide
(C) thick
(D) high

Warsaw 製薬会社での遺伝学上の進歩は，さまざまな種類の病気から人々を守ることがまもなく可能になるかもしれないことを意味する。

**正解 (B)**

a wide variety of ～で「幅広くさまざまな～」の意味。よって，(B) wide が正解。 　語彙

genetic [dʒənétik] 遺伝学的な
advance [ədvǽns] 進歩
pharmaceutical [fàːrməsjúːtikəl] 製薬
disease [dizíːz] 病気

### 103
Director Rao convinced the board to begin export sales to Europe this year, ------- at least lay the groundwork for doing so.

(A) while
(B) since
(C) but
(D) or

Rao 部長は，今年ヨーロッパに輸出販売を始めるように，あるいは少なくともそうするための基礎を築くように役員会を説得した。

**正解 (D)**

文意より，「または」「あるいは」という意味の接続詞 or でつなぐのがふさわしい。よって，正解は (D)。begin と lay が並列である。 　接続詞

convince O to do　～するよう O を説得する
groundwork [gráundwəːrk] 基礎

### 104
Alistair Properties Co. ------- to closing most deals in dollars, but due to client demand began accepting euros and yen as well.

(A) accustomed
(B) had been accustomed
(C) will accustom
(D) will have been accustomed

Alistair 不動産会社はほとんどの取引をいつもドルでまとめてきたが，顧客の要求で，ユーロと円も同様に受け入れ始めた。

**正解 (B)**

be accustomed to ～ing で「～するのに慣れている，～するのが習慣になっている」だとわかれば，(B) と (D) に絞られる。「受け入れ始めた」という過去の時点を基準として，それよりも以前からその時点まで「いつもしていた」と過去完了形にする必要がある。よって，正解は (B) had been accustomed である。 　時制

close a deal 取引をまとめる
demand [dimǽnd] 要求，需要

### 105
First Harbor Pharmaceutical Inc. is one of the top private caregivers in the province and ------- is a leader in advanced medical research.

(A) since
(B) whichever
(C) although
(D) moreover

First Harbor 製薬会社は，州で一流の民間介護施設のうちの1つで，さらには，高度な医療研究のリーダーである。

**正解 (D)**

文意より，「そのうえ」「さらに」という意味の接続副詞 moreover でつなぐのがふさわしい。よって，正解は (D)。 　接続副詞

caregiver [kéərgìvər] 介護者
province [prάvins] 州

| 問題文と訳 | 正解と解説 |
|---|---|

## 106

CEO Brian Greene stated at the meeting that an increase in sales of 13% by the end of the year was quite -------.

(A) attains
(B) attaining
(C) attainable
(D) attainably

最高経営責任者の Brian Greene は，年末までの13％の売り上げ増は十分達成できるとミーティングで述べた。

**正解 (C)**

空所の前に be 動詞の過去形 was と副詞 quite がある。動詞はすでに was があるので，(A) は不適切。また，副詞 attainably を空所に入れると，その後に補語がないために文が成り立たないので，(D) も不適切。文意より，形容詞 (C) attainable「達成できる」が正解。 品詞

attain [ətéin] ～を達成する

## 107

*Sun Lady* bath soap is certainly ------- than any similar product in fine stores today.

(A) fragrant
(B) more fragrant
(C) most fragrant
(D) fragrance

*Sun Lady* 浴用石けんは，今日高級店にあるどの類似製品より確かに香りがより良い。

**正解 (B)**

空所の直後に than があるので，比較級の (B) more fragrant が正解。最上級の (C) most fragrant には，空所の前に the が必要であるし，また，than と結びつくこともないので不適切。 比較

certainly [sə́ːrtənli] 確かに
similar [símələr] 似た
fragrant [fréigrənt] 香りの良い
fragrance [fréigrəns] 芳香

## 108

Mr. Ephron wished there ------- more funds for the company picnic, but the employees seemed satisfied with the snacks and beverages provided.

(A) is
(B) are
(C) would
(D) were

Ephron さんは会社のピクニックのための資金がもっとあればよいのにと思ったが，社員たちは出されたスナックと飲み物で満足しているように見えた。

**正解 (D)**

動詞 wish の後に仮定法過去が来て，現在の事実に反する願望を表す用法。there is [are] 構文の be 動詞の過去形である were が正解。 仮定法

fund [fʌnd] 資金
(be) satisfied with ～ ～に満足して（いる）
beverage [bévəridʒ] 飲み物

## 109

News reports indicate that some corporations are preparing ------- an economic upturn by making large investments now.

(A) for
(B) and
(C) to
(D) but

ニュース報道は，いくつかの企業が今大きな投資をすることによって経済的好転への準備をしていることを示している。

**正解 (A)**

prepare for ～で「～の準備をする」という意味。よって，正解は (A)。 前置詞

indicate [índəkèit] ～を示す
upturn [ʌ́ptəːrn] 好転；上昇
investment [invésmənt] 投資

## 110

Ms. Singh made it her personal ------- to track the company's profit margins in each of the major regions it operated in.

(A) interesting
(B) interest
(C) interestingly
(D) interested

Singh さんは，操業している主要な地域それぞれにおける会社の利益幅を追跡することに，個人的興味を持った。

**正解 (B)**

空所の直前に所有格 her と形容詞 personal があることから，空所には名詞が入るとわかる。よって，正解は (B) interest。made it の it は形式目的語で，空所直後の to 以下が真目的語である。 品詞

profit margin 利益幅
interestingly [íntəristiŋli] おもしろく

| 問題文と訳 | 正解と解説 |
|---|---|
| **111**<br>Evertrue Media Corporation is ------- the number one firm in the entertainment industry in terms of market share.<br><br>(A) responsively<br>(B) undoubtedly<br>(C) mutually<br>(D) compassionately<br><br>Evertrue メディア社は，市場占有率の点から見ると，エンターテイメント業界で間違いなくナンバーワンの企業である。 | **正解 (B)**<br>選択肢はすべて副詞であるが，空所の後の the number one firm を修飾するものとして最も文意に合うものは，(B) undoubtedly「疑いもなく」である。　　　　　　　　　　[語彙]<br><br>firm [fə:rm] 会社；企業<br>in terms of 〜　〜の点から見ると<br>responsively [rispánsivli] すぐに応じて<br>mutually [mjú:tʃuəli] 相互に<br>compassionately [kəmpǽʃənitli] 情け深く |
| **112**<br>Greater Vancouver, particularly during times of economic slowdowns, is ------- many Canadian IT companies locate their offices.<br><br>(A) how<br>(B) why<br>(C) when<br>(D) where<br><br>グレーターバンクーバーは，特に経済の減速時に，多くのカナダの IT 企業がオフィスを置く場所である。 | **正解 (D)**<br>文構造は，Greater Vancouver が主語で is が述語動詞，空所以下が補語である。主語が場所を表す語句であることから，空所には関係副詞の where が適切。先行詞 the place を含む用法である。　　　[関係副詞]<br><br>slowdown [slóudàun] 減速<br>locate [lóukeit] (店など)を構える |
| **113**<br>Mr. Anwar's design team was ------- on time with all its projects, causing the company to rely on it a great deal.<br><br>(A) invariable<br>(B) invariant<br>(C) invariably<br>(D) invariability<br><br>Anwar さんのデザインチームはすべてのプロジェクトにおいて必ず期限を守ったので，結果としてその会社は彼のチームを大いに頼りにした。 | **正解 (C)**<br>空所の直前に be 動詞の過去形 was があり，直後には副詞句として働く on time「時間通りに」がある。よって，副詞を修飾する副詞 (C) invariably「必ず」がふさわしい。　　[品詞]<br><br>rely on 〜　〜を頼りにする<br>a great deal 大いに<br>invariable [invέəriəbl] 不変の<br>invariant [invέəriənt] 変化しない<br>invariability [invὲəriəbíləti] 不変性 |
| **114**<br>Trainor Inc. maintains a competitive bonus system ------- order to motivate staff in all of its departments.<br><br>(A) in<br>(B) by<br>(C) from<br>(D) at<br><br>Trainor 社はすべての部署のスタッフにやる気を起こさせるために，他社に負けないボーナス制度を維持している。 | **正解 (A)**<br>in order to do で「〜するために」という意味である。よって，正解は (A)。　　　[語彙]<br><br>maintain [meintéin] 〜を維持する<br>competitive [kəmpétətiv] 他に負けない<br>motivate [móutəvèit] 〜にやる気を起こさせる |
| **115**<br>Five cents of every dollar ------- on goods in the Tyler Department Store goes toward local charities that help children.<br><br>(A) credited<br>(B) cashed<br>(C) paid<br>(D) spent<br><br>Tyler 百貨店の商品に支払われる 1 ドルにつき 5 セントが，子供を援助する地域の慈善事業に使われる。 | **正解 (D)**<br>選択肢はすべて動詞の過去分詞で，分詞の後置修飾である。(B) cashed は「現金に換えられた」の意味で文意に合わない。「〜の代金を払う」の意味では，pay には前置詞 for が必要なので (C) も不適切。(D) が正解で，spend A on B「A (金額)を B に費やす」の A が前に出て A spent on B「B に費やされる A (金額)」という構造。[語彙]<br><br>goods [gudz] 商品<br>charity [tʃǽrəti] 慈善事業<br>credit [krédit] 〜に信用貸しをする |

## 問題文と訳

### 116
Mr. M'Krumah is in ------- of the company's Lagos branch, operating all its major business activities in West Africa.

(A) responsibility
(B) touch
(C) charge
(D) engaged

M'Krumah さんは，その会社のラゴス支店の責任者で，西アフリカにおける主要な営業活動のすべてを管理している。

### 117
------- a sensation among teenagers, the *Jumping Box* online game rapidly became popular throughout East Asia.

(A) Creates
(B) Creating
(C) Created
(D) Create

10 代の少年少女の間でセンセーションを巻き起こしたので，*Jumping Box* オンラインゲームは急速に東アジア中で人気が高まった。

### 118
Director Kim is an ------- fine scholar in the field of robotics, as well as being a good businessman.

(A) intrusively
(B) oppositely
(C) exceptionally
(D) affordably

Kim 部長は優秀なビジネスマンであるだけでなく，ロボット工学分野で非常に優秀な学者である。

### 119
Real estate prices in Hanoi are expected to rise by as much as 15% ------- the local business boom continues.

(A) and
(B) but
(C) as
(D) or

ハノイの不動産価格は，地元産業の高度成長が続くにつれて，15％も上がると予想されている。

### 120
Mr. Armatelli feels that ------- is certainly the best way to resolve any problems among co-workers.

(A) talking
(B) has talked
(C) talks
(D) will talk

Armatelli さんは，話し合うことが間違いなく同僚間のどんな問題も解決する最良の方法だと感じている。

## 正解と解説

### 116
**正解 (C)**

in charge of ~ で「~を管理して，~を任されて」の意味。このイディオムを完成するために，空所には (C) charge を入れればよい。(B) は be in touch with ~ で「~と連絡を取る」，(D) は be engaged in ~ で「~に従事している」。　語彙

responsibility [rispὰnsəbíləti] 責任

### 117
**正解 (B)**

文頭に来る動詞を選んで「分詞構文」を完成させる問題。分詞構文の意味上の主語が，能動「~している」か，受け身「~された」かを判断しよう。主語は game で，game が「~を巻き起こしている」と能動の意味なので，正解は (B) Creating。　分詞構文

teenager [tíːnèidʒər] 10 代の少年少女
rapidly [rǽpidli] 急速に
throughout [θruː(ː)áut] ~の至る所に

### 118
**正解 (C)**

空所の後の形容詞 fine「優秀な」を強めて修飾するものとして，副詞の (C) exceptionally「並外れて，非常に」が最もふさわしい。よって，正解は (C)。　語彙

scholar [skάlər] 学者
intrusively [intrúːsivli] 出しゃばって
oppositely [άpəzitli] 反対の位置に
affordably [əfɔ́ːrdəbli] 購入しやすく

### 119
**正解 (C)**

空所の前後はいずれも〈主語＋動詞〉を含む文なので，空所には接続詞が入る。文意より「~につれて」の意味を表す (C) as が正解。　接続詞

real estate 不動産
boom [buːm] 急成長

### 120
**正解 (A)**

空所には that が導く名詞節の主語が入る。直後に be 動詞の is があることから，空所は名詞（相当語句）でなければならない。よって，名詞として働く動名詞の (A) talking が正解である。　動名詞

resolve [rizάlv] ~を解決する

| 問題文と訳 | 正解と解説 |
|---|---|
| **121**<br>Mr. Larson used to work for the Imperial Builders, but he found a new job with Central Constructions three years -------.<br><br>(A) else<br>(B) soon<br>(C) ago<br>(D) already<br><br>Larson さんは以前は Imperial 建設に勤めていたが，3 年前に Central 建設に転職した。 | **正解 (C)**<br>文末に入る副詞を選ぶ問題。but 以下は「3 年前に新しい仕事を見つけた」という文意がふさわしいので，(C) が正解。three years を見ただけで ago が選べるだろう。　語彙 |
| **122**<br>The marketing department came up with an excellent plan, but relied on local salespeople for proper ------- of it.<br><br>(A) execute<br>(B) execution<br>(C) executed<br>(D) executively<br><br>マーケティング部は素晴らしい企画を考え出したが，その適切な実行については現地の営業員に頼っていた。 | **正解 (B)**<br>空所は，前置詞 for 以下の名詞相当語句の一部であるが，形容詞 proper と前置詞 of に挟まれているので，名詞の (B) execution「実行」を入れるのがふさわしい。　品詞<br><br>come up with ～　～を考え出す<br>rely on ～　～に依存する<br>execute [éksəkjùːt] ～を実行する<br>executively [igzékjətivli] 実施上は |
| **123**<br>Passengers must show the boarding passes ------- were given to them in the ticketing area prior to boarding the aircraft.<br><br>(A) what<br>(B) whose<br>(C) that<br>(D) who<br><br>乗客は，飛行機への搭乗前に発券エリアで渡された搭乗券を見せなくてはならない。 | **正解 (C)**<br>適切な関係代名詞を選ぶ問題。空所の前の先行詞は「物」である boarding passes であり，後に were given という受動態が来ているので，主格である (C) that が正解。　関係代名詞<br><br>passenger [pǽsəndʒər] 乗客<br>boarding pass 搭乗券<br>prior to ～　～に先立って |
| **124**<br>Umagi Corporation's new steel ------- its shape and strength even when exposed to very high temperatures or pressures.<br><br>(A) sustenance<br>(B) sustains<br>(C) sustainably<br>(D) sustainable<br><br>Umagi 社の新しい鋼鉄は，非常に高い温度や圧力にさらされたときでさえ，その形状と強さを維持する。 | **正解 (B)**<br>空所の前の steel までが主語で，空所の後の its shape and strength は目的語である。よって，空所には述語動詞が入るのがふさわしい。(B) sustains が正解。　品詞<br><br>expose A to B　A を B にさらす<br>sustenance [sʌ́stənəns] 維持<br>sustain [səstéin] ～を維持する<br>sustainably [səstéinəbli] 維持できて<br>sustainable [səstéinəbl] 維持できる |
| **125**<br>This MP3 player is guaranteed against breakdowns caused by the manufacturer's ------- during shipping.<br><br>(A) warranty<br>(B) mindset<br>(C) default<br>(D) negligence<br><br>この MP3 プレイヤーは，輸送中メーカーの不注意によって引き起こされた故障に対して保証されている。 | **正解 (D)**<br>「メーカーの不注意によって引き起こされた故障」と考えるのが最も文意に合うので，正解は (D) negligence。　語彙<br><br>be guaranteed against ～　～に対して保証されている<br>breakdown [bréikdàun] 破損，故障<br>warranty [wɔ́ːrənti] 保証<br>mindset [máindsèt] 考え方，意見<br>default [difɔ́ːlt]（約束などの）不履行 |

| 問題文と訳 | 正解と解説 |
|---|---|

## 126

Mr. Nagy always brought a keen ------- perspective to trends in global manufacturing.

(A) analysis
(B) analyze
(C) analytic
(D) analytically

Nagy さんは，世界的な製造業における傾向に，いつも鋭い分析的な見通しを示した。

**正解 (C)**

空所の直前には冠詞 a と形容詞 keen があり，空所の直後には名詞 perspective「見通し；観点」がある。よって，名詞 perspective を修飾する形容詞がもう 1 つ入るとわかる。正解は (C) analytic「分析的な」。 品詞

keen [kiːn] 鋭い
analysis [ənǽləsis] 分析
analyze [ǽnəlàiz] 〜を分析する
analytically [ænəlítikəli] 分析的に

## 127

After successfully producing 20,000 units last year, the Rabo Corporation's Brazil subsidiary was able ------- on its own as a manufacturer.

(A) had stood
(B) to stand
(C) standing
(D) stood

昨年 2 万ユニットを無事に生産した後，Rabo 社のブラジル子会社は製造会社として独立することができた。

**正解 (B)**

be able to do で「〜することができる」という意味なので，空所には to 不定詞を入れるのがふさわしい。よって，正解は (B) to stand。 不定詞

subsidiary [səbsídièri] 子会社
stand on *one's* own 自立する

## 128

Connor Furniture Inc. has been selling top brands for over 21 ------- years in major cities across the country.

(A) straight
(B) direct
(C) connected
(D) totaled

Connor 家具会社は，全国の主要な都市で 21 年以上連続して一流のブランドを売ってきた。

**正解 (A)**

空所の直前に数字の 21，直後に years があるので，間に (A) の straight「連続した」を入れて for 21 straight years とすると「21 年間連続して」という意味になる。 語彙

direct [dirékt] 真っすぐな
connected [kənéktid] 接続した
totaled [tóutld] 合計した

## 129

Passengers ------- internationally must go to Terminal D, which houses all gates for overseas flights.

(A) travel
(B) to travel
(C) traveling
(D) traveled

国外へ渡航する乗客は，ターミナル D に行かなければならない。そこには国際線のためのすべてのゲートがある。

**正解 (C)**

空所の直前の名詞 Passengers を修飾する語として現在分詞の traveling が正解にふさわしい。文意より「乗客」は「渡航している」と能動の意味なので，受け身の意味を表す過去分詞 traveled は不適。不定詞の to travel も，「渡航する（ための）乗客」では意味を成さない。 現在分詞

internationally [ìintərnǽʃnəli] 国際的に
house [hauz] 〜を備える
overseas flight 国際線

## 130

Packages that ------- from Los Angeles may take up to five days to arrive in Cairo using Interprize Express Service.

(A) original
(B) originate
(C) originally
(D) originating

ロサンゼルスを出発した小包は，Interprize 速達サービスを利用してカイロに着くのに最長で 5 日かかる可能性がある。

**正解 (B)**

関係代名詞 that の直後に空所がある。Los Angeles までが文全体の主語で，この関係詞節を完成させるためには動詞が必要である。(B) originate には「（列車やバスが）始発する」という意味があり，これが正解。 品詞

up to 〜 （最高）〜まで
original [ərídʒənl] もともとの
originally [ərídʒənəli] 初めは

# PART 6

## 問題文

Questions 131-134 refer to the following letter.

January 14
Marie-Therese Deneuve
34 Rue de la Croce
Marseilles

Dear Ms. Deneuve,

We are pleased to present you with a business loan of up to €250,000. We are offering this ------- because you are one of our most valued customers with an excellent credit history.
**131.**

-------. You only have to pay an interest rate of 6.7%. This is a rate you are unlikely to find
**132.**
------- else. This special rate is available ------- to a selected group of valuable customers such
**133.**                                      **134.**
as yourself. If you would like to discuss this offer further, please call me at 008-7745-3009 ext. 19.

Sincerely,

Xavier Bayer
Senior Customer Service Representative
Bank of West Marseilles
The Bank to France, the Bank to Europe, the Bank to the World

---

**131.** (A) requirement
(B) inquiry
(C) request
(D) opportunity

**132.** (A) Your loan application is incomplete as it is.
(B) We would also like to inform you of another positive aspect.
(C) We cannot help you any further at this point.
(D) Interest rates are not favorable in today's economy.

**133.** (A) somewhere
(B) anywhere
(C) everywhere
(D) nowhere

**134.** (A) according
(B) close
(C) thanks
(D) only

## 問題文の訳

問題 131-134 は次の手紙に関するものです。

1月14日
Marie-Therese Deneuve
34 Rue de la Croce
Marseille

Deneuve 様

お客様に25万ユーロまでのビジネスローンをご提示できてうれしく思います。お客様は素晴らしいクレジット歴を持つ当行にとって最も大切な顧客のお1人なので,この機会をご提供いたしております。

また,お客様にもう1つ良い点をお知らせします。利率を6.7%しかお支払いいただかなくてよいのです。これは他のどこでも見つけることのできない利率です。この特別金利はお客様のような選り抜きの大切な顧客の方々にのみご利用いただけます。もしこの提供について詳しくお話しになりたいなら,私まで008-7745-3009 内線番号19にお電話ください。

敬具
Xavier Bayer
シニア・カスタマーサービス担当者
West Marseilles 銀行
フランスのための銀行,ヨーロッパのための銀行,世界のための銀行

---

## 正解と解説

### 131
**正解 (D)**

語彙の問題。空所の前にある offer「~を提供する」という動詞との組み合わせを考える。(A) requirement「要求」,(B) inquiry「問い合わせ」,(C) request「依頼」はいずれも合わない。「機会を提供する」という意味になる (D) opportunity が正解にふさわしい。

### 132
**正解 (B)**

文挿入問題。第1段落の目的は25万ユーロまでのビジネスローンを提示することで,第2段落の目的はローンの低利率を提示すること。よって,読み手である顧客にとって喜ばしい内容が続くので,(B) を入れると文脈に合う。(B) 以外は,すべて否定的な内容である。
(A) 「お客様のローン申請書は今のままでは不完全です」
(B) 「また,お客様にもう1つ良い点をお知らせします」
(C) 「当行は現時点ではこれ以上お客様のお役に立てません」
(D) 「利率は今日の経済において幸先よくありません」

### 133
**正解 (B)**

-where の形をした副詞の問題。主語の This は直前の an interest rate of 6.7% を指す。この利率はとても低いことから,「他では見つけられない」という文意にするのが適切。否定語の unlikely に注意して,(B) anywhere が正解。you are likely to find ならば,(D) の nowhere が入る。

### 134
**正解 (D)**

available to ~ は「~に利用可能な」という意味で,空所には後ろの to 以下の「お客様のような選び抜かれた大切な顧客」を修飾する語として only「~のみ」が適切。他の選択肢は仮に後ろの to と結び付けば according to ~「~によると」,close to ~「~と近い」,thanks to ~「~のおかげで」という意味だが,どれも文意に合わない。

## Vocabulary

☐ valued [vǽlju(:)d] 形 貴重な
☐ excellent [éksələnt] 形 素晴らしい
☐ credit history 信用 [クレジット] 履歴
☐ interest rate 利率

## 問題文

Questions 135-138 refer to the following e-mail.

---

To: Michael Chen <michael.chen@goldcrestbanking.ca>
From: Orianne Durand <orianne.Durand@tzdesign.com>
Subject: Update
Date: Wednesday, February 23

Dear Mr. Chen,

We ------- the revised visuals for the design of your company's new gym shoe, *Street Tiger*.
　　135.
Please see the PDF files attached ------- the composition of the materials and the internal structure.
　　　　　　　　　　　　　　　　　　136.
Our apologies for the extra time necessary to complete the revisions.

Our art directors are still ------- your suggestions from last week's meeting into the logo you want as
　　　　　　　　　　　　　　137.
well. -------.
　　138.

Thanks again for choosing us to create this very important new product for you.

Sincerely,

Orianne Durand
Chief Designer
TZ Design Ltd.

---

**135.** (A) will complete
(B) would have completed
(C) have completed
(D) have been completing

**136.** (A) show
(B) shows
(C) shown
(D) showing

**137.** (A) integrating
(B) articulating
(C) evaluating
(D) asserting

**138.** (A) Please make sure to keep it in a safe place.
(B) We hope to show you the selections during Monday's presentation.
(C) You might already have noticed some necessary changes.
(D) Apart from that, they were considered acceptable.

---

## 問題文の訳

問題 135-138 は次の E メールに関するものです。

宛先：Michael Chen <michael.chen@goldcrestbanking.ca>
送信者：Orianne Durand <orianne.Durand@tzdesign.com>
件名：最新情報
日付：2月23日水曜日

Chen 様

御社の新しい運動靴 *Street Tiger* のデザインの修正画像が完成しました。その素材構成と内部構造を示している添付の PDF ファイルをご覧ください。修正版を完成させるのに必要な余分な時間がかかってしまい申し訳ありませんでした。

なお、わが社のアートディレクターは先週のミーティングでのご提案の内容をまとめ、別途ご依頼のロゴに組み込んでいます。月曜のプレゼンで選り抜きのものをご披露したいと思っています。

この大変重要な新製品を御社のために作成することに、わが社をお選びいただきましたことを重ねて御礼申し上げます。

敬具
Orianne Durand
チーフデザイナー
TZ デザイン社

---

## 正解と解説

### 135
**正解 (C)**

時制を問う問題。後の文で「ファイルを添付している」と述べていることからデザインは「すでに完成した」と考えるのが自然。よって、現在完了形の (C) have completed が正解。

### 136
**正解 (D)**

適切な動詞の形を問う問題。Please see the PDF files attached「添付の PDF ファイルをご覧ください」までで英文が成り立っており、空所以下が前の the PDF files attached を修飾する構造。「その素材構成と内部構造を示している添付の PDF ファイル」という文意が適切なので、現在分詞の (D) showing が正解。

### 137
**正解 (A)**

語彙の問題。文中の into に注目すること。integrate A into B で「A を B にまとめる、A をまとめて B にする」という意味。ここでは「suggestions (提案) をまとめて logo (ロゴ) にする」ということ。

articulate [ɑːrtíkjəlèit] ～をはっきり述べる
evaluate [ivǽljuèit] ～を評価する
assert [əsə́ːrt] ～を断言する；～を強く主張する

### 138
**正解 (B)**

文挿入問題。直前の内容は「先週のミーティングでのご提案の内容をまとめ、別途ご依頼のロゴに組み込んでいます」という相手への報告で、この続きとしてふさわしいのは (B)。selections はここではロゴのことである。
(A)「必ず安全な場所にそれを保管してください」
(B)「月曜のプレゼンで選り抜きのものを御社に披露したいと思っています」
(C)「御社はすでにいくつかの必要な変更点にお気づきかもしれません」
(D)「その他、それらは許容できるものと見なされました」

## Vocabulary

- revised [riváizd] 形 修正された
- visual [víʒuəl] 名 (写真やデザインなどの)宣伝用ディスプレー資料
- attached [ətǽtʃt] 形 添付の
- composition [kɑ̀mpəzíʃən] 名 構成
- material [mətíəriəl] 名 素材、材料
- internal structure 内部構造
- create [kri(ː)éit] 動 ～を作る

## 問題文

Questions 139-142 refer to the following article.

According to the latest research, more and more employees are suffering from stress in the workplace. -------. In one study, 43% of employees ------- as being under heavy stress had weak concentration and poor work performance. Corporations operating in highly competitive environments commonly prefer to extend current employee work hours ------- hire new staff, but such long hours invariably lower employee productivity.
139.　　　　　　　　　　　　140.
141.

Women combining motherhood with careers were found to be at particular risk; -------, reports from workplaces imply that working mothers may experience exhaustion from the responsibility of balancing both homes and jobs. Experts recommend corporations expand the number of daycare centers to reduce their burdens.
142.

139. (A) Reports suggest it is a serious problem among all levels of workers.
(B) It has become of great importance to a successful job search.
(C) Both men and women have been found to be unaffected by such difficulties.
(D) Research shows that many employees are confused by this concept.

140. (A) are described
(B) will describe
(C) described
(D) to describe

141. (A) more than
(B) less than
(C) than not
(D) rather than

142. (A) specific
(B) specifically
(C) specify
(D) specification

## 正解と解説

### 139
**正解 (A)**

文挿入問題。前文は「最新の研究によると職場でストレスに苦しむ会社員が増えている」という内容で，空所の後もストレスに関する研究結果についての内容が続く。空所に適切なのは (A) で，it は前文の内容を指す。
(A)「報告によると，これはあらゆる地位の労働者の間で深刻な問題である」
(B)「これは就職活動を成功させることにおいて非常に重要なものとなっている」
(C)「男女ともにこのような困難によって影響を受けないことがわかっている」
(D)「研究によると，多くの会社員がこの概念に混乱している」

### 140
**正解 (C)**

分詞の後置修飾の問題。空所から stress までが前の名詞 employees を修飾する構造で，受け身の意味となる過去分詞 (C) described が正解。文の述語動詞として had があるので，(A) や (B) は選べない。

### 141
**正解 (D)**

前後の内容を適切につなぐ語句を問う問題。主語は Corporations (operating in highly competitive environments) で，動詞は (commonly) prefer。(D) が正解で，prefer A rather than B で「B よりむしろ A を好む」という意味。to extend current employee work hours と (to) hire new staff が，それぞれ A と B に当たる。

### 142
**正解 (B)**

品詞の問題。空所の後にカンマがあり，後には完全な文が続くことから，空所には文全体を修飾する副詞がふさわしい。よって，(B) specifically が適切。

## 問題文の訳

問題 139-142 は次の記事に関するものです。

最新の研究によると，ますます多くの会社員たちが職場のストレスに苦しんでいる。報告によると，これはあらゆる地位の労働者の間で深刻な問題である。ある研究では，強いストレス下にあると言われている会社員の 43% は，集中力が低く仕事の遂行能力が不十分であった。非常に競争の激しい環境下で操業する会社は，一般的に新しいスタッフを雇うよりも現社員の労働時間を延長したがるが，そのような長時間労働は必ず社員の生産性を低下させる。

母親であることと就業とを兼ねている女性は特別の危険にさらされていることが判明した。特に，職場からの報告は，働く母親は家庭と仕事の両方のバランスを取る責任から疲労困憊する可能性があることをほのめかしている。専門家は，企業が母親たちの負担を減らすために託児所の数を増やすことを提言している。

## Vocabulary

- according to 〜　〜によれば
- suffer from 〜　〜に苦しむ
- concentration [kùnsentréiʃən] 名 集中力
- environment [inváiərənmənt] 名 環境
- extend [iksténd] 動 〜を延長する
- invariably [invéəriəbli] 副 必ず
- productivity [pròudʌktívəti] 名 生産性
- imply [implái] 動 〜を示唆する
- exhaustion [igzɔ́:stʃən] 名 疲労困憊
- recommend [rèkəménd] 動 (〜すべきだと)提言する
- burden [bə́:rdn] 名 負担

## 問題文

Questions 143-146 refer to the following notice.

---

**Travel and Weather Update**
**EuroLine Bus Corporation**

*************** Update for the Eastern European Region ***************

Bus service on the Prague to Sofia route is currently experiencing severe delays due to sudden and heavy rainstorms. The ------- **143.** flooding has affected many places. Roads in such areas have become impassable because of these high waters, ------- **144.** have closed them to vehicle travel of any kind.

Travelers are advised to check the main terminal board for the latest information on arrival and departure times. Passengers preparing ------- **145.** on any buses at the gates are advised to wait. Buses there will leave only when the weather clears enough for them to do so.

-------. **146.**

---

143. (A) innocuous
 (B) anticipated
 (C) interrupted
 (D) consequent

144. (A) what
 (B) that
 (C) which
 (D) those

145. (A) departing
 (B) will depart
 (C) to depart
 (D) departed

146. (A) Finally, the scheduled departure times have now been posted.
 (B) Please continue to watch this board for further updates.
 (C) Thank you to all who have participated in our bus tour.
 (D) We hope you will continue to enjoy the weather during your trip.

## 問題文の訳

問題 143-146 は次のお知らせに関するものです。

旅と天気の最新情報
EuroLine バス株式会社

*************** 東ヨーロッパ地域の最新情報 ***************

プラハからソフィア行き路線のバスの運行は，現在，突然の激しい暴風雨により大幅な遅れを出しています。その結果として生じた洪水が多くの場所に被害を与えました。そうした地域の道路はこの洪水のため通行不能になり，いかなる種類の車両の通行に対しても道路が閉鎖されました。

旅行者の方は到着と出発時間の最新情報をメインターミナルの標示板で確認されることをお勧めします。いかなるバスであれ，乗車ゲートで出発しようと準備されている乗客の皆様にはお待ちいただくことをお勧めします。そちらのバスは出発に十分なほど天候が晴れたときにのみ出発いたします。

引き続きこの掲示板でさらなる最新情報をご確認ください。

## 正解と解説

### 143

**正解 (D)**

語彙の問題。空所には flooding「洪水」を修飾する形容詞が入る。前文は暴風雨が原因でバスが遅れているという内容である。(D) の consequent は「結果として生じる [発生する，起こる]」という意味で，これを入れると「暴風雨の結果として生じた洪水が～被害を与えた」となり，文意が通る。

innocuous [inάkjuəs] 無害の
anticipated [æntísəpèitid] 期待された
interrupted [ìntərʌ́ptid] 遮られた

### 144

**正解 (C)**

関係代名詞を問う問題。カンマの後にあることから非制限用法とわかるので，この用法では使われない that は除外する。先行詞について説明を付け加える非制限用法の (C) which が正解。この which は直前の these high waters を受けて，「そして，これらの洪水が道路を閉鎖した」となる。

### 145

**正解 (C)**

動詞の用法を問う問題。直前の動詞 prepare は to 不定詞を伴って，prepare to do「～する準備をする」という意味。(A) の動名詞，(D) の過去分詞は，preparing の後に置くことはできない。主語の Passengers に対する文の述語動詞は are advised なので，(B) の形も不適切である。

### 146

**正解 (B)**

文挿入問題。本文の最後に入る1文を選ぶパターン。文章の主旨が「悪天候によるバスの遅延」とわかれば，最後の締めとして最新情報を確認するよう促す (B) が適切だと判断できるだろう。
(A)「最後に，出発の予定時刻が今，掲示されました」
(B)「引き続きこの掲示板でさらなる最新情報をご確認ください」
(C)「弊社のバスツアーにご参加いただいた皆様にお礼を申し上げます」
(D)「ご旅行中，引き続き好天に恵まれることを願っております」

## Vocabulary

- update [ʌ́pdèit] 名 最新情報
- currently [kə́:rəntli] 副 目下
- severe [səvíər] 形 ひどい
- sudden [sʌ́dn] 形 突然の
- rainstorm [réinstɔ̀:rm] 名 暴風雨
- affect [əfékt] 動 ～に悪影響を及ぼす
- impassable [impǽsəbl] 形 通れない
- arrival [əráivəl] 名 到着
- departure [dipά:rtʃər] 名 出発

# PART 7

## 問題文

Questions 147-148 refer to the following table.

| **Travel information for The Irish Princess** | | | | |
|---|---|---|---|---|
| **Destinations (from Cork)** | **Gibraltar** | **Tenerife** | **Antigua** | **Aruba** |
| Estimated arrival date | 17th | 20th | 22nd | 24th |
| Present Travel Status | Arrival on Schedule | Updating | Updating | Two days late |
| Medical Certificate required | No | Yes | No | No |
| Visa Requirements | Not required for EU residents | Necessary for stays over 30 days | See Passenger Service for Updates | Not required for EU residents |

IRELAND-CARIBBEAN CRUISE LINES INC.

## 問題文の訳

問題 147-148 は次の表に関するものです。

| Irish Princess 号の運航情報 | | | | |
|---|---|---|---|---|
| 目的地（コークから） | ジブラルタル | テネリフェ島 | アンティグア島 | アルバ島 |
| 予定到着日 | 17日 | 20日 | 22日 | 24日 |
| 現在の運航状況 | 予定通りに到着 | 最新情報更新中 | 最新情報更新中 | 2日遅れ |
| 医療証明書の必要 | なし | あり | なし | なし |
| ビザの必要 | EU居住者は必要なし | 30日を超えて滞在する場合は必要 | 最新情報は乗客サービスを参照 | EU居住者は必要なし |

アイルランドーカリブ海 Cruise Lines 社

## Vocabulary

- □ estimated [éstəmèitid] 形 推定された；見積もられた  □ travel status 運航状況  □ medical certificate 医療証明書；診断書
- □ requirement [rikwáiərmənt] 名 必要条件  □ resident [rézədənt] 名 居住者

---

### 設問

**147**

On what date will passengers on The Irish Princess most likely arrive in Aruba?

(A) 20th
(B) 22nd
(C) 24th
(D) 26th

### 設問の訳

Irish Princess 号の乗客は何日にアルバ島に到着すると考えられますか。

(A) 20日
(B) 22日
(C) 24日
(D) 26日

### 正解と解説

**正解 (D)**

表を見ると、予定到着日は24日だが、運航状況は2日遅れとなっているので、(D) が正解。このように表問題は、引っ掛け問題になっていないかどうか、ざっとでよいから細部にも目を通すことが大切。

passenger [pǽsəndʒər] 乗客

---

**148**

Which destination requires a visa for stays over a month?

(A) Gibraltar
(B) Tenerife
(C) Antigua
(D) Aruba

1か月以上の滞在にビザが必要なのはどの目的地ですか。

(A) ジブラルタル
(B) テネリフェ島
(C) アンティグア島
(D) アルバ島

**正解 (B)**

表の「ビザの必要」の欄を確認すると、テネリフェ島に30日（つまり、1か月）を超えて滞在する場合はビザが必要であることがわかる。よって (B) が正解。

| 問題文 | 問題文の訳 |
|---|---|

Questions 149-150 refer to the following text message chain.

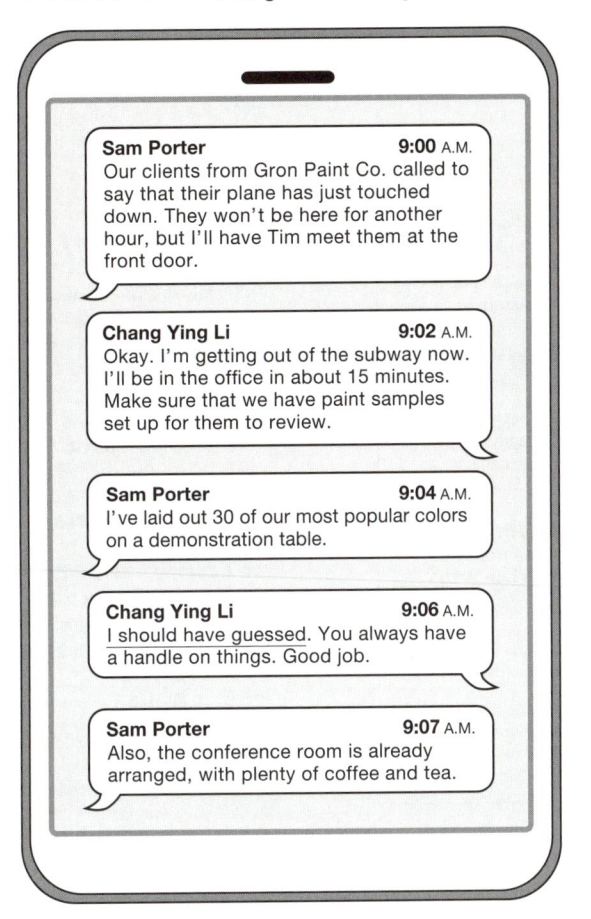

**Sam Porter** — 9:00 A.M.
Our clients from Gron Paint Co. called to say that their plane has just touched down. They won't be here for another hour, but I'll have Tim meet them at the front door.

**Chang Ying Li** — 9:02 A.M.
Okay. I'm getting out of the subway now. I'll be in the office in about 15 minutes. Make sure that we have paint samples set up for them to review.

**Sam Porter** — 9:04 A.M.
I've laid out 30 of our most popular colors on a demonstration table.

**Chang Ying Li** — 9:06 A.M.
I should have guessed. You always have a handle on things. Good job.

**Sam Porter** — 9:07 A.M.
Also, the conference room is already arranged, with plenty of coffee and tea.

---

問題149-150は次のテキストメッセージのやり取りに関するものです。

**Sam Porter** 午前9時
Gron 塗料社のお客様から，乗っている飛行機が着陸したと電話がありました。彼らは，あと1時間はここに到着しませんが，Tim に玄関で出迎えてもらいます。

**Chang Ying Li** 午前9時2分
わかりました。今，地下鉄から出るところです。15分ぐらいで事務所に着きます。彼らに見てもらう塗料サンプルを間違いなく用意しておくように。

**Sam Porter** 午前9時4分
展示テーブルの上に当社の最も人気のある色を30並べてあります。

**Chang Ying Li** 午前9時6分
そんなことだろうと思いました。あなたはいつでも物事をしっかりと把握していますね。よくやったわ。

**Sam Porter** 午前9時7分
それに，会議室もすでに準備を整えて，コーヒーも紅茶も十分にあります。

---

## Vocabulary
- lay out 〜  〜を配列する，陳列する
- plenty of 〜  多くの〜

---

| 設問 | 設問の訳 | 正解と解説 |
|---|---|---|

### 149
At 9:06 A.M., what does Chang Ying Li mean when she writes, "I should have guessed"?

(A) Mr. Porter often anticipates needs.
(B) Mr. Porter must make a decision.
(C) Mr. Porter requires further advice.
(D) Mr. Porter usually follows instructions.

午前9時6分に，Chang Ying Li が書いている "I should have guessed" は，何を意味していますか。

(A) Porter さんはニーズを予測することが多い。
(B) Porter さんは決断しなければならない。
(C) Porter さんはさらなる助言を必要とする。
(D) Porter さんはたいてい指示に従う。

**正解 (A)**

〈should have ＋過去分詞〉は過去の後悔や非難を表し，I should have guessed. は直訳すると「私は推測すべきだった」。後に続く内容から，Porter さんはふだんから用意周到なので聞くまでもなかったと思っていることがわかる。よって，(A) が正解。

### 150
What does Mr. Porter indicate that he will do?

(A) Call some clients
(B) Have someone meet a group
(C) Wait by a door
(D) Get some samples tested

Porter さんは何をすると述べていますか。

(A) 数名の顧客に電話をする
(B) 誰かにあるグループを出迎えてもらう
(C) ドアのそばで待つ
(D) いくつかのサンプルを検査してもらう

**正解 (B)**

Porter さんがこれから行う行動は，冒頭の I'll have Tim meet them at the front door にある。them は飛行機で到着した顧客（Our clients）のこと。(B) が正解で，clients を選択肢では a group と表している。〈have ＋ O ＋原形不定詞〉「O に〜させる，してもらう」や (D) の〈get ＋ O ＋過去分詞〉「O を〜してもらう」という表現も確認しておこう。

| 問題文 | 問題文の訳 |
|---|---|

Questions 151-152 refer to the following memo.

## MEMORANDUM

To: All Staff
From: Sven Bjorg
Time: 10:45 A.M., Wednesday
RE: Christian Jonson

Dear Staff,

As you already know, Christian is leaving us this Friday after more than 30 years with the firm. Before taking his present job as head of Research, he worked in various areas, including Production—both here and in Oslo—Design, and IT. Over the last 18 months, he has been overseeing the highly successful Z45-t drug trials in Zurich.

He has been an invaluable member of Lind Technologies and I know he will be sorely missed by his colleagues and friends. However, I am happy to say he has agreed to stay with us for the next four weeks in a part-time capacity so we will benefit from his expertise.

I hope you will join me and the rest of the Board of Directors for a Bread and Cheese Reception in the Premier Boardroom this Friday afternoon from 4:30 P.M. to formally congratulate Christian on his retirement and wish him every success in his new life!

Thank you,

Sven Bjorg
Managing Director
Lind Technologies

問題 151-152 は次のメモに関するものです。

社内連絡
宛先：全社員
発信者：Sven Bjorg
時刻：水曜日午前 10:45
件名：Christian Jonson

社員の皆様

ご存じの通り，Christian さんはこの金曜日に 30 年以上属ごしたわが社を退社されます。彼は現在の研究部の部長職に就く前に，生産部（こことオスロ），デザイン部，IT 部を含むさまざまな分野で働きました。この 18 ヵ月は，彼はチューリッヒで，大いに成功した薬品 Z45-t の臨床試験を監督してきました。

彼は Lind テクノロジーズの非常に貴重なメンバーでしたので，彼の同僚や友人はひどく寂しがることでしょう。しかし，うれしいことに，彼がこれから 4 週間パートタイムの立場でわが社に残ることに同意してくれたので，我々は彼の専門知識から得るものがあると思います。

皆さんにはぜひ，この金曜日の午後 4 時 30 分から第 1 役員室で行われる簡単な食事会に私や他の役員と一緒に参加していただき，Christian さんの退職を正式に祝い新生活の成功を祈りましょう。

よろしくお願いします。
Sven Bjorg
常務取締役
Lind テクノロジーズ

## Vocabulary

- oversee [òuvərsíː] 動 〜を監督する
- drug trial 治験
- invaluable [invǽljuəbl] 形 非常に貴重な
- sorely [sɔ́ːrli] 副 ひどく
- colleague [káliːg] 名 同僚
- capacity [kəpǽsəti] 名 立場
- expertise [èkspərtíːz] 名 専門技術[知識]
- bread and cheese 簡単な食事
- formally [fɔ́ːrməli] 副 正式に
- congratulate A on B　A を B のことで祝う

| 設問 | 設問の訳 | 正解と解説 |
|---|---|---|

### 151

Which department is Mr. Jonson working in now?

(A) Research
(B) Production
(C) Design
(D) IT

Jonson さんは現在どの部門で働いていますか。

(A) 研究部
(B) 生産部
(C) デザイン部
(D) IT 部

**正解 (A)**

第 1 段落に his present job as head of Research とあり，現在は研究部の部長であることがわかるので，(A) Research が正解である。(B) Production, (C) Design, (D) IT は，彼が過去にいたことのある部署である。

### 152

What will Mr. Jonson do over the coming month?

(A) Contribute personal knowledge
(B) Conduct a job search
(C) Hire part-time workers
(D) Attend a board meeting

Jonson さんは翌月にわたって何をしますか。

(A) 個人的知識を提供する
(B) 求職する
(C) パートタイム労働者を雇う
(D) 役員会に出席する

**正解 (A)**

第 2 段落から，Jonson さんはこれから 4 週間会社に残り，専門知識を伝えると判断できるので，正解は (A)。(C) は，Jonson さんはパートタイムの立場で働くのだから不適切。

contribute [kəntríbju(ː)t] 〜を与える；〜を寄与する
board meeting 役員会

46

| 問題文 | 問題文の訳 |
|---|---|
| Questions 153-154 refer to the following label. | 問題 153-154 は次のラベルに関するものです。 |

**Installation Guide for your Sparkle White Dishwasher**
Wonder Electronics Co.

Install the appliance in accordance with the instructions below.

- Ensure that the appliance is not connected to any power outlets during installation.
- Do not remove any of the metal plates covering electronic components or wiring inside.
- Confirm the power supply of the residence is compatible with this appliance. If it is not, a converter will be necessary (sold separately).
- Install this appliance on a flat surface. Failure to do so could severely affect its stability.
- Connect the appliance's water tubes to the main pipes beneath your sink. Check the diagram on the back of the appliance for the correct procedure.
- Following installation, please dispose of the packaging in an environmentally friendly way.

For more information on this and other fine appliances made by Wonder Electronics Co., go to www.wonderelectronicsonthenet.com.

---

Sparkle White 食器洗浄機の設置ガイド
Wonder 電器会社

以下の指示に従って器具を設置してください。

- 器具を設置中にいかなる電気コンセントとも接続されていないことを確認してください。
- 内部の電子部品や配線系統を覆っているいかなる金属板も外さないでください。
- 居住地の電力供給がこの器具と互換性があることを確認してください。互換性がなければ，変換器が必要です（別売り）。
- この器具は平らな面に設置してください。そうしないと器具の安定性にひどく影響します。
- 器具の水管を流しの下の本管に接続してください。正しい手順については器具の背面の図を確認してください。
- 設置の後で，環境に優しい方法で包装物を処分してください。

これについての詳細と，Wonder 電器会社によって製造された他の素晴らしい器具の詳細については，www.wonderelectronicsonthenet.com をお訪ねください。

## Vocabulary

- installation [instəléiʃən] 名設置
- appliance [əpláiəns] 名器具
- in accordance with ~ ~に従って
- instruction [instrʌ́kʃən] 名指示
- ensure [inʃúər] 動~を確かにする
- power outlet 電気コンセント
- remove [rimúːv] 動~を取り除く
- component [kəmpóunənt] 名部品
- residence [rézədəns] 名居住地
- compatible [kəmpǽtəbl] 形互換性のある
- converter [kənvə́ːrtər] 名変換器
- stability [stəbíləti] 名安定性
- sink [siŋk] 名流し
- diagram [dáiəgræm] 名図表
- dispose of ~ ~を捨てる
- environmentally friendly 環境に優しい

| 設問 | 設問の訳 | 正解と解説 |
|---|---|---|
| **153**<br>What is NOT listed as an installation step for the appliance?<br>(A) Checking that the electrical supply is suitable<br>(B) Contacting company technicians<br>(C) Ensuring positioning is on a surface that is level<br>(D) Referring to graphs on the device | 器具の設置手順として挙げられていないことは何ですか。<br>(A) 電気供給が適切であることを確認すること<br>(B) 会社の技術者に連絡すること<br>(C) 水平な面に置かれていることを確認すること<br>(D) 装置の図表を参照すること | **正解 (B)**<br>(A), (C), (D) についてはそれぞれ 3 つ目から 5 つ目の項目に記載されている。(B) のみが文中に記載がないので，正解は (B)。<br><br>electrical supply 電気供給<br>refer to ~ ~を参照する<br>device [diváis] 装置 |
| **154**<br>What are users suggested to do?<br>(A) Test the appliance when installation is complete<br>(B) Replace the water pipes beneath the sink if necessary<br>(C) Disconnect the power supply when not in use<br>(D) Consider the environment when discarding items | ユーザーは何をするように勧められていますか。<br>(A) 設置が終了したら器具をテストする<br>(B) 必要なら流しの下の水管を交換する<br>(C) 使用しないときは電力供給を切る<br>(D) 品物を捨てるときは環境に配慮する | **正解 (D)**<br>最後の項目に please dispose of the packaging in an environmentally friendly way とあり，その言い換えである (D) が正解。<br><br>disconnect [dìskənékt] ~の電源を切る<br>discard [diskɑ́ːrd] ~を捨てる |

| 問題文 | 問題文の訳 |
|---|---|

Questions 155-157 refer to the following e-mail.

**E-mail**

From: Thiago de Silva <tdesilva@ozatmail.net>
To: Lucia Morais <lucia.morais@olivehotel.fr> Manager, Olive Hotel
Date: Wednesday, October 7
Subject: My room

Dear Ms. Morais,

Two weeks ago I e-mailed you to reserve accommodations, along with an online deposit to secure them. — [1] —. I was scheduled to check in tomorrow, so that I can attend the European Manufacturing Conference there in Lyons.

However, I have recently been accepted into a 1-week international management development course in Switzerland, so I would like to cancel my reservation. — [2] —. One of the original team members has had to drop out for health reasons and I have been offered his spot. — [3] —. I realize this is extremely short notice, but considering these circumstances I am hoping I can still get my money back.

Please e-mail as soon as possible to let me know. — [4] —. I hope to hear from you before then.

Kind regards,
Thiago de Silva

問題 155-157 は次の E メールに関するものです。

送信者：Thiago de Silva <tdesilva@ozatmail.net>
宛先：Lucia Morais <lucia.morais@olivehotel.fr>
　　　Olive ホテル マネージャー
日付：10 月 7 日水曜日
件名：私の部屋

Morais 様

2 週間前，私は部屋を確保するため，オンラインの保証金と一緒に部屋を予約する E メールをあなたに送りました。— [1] — そちらリヨンでのヨーロッパ製造者会議に出席できるように明日チェックインする予定でした。

しかし，先ほどスイスでの 1 週間の国際経営開発コースに受け入れられましたので，予約をキャンセルしたいと思います。— [2] — 本来のチームメンバーの 1 人が健康上の理由で抜けなければならなくなったので，穴埋めに私に声がかかったのです。— [3] — これがきわめて急な通知だと理解していますが，この事情を考慮されて，やはり返金していただけたらと願っております。

できるだけ早く E メールでお知らせください。今から 12 時間以内に私は研修プログラムに向けて出発しなければなりません。その前にご連絡いただけることを願っています。

敬具
Thiago de Silva

## Vocabulary

- accommodation [əkùmədéiʃən] 名（米国では通常複数形で）宿泊(設備)，（客）室
- along with ～ ～と一緒に
- deposit [dipázit] 名保証金，前金
- secure [sikjúər] 動～を確保する
- drop out 抜ける
- spot [spɑt] 名立場，職
- short notice 急な通知
- considering [kənsídəriŋ] 前～を考慮すれば
- circumstance [sə́ːrkəmstæns] 名（通常複数形で）周囲の事情

| 設 問 | 設問の訳 | 正解と解説 |
|---|---|---|

### 155
What is the purpose of the e-mail?

(A) To schedule an arrival
(B) To confirm a transaction
(C) To state a change
(D) To make a payment

E メールの目的は何ですか。

(A) 到着の予定を決めること
(B) 取引を確認すること
(C) 変更を知らせること
(D) 支払いをすること

**正解 (C)**

会議に出席するためにホテルの予約をしたのだが，行けなくなったのでキャンセルを申し出ている。つまり，変更を知らせているのだから，正解は (C)。

transaction [trænzǽkʃən] 取引
make a payment 支払いをする

### 156
What is a stated concern of Mr. de Silva?

(A) Room availability
(B) Hotel amenities
(C) Refund policy
(D) Cancellation deadlines

de Silva さんの懸念として述べられていることは何ですか。

(A) 部屋が利用できる可能性
(B) ホテルの設備
(C) 返金規定
(D) キャンセルの期限

**正解 (C)**

前日のキャンセルというきわめて急な通知のために，I am hoping I can still get my money back と言って「返金してもらえる」かどうか心配していることがわかる。よって，正解は (C)。

amenity [əménəti]（通常複数形で）娯楽設備
refund [ríːfʌnd] 払い戻し

### 157
In which of the positions marked [1], [2], [3] and [4] does the following sentence best belong?
"I have to leave for the training program within the next 12 hours."

(A) [1]
(B) [2]
(C) [3]
(D) [4]

[1]，[2]，[3]，[4] と記載された箇所のうち，次の文が入るのに最もふさわしいのはどれですか。

「今から 12 時間以内に私は研修プログラムに向けて出発しなければなりません」

(A) [1]
(B) [2]
(C) [3]
(D) [4]

**正解 (D)**

空所 [4] の直後の before then に着目。de Silva さんは相手に「その前に連絡が欲しい」と言っているが，前の Please e-mail as soon as possible to let me know. とうまくつながっていない。そこで挿入文を [4] に入れると，de Silva さんがこのメールを送った後 12 時間以内にメールが欲しいという意味になり，文脈がつながる。

| 問題文 | 問題文の訳 |
|---|---|

Questions 158-160 refer to the following instructions.

問題 158-160 は次の使用説明書に関するものです。

### How to use Eazee Breeze in your washing machine

Measure out Eazee Breeze Detergent concentrate (1 scoop per medium load of clothes) into a cup of lukewarm water and allow it to dissolve completely for about 5-10 minutes or until it can no longer be seen. Turn on your washing machine, choosing the shortest cycle and making sure your soiled clothes are fully immersed in water. Next, pour the Eazee Breeze mixture onto the clothes. Let clothes soak for at least 15 minutes to allow Eazee Breeze's fast-penetrating formula to work on grime, stains and odors.* Next, close the lid and continue the cycle. With Eazee Breeze you can say goodbye to scrubbing, cut down on wash time and save on electricity.

* Eazee Breeze is safe for all types of fabrics, but as a precaution do not soak dark clothes and whites together.

洗濯機での Eazee Breeze の使い方

Eazee Breeze 濃縮洗剤を量って（衣服の量が中くらいの場合計量スプーン1杯）1カップのぬるま湯に入れ、約5～10分間、あるいは、洗剤が見えなくなるまで完全に溶かしてください。洗濯機の電源を入れ、一番短い洗濯コースを選んだ後、汚れた衣服は必ず完全に水に浸しておいてください。次に、Eazee Breeze 混合液を衣服に注いでください。汚れ、染み、においに Eazee Breeze の即効浸透処方を効かせるため、少なくとも衣服を15分間浸したままにしてください*。次に、ふたを閉めて洗濯機を回してください。Eazee Breeze を使えば、ごしごしとこすることに別れを告げ、洗濯時間を減らして電気を節約できます。

*Eazee Breeze はあらゆる種類の生地に安全ですが、念のため色の濃い衣服と白物を一緒に浸さないでください。

## Vocabulary

- measure out ～ ～を量り分ける
- detergent [ditə́ːrdʒənt] 洗剤
- concentrate [kάnsəntrèit] 濃縮物
- scoop [skuːp] 一すくい（の量）
- load [loud] 1回分の量
- lukewarm [lùːkwɔ́ːrm] 生ぬるい
- dissolve [dizάlv] 溶ける
- soiled [sɔild] 汚れた
- immerse [imə́ːrs] ～を浸す
- soak [souk] （液体に）浸す, つける
- fast-penetrating [fæstpénətrèitiŋ] 速く浸透する
- formula [fɔ́ːrmjələ] 処方
- grime [graim] 汚れ
- stain [stein] 染み
- odor [óudər] におい, 臭気
- precaution [prikɔ́ːʃən] 予防措置

| 設問 | 設問の訳 | 正解と解説 |
|---|---|---|

### 158

What is the first step in using Eazee Breeze?

(A) Letting the substance melt
(B) Soaking clothes in water
(C) Letting water sit for 15 minutes
(D) Washing clothes for 5 minutes

Eazee Breeze を使用するときの第1段階は何ですか。

(A) 物質を溶かすこと
(B) 水に衣服を浸すこと
(C) 15分間水をそのままにしておくこと
(D) 5分間衣服を洗うこと

**正解 (A)**

第1文から、最初の段階でやるべきことは、規定の量の濃縮洗剤をぬるま湯で完全に溶かすことであるとわかる。よって、正解は (A)。

substance [sʌ́bstəns] 物質

### 159

The word "soiled" in line 5 is closest in meaning to

(A) rough
(B) shabby
(C) dirty
(D) old

5行目の "soiled" に最も意味が近いのは

(A) 粗い
(B) ぼろぼろの
(C) 汚れた
(D) 古い

**正解 (C)**

「～な衣服が水に浸るようにする」という文脈。soiled は「汚れた」という意味で、一番近い意味の語は (C) dirty。

### 160

What are people using Eazee Breeze advised NOT to do?

(A) Add extra concentrate
(B) Scrub items before washing
(C) Use together with other products
(D) Combine colors and whites

Eazee Breeze を使用する人々は何をしないように助言されていますか。

(A) 余分な濃縮物を加える
(B) 洗濯物を洗う前にごしごしこする
(C) 他の製品と一緒に使う
(D) 色物と白物を組み合わせる

**正解 (D)**

最後の * の部分を見ると、but as a precaution do not soak dark clothes and whites together とあり、色の濃い衣服と白物を混合しないように助言しているので、正解は (D)。(B) は「Eazee Breeze を使えば、ごしごし洗うことから解放される」とは書いてあるが、「こすってはいけない」とは書いていないので、不適切。

| 問題文 | 問題文の訳 |
|---|---|

Questions 161-164 refer to the following online chat discussion.

**Alvarez, Hector** [11:05 A.M.]
Hi everyone. I went over the last report on our sales. They are still too low. Give me your thoughts.

**Terao, Katsuya** [11:06 A.M.]
Our sales staff needs more training in how to approach customers—especially because many of them are new.

**Dean, Andrew** [11:10 A.M.]
We could focus more on online sales. With big upgrades to our Web site, we could generate more revenue online. Elisa Smythe has shown me several revenue projections that seem to indicate that.

**Alvarez, Hector** [11:13 A.M.]
I can see that. We're not getting the level of sales online that our competitors are.

**Rao, Manisha** [11:15 A.M.]
I have to caution you that changes to our Web site wouldn't be cheap. It would impact my teams the most, because we'd have to devote a lot of IT resources to that.

**Baldwin, Veronica** [11:17 A.M.]
We might also have to adjust our product line. Rick Jones has plenty of data showing that online shoppers and in-store shoppers sometimes have different preferences.

**Alvarez, Hector** [11:20 A.M.]
Nevertheless, I'd like to explore that option. Have Elisa share her information with Rick. Then I want both of them—and all of you—to join me in my office tomorrow at 2:00 P.M.

---

問題 161-164 は次のオンライン・チャットでの話し合いに関するものです。

Alvarez, Hector [ 午前 11 時 5 分 ]
こんにちは，皆さん。当社の売上高についての最終報告書を見直しました。まだ低すぎますね。考えを聞かせてください。

Terao, Katsuya [ 午前 11 時 6 分 ]
うちの販売員には接客の訓練がもっと必要だ。特に，彼らの多くが新人だからな。

Dean, Andrew [ 午前 11 時 10 分 ]
オンライン販売にもっと注力すればいい。当社のウェブサイトを大幅に刷新すれば，オンラインでもっと収益を生み出せる。Elisa Smythe が，それを示すような収益予測をいくつか見せてくれたよ。

Alvarez, Hector [ 午前 11 時 13 分 ]
それはわかります。競合他社のオンラインの売り上げのレベルに当社は及びません。

Rao, Manisha [ 午前 11 時 15 分 ]
ウェブサイトの変更は安くはないと忠告しておくわ。私のチームに最も影響するわね。多くの IT 資源をそれに割かなくてはいけなくなるから。

Baldwin, Veronica [ 午前 11 時 17 分 ]
製品ラインも調整しなければならないかもしれないわね。オンラインでの購入者と店舗での購入者とでは，ときどき嗜好が違うことを示すデータを Rick Jones がたくさん持っているわ。

Alvarez, Hector [ 午前 11 時 20 分 ]
いろいろありますが，その選択肢を検討してみたいと思います。Elisa に彼女の情報を Rick と共有するようにさせてください。それからその 2 人と，あなた方全員，明日午後 2 時に私のオフィスに集合してください。

## Vocabulary

- ☐ focus on ～　～に焦点を当てる
- ☐ generate [dʒénərèit] 動 ～を生み出す，引き起こす
- ☐ projection [prədʒékʃən] 名 予測
- ☐ caution [kɔ́ːʃən] 動 ～に警告する
- ☐ devote A to B　A を B に充てる
- ☐ preference [préfərəns] 名 嗜好
- ☐ nevertheless [nèvərðəlés] 副 それでもやはり

| 設 問 | 設問の訳 | 正解と解説 |
|---|---|---|

### 161

At 11:05 A.M., what does Mr. Alvarez mean when he writes, "Give me your thoughts"?

(A) He has to meet a deadline.
(B) He needs to update an account.
(C) He hopes to persuade a supervisor.
(D) He wants to gather some opinions.

午前 11 時 5 分に，Alvarez さんが書いている "Give me your thoughts" は，何を意味していますか。

(A) 締め切りに間に合わせなければならない。
(B) アカウントを更新しなければならない。
(C) 上司を説得したいと思っている。
(D) いくらか意見を集めたいと思っている。

**正解 (D)**

thought は think の名詞形で「考え，意見」という意味で，(D) が正解。この後，売り上げについて他の人たちが意見を述べていることからも判断できる。

meet a deadline 期限に間に合う
persuade [pərswéid] ～を説得する
supervisor [súːpərvàizər] 上司
gather [gǽðər] ～を集める

### 162

For what type of company do these people most likely work?

(A) A retail outlet
(B) A consulting agency
(C) A cyber security firm
(D) An event planning company

彼らはどんな業種の会社で働いていると考えられますか。

(A) 小売店
(B) コンサルティング会社
(C) サイバーセキュリティ会社
(D) イベント企画会社

**正解 (A)**

5 人の発言内容から，店舗やオンラインで商品を売っている会社と推測できる。Terao さんの Our sales staff needs more training in how to approach customers や Baldwin さんの online shoppers and in-store shoppers sometimes have different preferences という発言から，(A) が正解。

### 163

According to the discussion, whose department would be most affected by Mr. Dean's suggestion?

(A) Mr. Terao's department
(B) Ms. Rao's department
(C) Ms. Baldwin's department
(D) Mr. Jones' department

この話し合いによると，誰の部署が Dean さんの提案に最も影響を受けますか。

(A) Terao さんの部署
(B) Rao さんの部署
(C) Baldwin さんの部署
(D) Jones さんの部署

**正解 (B)**

オンライン販売に力を注ぐべきという Dean さんの提案に対し，Rao さんは I have to caution ～. It would impact my teams the most と言っている。impact は「～に影響を及ぼす」という意味で，最も影響を受けるのは Rao さんの部署とわかる。

### 164

What information will Ms. Smythe most likely share with Mr. Jones?

(A) Training methods
(B) Customer profiles
(C) Financial statistics
(D) Team organization

Smythe さんはどのような情報を Jones さんと共有すると考えられますか。

(A) 研修方法
(B) 顧客プロフィール
(C) 財務統計
(D) チーム構成

**正解 (C)**

Alvarez さんは最後に Have Elisa share her information with Rick. と指示している。Elisa Smythe さんはオンライン販売の収益予測を持っているので，Rick Jones さんに教える情報は，(C) の Financial statistics である。

Questions 165-168 refer to the following advertisement.

# Shanghai Romance

**MUSICAL LOVERS WILL LOVE THIS NEW PRODUCTION FROM THE RED BALLOON PERFORMANCE COMPANY.**

◆

**Chosen Best Musical by the Evening Star Monthly!**

Set in China in the 1920s, this lavish extravaganza will thrill and excite you!

Read what people are saying about it:

"I'm not much of a theatergoer, but I loved it!"
–Amy Winters, university student, Edinburgh

"If you want lighthearted entertainment for the whole family, this show is for you. We and the kids had a grand time seeing it."
–Frank Coswell, business owner, London

Don't miss out on Helen McTavish's performance as Eleanor Gantry. Also starring Richard Mace as Ewan Lockhart.

Tickets are available at the box office from May 18, with online sales starting the day before. Reserve yours anytime until June 20. Seats can otherwise be obtained at the door. The final performance will be on June 27 unless extended.

Discounted matinee performances are held at 2:00 P.M. every Saturday and Wednesday for £35-£40. These cannot be purchased online or used in combination with group discounts or season passes.
For more details, call the Box Office (9:30 A.M. – 11:00 P.M., Monday through Saturday), at 0845-671-1200 or visit us online at www.thamestheater.co.uk.

\* Refunds available up to half an hour before each performance begins, less fees.

| 設 問 | 設問の訳 | 正解と解説 |
|---|---|---|
| **165**<br>What is indicated about Shanghai Romance?<br><br>(A) It has an international cast.<br>(B) It is a show for adults.<br>(C) It is a long running show.<br>(D) It has received favorable reviews. | 上海ロマンスについて何が示されていますか。<br><br>(A) 国際的な出演者がいる。<br>(B) 大人向けのショーである。<br>(C) 長く興行されているショーである。<br>(D) 好評を得ている。 | **正解 (D)**<br>キャストの国籍には触れていないので (A) は不適切。子供も気に入ったと感想に書いてあるので (B) も不適切。新作であることから判断して、(C) もまた不適切。月刊誌からベストミュージカルに選ばれ、観客から良いコメントが寄せられているので、(D) It has received favorable reviews. が正解。<br><br>favorable [féivərəbl] 好意的な<br>review [rivjúː] 評論、批評 |
| **166**<br>Who has praised Shanghai Romance?<br><br>(A) The theater owner<br>(B) Audience members<br>(C) Play writers<br>(D) Stage actors | 誰が上海ロマンスを称賛しましたか。<br><br>(A) 劇場所有者<br>(B) 観客<br>(C) 劇作家<br>(D) 舞台俳優 | **正解 (B)**<br>コメントしているのは大学生と会社経営者という「一般人」である。専門家ではなく観客であることがわかるので、正解は (B)。<br><br>praise [preiz] 〜を称賛する |
| **167**<br>When can the earliest tickets be purchased?<br><br>(A) May 17<br>(B) May 18<br>(C) June 20<br>(D) June 27 | 一番早くチケットが買えるのはいつですか。<br><br>(A) 5月17日<br>(B) 5月18日<br>(C) 6月20日<br>(D) 6月27日 | **正解 (A)**<br>Tickets are available at the box office from May 18, with online sales starting the day before. に注目。チケット売り場では5月18日から入手できるが、オンラインでは前日に入手できるとある。つまり、5月17日が一番早くチケットを入手できる日である。よって、正解は (A)。6月20日は予約できる最終日、6月27日は最終公演予定日である。 |
| **168**<br>How can guests get lower prices?<br><br>(A) By attending afternoon performances<br>(B) By purchasing tickets online<br>(C) By seeing the performance twice<br>(D) By contacting the performers | 観客はどのようにすればより安く済ますことができますか。<br><br>(A) 午後の公演を見ることによって<br>(B) オンラインでチケットを買うことによって<br>(C) 公演を2回見ることによって<br>(D) 公演者と連絡を取ることによって | **正解 (A)**<br>本文の matinee performances「昼公演」を言い換えている (A) By attending afternoon performances が正解。マチネーという言葉を知らなくても、午後の公演時間に安くなると明記してあるので、正解とわかるはず。 |

Questions 169-171 refer to the following e-mail.

---

**E-mail**

**From:** Joseph Mooresville <joseph@gentryparts.au>  President & CEO  Gentry Car Parts Inc.
**To:** Emiko Takeda <emiko.takeda@ichigoauto.co.jp>  Purchasing Director  Ichigo Automobile Corporation
**Date:** September 4
**Subject:** Your visit

Dear Ms. Takeda,

Here are the directions you requested. They should bring you directly to our main factory outside Melbourne.

As you drive out of the airport, get onto Highway Nine going west. Take that for about 15 kilometers, until you reach the Pettigrew Overpass. Continue on for an additional 3 kilometers to Exit 3. Take that exit and it will lead you to Coldicote Road. Turn right there, and head north for about 4 more kilometers.

After you pass the Herald Hotel on your right, you'll only be a minute or two away from us. If you see Blake Stadium, you'll know you've gone too far, so make a U-turn at Carlton Park or East Pacific Bank and come back toward us.

Guest parking inside the facility is free, but please be sure to enter one of the spaces marked for visitors. My assistants, Marsha Jensen and William Marsden, will meet you at the gate and see you through security. You'll be able to see them as soon as you pull up.

If you have any questions at any time, please e-mail me at the address above. Or you are welcome to contact me by phone. I look forward to seeing you soon.

Sincerely,

Joseph Mooresville

*World Specialists in Car Parts Design*

---

## Vocabulary

- direction [dirékʃən] 名 道順
- directly [diréktli] 副 真っすぐに
- pull up （車を）止める

| 設問 | 設問の訳 | 正解と解説 |
|---|---|---|
| **169**<br>How far is Ms. Takeda instructed to drive down Highway Nine?<br><br>(A) Three kilometers<br>(B) Four kilometers<br>(C) Fifteen kilometers<br>(D) Eighteen kilometers | Takeda さんは9号線をどのくらい走るように指示されていますか。<br><br>(A) 3 キロメートル<br>(B) 4 キロメートル<br>(C) 15 キロメートル<br>(D) 18 キロメートル | **正解 (D)**<br>計算問題。9号線をまず Pettigrew 高架道に至るまで約15キロ, そこから3番出口までさらに3キロ進み続けるのであるから, 15＋3＝18キロで (D) が正解。 |
| **170**<br>What landmark will Ms. Takeda see before she reaches the Melbourne factory?<br><br>(A) Herald Hotel<br>(B) Blake Stadium<br>(C) Carlton Park<br>(D) East Pacific Bank | Takeda さんはメルボルン工場に着くまでにどんな目印を見ますか。<br><br>(A) Herald ホテル<br>(B) Blake スタジアム<br>(C) Carlton 公園<br>(D) East Pacific 銀行 | **正解 (A)**<br>「右手に Herald ホテルを通り過ぎればもう1, 2分」と Herald ホテルを目印に挙げているので, 正解は (A)。Blake スタジアムは行き過ぎ, Carlton 公園と East Pacific 銀行は行き過ぎた場合のUターンポイントなので, 他の選択肢は不適切。<br><br>landmark [lǽndmàːrk] 目印 |
| **171**<br>What should Ms. Takeda do upon arriving?<br><br>(A) Park outside the facility<br>(B) Show her guest pass<br>(C) Contact security<br>(D) Look for Mr. Mooresville's staff | Takeda さんは到着時に何をすべきですか。<br><br>(A) 施設の外に駐車する<br>(B) 来客証を見せる<br>(C) 警備員に連絡する<br>(D) Mooresville さんのスタッフを探す | **正解 (D)**<br>駐車後, Mooresville さんの助手である Marsha Jensen と William Marsden が入口で出迎えてくれるので, 彼らの姿を探すことになる。よって, 正解は (D)。「施設内の来客用駐車場は無料」とあり, 施設内に駐車してよいことがわかるので, (A) は不適切。<br><br>guest pass 来客証 |

## 問題文

Questions 172-175 refer to the following newspaper article.

### Big Changes at Diaz Motors

Diaz Motors yesterday announced substantial changes at the company's assembly plants in Guadalajara, where it employs 3,200 people, and Veracruz, where it employs 1,200. From April 1, staff will work four-day weeks and take 20% reductions in base salaries. — [1] —. This policy will be subject to a 12-month review, at which time it will be decided whether to continue it.

CEO Felipe Kahlo said the move was designed to secure the long-term competitiveness of the company. — [2] —. Earlier this month, Diaz introduced a voluntary layoff program and eliminated 300 part-time jobs at its subsidiary component plant just outside of Mexico City. Diaz's board of directors has also reportedly discussed outsourcing some processes to lower-cost Guatemala.

— [3] —. According to the latest statistics, car purchases from Diaz and other South American automakers have fallen by 63% over the past three months. This decline is despite a $US 200 million investment the company made recently in advanced production technologies. Diaz stock held steady in light trading on the announcement.

Union officials are reported to be in negotiations with company representatives over ways to avoid further layoffs or outsourcing. — [4] —. Senior union director Miguel Hayek said he was willing to work with management to safeguard jobs in the face of current uncertainty in the market.

## 問題文の訳

問題 172-175 は次の新聞記事に関するものです。

### Diaz 自動車で大改革

Diaz 自動車は昨日，3,200 人を雇用しているグアダラハラと 1,200 人を雇用しているベラクルスにある自社組立工場の大幅な改革を発表した。4 月 1 日から社員は週に 4 日勤務となり，基本給は 20% 減額される。— [1] — この方針は，12 か月後の再検討を前提としており，そのときその方針を維持するかどうかが決定される。

最高経営責任者 Felipe Kahlo は，この動きは会社の長期的な競争力を確固たるものにするために立案されたものだと述べた。— [2] — 今月初旬，Diaz は自発的退職制度を導入し，メキシコシティーの少し外れにある系列の部品工場で 300 人のパートタイム社員を削減した。Diaz の取締役会はまた，伝えられるところによれば，低コストのグアテマラへいくつかの製造工程を外部委託することを討議している。

このニュースは，このメキシコの自動車メーカーが地域の景気後退と闘っているのと時を同じくして報じられている。最新の統計によると，Diaz および他の南アメリカの自動車メーカー製の車の購入は，ここ 3 か月で 63% 下落している。この減少は，最近会社が行った先進生産技術への 2 億米ドルの投資にもかかわらず起こっている。発表時には，Diaz の株価は薄商いで安定を保った。

労働組合の役員は，これ以上の解雇や外部委託を避ける方法について会社の代表者と交渉中だと報道されている。— [4] — 上級組合委員長 Miguel Hayek は，市場における現在の不安定さに直面して，職を守るためには経営陣と協力することもいとわないと述べた。

## Vocabulary

- substantial [səbstǽnʃəl] 形 大幅な；実質的な
- assembly plant 組み立て工場
- reduction [rɪdʌ́kʃən] 名 削減
- base salary 基本給
- be subject to ~ ～を条件としている，～の対象となる
- competitiveness [kəmpétətɪvnɪs] 名 競争力，競合性
- voluntary [vɑ́ləntèri] 形 自発的な；自由志願の
- layoff [léɪɔːf] 名 解雇
- eliminate [ɪlímənèɪt] 動 ～を排除する
- subsidiary [səbsídièri] 形 系列の；子会社の
- component plant 部品工場
- reportedly [rɪpɔ́ːrtɪdli] 副 伝えられるところによれば
- outsource [áʊtsɔːrs] 動 ～を外部委託する
- statistics [stətístɪks] 名 統計（の数字）
- despite [dɪspáɪt] 前 ～にもかかわらず
- light trading （株式の）薄商い
- union [júːnjən] 名 組合
- in negotiations with ~ ～と交渉中で
- representative [rèprɪzéntətɪv] 名 代表者；代理人
- be willing to *do* ～することに前向きである；快く～する
- safeguard [séɪfgɑ̀ːrd] 動 ～を守る；～を保護する
- in the face of ~ ～に直面して
- uncertainty [ʌnsɔ́ːrtənti] 名 不確実性

| 設問 | 設問の訳 | 正解と解説 |
|---|---|---|
| **172**<br>What is the article mainly about?<br>(A) Economic trends in South America<br>(B) Labor relations at auto companies<br>(C) Productivity changes in car factories<br>(D) Ongoing corporate reorganizations | 主に何についての記事ですか。<br>(A) 南アメリカの経済動向<br>(B) 自動車会社での労使関係<br>(C) 自動車工場の生産性の変化<br>(D) 進行中の会社の再編 | **正解 (D)**<br>冒頭に Diaz Motors yesterday announced substantial changes at the company's assembly plants ～, とあり, 会社は「大幅な改革」を行うことで「会社の再編」を行おうとしていることがわかるので, 正解は (D)。南アメリカの景気後退や労働者の解雇に関する話題も出てくるが, 主に会社の具体的な再編策を述べているので, (D) が最も正解にふさわしい。<br><br>ongoing [ángòuiŋ] 進行中の<br>reorganization [ri:ɔ̀:rgənəzéiʃən] 再編成 |
| **173**<br>The word "subsidiary" in paragraph 2, line 7, is closest in meaning to<br>(A) divisional<br>(B) remaining<br>(C) partial<br>(D) sequential | 第 2 段落・7 行目の "subsidiary" に最も意味が近いのは<br>(A) 部門の<br>(B) 残りの<br>(C) 一部の<br>(D) 連続して起こる | **正解 (A)**<br>文中の subsidiary「系列の, 子会社の」は component plant「部品工場」を修飾する形容詞として用いられている。これに一番近い意味の語は, (A) divisional「部門の, 支社の」である。 |
| **174**<br>What problem is Diaz Motors facing?<br>(A) A lack of competitive technologies<br>(B) Sharp decreases in stock prices<br>(C) A reduction of market share<br>(D) A slump in consumer demand | Diaz 自動車はどんな問題に直面していますか。<br>(A) 競争力のある技術の欠如<br>(B) 株価の急激な下落<br>(C) 市場占有率の低落<br>(D) 消費者需要の不振 | **正解 (D)**<br>第 3 段落に car purchases from Diaz and other South American automakers have fallen by 63% とあり,「消費者需要の不振」に悩まされていることがわかるので, 正解は (D)。Diaz stock held steady ～とあり, 株価は安定を保ったとわかるので, (B) は不適切。<br><br>slump [slʌmp] 不振, 落ち込み |
| **175**<br>In which of the positions marked [1], [2], [3] and [4] does the following sentence best belong?<br><br>"The news comes as the Mexican car manufacturer battles a regional recession."<br><br>(A) [1]<br>(B) [2]<br>(C) [3]<br>(D) [4] | [1], [2], [3], [4] と記載された箇所のうち, 次の文が入るのに最もふさわしいのはどれですか。<br><br>「このニュースは, このメキシコの自動車メーカーが地域の景気後退と闘っているのと時を同じくして報じられている」<br><br>(A) [1]<br>(B) [2]<br>(C) [3]<br>(D) [4] | **正解 (C)**<br>文脈から, Diaz はメキシコの自動車メーカーであることが推測される。段落ごとの内容を捉えていくと, 空所 [3] より前の部分は Diaz の再編, 解雇や外部委託が話題。一方 [3] の次の文は Diaz および他の南アメリカの自動車メーカーの不景気の話である。挿入文の a regional recession に着目して, [3] に入れるのが最適。<br><br>regional [rí:dʒnəl] 地域(全体)の<br>recession [riséʃən] (一時的な)景気後退 |

| 問題文 | 問題文の訳 |
|---|---|

Questions 176-180 refer to the following survey and e-mail.

## Car4U Inc.
### Customer Survey

Customer Name: (Mr.)/Ms.) _Ibrahim Rafsanjani_
Address: _17 Rue De Mons, Lyons, France  90A-E7K_
E-mail: _Rafsanjani2947@francotel.com_
Date of Car Rental: From _8 June_ to _15 June_
Applicable rules, fees or other information regarding your rental: _N/A_

Please indicate your level of service satisfaction with Car4U Inc. by rating us in each of the categories below, from 1 to 5.   1= Very unsatisfied   5 = Very satisfied

| Category | Condition of car at time of rental | Cost per day | Service Staff Helpfulness | Car Model Options | Drop-off and Pick-up convenience |
|---|---|---|---|---|---|
| Rating | 4 | 3 | 3 | 1 | 3 |

Comments: _I think my responses above show my opinion about renting from you. I have also rented from Falcon Rental Co., and frankly I believe they do a better job. It's easy to see why they're the number one car rental agency in Europe. I would recommend that you work to improve your service if you want to compete with them._

Thank you for taking the time to fill out our survey. Fully completed surveys earn 200 Frequent Flier Miles on World Wings Airlines. Let World Wings fly you across the globe—and choose Car4U when you land.

---

**E-mail**

From: eva.veblen@car4u.net
To: robert.heller@car4u.net
Date: 18 July
Subject: Survey

Dear Mr. Heller,

We completed a survey of customer satisfaction last month: over 3,000 respondents were included. I have a broad statistical analysis of the results I will send later. However, I have attached this particular response because the scores are representative of many of the surveys we collected. Furthermore, the respondent offered a succinct written summary of what other customers might also feel.

As you can see, it indicates that we have varying levels of performance in different areas. I spoke with some analysts in the company who said it is "impossible" to perform well in all areas.

However, I don't accept this as necessarily true. Instead, I would like to suggest that we try to make improvements in our worst area of performance, clearly shown in the survey, by expanding our budget in that area. I know that it's not easy to increase expenses, but in my opinion it would be a very positive move that would result in the long-term success of our company.

Yours truly,
Eva Veblen
Director of Operations

---

## Vocabulary

- □ customer survey 顧客調査　□ applicable [ǽpləkəbl] 形 適用される　□ regarding [rigɑ́ːrdiŋ] 前 〜に関して　□ category [kǽtəgɔ̀ːri] 名 部門
- □ frankly [frǽŋkli] 副 正直なところ　□ compete with 〜　〜と競合する　□ respondent [rispándənt] 名 回答者
- □ broad [brɔːd] 形 幅広い　□ statistical [stətístikəl] 形 統計的な　□ representative of 〜　〜を代表する　□ succinct [səksíŋkt] 形 簡潔な
- □ varying [véəriiŋ] 形 さまざまな　□ budget [bʌ́dʒit] 名 予算　□ positive [pázətiv] 形 積極的な、前向きな

| 設問 | 設問の訳 | 正解と解説 |
|---|---|---|
| **176**<br>What is Mr. Rafsanjani most satisfied with?<br>(A) The state of the cars<br>(B) Rental fees<br>(C) The quality of customer service<br>(D) Car models available | Rafsanjani さんは何に最も満足していますか。<br><br>(A) 車の状態<br>(B) レンタル料<br>(C) 顧客サービスの質<br>(D) 利用可能な車種 | **正解 (A)**<br>調査の満足度の表で Rafsanjani さんは Condition of car at time of rental に 4 を入れていることから、車の状態に最も満足したことがわかる。(A) が正解で、condition を state と言い換えている。<br><br>state [steit] 状態 |
| **177**<br>Why does Mr. Rafsanjani mention Falcon Rental Co.?<br>(A) To provide a comparison<br>(B) To comment on a car he rented<br>(C) To support his comments on price<br>(D) To complain about the company's service | Rafsanjani さんが Falcon レンタカー社に言及しているのはなぜですか。<br><br>(A) 比較対照を提供するため<br>(B) 彼が借りた車についてコメントするため<br>(C) 価格についての彼のコメントを立証するため<br>(D) 会社のサービスに苦情を述べるため | **正解 (A)**<br>競争会社のレベルを述べることによって、彼が求める水準の例を挙げたのであるから、正解は (A)。 |
| **178**<br>What do people who answer the survey get?<br>(A) Lower rental prices<br>(B) Complimentary airline upgrades<br>(C) Frequent flier miles<br>(D) Discounted accommodations | 調査に答える人は何を得られますか。<br><br>(A) 低いレンタル価格<br>(B) 無料の飛行機のアップグレード<br>(C) フリクエントフライヤーのマイレージ<br>(D) 宿泊施設の割引 | **正解 (C)**<br>調査の下部に、Fully completed surveys earn 200 Frequent Flier Miles on World Wings Airlines. とあるので、正解は (C)。このように欄外の小さな文に正解のポイントが含まれていることも多いので、見落とさないようにしよう。frequent flier miles とは、航空会社のマイレージサービスを受けるためのマイルのことで、飛行機の利用距離に応じてポイントがもらえる。<br><br>complimentary [kàmpləméntəri] 無料の |
| **179**<br>Why did Ms. Veblen attach the single response?<br>(A) It answers her boss' request.<br>(B) It is a good example of the overall survey results.<br>(C) It corrects a previous statistical error.<br>(D) It solicits approval for more responses. | Veblen さんはなぜ1つだけ回答を添付したのですか。<br><br>(A) 上司の要望に応えるものだから。<br>(B) 全体の調査結果を示す良い例だから。<br>(C) 以前の統計ミスを修正するものだから。<br>(D) もっと多くの回答の承認を求めるものだから。 | **正解 (B)**<br>質問文の the single response とは Rafsanjani さんが書いた調査のこと。これを添付した理由は、E メール第1段落の I have attached this particular response because 〜以下にある。Veblen さんはこの Rafsanjani さんによる評価が他の多くの顧客にも当てはまると考えていることから、(B) が正解。 |
| **180**<br>What does Ms. Veblen suggest doing to improve the company's performance?<br>(A) Conducting market research<br>(B) Cutting down on labor expenses<br>(C) Increasing the variety of cars<br>(D) Analyzing the results of the survey | Veblen さんは会社の業績を向上させるために何をすることを提案していますか。<br><br>(A) 市場調査を行うこと<br>(B) 人件費を抑えること<br>(C) 車の種類を増やすこと<br>(D) 調査結果を分析すること | **正解 (C)**<br>Veblen さんは、E メール第3段落の I would like to suggest that 〜以下で具体的な提案をしている。our worst area of performance, clearly shown in the survey「調査で明確に示されている成果が最悪の分野」とは何かを調査から読み取る。満足度の表を見ると、Car Model Options の 1 が最も低いので、(C) が正解。 |

## 問題文

Questions 181-185 refer to the following Web page and e-mail.

www.cheshirefoods.com/raspberryleaftea/

Thank you for visiting Cheshire Foods. See our main Internet homepage for exciting links to other great Cheshire products.

**Recommended! Raspberry Leaf Tea**

A delicate blend of raspberry leaf, natural flavor and real pieces of apple comes together to make this deliciously fragrant tea.
Completely organic, without artificial flavorings, colors or preservatives.

**What's inside?**
Raspberry Leaves, Hibiscus, Blackberry Leaves, Natural Raspberry Flavor, Tartaric Acid, Rosehips, Raspberries, Apple pieces.
**CAFFEINE-FREE**

**How to enjoy it?**
Place the teabag in a cup or teapot of boiled water (one bag per person). Immerse for 3-5 minutes to bring out the full flavor. Best drunk without adding milk, cream or any other liquids or condiments.

Unfortunately, we are unable to make direct sales.
Please pick up some at your local grocery store.

---

* E-mail *

**To:** CustomerService@Cheshirefoods.com
**From:** gloria7902@laketel.com
**Date:** Wednesday, May 3
**Subject:** Ordering raspberry tea

Dear Cheshire Foods,

I have enjoyed your Raspberry Leaf Tea for many years. I usually take mine with a bit of Korean or Chinese ginseng, and find it delicious. I even check for product updates regularly on your Web site.

Indeed, I think it would be ideal if I were able to buy it there directly. That's because I sometimes forget to pick it up when I'm out shopping. At other times, your tea may not be available at a particular store I go to. In such cases, I purchase other products, though they are not as enjoyable as yours.

Is there any way that I could order directly from your company—perhaps by catalog or phone? If you have no way for customers to do so at this time, I suggest you consider making such an option available. You would certainly benefit through increased sales, and customers like me would benefit through the convenience of the product being brought right to our doors. I should tell you that Longfellow Grey Tea does provide such a service already.

Sincerely,

Gloria Han

---

## Vocabulary

- delicate [déləkit] 繊細な
- blend [blend] ブレンド；混合物
- flavor [fléivər] 味；風味
- organic [ɔːrgǽnik] 有機農法による
- artificial [àːrtəfíʃəl] 人工的な
- preservative [prizə́ːrvətiv] 保存料
- immerse [imə́ːrs] ～を浸す
- bring out ～ ～を引き出す
- liquid [líkwid] 液体
- condiment [kándəmənt] 香辛料
- pick up ～ ～を手に入れる，買う
- grocery store 食品雑貨店
- ginseng [dʒínseŋ] 朝鮮人参
- indeed [indíːd] 実は
- benefit [bénəfit] 利益を得る

| 設問 | 設問の訳 | 正解と解説 |
|---|---|---|
| **181**<br>What is a stated feature of Cheshire Foods Raspberry Leaf Tea?<br>(A) Low price<br>(B) New flavors<br>(C) Natural ingredients<br>(D) Wide popularity | Cheshire 食品のラズベリーリーフティーの特徴として述べられているものは何ですか。<br>(A) 低価格<br>(B) 新しい風味<br>(C) 自然の材料<br>(D) 幅広い人気 | **正解 (C)**<br>ウェブサイトにある Completely organic, without artificial flavorings, colors or preservatives. から「自然の材料」を使っていることが特徴とわかる。よって、正解は (C)。他の選択肢については文中で明記されていない。<br><br>ingredient [ingríːdiənt] 材料 |
| **182**<br>What suggestion does the Web site offer?<br>(A) To add apple pieces to the tea<br>(B) To allow to cool before consuming<br>(C) To use the appropriate type of teapot<br>(D) To avoid adding any dairy products | ウェブサイトはどのような提案をしていますか。<br>(A) リンゴ片を紅茶に加えること<br>(B) 飲む前に冷やしておくこと<br>(C) 適切なタイプのティーポットを使うこと<br>(D) どんな乳製品も加えるのを避けること | **正解 (D)**<br>ウェブサイトの最後の方に Best drunk without adding milk, cream 〜 とあり、「乳製品を加えない」ことを勧めているので、(D) が正解とわかる。(A) は、リンゴ片はもうすでに製品に含まれているので不適切。<br><br>appropriate [əpróupriit] 適切な<br>dairy product 乳製品 |
| **183**<br>What is indicated about Ms. Han?<br>(A) She enjoys tea in a different way from the producer's instructions.<br>(B) She prefers ginseng to raspberry leaf tea.<br>(C) She purchases tea in large quantities.<br>(D) She goes shopping for tea at a certain store. | Han さんについて何が示されていますか。<br>(A) 生産者の指示とは違う方法で紅茶を楽しんでいる。<br>(B) ラズベリーリーフティーより薬用人参の方が好みである。<br>(C) 大量に紅茶を買う。<br>(D) ある決まった店に紅茶を買いに行く。 | **正解 (A)**<br>Han さんは E メールの第 1 段落で紅茶の楽しみ方について I usually take mine with a bit of Korean or Chinese ginseng と書いている。これはウェブサイトの How to enjoy it? の部分に書かれている紅茶の楽しみ方とは異なるので、(A) が正解。ふだん行く店のうちある特定の店では入手できないことがあると言っているのであって、決まった店に紅茶を買いに行くのではないので (D) は不適。<br><br>prefer A to B B より A を好む<br>in large quantities 大量に |
| **184**<br>What does Ms. Han ask Cheshire Foods to do?<br>(A) Post product updates on their Web site<br>(B) Provide product details<br>(C) Use larger tea boxes<br>(D) Increase their products' availability | Han さんは Cheshire 食品にどうするように頼んでいますか。<br>(A) ウェブサイトに製品の最新情報を掲載する<br>(B) 製品の詳細を提供する<br>(C) より大きな紅茶の箱を使う<br>(D) 製品の入手可能性を増やす | **正解 (D)**<br>Han さんは、自分が行った店で製品を入手できないことがあるため、Is there any way that I could order directly from your company 〜? と直接入手できる方法はないか尋ねている。入手の可能性を増やすように頼んでいるので、正解は (D)。<br><br>post [poust] 〜を掲示する |
| **185**<br>How does Ms. Han try to persuade Cheshire Foods to consider her suggestion?<br>(A) By mentioning a competitor<br>(B) By threatening to shop elsewhere<br>(C) By illustrating a business mistake<br>(D) By showing past losses | Han さんは、自分の提案を検討させるために Cheshire 食品をどのように説得しようとしていますか。<br>(A) 競合他社に言及することによって<br>(B) どこか他で買うと言って脅すことによって<br>(C) ビジネス上のミスを説明することによって<br>(D) 過去の損失を示すことによって | **正解 (A)**<br>Han さんは最後に、I should tell you that Longfellow Grey Tea does provide such a service already. と書いて、他社はすでに直接販売を始めていると述べている。(A) が正解で、Longfellow Grey Tea を a competitor と表している。(B) は、入手困難なときは他の製品を購入すると述べているが、他社商品を買うと伝えることで提案を受け入れさせようと脅しているわけではない。<br><br>competitor [kəmpétətər] 競合他社<br>threaten to do 〜するぞと脅す |

Questions 186-190 refer to the following list, schedule, and memo.

**Starden Foods, Inc.**

Created by Consumer Research Department
June 29

### Comparison of marketing expenses on food categories with sales changes

Study covered all 637 stores in the European Union. A comparison next quarter will focus on stores in the Americas and the Asia Pacific.

| Department | Amount spent on marketing (in millions) | Change in unit sales from last year |
| --- | --- | --- |
| Fruits and Vegetables | €4.3 | +4.2% |
| Breads | €12.8 | +3.8% |
| Dry Goods | €26.6 | -1.9% |
| Meats | €18.2 | +0.5% |
| Dairy | €31.4 | -2.2% |
| Seafood | €12.6 | +0.1% |

Note: Scheduled for discussion at the Marketing Plans Meeting on July 25. There will be an updated schedule soon.

---

**Starden Foods, Inc.**

### Division Manager Committee Meetings for the Month of July

Final agendas for each meeting will be issued at least 3 days ahead of time. Attendance at all meetings is mandatory, unless urgent client-related or other business arises.

| Date | Topic |
| --- | --- |
| July 4 | Supplier Review |
| July 11 | Marketing Plans |
| July 18 | Store Maintenance Issues |
| July 25 | Quality Control |
| July 31 | Human Resources |

Board directors may attend any meeting with little or no advance notice.

## 問題文

**MEMO**

To: Division Managers
From: Brenda Phan, COO
Date: July 12
Subject: Business Report

Colleagues,

In yesterday's meeting, we discussed whether there is a correlation between the amount of money spent on marketing certain products and the revenue generated from those products. Currently, we can say that the connection is not very clear. We reviewed the list that compares shopper spending traits, and found some surprises. Helen Smith had to miss the meeting, but we talked afterwards. She pointed out products that experienced high sales growth.

You might intuitively feel that we have to spend more money on our products experiencing the lowest sales. However, I think it would be better instead to increase marketing support for our products experiencing the highest sales.

If a product category is experiencing weak sales, I do not think that more advertising alone can improve the situation. Instead, we have to look at other factors, such as quality or price. That is what I tried to stress to Evan Lee, who unexpectedly but fortunately was able to join the meeting. He seemed to agree with my analysis. In any event, I have attached a report detailing this idea, which I'd like to discuss at our next meeting. I don't think that we should put it off until the last gathering of the month.

Thank you,
Brenda Phan

## 問題文の訳

メモ

宛先：部門長
差出人：Brenda Phan 最高執行責任者
日付：7月12日
件名：業務報告

皆さま

昨日の会議では，特定の製品のマーケティングに支出した金額と該当製品から得られた収益との間に相関があるか議論しました。現在のところ，関係はあまり明らかではないと言えます。買い物客の購買特性を比較したリストを吟味したところ，いくつか意外なことがわかりました。Helen Smith は会議を欠席しなければなりませんでしたが，私たちは後で話し合いました。彼女は売り上げが大きく伸びた製品を指摘しました。

売り上げの最も低い製品にもっとお金をかけなければいけないと直感的に思われるかもしれませんが，むしろ，売り上げが最も多い製品に対するマーケティング支援を増やす方が良いだろうと思います。

ある製品カテゴリーの売り上げが低迷しているのであれば，ただ宣伝を強化するだけでは状況は改善しないと思います。そうではなく，品質や価格などの他の要素を見てみる必要があります。予想外でしたが幸運にも会議に参加できた Evan Lee に私が強調しようとしたのがこれです。彼は，私の分析に同意してくれたようでした。ともかく，このアイデアについて詳細を記したレポートを添付していますので，次回の会議で話し合いたいと思います。今月の最後の集まりまで先送りにするべきではないと考えます。

よろしくお願いします。
Brenda Phan

## Vocabulary

- comparison [kəmpǽrisn] 名 比較
- agenda [ədʒéndə] 名 議題（一覧），議事日程（表）
- issue [íʃuː] 動 ～を公表する
- ～ ahead of time 定刻の～前に
- attendance [əténdəns] 名 出席
- mandatory [mǽndətɔ̀ːri] 形 強制的な，必須の
- urgent [ə́ːrdʒənt] 形 緊急の
- correlation [kɔ̀ːrəléiʃən] 名 相互関係
- trait [treit] 名 特性
- afterwards [ǽftərwərdz] 副 後で，後ほど
- intuitively [intjúːətivli] 副 直感的に
- unexpectedly [ʌ̀nikspéktidli] 副 予想外に
- in any event ともかく
- put ～ off ～を延期する

| 設問 | 設問の訳 | 正解と解説 |
|---|---|---|
| **186**<br>According to the list, what is true about the research?<br>(A) It compares different shopper categories.<br>(B) It spans several quarters.<br>(C) It includes many Asian stores.<br>(D) It covers a single region. | リストによると，調査について正しいことは何ですか。<br>(A) 異なる買い物客カテゴリーを比較している。<br>(B) 数四半期に及ぶ。<br>(C) 多くのアジアの店舗を含む。<br>(D) 1つの地域を対象にしている。 | **正解 (D)**<br>リストの Study covered all 637 stores in the European Union. の部分より，(D) が正解。「欧州連合」を選択肢では a single region と表している。異なるカテゴリーの比較は買い物客ではなく食品なので，(A) は誤り。(B) はリストの A comparison next quarter will ～の部分から，誤答と判断する。(C) の Asian stores は次四半期に比較されるので誤り。<br><br>span [spæn] ～の(期間)に及ぶ |
| **187**<br>What is suggested about the list?<br>(A) It was created by an outside firm.<br>(B) It will be distributed at a meeting.<br>(C) A meeting about it was rescheduled.<br>(D) A report about it has been written. | リストについて何がわかりますか。<br>(A) 外部会社によって作成された。<br>(B) 会議で配られる。<br>(C) それに関する会議の予定が変更された。<br>(D) それに関する報告書が書かれた。 | **正解 (C)**<br>リストの下に書かれた Note によると，このリストについて討論をする Marketing Plans の会議は，7月25日に開催されることがわかる。しかし，予定表を見ると，Marketing Plans の日程が July 11 となっているので，会議の予定日が変更されたと判断できる。よって，(C) が正解。メモの日付 July 12 と本文冒頭の In yesterday's meeting, ～もヒントになる。 |
| **188**<br>What is indicated about the July 11 meeting?<br>(A) A member had urgent business.<br>(B) A rule was revised.<br>(C) A maintenance issue was solved.<br>(D) An important client was invited. | 7月11日の会議について何が示されていますか。<br>(A) 委員の1人に緊急の業務があった。<br>(B) ルールが改正された。<br>(C) メンテナンス上の課題が解消された。<br>(D) 重要な顧客が招かれた。 | **正解 (A)**<br>メモは，日付が July 12 で本文が In yesterday's meeting, ～と始まることから，July 11 の会議について書かれていることがわかる。第1段落の Helen Smith had to miss the meeting, but ～から，Helen Smith という人が会議を欠席したことがわかるが，予定表を見ると，Attendance at all meetings is mandatory, unless urgent client-related or other business arises. とあることから，この人物は緊急の業務があったと推測できる。よって，(A) が正解。 |
| **189**<br>In the memo, the word "connection" in paragraph 1, line 3, is closest in meaning to<br>(A) termination<br>(B) wire<br>(C) relationship<br>(D) payment | メモの第1段落・3行目の "connection" に最も意味が近いのは<br>(A) 結末<br>(B) 電線<br>(C) 関係<br>(D) 支払い | **正解 (C)**<br>何があまり明らかではない (not very clear) かというと，直前の内容から，「特定の製品のマーケティングに支出した金額と該当製品から得られた収益との間の関係」である。connection と (C) の relationship には，いずれも「関係」という意味がある。 |
| **190**<br>Who most likely is Evan Lee?<br>(A) A marketing expert<br>(B) A senior executive<br>(C) A consumer analyst<br>(D) A dairy manufacturer | Evan Lee は誰だと考えられますか。<br>(A) マーケティングの専門家<br>(B) 上級幹部<br>(C) 消費者アナリスト<br>(D) 乳製品製造者 | **正解 (B)**<br>メモの第3段落にある Evan Lee, who unexpectedly but fortunately was able to join the meeting から，Evan Lee は予想外に，幸運にも会議に出席した (=本来会議に出なければならない人物ではない) ことが推測できる。そこで予定表を見ると，下部に Board directors may attend any meeting with little or no advance notice. とあるので，Evan Lee は board director であるとわかる。これを senior executive と表した (B) が正解。 |

Questions 191-195 refer to the following product information, online review, and response.

# H-3000 Mobile Phone

**Karn Telecom**

This best-selling device is easy to use to surf the Web, download apps, talk, text, and perform many other functions. Its most valuable feature is its ability to link to wireless systems even in remote locations.

The device is only compatible with Karn Telecom hardware. This extends to chargers, power cords, and batteries.

A product warranty is enclosed, covering all internal components for 3 years. External surfaces and damage from dropping or ordinary wear and tear are excluded.

---

www.electronicshopper.net/reviews/892361/

**Customer comment**

Product: The H-3000 Mobile Phone
Customer: Blake Woods
Verified Purchase:

I can say that the device is basically good. I enjoy it in most respects. The price is a little high, and the design isn't particularly elegant, but it does have excellent reception, just as advertised. I am very pleased with that.

I was disappointed, however, because the screen scratched too easily—after only a month of use. I took it to a Karn Telecom store, but the Customer Service representative there only cited the warranty information. In my opinion, the company should reevaluate what "ordinary wear and tear" means.

## 問題文

www.electronicshopper.net/reviews/892361/

**Customer comment**

Product: The H-3000 Mobile Phone
Customer: Blake Woods
Response from: Karn Telecom Customer Service

Thank you very much for your review. Your feedback is very important to us. Unfortunately, our 3-year warranty is explicit on the subject of surface wear, and the response given to you by the Customer Service representative you spoke with is consistent with that. However, if you do opt for a replacement, we recommend our Z-1X model, which has a stronger screen and is more scratch-resistant. Additionally, we would suggest enrolling in our Extended Care Program. This will warranty your internal components for 2 additional years. The cost for this program is only $175. We want to make sure that you receive the very best support for your product, and we look forward to your continued patronage and feedback.

## 問題文の訳

www.electronicshopper.net/reviews/892361/
お客様コメント：

製品：H-3000 携帯電話
投稿者：Blake Woods
返答者：Karn Telecom カスタマーサービス

レビューをありがとうございました。お客様のご意見は，当社にとって大変貴重です。残念ながら，当社の3年保証は外面の摩耗の問題について明確にしており，またお客様が話されたカスタマーサービス担当者による返答も，これに沿っています。しかし，交換を選ばれるなら，画面の強度が高く傷のつきにくいZ-1Xモデルをお勧めします。さらに，当社の延長保証プログラムに加入されることを提案いたします。これによって，お使いの機器の内部部品を2年間追加保証いたします。このプログラムの料金はたったの175ドルです。当社は，お客様がお使いの製品に対して最良のサポートを受けられるように最善を尽くします。お客様の変わらぬご愛顧とご意見をお願いいたします。

## Vocabulary

- app [æp] 名 アプリ（application program の省略形）
- function [fʌ́ŋkʃən] 名 機能
- remote [rimóut] 形 遠隔の
- compatible [kəmpǽtəbl] 形 互換性のある
- extend to ～ ～にまで及ぶ
- product warranty 製品保証（書）
- internal [intə́ːrnl] 形 内部の
- external [ikstə́ːrnl] 形 外部の
- surface [sə́ːrfəs] 名 表面
- exclude [iksklúːd] 動 ～を除く
- cite [sait] 動 ～に言及する
- reevaluate [riivǽljuèit] 動 ～を見直す，再評価する
- feedback [fíːdbæ̀k] 名 感想，意見
- explicit [iksplísit] 形 明確な
- be consistent with ～ ～と一致する
- opt for ～ ～を選ぶ，～に決める
- replacement [ripléismənt] 名 代替品
- scratch-resistant [skrǽtʃrizìstənt] 形 傷のつきにくい
- enroll in ～ ～に登録する
- continued patronage 変わらぬご愛顧

| 設問 | 設問の訳 | 正解と解説 |
|---|---|---|
| **191**<br>What is NOT mentioned in the product information?<br>(A) Internet use<br>(B) Access security<br>(C) Battery components<br>(D) Sales ranking | 製品情報で述べられていないことは何ですか。<br>(A) インターネットの利用<br>(B) アクセス保護<br>(C) 電池部品<br>(D) 売上ランキング | **正解 (B)**<br>質問文の the product information は1つ目の文書のこと，product は H-3000 携帯電話のことである。第1段落の This best-selling device が (D)，surf the Web が (A)，第2段落の 〜, and batteries が (C) とそれぞれ一致する。文書内に情報のない (B) が正解。 |
| **192**<br>In the online review, the word "respects" in paragraph 1, line 1, is closest in meaning to<br>(A) predictions<br>(B) transmissions<br>(C) aspects<br>(D) patterns | オンライン・レビューの第1段落・1行目の "respects" に最も意味が近いのは<br>(A) 予測<br>(B) 送信<br>(C) 側面<br>(D) 模様 | **正解 (C)**<br>オンライン・レビューを書いた Woods さんが，直前の文で，製品について basically good と述べ，続く The price is 〜の文ではデメリットを挙げていることから，「私はほとんどの面でこの製品に満足している」という文脈がふさわしい。respect と (C) の aspect にはいずれも「側面」という意味がある。 |
| **193**<br>What is Mr. Woods particularly pleased with about the mobile phone?<br>(A) Its connectivity<br>(B) Its compatibility<br>(C) Its design<br>(D) Its price | Woods さんがこの携帯電話で特に満足している点は何ですか。<br>(A) （通信ネットワークの）接続性<br>(B) 互換性<br>(C) デザイン<br>(D) 価格 | **正解 (A)**<br>Woods さんが特に満足している点はレビュー第1段落の it does have excellent reception, just as advertised. I am very pleased with that. の部分にヒントがある。この reception を1つ目の文書（製品情報）から読み取る。第1段落に Its most valuable feature is its ability to link to wireless systems even in remote locations. とあり，「遠隔地でもワイヤレスシステムにつながる能力」が reception だとわかる。それを connectivity と表した (A) が正解。 |
| **194**<br>What is the total warranty length Karn Telecom can offer?<br>(A) 1 year<br>(B) 3 years<br>(C) 4 years<br>(D) 5 years | Karn Telecom が提供できる最長の保証期間はどれくらいですか。<br>(A) 1年間<br>(B) 3年間<br>(C) 4年間<br>(D) 5年間 | **正解 (D)**<br>製品の保証期間は，1つ目の文書（製品情報）の第3段落から3年間とわかる。また，カスタマーサービスは Woods さんのレビューを受けて，3つ目の文書の中ほどで Additionally, we would suggest enrolling in our Extended Care Program. This will warranty 〜 for 2 additional years. と言って，延長保証プログラムに加入すると2年間の追加保証が受けられると述べている。よって，最長の保証期間は 3＋2 ＝ 5 年である。 |
| **195**<br>What was the Customer Service representative correct about?<br>(A) The method to avoid scratches<br>(B) The need for program enrollment<br>(C) The coverage for a device<br>(D) The best kind of mobile phone screen | カスタマーサービス担当者はどんな点で正しかったのですか。<br>(A) 傷を防ぐ方法<br>(B) プログラム加入の必要性<br>(C) 機器の保証範囲<br>(D) 携帯電話の画面の最高の種類 | **正解 (C)**<br>質問文の意図は，3つ目の文書に「当社の3年保証は外面の摩耗の問題について明確にしており，またお客様が話されたカスタマーサービス担当者による返答も，これに沿っています」とある。担当者は，Woods さんが店舗に持ち込んだ携帯電話の画面の傷について対応したのだが，2つ目の文書に「カスタマーサービス担当者は保証内容を示しただけでした」とあり，また続く「ordinary wear and tear の意味を見直すべき」の ordinary wear and tear という表現は1つ目の文書の最後にあり，「通常の使用による損耗は保証に含まれていない」と書かれている。これらの情報を総合して，(C) が正解。 |

Questions 196-200 refer to the following notice, e-mail, and article.

## Jowel Community Center
17 Lakeland Street
www.jowelccenter.org

**Special Event: Building Your Wealth — Tips for Ordinary People**
Speaker: Joseph Steinz, Personal Financial Consultant
April 23

Free and open to the public

Learn: Home budget management skills
　　　　Choosing the right bank or financial institution
　　　　The basics of stocks, bonds, and other investing or reinvesting options

30-Minute Question and Answer Session to follow the talk
Tea, coffee and snacks provided

While the event is free and open to the public, space is limited, and guaranteed seating can be assured only to the first 75 people who register. Please visit the Web site above to register. For more information, contact Bozena Kovac, special event organizer: bozena@jowelccenter.org.

---

* E-mail *

To: bozena@jowelccenter.org
From: joseph.steinz@zoneumail.net
Date: April 11
Subject: Second Reminder: Certification

Dear Ms. Kovac,

I regret to inform you that I will not be able to speak at your April 23 Community Center event on finance management. I have an urgent business matter that I have to attend to on that day. I do not want to let down your attendees, so I have arranged a colleague of mine to take my place. I can guarantee that he is more than qualified to do so as he has both taught and written extensively on this topic. Details are in the attachment.

I apologize for this situation, and trust the event will work out well. If I can help in any other way, please do not hesitate to let me know.

Yours sincerely,

Joseph Steinz

## 問題文

# NEWS DAILY

### Special Event at Jowel Community Center
By Eve Sanders, Special Correspondent

It was a pleasure to hear Wazir Sanjrani speak at the April 23 financial planning event at the Jowel Community Center. This highly accomplished investor took complex topics such as stocks, bonds, and mutual funds, and simplified them so that everyone could understand. He did this repeatedly and in a friendly way, making the talk not only informative but pleasant.

He also explained clearly how people could slowly grow their money starting with just a low sum. This was encouraging, since most of the attendees were simple working men and women. I think all of the attendees also appreciated the fact that Mr. Sanjrani allowed a full one-hour question and answer session.

However, I believe the audiovisual system of the center could benefit from renovation. Several times, it faded out and it was difficult to understand what the speaker was saying.

## 問題文の訳

News Daily 誌
Jowel コミュニティセンターでの特別イベント
Eve Sanders 特派員記

4月23日に Jowel コミュニティセンターで開催された財政計画イベントで Wazir Sanjrani の話を聞くことができて光栄であった。この非常に優れた投資家は、株式、債券、投資信託などの複雑なテーマを取り上げ、誰でも理解できるように平易な言葉で話した。彼はこれを何度も、親しみやすく行って、講演を有益なだけではなく楽しくしていた。

彼はさらに、少ない金額から始めても、ゆっくりお金を増やせる方法を明確に説明した。出席者の大多数は普通の働く男女であったため、これは励みになった。Sanjrani 氏が質疑応答に丸1時間とったことも、出席者は全員歓迎したことだろう。

しかし、同センターの AV システムは修理した方がよいのではなかろうか。幾度かフェードアウトし、講演者が言っていることを聞き取るのが困難だった。

## Vocabulary

- tip [tip] 名(有益な)ヒント，助言
- public [pʌ́blik] 名(the をつけて)一般人
- institution [ìnstətjúːʃən] 名機関
- stock [stɑk] 名株，株式
- bond [bɑnd] 名債券
- option [ɑ́pʃən] 名選択肢
- assure [əʃúər] 動〜を保証する
- I regret to inform you (that)〜 残念ながら〜をお知らせします
- matter [mǽtər] 名こと，問題
- let down 〜 〜をがっかりさせる
- attendee [ətèndíː] 名出席者
- colleague [kɑ́liːg] 名同僚
- take someone's place 〜の代わりをする
- qualified [kwɑ́ləfàid] 形資格[能力]のある
- extensively [iksténsivli] 副幅広く
- attachment [ətǽtʃmənt] 名添付書類
- work out うまくいく
- Please do not hesitate to do 遠慮なく〜してください
- correspondent [kɔ̀ːrəspɑ́ndənt] 名特派員
- accomplished [əkɑ́mpliʃt] 形熟達した
- complex [kɑmpléks] 形複雑な
- simplify [símpləfài] 動〜を簡潔化する
- so that S can 〜 S が〜できるように
- repeatedly [ripíːtidli] 副繰り返し
- informative [infɔ́ːrmətiv] 形有益な
- sum [sʌm] 名(お金の)額
- appreciate [əpríːʃièit] 動〜をありがたく思う
- the fact that 〜 〜という事実
- audiovisual [ɔ̀ːdiouvíʒuəl] 形AV[音響と映像]の
- renovation [rènəvéiʃən] 名修繕

| 設問 | 設問の訳 | 正解と解説 |
|---|---|---|
| **196**<br>What information is NOT mentioned in the notice?<br>(A) Photo IDs<br>(B) Participant registration<br>(C) Refreshment items<br>(D) Event location | お知らせで述べられていない情報は何ですか。<br><br>(A) 写真付きの身分証明書<br>(B) 参加者の登録<br>(C) 軽食類<br>(D) イベントの場所 | **正解 (A)**<br>NOT 問題は消去法で解くとよい。お知らせのヘッダーの 17 Lakeland Street が (D)、Tea, coffee and snacks provided が (C)、guaranteed seating can be assured only to the first 75 people who register が (B) とそれぞれ一致する。本文に記述がない (A) が正解。 |
| **197**<br>What is indicated about Wazir Sanjrani?<br>(A) He updated a Web site.<br>(B) He earned speaker fees.<br>(C) He works at a bank.<br>(D) He replaced a presenter. | Wazir Sanjrani について何が示されていますか。<br><br>(A) ウェブサイトを更新した。<br>(B) 講演料を稼いだ。<br>(C) 銀行で働いている。<br>(D) 講演者と交替した。 | **正解 (D)**<br>Wazir Sanjrani は記事の冒頭の It was a pleasure to hear Wazir Sanjrani speak 〜から、イベントで話した人物である。お知らせの Speaker: Joseph Steinz, Personal Financial Consultant と E メール第 1 段落の I have arranged a colleague of mine to take my place から、Wazir Sanjrani は当初話す予定だった Joseph Steinz の代理であることがわかる。よって、(D) が正解。 |
| **198**<br>What is indicated about the event?<br>(A) The main topic of the session was changed.<br>(B) The payment to sign up was increased.<br>(C) Entrance to the location was unrestricted.<br>(D) The question and answer time was extended. | イベントについて何が示されていますか。<br><br>(A) イベントの主要テーマが変更された。<br>(B) 申し込み費用が値上げされた。<br>(C) 会場への入場が制限されていなかった。<br>(D) 質疑応答時間が延長された。 | **正解 (D)**<br>質疑応答の時間について、お知らせには 30 分とあるが (30-Minute Question and Answer Session to follow the talk)、記事によると、実際は 1 時間だった (a full one-hour question and answer session)。よって、時間が延長されたと判断して、(D) が正解。<br><br>unrestricted [ʌ̀nrɪstríktɪd] 制限されていない |
| **199**<br>In the article, what does Ms. Sanders say the speaker did well?<br>(A) He summarized his financial accomplishments.<br>(B) He reviewed the best financial markets.<br>(C) He put difficult topics into plain terms.<br>(D) He made individual investment portfolios. | 記事の中で、講演者は何をうまくやったと Sanders さんは述べていますか。<br><br>(A) 財務の業績をまとめた。<br>(B) 最良の金融市場をレビューした。<br>(C) 難しいテーマをわかりやすい言葉で説明した。<br>(D) 個別の投資ポートフォリオを作った。 | **正解 (C)**<br>Sanders さんは記事を書いた人物。記事の第 1 段落の This highly accomplished investor took complex topics 〜, and simplified them so that everyone could understand. から、(C) が正解。complex topics を選択肢では difficult topics と表している。<br><br>summarize [sʌ́məràɪz] 〜を要約する<br>accomplishment [əkɑ́mplɪʃmənt] 業績<br>put A into B  A を B の状態に変える<br>term [tɚːrm]（複数形で）言葉遣い、表現<br>investment portfolios 投資ポートフォリオ、有価証券明細書 |
| **200**<br>What problem is mentioned in the article?<br>(A) Attendees were fewer than expected.<br>(B) Some equipment was defective.<br>(C) Some topics were omitted.<br>(D) Financial analyses were unclear. | 記事ではどんな問題が述べられていますか。<br><br>(A) 出席者が予想よりも少なかった。<br>(B) 設備に不備があった。<br>(C) いくつかのテーマが省かれた。<br>(D) 財務分析が不明確であった。 | **正解 (B)**<br>イベントの問題点については記事の第 3 段落に書かれている。この部分の内容を短く表した (B) が正解。本文の audiovisual system「AV システム」を選択肢では some equipment に言い換え、「幾度かフェードアウトし、聞き取りが困難」という状況を defective「欠陥がある」と表している。<br><br>omit [oʊmít] 〜を省略する |

# 第2回 模擬試験 解答・解説

**解答一覧**

| 設問番号 | 正解 | 設問番号 | 正解 | 設問番号 | 正解 | 設問番号 | 正解 | 設問番号 | 正解 |
|---|---|---|---|---|---|---|---|---|---|
| 1 | D | 41 | C | 81 | D | 121 | C | 161 | C |
| 2 | A | 42 | D | 82 | C | 122 | B | 162 | B |
| 3 | A | 43 | B | 83 | C | 123 | D | 163 | C |
| 4 | D | 44 | B | 84 | B | 124 | B | 164 | B |
| 5 | B | 45 | A | 85 | D | 125 | C | 165 | D |
| 6 | C | 46 | B | 86 | A | 126 | C | 166 | A |
| 7 | B | 47 | C | 87 | A | 127 | A | 167 | C |
| 8 | B | 48 | B | 88 | B | 128 | A | 168 | D |
| 9 | A | 49 | D | 89 | B | 129 | C | 169 | A |
| 10 | C | 50 | B | 90 | A | 130 | A | 170 | A |
| 11 | B | 51 | C | 91 | C | 131 | A | 171 | D |
| 12 | A | 52 | A | 92 | B | 132 | D | 172 | D |
| 13 | C | 53 | C | 93 | A | 133 | B | 173 | D |
| 14 | A | 54 | A | 94 | A | 134 | B | 174 | A |
| 15 | A | 55 | D | 95 | B | 135 | C | 175 | B |
| 16 | C | 56 | B | 96 | A | 136 | D | 176 | A |
| 17 | B | 57 | C | 97 | B | 137 | C | 177 | B |
| 18 | B | 58 | A | 98 | B | 138 | A | 178 | D |
| 19 | C | 59 | B | 99 | C | 139 | D | 179 | A |
| 20 | C | 60 | B | 100 | D | 140 | C | 180 | D |
| 21 | B | 61 | D | 101 | B | 141 | B | 181 | C |
| 22 | C | 62 | C | 102 | D | 142 | D | 182 | D |
| 23 | A | 63 | B | 103 | A | 143 | B | 183 | B |
| 24 | C | 64 | D | 104 | D | 144 | B | 184 | C |
| 25 | A | 65 | C | 105 | B | 145 | D | 185 | A |
| 26 | C | 66 | A | 106 | D | 146 | A | 186 | D |
| 27 | A | 67 | D | 107 | D | 147 | B | 187 | B |
| 28 | B | 68 | C | 108 | A | 148 | B | 188 | A |
| 29 | C | 69 | B | 109 | B | 149 | D | 189 | C |
| 30 | A | 70 | D | 110 | C | 150 | A | 190 | D |
| 31 | C | 71 | C | 111 | A | 151 | D | 191 | B |
| 32 | B | 72 | B | 112 | D | 152 | C | 192 | C |
| 33 | D | 73 | D | 113 | B | 153 | C | 193 | A |
| 34 | A | 74 | A | 114 | C | 154 | D | 194 | A |
| 35 | C | 75 | C | 115 | A | 155 | C | 195 | A |
| 36 | A | 76 | B | 116 | D | 156 | C | 196 | D |
| 37 | C | 77 | A | 117 | B | 157 | B | 197 | A |
| 38 | D | 78 | C | 118 | C | 158 | C | 198 | A |
| 39 | D | 79 | A | 119 | B | 159 | D | 199 | B |
| 40 | B | 80 | A | 120 | B | 160 | C | 200 | D |

# PART 1

## 放送文と訳

### 1

(A) The man is entering a building.
(B) The man is using a vending machine.
(C) The man is looking for a parking lot.
(D) The man is standing beside the road.

(A) 男性は建物に入っていくところである。
(B) 男性は自動販売機を使っている。
(C) 男性は駐車場を探している。
(D) 男性は道路の脇に立っている。

### 2

(A) A clock is attached to the building.
(B) A clock is lying on its face.
(C) An alarm clock's hands are turning.
(D) A clock hand has been taken off the wall.

(A) 時計が建物に取り付けられている。
(B) 時計が文字盤を伏せて置いてある。
(C) 目覚まし時計の針が回っている。
(D) 時計の針が壁から取り外されている。

### 3

(A) They're by a post.
(B) They're under a tree.
(C) They're in a building.
(D) They're in a driveway.

(A) 彼女たちは柱のそばにいる。
(B) 彼女たちは木の下にいる。
(C) 彼女たちは建物の中にいる。
(D) 彼女たちは私有車道にいる。

## 正解と解説

### 正解 (D)

男性がパーキングメーターにコインを投入している。(B) の vending machine は使用していない。(C) は parking lot に惑わされずに「動作」をよく聞き取ろう。「男性は道路の脇に立っている」ので，正解は (D)。TOEICでは，「コインを投入する」などの細かい「動作」ではなく，「立っている」などのシンプルな「状態」を問うパターンが多い。

vending machine 自動販売機
parking lot 駐車場

### 正解 (A)

建物の壁に時計が取り付けられている状態を適切に表している (A) が正解。文字盤は表を向いているので，(B) は不適切。(C) は alarm clock「目覚まし時計」という主語を聞いた時点で誤答とわかる。(D) も写真の時計には針がついているので不適切。

attach [ətǽtʃ] ~を取り付ける
hand [hǽnd] （時計の）針

### 正解 (A)

2人の女性が街灯のように見える「柱」のそばにいるので，正解は (A)。post には「郵便ポスト」だけでなく「柱」の意味もあるので要注意。彼女たちは木の下にいないし，屋外にいるので，(B), (C) は不適切。また私有道路にもいないので，(D) も不適切。

driveway [dráivwèi] 私有車道

## 放送文と訳

**4** 🇬🇧

(A) The oar is in the water.
(B) Water is being drained from the boat.
(C) A hole is being drilled.
(D) The boat is tied up.

(A) オールが水の中にある。
(B) 水がボートから抜かれているところである。
(C) 穴がドリルで開けられているところである。
(D) ボートは係留されている。

**5** 🇦🇺

(A) The woman is opening a cabinet drawer.
(B) The woman is taking out a file.
(C) The woman is folding paper.
(D) The woman is crossing her fingers.

(A) 女性はキャビネットの引き出しを開けている。
(B) 女性はファイルを取り出している。
(C) 女性は紙を折っている。
(D) 女性は幸運を祈っている。

**6** 🇺🇸

(A) They're operating an oven.
(B) They're selling baked goods.
(C) They're working opposite each other.
(D) They're putting bread on shelves.

(A) 彼らはオーブンを操作している。
(B) 彼らは焼き菓子を売っている。
(C) 彼らは向かい合って作業をしている。
(D) 彼らはパンを棚に載せている。

## 正解と解説

**正解 (D)**

ボートがロープで係留されているので、正解は (D)。オールはボートの中にあり、穴のように見えるものはあっても水が抜かれているところではなく、また穴が開けられているところでもない。よって、他の選択肢は不適切とわかる。

oar [ɔːr] オール；櫂
drain [drein] (液体)を(〜から)排出させる
tie up 〜 〜を係留する；〜を停泊させる

**正解 (B)**

女性が引き出しからファイルを取り出そうとしているので、正解は (B)。引き出しは開いてはいるが、女性が開けているところではないので、(A) は不正解。(C), (D) は写真に写っている paper や fingers を利用した誤答である。

cabinet [kǽbənit] 戸棚
drawer [drɔ́ːər] 引き出し
fold [fould] 〜を折りたたむ
cross one's fingers 幸運を祈る；成功を祈る

**正解 (C)**

屋内で2人が向かい合わせで作業をしている。よって、正解は (C)。写真のイメージから oven, baked goods, putting bread on shelves に惑わされないようにしよう。写真で人物が実際に明確に行っていない「動作」はすべて誤答である。

baked goods 焼いてある食べ物，焼き菓子
opposite [ɑ́pəzit] 〜に向かい合って

# PART 2  CD2 8-13

## 放送文と訳

### 7  M 🇨🇦  W 🇬🇧

**M**: Where is the film showing?
**W**: (A) Yes, I really like that show.
　　(B) At the Roxy Theater downtown.
　　(C) Tomorrow evening at 7:30.

M：どこでその映画は上映されていますか。
W：(A) はい，私はそのショーが大好きです。
　　(B) 中心街の Roxy 劇場です。
　　(C) 明日の夜 7 時 30 分に。

### 正解と解説

**正解 (B)**

Where ～? で「場所」について尋ねている。疑問詞の疑問文に Yes で答えている (A) はまず除外する。「時」を答えている (C) も不適切。「映画が上映される場所」を具体的に答えている (B) が正解である。

downtown [dàuntáun] 中心街に［の］

---

### 8  M 🇨🇦  M 🇦🇺

**M**: You're from the local office, aren't you?
**M**: (A) I'll locate the officer.
　　(B) No, headquarters.
　　(C) Great, it does look official.

M：地方のオフィスから来られたのですよね。
M：(A) その警官の居場所を探します。
　　(B) いいえ，本社です。
　　(C) いいですね，確かに公式のものに見えます。

**正解 (B)**

「～ですよね」と念押しや確認をする「付加疑問文」。(A) は office と officer で，(C) は office と official で混乱させようとしている。No, headquarters. 「いいえ，本社（から）です」と答えている (B) が正解。

locate [lóukeit] （～の場所）を探す
official [əfíʃəl] 公式の

---

### 9  M 🇦🇺  W 🇺🇸

**M**: What did Mr. Kamal talk with Barbara about?
**W**: (A) Our year-end report.
　　(B) They met for about an hour.
　　(C) Yes, I talked to them about it.

M：Kamal さんは Barbara と何について話したのですか。
W：(A) わが社の会計年度末報告書です。
　　(B) 彼らは約 1 時間会いました。
　　(C) はい，私は彼らにそれについて話しました。

**正解 (A)**

「何を話したのか」を尋ねている。(B) は質問文と同じ about が含まれているが，「話した内容」を答えていないので正解ではない。(C) には talked が含まれているが，疑問詞の疑問文には Yes で答えられないので不適切。「話した内容」を答えている (A) が正解。

year-end [jìərénd] 会計年度末の，年末の

---

### 10  W 🇺🇸  M 🇦🇺

**W**: When is the summer sale supposed to begin?
**M**: (A) Yes, it's some kind of sale, isn't it?
　　(B) 17 percent off everything.
　　(C) It's still being decided.

W：夏のセールはいつ始まる予定ですか。
M：(A) はい，それは何かのセールですよね。
　　(B) すべて 17%引です。
　　(C) まだ決めているところです。

**正解 (C)**

When ～? で「時」について尋ねている。質問文と同じ sale を利用した (A) を選ばないように注意しよう。「セールの割引率」は聞かれていないので (B) も正解ではない。「まだ（いつ始めるか）決めているところ」と答えている (C) が正解である。

be supposed to do ～することになっている
decide [disáid] ～を決める

---

### 11  M 🇨🇦  W 🇬🇧

**M**: Was Marla given the new supervisory position?
**W**: (A) She's worked here about a year.
　　(B) Yes, hadn't you heard?
　　(C) Because of the higher pay.

M：Marla は新しい管理職を与えられたのですか。
W：(A) 彼女は約 1 年ここで働いています。
　　(B) はい，聞いていなかったのですか。
　　(C) 給料が上がるからです。

**正解 (B)**

「Marla は与えられたのか」に対して，Yes, hadn't you heard?「はい，聞いていなかったのですか」と聞き返している (B) が正解にふさわしい。(A) は new supervisory position から連想される work で引っ掛けようとしている。(C) は「役職任命」と「給料」の関連が不明確。

supervisory [sùːpərváizəri] 監督の，管理の

## 放送文と訳

### 12  M 🇦🇺 W 🇬🇧

**M**: Has Bill asked you about your new job?
**W**: (A) Not yet.
　　(B) It's in Sales.
　　(C) I'll start next week.

**M**: Bill はあなたの新しい仕事について尋ねましたか。
**W**: (A) まだです。
　　(B) それは営業部にあります。
　　(C) 来週始めます。

### 13  W 🇺🇸 M 🇦🇺

**W**: Do you want me to have Mr. Jackson call you when he returns later today?
**M**: (A) I'd like to return the item.
　　(B) Yes, I'll be back tomorrow.
　　(C) No thanks, I'll call again tomorrow.

**W**: Jackson さんが本日この後戻りましたら、あなたにお電話させましょうか。
**M**: (A) この商品を返品したいのですが。
　　(B) はい、私は明日戻ってきます。
　　(C) いえ、大丈夫です。明日また電話します。

### 14  M 🇨🇦 W 🇬🇧

**M**: Why are you skipping your break to stay in the office?
**W**: (A) I have to finish this report.
　　(B) I stayed for breakfast.
　　(C) Yes, he's still at the office.

**M**: なぜあなたは休憩を抜いてオフィスにいるのですか。
**W**: (A) このレポートを仕上げなければならないからです。
　　(B) 私は朝食のためにとどまりました。
　　(C) はい、彼はまだオフィスにいます。

### 15  W 🇬🇧 M 🇨🇦

**W**: Would you like to stop and rest for a while?
**M**: (A) Good idea.
　　(B) She's in the restroom.
　　(C) The next stop's mine.

**W**: 中断して少し休憩しませんか。
**M**: (A) いい考えですね。
　　(B) 彼女は化粧室にいます。
　　(C) 次が私の降りる停留所です。

### 16  W 🇬🇧 M 🇦🇺

**W**: I got my accounting certification yesterday.
**M**: (A) After I did well on the test.
　　(B) Yes, you can count on it.
　　(C) Congratulations!

**W**: 昨日、会計士の資格を取りました。
**M**: (A) テストで良い成績を取った後です。
　　(B) はい、期待しておいてください。
　　(C) おめでとう！

## 正解と解説

### 正解 (A)

Has Bill asked you about ~? 「Bill はあなたに~について尋ねたか」の質問に対して、Not yet. 「まだ」と答えている (A) が正解である。「どこの部署で働くのか」を聞いているのではないので、(B) は不適切。また、「いつ始めるのか」という質問でもないので、(C) も正解ではない。

### 正解 (C)

Do you want [Would you like] me to ~? は「(私が)~しましょうか」という申し出の表現。「Jackson さんに電話させましょうか」という申し出に対し、「明日電話します(のでその必要はありません)」と断っている (C) が正解。

### 正解 (A)

Why ~? で「理由」について尋ねている。(B) は breakfast で、(C) は office で引っ掛けようとしている。(C) は Why で聞かれて Yes で答えていることも不正解の理由。「レポートを仕上げなければならない」→「時間がない」→「休憩を抜く」と「理由」の返答として成り立つので、(A) が正解。

skip [skip] ~を抜く

### 正解 (A)

Would you like to ~? は「~しませんか」とていねいに勧誘する表現。Good idea. 「いい考えですね」と同意している (A) が正解。(B) は rest と restroom で、(C) は stop と stop's で音の混乱をねらっている。

rest [rest] 休む
for a while しばらくの間
restroom [réstrù(:)m] 化粧室
stop [stɑp] 停留所

### 正解 (C)

「会計士の資格を取った」という平叙文に対して、Congratulations!「おめでとう」と祝福している (C) が正解。(B) は accounting と count で音の混乱をねらっている。

certification [sɜ̀ːrtəfəkéiʃən] 資格
count on ~ ~を頼りにする、あてにする

| 放送文と訳 | 正解と解説 |
|---|---|

## 17  W 🇬🇧  M 🇦🇺

**W**: How can we reduce costs?
**M**: (A) It costs 32 dollars.
　　(B) Let's discuss that later.
　　(C) By about 18 percent.

W: 私たちはどのようにすれば費用を削減できますか。
M: (A) 32 ドルかかります。
　　**(B) 後ほど話し合いましょう。**
　　(C) 約 18% の差です。

**正解 (B)**

How ～? で「どうやったら減らせるのか」と「方法」を尋ねている。(A) は costs で混乱させようとしている。(C) は How much ～?「どのくらい」とは聞かれていないので，正解ではない。「後で話し合おう」と答えている (B) が正解。

reduce [ridjúːs] ～を減らす
cost [kɔːst/kɔst] 名 費用
　　　　　　　　　 動 (費用)がかかる

## 18  M 🇨🇦  W 🇬🇧

**M**: How about something cool to drink?
**W**: (A) It's only 4 degrees Celsius.
　　(B) Sounds nice.
　　(C) Thanks, it was refreshing.

M: 何か冷たい飲み物はいかがですか。
W: (A) たったセ氏 4 度です。
　　**(B) いいですね。**
　　(C) ありがとう，さわやかでした。

**正解 (B)**

How about ～? は「～はいかがですか」と提案する表現。「冷たい飲み物はいかがですか」という提案を Sounds nice.「いいですね」と言って受け入れている (B) が正解。cool につられて，4 degrees を含む (A) を選ばないように注意しよう。(C) は Thanks，まではよいが，その後の内容が質問とかみ合わない。

degree [digríː] (温度などの)度
refreshing [rifréʃiŋ] さわやかな

## 19  W 🇺🇸  M 🇦🇺

**W**: Who put all these papers on my desk?
**M**: (A) Oh, did you?
　　(B) No, they're hard to describe.
　　(C) Probably Beth.

W: これらの全書類を私の机の上に置いた人は誰ですか。
M: (A) ああ，あなたがやったのですか。
　　(B) いいえ，それらは説明しにくいです。
　　**(C) たぶん Beth です。**

**正解 (C)**

Who ～? で「人」について尋ねている。疑問詞の疑問文には Yes/No では答えられないので，(B) は不適切とすぐにわかる。また，desk と describe の音の混乱もねらっている。「人名」を答えている (C) が正解。

describe [diskráib] ～を説明する

## 20  W 🇬🇧  M 🇨🇦

**W**: Aren't you going to take the shuttle bus back to the hotel?
**M**: (A) It only takes about 10 minutes.
　　(B) I reserved a suite.
　　(C) No, I'll just walk.

W: ホテルまで帰るのにシャトルバスに乗るつもりはないのですか。
M: (A) 10 分ほどかかるだけです。
　　(B) スイートルームを予約しました。
　　**(C) はい，歩いて行きます。**

**正解 (C)**

Aren't you ～?「～ではないのですか」と相手に確認する否定疑問文。「乗るつもりはないのか」と聞かれて，「はい (乗るつもりはありません)，歩きます」と答えている (C) が正解。否定疑問文に対しては，「はい」の意味では No で答えることに要注意。(A) は take で，(B) は hotel から連想される reserved や suite で引っ掛けようとしている。

shuttle bus シャトルバス　reserve [rizɔ́ːrv] ～を予約する　suite [swiːt] スイートルーム

## 21  M 🇦🇺  W 🇺🇸

**M**: How soon can I get an update on our sales this month?
**W**: (A) It went well.
　　(B) Give me an hour.
　　(C) Uh … it's not for sale.

M: 今月の売り上げの最新情報をどのくらいでもらえますか。
W: (A) うまくいきました。
　　**(B) 1 時間ください。**
　　(C) ええと，それは非売品です。

**正解 (B)**

How soon ～? で「どのくらい早く～か」を尋ねている。(C) は sales と sale で混乱を誘っている。(B) Give me an hour.「1 時間ください」は，「1 時間くれたら最新情報を渡せる」という意味なので正解としてふさわしい。

update [ʌ́pdèit] 最新情報

## 放送文と訳

### 22

**M**: Who will take over the research and development division during Mr. Jang's absence next month?
**W**: (A) I haven't asked about any takeover.
　　(B) He's been in charge for three years.
　　(C) Ashley Garner would be ideal.

M: Jang さんが来月不在の間，誰が研究開発部を引き継ぐのですか。
W: (A) 私は引き継ぎについて尋ねていません。　(B) 彼は3年間担当しています。
　　(C) Ashley Garner が理想的でしょう。

### 正解 (C)

Who ～? で「人」について尋ねている。(A) は質問に出てくる take over と takeover で混乱させようとしている。(B) は take over から連想される in charge で引っ掛けようとしている。「人名」を具体的に答えている (C) が正解。

take over ～（仕事など）を引き継ぐ
research and development division 研究開発部
takeover [téikòuvər] 引き継ぎ，企業買収
in charge 担当して

---

### 23

**M**: You haven't filed that report yet.
**W**: (A) Sorry, I've been too busy.
　　(B) Yes, it's very boring.
　　(C) There's a reporter outside.

M: まだそのレポートをファイルしていませんね。
W: (A) すみません，あまりに忙しくて。
　　(B) はい，それはとても退屈です。
　　(C) レポーターが外にいます。

### 正解 (A)

「まだそのレポートをファイルしていませんね」という，相手をやや責めるような平叙文に対して，Sorry, I've been too busy. 「すみません，あまりに忙しくて（まだやっていません）」と弁解している (A) が正解。(B) は内容が質問とかみ合わない。(C) は report と reporter で音の混乱をねらっている。

file [fail] ～をファイルする
boring [bɔ́:riŋ] 退屈な

---

### 24

**M**: Why didn't you take the 12:15 train?
**M**: (A) About 12 to 15 hours to get there.
　　(B) Yes, we trained there, too.
　　(C) I changed my plans.

M: なぜ12時15分発の列車に乗らなかったのですか。
M: (A) そこへ行くのに約12時間から15時間です。
　　(B) はい，私たちもそこで訓練を受けました。
　　(C) 予定を変更したからです。

### 正解 (C)

Why ～? で「理由」について尋ねている。所要時間は聞かれていないので (A) は不適切。(A) の 12 と 15 や (B) の train と trained のような音の引っ掛けに注意。「列車に乗らなかった理由」として「予定を変更した」と答えている (C) が正解。

train [trein] 訓練を受ける

---

### 25

**W**: Where are the new employees supposed to go for orientation?
**W**: (A) The main auditorium in the west wing.
　　(B) Your presentation proposals are fine.
　　(C) It's a good way to meet new co-workers.

W: 新入社員はオリエンテーションのためにどこに行くことになっているのですか。
W: (A) 西棟の大ホールです。
　　(B) あなたのプレゼンテーション案は大丈夫です。
　　(C) それは新しい同僚に会うのに良い方法です。

### 正解 (A)

Where ～? に対して具体的に「場所」を答えている (A) が正解。(B), (C) には employees, orientation から連想されるビジネス関連語の presentation, co-workers が含まれているが，質問の答えになっていないので不適切。

orientation [ɔ̀:riəntéiʃən] オリエンテーション
auditorium [ɔ̀:dətɔ́:riəm] ホール，講堂
wing [wiŋ]（建物などの）翼，棟

---

### 26

**W**: Would you like a blueberry muffin or a banana one?
**W**: (A) Yes, a blue bandanna.
　　(B) They are delicious.
　　(C) Hmm … either would be fine.

W: ブルーベリーマフィンかバナナマフィンはいかがですか。
W: (A) はい，青いバンダナです。
　　(B) それらはとてもおいしいです。
　　(C) うーん，どちらでも構いません。

### 正解 (C)

Would you like ～? は物をていねいに勧める表現。A or B? の二者択一の問いには，本来はどちらかを明確に答えることになるが，ここでは either would be fine 「どちらでも構わない」と答えている (C) が正解。(B) は「食べ物」から連想される delicious で引っ掛けようとしている。新形式の TOEIC で意識されている Hmm … のような言い淀みにも慣れておこう。

| 放送文と訳 | 正解と解説 |
|---|---|

## 27  M 🇨🇦  W 🇬🇧

**M**: What attracts you to working the night shift?
**W**: (A) Nothing in particular.
　　(B) Yes, that track's being worked on.
　　(C) Until 11:00 at night.

M：何があなたを夜勤で働くことに引きつけるのですか。
W：**(A) 特にありません。**
　　(B) はい，その線路は修理されています。
　　(C) 夜の 11 時までです。

### 正解 (A)

質問は What ～? だが，「何があなたを夜勤で働くことに引きつけるのですか」は，夜勤で働きたい「理由」を尋ねている。「(理由は) 特にない」と答えている (A) が正解。

attract [ətrǽkt] ～を引きつける
night shift 夜勤
in particular 特に
track [trǽk] 鉄道線路

## 28  M 🇦🇺  W 🇺🇸

**M**: Hasn't the deadline for the project passed?
**W**: (A) We project 4 percent.
　　(B) No, we've still got 2 days.
　　(C) Line up here, please.

M：プロジェクトの締め切りは過ぎたのではないですか。
W：(A) 私たちは 4％ と見積もっています。
　　**(B) いいえ，まだ 2 日あります。**
　　(C) ここに並んでください。

### 正解 (B)

Hasn't ～ passed?「～は過ぎたのではないですか」は，相手に確認する否定疑問文。No, we've still got 2 days.「いいえ，まだ 2 日あります (ので過ぎていません)」と答えている (B) が正解。(A) は質問と同じ project を使っているが，品詞と意味が異なる。

deadline [dédlàin] 締め切り
project [prɑ́dʒekt] 名 プロジェクト
　　　　[prədʒékt] 動 ～を見積もる
line up 一列に並ぶ

## 29  W 🇬🇧  W 🇺🇸

**W**: Could you show me how to work the copier, please?
**W**: (A) I bought a copy of that book yesterday.
　　(B) Tea, not coffee.
　　(C) Sorry, I'm on my way out.

W：コピー機の動かし方を教えていただけませんか。
W：(A) 昨日その本を 1 冊買いました。
　　(B) コーヒーではなくて紅茶です。
　　**(C) すみません，出掛けるところなのです。**

### 正解 (C)

Could you show me how to ～?「～の仕方を教えてくださいませんか」は，ていねいに依頼する表現。Sorry, I'm on my way out.「すみません，出掛けるところなのです」と断っている (C) が正解。(A) は copier と copy で，(B) は copier と coffee で音の混乱をねらっている。

copier [kɑ́piər] コピー機
copy [kɑ́pi] (本の) 冊
on *one's* way out 出掛ける途中で

## 30  W 🇺🇸  M 🇨🇦

**W**: Are you going to read through even the minor details of the contract yourself?
**M**: (A) No, a specialist will.
　　(B) I'll contact them later.
　　(C) It's for three years.

W：契約の重要ではない細目についてまで自分で目を通すつもりですか。
M：**(A) いいえ，専門家がします。**
　　(B) 後で彼らに連絡を取ります。
　　(C) 3 年間です。

### 正解 (A)

「細目についてまで自分で目を通すのか」に対して，No, a specialist will.「いいえ，専門家がします」と答えている (A) が正解。(B) は contract と似た音の contact を用いた引っ掛け。「期間」を聞かれてはいないので，(C) は不適切。

read through ～ ～によく目を通す
detail [díːteil] 詳細
contract [kɑ́ntrækt] 契約

## 31  W 🇬🇧  M 🇦🇺

**W**: When's the earliest we could pick up the office supplies?
**M**: (A) I've picked up the list.
　　(B) I always get up early.
　　(C) Next Tuesday, I think.

W：事務用品を一番早く受け取れるのはいつですか。
M：(A) リストを受け取りました。
　　(B) 私はいつも早く起きます。
　　**(C) 来週の火曜日だと思います。**

### 正解 (C)

When ～? で「時」について尋ねている。pick up につられて (A) を，earliest につられて early を含む (B) を選ばないように注意しよう。「来週の火曜日だと思う」と具体的に「時」を答えている (C) が正解である。

pick up ～ ～を受け取る

# PART 3  CD2 34-35  W 🇬🇧  M-1 🇨🇦  M-2 🇦🇺

## 放送文

Questions 32 through 34 refer to the following conversation with three speakers.

**W**: Steve, can you send these documents to Michelle in Dublin, please?
**M-1**: Sure. Are they important?
**W**: Yeah. I need her to review the graphics before I go any further with this project.
**M-2**: Actually, you can give them to her in person, Ms. Grady.
**W**: What do you mean, Ted?
**M-2**: She's in a meeting on the fifth floor at the moment.
**W**: Oh, I didn't realize she was here in our London office. No wonder she didn't answer my calls. Then, Steve, could you ask her to drop by my office later, please? I'm on a tight deadline.
**M-1**: No problem.
**M-2**: The meeting's due to end in a few minutes. She's reserved a seat on the train for Brussels this evening and then she's going to Paris, so now's a good time to see her.

## 放送文の訳

問題 32-34 は 3 人の話し手による次の会話に関するものです。

W：Steve, ダブリンの Michelle にこの書類を送ってもらえる？
M-1：いいですよ。それは重要なものですか。
W：そうなの。このプロジェクトを先へ進める前に，彼女にグラフィックを見直してもらう必要があるのよ。
M-2：実は，彼女に直接渡せますよ，Grady さん。
W：どういうこと，Ted？
M-2：ちょうど今，彼女は 5 階でミーティング中です。
W：あら，彼女がこのロンドン事務所にいるとは気づかなかったわ。どうりで私の電話に出なかったはずね。じゃあ，Steve，彼女に後で私のオフィスに寄るように頼んでくれる？ 私には厳しい締め切りがあるの。
M-1：いいですよ。
M-2：ミーティングはあと数分で終わる予定です。彼女は今夜ブリュッセル行きの列車の席を予約していて，その後はパリに行きます。ですから，彼女に会うのは今が良い機会です。

## Vocabulary

- □ review [rivjúː] 動 〜を見直す
- □ graphics [grǽfiks] 名 グラフィック，画像
- □ in person 直接に，じかに
- □ at the moment ちょうど今
- □ realize [ríː(ː)əlàiz] 動 〜に気づく
- □ no wonder 〜 〜も無理はない
- □ drop by 〜 〜に立ち寄る
- □ tight [tait] 形 厳しい
- □ deadline [dédlàin] 名 締め切り
- □ be due to *do* 〜する予定である

---

### 32
Where are the speakers?

(A) In Dublin
(B) In London
(C) In Brussels
(D) In Paris

**設問の訳**
話し手たちはどこにいますか。

(A) ダブリン
(B) ロンドン
(C) ブリュッセル
(D) パリ

**正解 (B)**

女性は I didn't realize she was here in our London office と言って，Michelle が今話し手たちがいるロンドン事務所にいることを知り，自分に会いに来るように頼んでいる。つまり，女性も男性 2 人もロンドン事務所にいるということなので，正解は (B)。3 人による会話が PART 3 の最初に来ても，慌てないように心の準備をしておこう。

---

### 33
What does the woman want Michelle to do?

(A) Send her an e-mail
(B) Call her directly
(C) Fax her some files
(D) Come to see her

**設問の訳**
女性は Michelle に何をしてもらいたいのですか。

(A) 自分に E メールを送る
(B) 自分に直接電話する
(C) 自分に書類をファックスする
(D) 自分に会いに来る

**正解 (D)**

女性は Steve, could you ask her to drop by my office later, please? と言って，Steve (M-1) に依頼をしている。この her は Michelle のことなので，女性が Michelle にしてもらいたいこととして適切なのは (D)。

---

### 34
What does one of the men say will happen in a few minutes?

(A) A conference will end.
(B) A train will leave.
(C) A deadline will arrive.
(D) A project will be launched.

**設問の訳**
男性の 1 人は数分後に何が起こると言っていますか。

(A) 会議が終わる。
(B) 列車が出発する。
(C) 締め切りが来る。
(D) プロジェクトが開始される。

**正解 (A)**

Ted (M-2) が最後の発言で The meeting's due to end in a few minutes. と述べている。よって，正解はその言い換えである (A) A conference will end. である。

launch [lɔːntʃ] 〜を開始する

## 放送文

Questions 35 through 37 refer to the following conversation.

W: Good morning. Welcome to SunCrest Mutual. How can I help you?
M: I'm going to Thailand on business soon and I'd like to know if I'll be able to use my SunCrest Debit Card there. I prefer to use that over cash or traveler's checks.
W: You can use your card overseas to pay for everything from plane tickets to travel insurance. Just look for the SunCrest logo on ATMs and on buildings. Any place you see that, the card is valid.

## 放送文の訳

問題 35-37 は次の会話に関するものです。

W: おはようございます。SunCrest Mutual へようこそ。ご用件をお伺いします。
M: もうすぐ出張でタイに行くので，私の SunCrest デビットカードがそこで使えるかどうかを知りたいのですが。私は現金やトラベラーズチェックよりカードを使いたいのです。
W: お客様のカードは，飛行機のチケットから旅行保険まで，すべてのお支払いに対して海外で使うことができます。ATM や建物で SunCrest のロゴを探すだけです。それがあるところならどこでもカードは有効です。

### Vocabulary
- prefer A over B　B よりむしろ A を選ぶ
- overseas [ðuvɚsíːz] 海外で
- insurance [inʃúərəns] 保険
- valid [vǽlid] 有効な

## 設問

**35**
Who most likely is the woman?

(A) A tour agent
(B) An airline clerk
(C) A bank representative
(D) An insurance salesperson

**36**
What would the man prefer to take on his trip?

(A) A debit card
(B) A credit card
(C) Cash
(D) Traveler's checks

**37**
What does the SunCrest logo on ATMs and buildings indicate?
(A) The brand is popular.
(B) The usage fee is low.
(C) Debit cards can be used.
(D) The machine is new.

## 設問の訳

女性は誰だと考えられますか。

(A) 旅行業者
(B) 航空会社の職員
(C) 銀行員
(D) 保険の外交員

男性が旅行に持っていきたいものは何ですか。

(A) デビットカード
(B) クレジットカード
(C) 現金
(D) トラベラーズチェック

ATM や建物の SunCrest のロゴは，何を意味しますか。
(A) そのブランドは人気がある。
(B) 使用料が安い。
(C) デビットカードが使える。
(D) 機械が新しい。

## 正解と解説

**正解 (C)**
女性がデビットカードが使える場所や ATM や建物のロゴについて説明していることから，選択肢の中では，(C) A bank representative が正解に最もふさわしい。

tour agent 旅行業者

**正解 (A)**
男性は，I'd like to know if I'll be able to use my SunCrest Debit Card there. I prefer to use that over cash or traveler's checks. と述べており，デビットカードを使いたがっていることがわかる。よって，正解は (A)。

**正解 (C)**
女性の最後の発言の，Just look for the SunCrest logo on ATMs and on buildings. Any place you see that, the card is valid. が正解の決め手。ロゴのあるところではデビットカードが使えるということなので，正解は (C)。

usage fee 使用料

## 放送文

Questions 38 through 40 refer to the following conversation.

W: Excuse me, conductor. Do you know which station is next? I must have fallen asleep after we left Boston.
M: Actually, we just left New York, so we're headed toward Philadelphia as our next major stop, before continuing on to the last stop, Washington, D.C.
W: How long will it take us to get to D.C.? About two more hours?
M: I guess, closer to three, assuming that all this snow on the rail tracks doesn't slow us down.

## 放送文の訳

問題 38-40 は次の会話に関するものです。

W：すみません，車掌さん。次の駅がどこかわかりますか。ボストンを出た後眠り込んでしまったみたいです。
M：実は，ちょうどニューヨークを出たばかりで，次の主要な停車駅のフィラデルフィアに向かっています。それから，終点のワシントン DC へと向かいます。
W：ワシントン DC に着くのにどれくらいかかりますか。あと 2 時間くらいですか。
M：線路に積もった雪によって減速しないと仮定して，3 時間近くだと思います。

## Vocabulary

- fall asleep 眠り込む
- actually [ǽktʃuəli] 副 実は
- be headed toward ~ ~に向かう
- major [méidʒər] 形 主要な
- assuming that ~ ~だと仮定して
- rail track 線路

### 38
Where most likely are the speakers?

(A) On an airplane
(B) On a bus
(C) On a ship
(D) On a train

**設問の訳**
話し手たちはどこにいると考えられますか。

(A) 飛行機
(B) バス
(C) 船
(D) 列車

**正解 (D)**

station という単語が会話に含まれていることと，all this snow on the rail tracks doesn't slow us down という部分から判断して，(D) On a train が正解。

### 39
What is the final destination?

(A) Philadelphia
(B) Boston
(C) New York
(D) Washington, D.C.

**設問の訳**
最終の行き先はどこですか。

(A) フィラデルフィア
(B) ボストン
(C) ニューヨーク
(D) ワシントン DC

**正解 (D)**

男性の最初の発言に we're headed toward Philadelphia as our next major stop, before continuing on to the last stop, Washington, D.C. とあり，Washington, D.C. が最終の行き先とわかるので，正解は (D)。本文中の the last stop を質問文では final destination と言い換えている。

final destination 終点

### 40
When is the woman likely to reach her destination?

(A) In about two hours
(B) In about three hours
(C) In about four hours
(D) In about five hours

**設問の訳**
女性は目的地にいつ到着すると考えられますか。

(A) 約 2 時間後
(B) 約 3 時間後
(C) 約 4 時間後
(D) 約 5 時間後

**正解 (B)**

女性にワシントン DC までの所要時間を聞かれて，男性は I guess, closer to three と答えているので，正解は (B)。(A) の In about two hours は，女性が予想した時間なので引っ掛からないようにしよう。

## 放送文

Questions 41 through 43 refer to the following conversation.

W: I hear the workshop schedule for new recruits has been put up. Have you seen it yet?
M: Yes, it's for the week beginning June 25. Each division will hold workshops in different rooms, but the main presentations will be held in Conference Room 21D.
W: So do we need to register for them somewhere or submit our names to someone?
M: Yes, we have to confirm we'll be going through our managers by this afternoon. They'll give us brochures containing all the information we need.

## 放送文の訳

問題 41-43 は次の会話に関するものです。

W：新入社員のための研修スケジュールがもう貼り出されているそうよ。あなたはもう見た？
M：うん。6月25日から始まる週だよ。それぞれの部門が違う部屋で研修を開くんだけど，中心となるプレゼンテーションは 21D 会議室で開かれるんだ。
W：それで私たちはどこかで登録するか，名前を誰かに提出しなければならないの？
M：うん。今日の午後までに課長の許可が得られることを確認しなければならない。必要な情報がすべて含まれたパンフレットをもらえるよ。

### Vocabulary

- workshop [wə́ːrkʃɑ̀p] 名ワークショップ，研修会
- recruit [rikrúːt] 名新人
- division [divíʒən] 名部門
- conference [kɑ́nfərəns] 名会議
- register for ~ ～に登録する
- submit [səbmít] 動～を提出する
- confirm [kənfə́ːrm] 動～を確認する
- brochure [brouʃúər] 名パンフレット
- contain [kəntéin] 動～を含む

---

### 41

Where most likely are the speakers?

(A) At a conference
(B) At a presentation
(C) At a workplace
(D) At a library

話し手たちはどこにいると考えられますか。

(A) 会議
(B) プレゼンテーション
(C) 職場
(D) 図書館

**正解 (C)**

研修スケジュールのことなどを詳細に話していることから，「職場」で話していると思われる。話題は，会議中やプレゼン中に公的に話す内容でもない。よって，正解は (C)。

---

### 42

What will happen on June 25?

(A) New employees will start work.
(B) A department will relocate.
(C) Presentations will end.
(D) Training will begin.

6月25日に何が起こりますか。

(A) 新入社員が仕事を始める。
(B) 部署が移転する。
(C) プレゼンテーションが終わる。
(D) 研修が始まる。

**正解 (D)**

女性が新入社員の研修スケジュールに言及して，それに対して男性が it's for the week beginning June 25 と述べている。つまり，新入社員が研修を始めるのが6月25日なので，正解は (D)。

department [dipɑ́ːrtmənt] （会社などの）部
relocate [rìːlóukeit] 移転する

---

### 43

What must the speakers do today?

(A) Alter the program schedule
(B) Verify attendance
(C) Hand in their brochures
(D) Go to a conference

話し手たちは今日何をしなければなりませんか。

(A) プログラムのスケジュールを変更する
(B) 参加を確実にする
(C) パンフレットを提出する
(D) 会議に行く

**正解 (B)**

男性の最後の発言に we have to confirm we'll be going through our managers by this afternoon とあり，課長を通して参加を確定させる必要があると述べている。よって，正解は (B)。

alter [ɔ́ːltər] ～を変更する
verify [vérəfài] ～を確実にする
hand in ~ ～を提出する

## 放送文

Questions 44 through 46 refer to the following conversation.

**M**: The total will be 25 dollars and 30 cents, please. How would you like to pay?
**W**: Oh, that's more expensive than I thought. Is that the amount before, or after my store card discount?
**M**: After. You received 10 percent off your purchase. Here it is printed on your receipt.
**W**: Oh, I see. I guess that dress was more than I thought. I'd like to pay by credit card if that's OK.

## 放送文の訳

問題 44-46 は次の会話に関するものです。

M：合計 25 ドル 30 セントになります。どのようにお支払いになりたいですか。
W：あら，思ったより高いんですね。それって店のカード割引の前の総額ですか，それとも後の総額ですか。
M：後のです。お買い上げの品物について 10％引きを受けられました。このようにお客様のレシートに印字されています。
W：ああ，なるほど。あのドレスが思ったより高かったようですね。もしよろしければクレジットカードで支払いたいんですけど。

## Vocabulary

- expensive [ikspénsiv] 形 高価な
- amount [əmáunt] 名 総額
- discount [dískaunt] 名 割引
- purchase [pə́ːrtʃəs] 名 購入
- receipt [risíːt] 名 レシート
- guess [ges] 動 〜と推測する

---

### 設問 44

What is the woman doing?

(A) Returning goods
(B) Concluding a transaction
(C) Applying for credit
(D) Explaining about products

**設問の訳**

女性は何をしていますか。

(A) 商品を返品している
(B) 取引を終えようとしている
(C) 信用貸しを申し込んでいる
(D) 製品について説明をしている

**正解 (B)**

レジで精算中に交されている会話である。女性は商品の代金を支払うことで「取引を終えようとしている」と言えるので，正解は (B)。

conclude [kənklúːd] 〜を終える
transaction [trænsǽkʃən] 取引
explain [ikspléin] 説明する

---

### 設問 45

How much did the woman save?

(A) 10 percent
(B) 20 percent
(C) 25 percent
(D) 30 percent

**設問の訳**

女性はいくら得をしましたか。

(A) 10％
(B) 20％
(C) 25％
(D) 30％

**正解 (A)**

男性が女性に You received 10 percent off your purchase. と言っているので，10％の割引を受けたとわかる。よって，正解は (A)。

---

### 設問 46

What did the woman misunderstand?

(A) The credit card limit
(B) The item price
(C) The location of the store
(D) The refund policy

**設問の訳**

女性は何を勘違いしたのですか。

(A) クレジットカードの限度額
(B) 品目の値段
(C) 店の場所
(D) 代金返却の規定

**正解 (B)**

最初に女性は思ったよりも合計金額が高いことに驚いている。そして，男性にレシートを見せてもらった女性は I guess that dress was more than I thought. と言っているので，ドレスの値段を勘違いしていたことが推測できる。よって，正解は (B)。

location [loukéiʃən] 場所
policy [páləsi] 規定，方針

## 放送文

Questions 47 through 49 refer to the following conversation.

W: As you know, the supplier's still refusing to increase our discount. I've been researching the market online and I think we can get the raw materials we need cheaper elsewhere.
M: That'd be great. We need to reduce costs to the level of our competitors if we're going to survive.
W: Exactly! I'd like us to buy from eastern Europe from now on. I had Ricardo in Operations look at the figures. He confirmed my research. He said we could save up to 32 percent that way.

## 放送文の訳

問題 47-49 は次の会話に関するものです。

W：知っての通り，供給業者がまだ私たちの会社の割引を引き上げることを拒否しているのよ。オンラインでずっと市場を調査しているけど，必要な原材料を他でもっと安く手に入れられると思うわ。
M：それはいいね。生き残るつもりなら，ライバル社のレベルまでコストを削減する必要があるし。
W：その通りよ！ これからは私たちの会社には東ヨーロッパから買ってほしいわ。業務部の Ricardo に数値を見てもらったの。彼は私の調査が正しいと確認してくれたわ。彼が言うには，私たちはその方法で最大32%まで節約できるそうよ。

### Vocabulary
- supplier [səpláiər] 名 供給業者
- refuse to *do* 〜するのを拒否する
- research [rísəːrtʃ] 動 〜を調査する 名 調査；研究
- raw material 原材料
- reduce [ridjúːs] 動 〜を減らす
- competitor [kəmpétətər] 名 競合他社
- survive [sə(ː)rváiv] 動 生き残る
- from now on 今後は
- up to 〜 最大〜まで

## 設問

**47**
What are the speakers mainly discussing?
(A) Expanding their market share
(B) Offering a discount
(C) Lowering expenses
(D) Selling new products

**48**
Why does the man think that they need to change their supplier?
(A) To access better materials
(B) To remain competitive
(C) To order online
(D) To raise product prices

**49**
What did Ricardo do?
(A) Transferred to eastern Europe
(B) Simplified operations
(C) Saved money
(D) Reviewed the data

## 設問の訳

話し手たちは主に何について話していますか。
(A) 市場占有率を拡大すること
(B) 割引を申し出ること
(C) 出費を減らすこと
(D) 新製品を売ること

男性はなぜ供給業者を変更する必要があると思っているのですか。
(A) より良い材料を入手するため
(B) 競争力を保つため
(C) オンラインで注文するため
(D) 製品の価格を上げるため

Ricardo は何をしましたか。
(A) 東ヨーロッパに転勤した
(B) 業務を簡略化した
(C) 金を貯めた
(D) データを見直した

## 正解と解説

**正解 (C)**
話し手たちは，いかにコストを削減するかを話し合っている。男性の言葉にある to reduce costs を言い換えた (C) Lowering expenses が正解。

- expand [ikspǽnd] 〜を拡大する
- market share 市場占有率
- lower [lóuər] 〜を減らす

**正解 (B)**
男性は，供給業者を変更するという女性の意見に同意した後に，その理由として We need to reduce costs to the level of our competitors if we're going to survive. とライバル社に対抗するためだと述べているので，正解は (B)。

**正解 (D)**
女性は最後の発言で，Ricardo がしたこととして，He confirmed my research. と言っている。これを言い換えた (D) Reviewed the data が正解。

- transfer to 〜 〜に転勤する
- simplify [símpləfài] 〜を簡略化する

## 放送文

Questions 50 through 52 refer to the following conversation.

W: Excuse me, do you have the latest Red Wolf?
M: I'm sorry ma'am, that product won't be released until Friday. Would you like to pre-order one?
W: Um … I'm not sure. I'd like to take a look at it first. I only want it to make calls. So, the simpler, the better.
M: Red Wolf comes in a variety of models, from the very basic to the very sophisticated. They can also be upgraded later if you want. I can get some of the previous models out for you to look at if you like.

## 放送文の訳

問題 50-52 は次の会話に関するものです。

W：すみません。最新型の Red Wolf はありますか。
M：申し訳ありませんが，そちらの商品は金曜まで発売されません。予約注文されますか。
W：うーん…どうかな。まずはちょっと見てみたいです。私はただ電話をかけるのに欲しいだけなんです。だから，シンプルであればあるほどいいのです。
M：Red Wolf は，とてもベーシックなものからとても凝ったものまで，いろいろなモデルがあります。もしお望みなら後でアップグレードすることもできます。よろしければ，前のモデルをいくつかお見せしましょう。

### Vocabulary

- latest [léitist] 形 最新の
- release [rilí:s] 動 〜を発売する
- pre-order [pri(:)ɔ́:rdər] 動 〜を先行予約する
- a variety of 〜 いろいろな〜
- basic [béisik] 形 基本的な
- sophisticated [səfístəkèitid] 形 凝った
- upgrade [ʌpgréid] 動 〜をアップグレードする

---

### 50
What most likely is the Red Wolf?

(A) A radio
(B) A mobile phone
(C) A Web site
(D) A television set

**設問の訳**
Red Wolf とは何だと考えられますか。

(A) ラジオ
(B) 携帯電話
(C) ウェブサイト
(D) テレビ受像機

**正解 (B)**

女性の I only want it to make calls. という発言が正解のポイント。「電話をかけるもの」であるから，(B) A mobile phone が正解にふさわしい。

---

### 51
What does the man offer to do for the woman?

(A) Exchange a model
(B) Upgrade a component
(C) Show her some products
(D) Order a product

**設問の訳**
男性は女性に何をすることを申し出ていますか。

(A) モデルを交換する
(B) 部品をアップグレードする
(C) 彼女にいくつか製品を見せる
(D) 製品を注文する

**正解 (C)**

男性が最後の発言で I can get some of the previous models out for you to look at if you like. と述べており，製品を見せることを提案しているので，正解は (C)。

component [kəmpóunənt] 部品

---

### 52
Why does the woman say, "the simpler, the better"?

(A) She does not need a lot of extra functions.
(B) She wants to acquire the product promptly.
(C) She values unique design features.
(D) She strongly believes in quality over quantity.

**設問の訳**
女性はなぜ "the simpler, the better" と言っていますか。

(A) 余分な機能があまり必要ないから。
(B) 早急に製品を手に入れたいから。
(C) 独特なデザイン上の特徴を評価しているから。
(D) 量より質を強く信じているから。

**正解 (A)**

the simpler, the better は「シンプルであればあるほどよい」という意味。〈the ＋比較級 〜, the ＋比較級 …〉で「〜であればあるほど，…」という意味である。女性は直前で I only want it to make calls.「電話をかけるのに欲しいだけだ」と言っていることから，(A) が正解。

function [fʌ́ŋkʃən] 機能
acquire [əkwáiər] 〜を獲得する
promptly [prɑ́mptli] すぐに
value [vǽlju(:)] 〜を評価する
feature [fí:tʃər] 特徴

## 放送文

Questions 53 through 55 refer to the following conversation.

W: I'd like two tickets for the 1:00 showing of *Jack the Pirate*, please.
M: I'm sorry, but that's sold out right now. We still have tickets for the 3:00 show.
W: My son and I don't really want to wait around for two hours. What else could you recommend for children under 10?
M: *Secret Forest* might interest both of you. It's an exciting mystery based on a book. Would you like two tickets?

## 放送文の訳

問題 53-55 は次の会話に関するものです。

W：*Jack the Pirate*（海賊ジャック）の 1 時上映のチケットを 2 枚お願いします。
M：申し訳ありませんが，ただ今売り切れています。3 時の上映なら，まだチケットがあります。
W：息子と私は 2 時間もぶらぶら待ちたくないのです。10 歳未満の子供にお勧めのものは他にありますか。
M：*Secret Forest*（秘密の森）ならお 2 人とも興味を持たれるかもしれません。本を原作にした手に汗握るミステリーです。チケットを 2 枚いかがですか。

### Vocabulary

- right now 現在，たった今
- recommend [rèkəménd] 動 ～を勧める
- (be) based on ～ ～に基づいた

---

### 53
**Where most likely are the speakers?**
(A) At an amusement park
(B) At a bus terminal
(C) At a movie theater
(D) At a bookstore

**設問の訳**：話し手たちはどこにいると考えられますか。
(A) 遊園地
(B) バスターミナル
(C) 映画館
(D) 書店

**正解 (C)**
女性が最初の発言で I'd like two tickets for the 1:00 showing of *Jack the Pirate*, please. と言っているので，(C) At a movie theater「映画館」が正解に最もふさわしい。

amusement park 遊園地

---

### 54
**What is the woman's preferred time?**
(A) 1:00
(B) 3:00
(C) 7:00
(D) 10:00

**設問の訳**：女性の希望時間は何時ですか。
(A) 1 時
(B) 3 時
(C) 7 時
(D) 10 時

**正解 (A)**
最初に女性は 1 時の上映を希望している。よって，正解は (A)。(B) の 3 時は，見たい映画のチケットが手に入る上映時間であり，don't really want to wait around「待ちたくない」と言っていることからも，女性が希望している時間ではないとわかる。

---

### 55
**What does the man suggest the woman do?**
(A) Wait for two hours
(B) Check another area
(C) Get a refund
(D) Accept an alternative

**設問の訳**：男性は女性にどうするよう提案していますか。
(A) 2 時間待つ
(B) 別の地域をあたる
(C) 返金を受ける
(D) 代案を受け入れる

**正解 (D)**
男性は，まず 3 時の上映に空きがあることを伝えたが，女性が「2 時間待ちたくない」と言い，他の子供向きの映画を勧めている。代案を出していると言えるので，正解は (D)。

refund [ríːfʌnd] 払い戻し
alternative [ɔːltớːrnətiv] 代案

## 放送文

Questions 56 through 58 refer to the following conversation.

M: I'm going to the reception desk to find out the earliest time we can set up at the exhibition hall. Do you want to come along?
W: Umm ... I think I'd rather not.
M: Why is that?
W: Well, I need to stay here in the office and finish writing my notes. I have a meeting with Cirrus Planning at 2:00. They want to confirm the schedule for tomorrow and talk to me about the complimentary gifts and refreshments.
M: Oh really. That sounds pretty expensive for an investors' conference.
W: Maybe, but it's what Mr. Gupta wants, and he's the CEO. He wants everything to go as smoothly as possible.

## 放送文の訳

問題 56-58 は次の会話に関するものです。

M：受付に行って展示会場で僕たちが設置できる一番早い時間を確認してくる。君も一緒に来るかい？
W：うーん…私はいいわ。
M：どうして？
W：ええと，私はここのオフィスにいてメモを書き上げなくちゃ。Cirrus プランニングと2時にミーティングがあるの。彼らは明日のスケジュールを確認することと，無料の手土産と軽食について私と話すことを望んでいるの。
M：あ，そうなんだ。投資家の会議にしては，とてもぜいたくだね。
W：そうかもね，でも，Gupta さんがそう望んでいて，彼は最高経営責任者だし。彼は何もかもできる限りスムーズに運ばせたいのよ。

## Vocabulary

- reception [risépʃən] 名 受付
- find out 〜 〜を突き止める
- set up 設置する
- exhibition [èksəbíʃən] 名 展示会
- come along 一緒に行く[来る]
- complimentary [kàmpləméntəri] 形 無料の
- refreshment [rifréʃmənt] 名（複数形で）軽食
- investor [invéstər] 名 投資家

---

### 56

What are the speakers doing?

(A) Touring a site
(B) Preparing for an event
(C) Taking a break
(D) Making a presentation

**設問の訳**

話し手たちは何をしていますか。

(A) 現場を見て回っている
(B) イベントの準備をしている
(C) 休憩を取っている
(D) プレゼンテーションを行っている

**正解 (B)**

男性が冒頭で I'm going to the reception desk to find out the earliest time we can set up at the exhibition hall. と述べており，また女性も明日のスケジュールを確認するためにミーティングをすると述べていることから，イベントの準備をしていることがわかるので，正解は (B)。

tour [tuər] 〜を見て回る

---

### 57

What does the woman mean when she says, "I think I'd rather not"?

(A) She is not interested in the exhibition.
(B) She hopes that she will quit her job soon.
(C) She wants to stay and work in the office.
(D) She might be able to accompany the man.

**設問の訳**

女性が "I think I'd rather not" と言う際，何を意図していますか。

(A) 展示会に興味がない。
(B) もうすぐ仕事を辞めることを望んでいる。
(C) オフィスに残って作業をしたい。
(D) 男性に同行することができるかもしれない。

**正解 (C)**

I'd は I would の短縮形で，would rather not で「（どちらかというと）〜したくない」という意味。do not want to の控えめな表現である。ここでは not の後に come along が省略されており，男性と一緒に行かない理由として I need to stay here in the office 〜と言っていることから，(C) が正解。

accompany [əkʌ́mpəni] 〜に同行する

---

### 58

What will the attendees receive?

(A) Presents
(B) Complimentary tickets
(C) Gift certificates
(D) Conference brochures

**設問の訳**

出席者は何を受け取りますか。

(A) 贈り物
(B) 無料のチケット
(C) 商品券
(D) 会議のパンフレット

**正解 (A)**

女性が無料の手土産に言及しているので，その言い換えである (A) Presents が正解にふさわしい。(B) Complimentary tickets と (C) Gift certificates は会話中の complimentary gifts と混乱しないようにしよう。

attendee [ətèndíː] 出席者
gift certificate 商品券

| 放送文 | 放送文の訳 |
|---|---|
| Questions 59 through 61 refer to the following conversation.<br><br>W: Something's wrong with this door. When I enter the code, nothing happens.<br>M: Haven't you heard?<br>W: Heard what?<br>M: The procedure changed last night. Now you need to swipe a security card through a reader to open the entrance.<br>W: Do you mean my ID card?<br>M: Not that one. You'll need to pick up a new one with a magnetic strip on the back. Talk to Susan in human resources. She'll explain everything. Then, go to IT to pick up your card. | 問題 59-61 は次の会話に関するものです。<br><br>W：このドアは何かおかしいわ。コードを入力しても何も起きないわ。<br>M：聞かなかった？<br>W：何を？<br>M：昨夜，手順が変わったんだよ。これからは，入り口を開けるにはセキュリティカードを読み取り機に通す必要があるんだよ。<br>W：私の ID カードのこと？<br>M：それじゃないよ。裏に磁気ストリップがついた新しいカードを受け取らないといけないんだ。人事部の Susan と話してごらん。彼女が全部説明してくれるよ。それから IT 部に行ってカードをもらうんだ。 |

## Vocabulary

- procedure [prəsíːdʒər] 图手順
- swipe a card through ～ ～にカードを通す
- reader [ríːdər] 图読み取り機
- entrance [éntrəns] 图入り口
- magnetic strip 磁気ストリップ
- human resources 人事部

| 設問 | 設問の訳 | 正解と解説 |
|---|---|---|
| **59**<br>What happened last night?<br><br>(A) A door was installed.<br>(B) A system was changed.<br>(C) An entrance was closed.<br>(D) A code was updated. | 昨夜何が起きましたか。<br><br>(A) ドアが設置された。<br>(B) システムが変わった。<br>(C) 入り口が閉鎖された。<br>(D) コードが更新された。 | **正解 (B)**<br>男性の発言に The procedure changed last night. とあり，その言い換えである (B) A system was changed. が正解である。<br><br>install [instɔ́ːl] ～を設置する |
| **60**<br>What does the man say about the woman's ID card?<br>(A) It needs a new magnetic strip.<br>(B) It needs to be replaced.<br>(C) It works when slid through a reader.<br>(D) It works at another entrance. | 男性は女性の ID カードについて何と言っていますか。<br>(A) 新しい磁気ストリップが必要である。<br>(B) 取り換える必要がある。<br>(C) 読み取り機に通すと機能する。<br>(D) 別の入り口で機能する。 | **正解 (B)**<br>男性の発言に You'll need to pick up a new one with a magnetic strip on the back. とあり，新しいものと古いものを交換する必要があるので，正解は (B)。新しい磁気ストリップではなく，磁気ストリップが裏についた新しいカードが必要なので，(A) は不適切。 |
| **61**<br>Why does the man recommend seeing Susan?<br>(A) She supervises human resources.<br>(B) She manages IT.<br>(C) She makes repairs.<br>(D) She has more details. | 男性はなぜ Susan に会うことを勧めていますか。<br>(A) 彼女は人事部を監督しているから。<br>(B) 彼女は IT 部を管理しているから。<br>(C) 彼女は修理をするから。<br>(D) 彼女は詳しい情報をもっと持っているから。 | **正解 (D)**<br>男性は最後の発言で Talk to Susan in human resources. She'll explain everything. と述べており，Susan がすべてを説明してくれるから，彼女のところに行くよう勧めている。よって，正解は (D)。<br><br>supervise [súːpərvàiz] ～を監督する<br>make repairs 修理する |

## 放送文

Questions 62 through 64 refer to the following conversation and map.

**W**: Don, would you mind going to the downtown branch office to pick up the Halvorsen portfolio for me? Sorry to ask you on such short notice. I had no idea I'd get called to an emergency meeting.
**M**: I think I can do that. Hopefully I won't get lost. What's the quickest way to get there?
**W**: After you get off the Interstate at Exit 57, just keep going straight until you hit 3rd Street, then take a left. About two blocks down you'll see a ... some kind of a dry cleaners on the right. It's got a huge sign.
**M**: So, it's by the cleaners?
**W**: Right. It's right across the street from that. 562 3rd Street is the address.

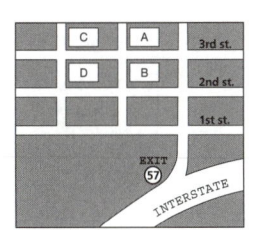

## 放送文の訳

問題 62-64 は次の会話と地図に関するものです。

**W**: Don, Halvorsen のポートフォリオを受け取りに, 中心街の支店に行ってもらえない？ こんなに急に頼んでごめんなさい。緊急会議に呼ばれるなんて思わなかったから。
**M**: できると思うよ。迷わないといいのだけれど。そこに一番早く着ける行き方は？
**W**: 州間高速を出口 57 で降りた後, 3 番通りにぶつかるまでずっと真っすぐ進んだら, そこで左に曲がって。2 ブロックほど行くと…, 何かのドライクリーニング店が右手に見えるわ。巨大な看板があるから。
**M**: つまり, クリーニング店のそばというわけ？
**W**: そう。そこから道をはさんで真向かいにあるわ。住所は 3 番通り 562 よ。

## Vocabulary

- portfolio [pɔːrtfóuliòu] 名ポートフォリオ
- get called to ～ ～に呼び出しを受ける
- emergency [imə́ːrdʒənsi] 名緊急事態
- interstate [ìntərstéit] 名(米国の)州間高速道路
- go straight 真っすぐ進む
- take a left 左に曲がる
- huge [hjúːdʒ] 形とても大きな
- be right across the street from ～ ～から通りをはさんで真向かいにある

---

### 62

**設問**
What is probably the woman's problem?
(A) She has lost some documents.
(B) She cannot find a location.
(C) She has to change plans quickly.
(D) She does not have a car.

**設問の訳**
女性の問題はおそらく何ですか。
(A) いくつか書類をなくした。
(B) 場所を見つけられない。
(C) 急いで予定を変更しなければならない。
(D) 車を持っていない。

**正解 (C)**

女性は冒頭で, 自分の代わりに男性に中心街の支店に行くよう頼んでいる。for me は「私の代わりに」ということ。続く Sorry to ask you ～ や I had no idea I'd get called ～ という内容から, 女性は急な予定変更に対応しなければならない状況にあることがわかる。よって, (C) が正解。

### 63

**設問**
What is the man being asked to do?
(A) Attend a meeting
(B) Travel downtown
(C) Clean an office
(D) Sign some papers

**設問の訳**
男性は何をするように依頼されていますか。
(A) 会議に出席する
(B) 中心街に行く
(C) 事務所を掃除する
(D) 書類に署名する

**正解 (B)**

女性の男性への依頼は冒頭の 1 文にある。Would you mind ～ing? は,「～してもらえませんか」という意味の依頼表現である。going to the downtown branch office を簡潔に表した (B) が正解。

paper [péipər]（複数形で）書類

### 64

**設問**
Look at the graphic. Where is the downtown branch office located?
(A) Building A
(B) Building B
(C) Building C
(D) Building D

**設問の訳**
図を見てください。中心街の支店はどこにありますか。
(A) 建物 A
(B) 建物 B
(C) 建物 C
(D) 建物 D

**正解 (D)**

図表問題では, 放送を聞く前にざっと図表の内容を確認しておきたい。ここでは地図を見ておくと道案内の会話だと予測がつく。女性の「Interstate を Exit 57 で降りて 3rd street まで真っすぐ進み, 左に曲がる。2 ブロック進むと右手にドライクリーニング店がある」という説明から, ドライクリーニング店の場所は C。その後,「オフィスは道をはさんで真向かいにある」と言っていることから, 正解は (D)。

| 放送文 | 放送文の訳 |
|---|---|
| Questions 65 through 67 refer to the following conversation and label.<br><br>**M**: Hi, I just bought this shirt three days ago. I washed it only once, and didn't put it in the dryer, but still it shrunk two sizes. It's too small now. Is there any way I could exchange it for a new one?<br>**W**: I'm sorry, our refund policy only covers unused items, with the tag still on them. As to why it shrunk, let's see what the label says.<br>**M**: Oh. It must've been the water temperature. Oh well, live and learn, I guess.<br>**W**: The good news is, those shirts are now on sale. Half off. We have size large in stock, too.<br>**M**: Really? Well then, maybe I'll try again. | 問題 65-67 は次の会話とラベルに関するものです。<br><br>**M**：こんにちは。このシャツを3日前に買ったばかりなのですが，たった1回洗っただけで，乾燥機にも入れなかったのですが，それでも2サイズ分縮みました。これはもう小さすぎます。新しいものと交換してもらうことはできますか。<br>**W**：申し訳ありませんが，当店の返金ポリシーは，値札の付いたままの未使用の品物のみが対象となります。なぜ縮んだのかについては，ラベルに何て書いてあるか見てみましょう。<br>**M**：ああ，水温のせいだったのでしょう。仕方ないですね，失敗から学んだと思いましょう。<br>**W**：良いことに，そのシャツは今セール中なんですよ。半額です。Lサイズも在庫がございます。<br>**M**：本当ですか。それなら，もう1回試してみましょうかね。 |

```
STYLE #55xl-navy
100% COTTON
Dry clean or machine
wash cold. Inside out
with like colors. Tumble
dry low. Non-chlorine
bleach only.

Made in U.S.A.
L
$16.99
```

```
STYLE #55xl-ネイビー
綿100%
ドライクリーニングまたは
洗濯機で水洗いしてください。裏返して同系色と洗ってください。乾燥機使用時，
低温設定。非塩素系漂白剤のみ可。
アメリカ製
L
16ドル99セント
```

## Vocabulary

- dryer [dráiɚ] 名乾燥機
- shrunk [ʃrʌŋk] 動shrink「縮む」の過去形
- unused [ʌnjúːzd] 形未使用の
- as to ～ ～に関しては
- live and learn 経験で知る

| 設問 | 設問の訳 | 正解と解説 |
|---|---|---|
| **65**<br>What is the conversation mainly about?<br>(A) An incorrect purchase<br>(B) Overpayment for an item<br>(C) A problem with an item<br>(D) An item being out of stock | 会話は主に何に関するものですか。<br>(A) 購入間違い<br>(B) ある品物に対する過払い<br>(C) ある品物に関する問題<br>(D) 在庫がないある品物 | **正解 (C)**<br>男性客と女性店員の会話。新形式のTOEICの対策として，従来よりもややカジュアルな口調にも慣れておこう。男性の冒頭の発言から，自分が買ったシャツを店に持ち込み，洗濯したらシャツが縮んだとクレームをつけている場面が想像できる。これを「品物に関する問題」と抽象的に表した (C) が正解。an item は shirt のこと。 |
| **66**<br>Look at the graphic. How could the problem have been avoided?<br>(A) By using cold water<br>(B) By using hot water<br>(C) By using bleach<br>(D) By drying the item | 図を見てください。問題はどうしたら回避することができましたか。<br>(A) 冷水を使うことにより<br>(B) 温水を使うことにより<br>(C) 漂白剤を使うことにより<br>(D) 品物を乾かすことにより | **正解 (A)**<br>シャツが縮んだと聞いた店員がラベルを確認したところ，男性は It must've been the water temperature.「問題は水温だったに違いない」と言っている。must've は must have の短縮形で，発音を確認しておくとよい。ラベルを見ると，machine wash cold「洗濯機で水洗い」とあり，男性は冷水 (cold water) ではなく温水 (hot water) で洗ったと推測できる。つまり，冷水を使えばシャツは縮まなかったと考えて，(A) が正解。 |
| **67**<br>What does the woman suggest the man do?<br>(A) Buy a different size<br>(B) Wash the item again<br>(C) Get a refund for the item<br>(D) Purchase another item | 女性は男性に何をするように提案していますか。<br>(A) 違うサイズを買う<br>(B) 品物をもう1度洗う<br>(C) 品物に対して返金を受ける<br>(D) 別の品物を購入する | **正解 (D)**<br>女性は The good news is, ～の部分で，同じシャツが半額になっていることを伝えている。女性は男性に半額のシャツ (= another item) を買うよう提案しているので，(D) が正解。 |

## 放送文

Questions 68 through 70 refer to the following conversation and coupon.

W: Hi, I can use this coupon on more than one jar, right?
M: Yes, ma'am. You can only use the coupon one time, but you can use it on as many jar candles as you'd like.
W: I'd like six: four vanilla and two lavender. I could only find one lavender on the shelf. Is there another one somewhere?
M: We might have one in the stock room. If we don't, I could probably have one sent over from one of our other stores.
W: Oh, that won't be necessary. But if you have one in the back, I'll take it. Otherwise I'll take another vanilla one instead.
M: I'll go check right now.

**Candie's Candleworks**
**$4 Jar Candles**
**Buy One, Get One FREE**
Present this coupon to receive one jar candle of equal or lesser value with the purchase of one at regular price.
Must be presented at time of purchase.
Limit one coupon per customer.

## 放送文の訳

問題 68-70 は次の会話とクーポンに関するものです。

W：こんにちは，このクーポンは 2 本以上のジャーに使えますよね？
M：はい，お客様。クーポンは 1 度しか使えませんが，お好きな数のジャーキャンドルに使えますよ。
W：6 本ください，バニラを 4 本とラベンダー 2 本。棚には 1 本しかラベンダーがありませんでした。どこかにもう 1 本ありますか。
M：倉庫に 1 本あるかもしれません。もしなかったら，別の店舗から送らせることができると思います。
W：ああ，それは必要ありません。でも裏に 1 本あるなら，それをもらいます。なければ，代わりにもう 1 本バニラをください。
M：今すぐ確認してきます。

Candie のキャンドル工房
ジャーキャンドル　4 ドル
1 本お買い上げでもう 1 本プレゼント
このクーポン提示で，ジャーキャンドルを定価で 1 本お買い上げいただくと，同額以下のジャーキャンドル 1 本を無料サービスいたします。
ご購入時に提示してください。お 1 人様につき 1 枚ご利用いただけます。

## Vocabulary

- more than ~　～より多い（"～"の数は含まない）
- as many ~ as you like　あなたが好きなだけの数の～
- necessary [nésəsèri] 形 必要な
- back [bæk] 名 裏
- otherwise [ʌ́ðərwàiz] 副 そうでなければ
- right now 今すぐに

---

### 68

What is the woman's problem?

(A) She cannot use a coupon.
(B) She does not have enough money.
(C) She cannot find an item.
(D) She cannot get a refund.

**設問の訳**

女性の問題は何ですか。

(A) クーポンを使えない。
(B) お金が足りない。
(C) 商品が見つからない。
(D) 返金を受けられない。

**正解 (C)**

女性の抱える問題は I could only find one lavender on the shelf. Is there another one somewhere? の部分にある。another one はラベンダーのジャーキャンドルのことで，これを an item と抽象的に表した (C) が正解。

---

### 69

Look at the graphic. How many free candles will the woman get?

(A) Two
(B) Three
(C) Four
(D) Six

**設問の訳**

図を見てください。女性は無料のキャンドルを何本受け取りますか。

(A) 2 本
(B) 3 本
(C) 4 本
(D) 6 本

**正解 (B)**

冒頭から，このクーポンは複数のジャーキャンドルに使える。I'd like six から，女性が欲しいのは 6 本。そこでクーポンを見ると，Buy One, Get One FREE「1 本買えば，もう 1 本は無料」とあるので，3 本分のお金を払えば 3 本無料でもらえることになる。なお，図表内には情報がいろいろ書かれているが，ここでは Buy One, Get One FREE さえ押さえることができれば解ける。必ずしもすべての情報を読み取る必要はないので，効率よく解くことが重要。

---

### 70

What will the man most likely do next?

(A) Contact another store
(B) Wrap some items
(C) Take a customer's order
(D) Look for another candle

**設問の訳**

男性は次に何をすると考えられますか。

(A) 別の店に連絡する
(B) いくつかの商品を包む
(C) 客の注文を取る
(D) もう 1 本キャンドルを探す

**正解 (D)**

男性店員は女性が求めているラベンダーのジャーキャンドルについて，「倉庫にあるかもしれない」と言っている。最後に I'll go check right now. と言っていることからも，(D) が正解。(A) は，別の店舗から取り寄せるという男性店員の提案に対して，女性が that won't be necessary と言っているので誤り。

# PART 4

## 放送文

Questions 71 through 73 refer to the following talk.

Welcome to Leighton's Investment Division. As you'll know from reading the employee training materials we sent you, this is one of our areas of expertise, the other two being Retail and Corporate Banking. Our goals are simple: to help our clients grow their personal or business success through sound financial management. Our strategy has helped us through many decades, even in times when our competitors have struggled or failed. You'll learn more about that later. First, please switch off your phones and make sure your ID badges are visible while I take you through our secure trading floor.

## 放送文の訳

問題 71-73 は次の話に関するものです。

Leighton の投資部へようこそ。お送りした社員研修資料を読めばわかるように、ここがわが社の専門知識分野のうちの1つで、他の2つは小売り部と企業金融部です。我々の目標はシンプルで、堅実な財政管理を通して、顧客が個人的に、あるいはビジネス上で成功できるよう手助けすることです。我々の戦略は、競合他社が苦しんだり失敗したりしたときでさえ、何十年にもわたって我々を助けてきました。それについては後で詳しく知ることになります。まず携帯電話の電源を切り、厳重に管理された取引フロアを案内する間、身分証明バッジが目につきやすいようにしておいてください。

## Vocabulary

- material [mətíəriəl] 名 資料
- expertise [èkspərtíːz] 名 専門知識[技術]
- retail [ríːteil] 名 小売り
- corporate banking 企業金融
- sound [saund] 形 堅実な
- strategy [strǽtədʒi] 名 戦略
- struggle [strʌ́gl] 動 苦闘する
- fail [feil] 動 失敗する
- visible [vízəbl] 形 目に見える
- secure [sikjúər] 形 厳重に管理された

---

### 71

**設問**
According to the speaker, what can be found in the training materials?
(A) Locations of all the divisions
(B) Names of their competitors
(C) Information about the company's expertise
(D) Advice on investments

**設問の訳**
話し手によると、研修資料に何が載っていますか。
(A) すべての部署の場所
(B) 競合他社の社名
(C) 会社の専門知識に関する情報
(D) 投資に関する助言

**正解 (C)**
最初の方の As you'll know from reading the employee training materials we sent you, this is one of our areas of expertise, ~ の部分から、研修資料には会社の専門知識分野に関する情報が載っていることが推測できる。よって、正解は (C)。

---

### 72

**設問**
What is implied about Leighton?
(A) It has gained a large market share.
(B) It has existed for a long time.
(C) It has used complex strategies.
(D) It has recruited new managers.

**設問の訳**
Leighton について何がわかりますか。
(A) 大きな市場占有率を獲得した。
(B) 長い間存在してきた。
(C) 複雑な戦略を使った。
(D) 新しいマネージャーを採用した。

**正解 (B)**
中盤の、Our strategy has helped us through many decades, ~ から、この会社は何十年もの歴史があることがわかる。よって、(B) It has existed for a long time. が正解。

gain [gein] ~を得る　　exist [igzíst] 存在する
complex [kɑmpléks] 複雑な
recruit [rikrúːt] ~を採用する

---

### 73

**設問**
What will the listeners do next?
(A) Take off their ID badges
(B) Retrieve their mobile phones
(C) Go up to the second floor
(D) Tour the trading area

**設問の訳**
聞き手は次に何をしますか。
(A) 身分証明バッジを外す
(B) 携帯電話を取り戻す
(C) 2階に上がる
(D) 取引エリアを見学する

**正解 (D)**
最後に、First, ~ while I take you through our secure trading floor. と、取引フロアを回る前の注意点を述べている。つまり、この後取引エリアの見学を始めるので、正解は (D)。次の行動を問う問題のヒントはたいてい終盤にあるので、最後まで集中力を切らさないようにしよう。

retrieve [ritríːv] ~を取り戻す

## 放送文

Questions 74 through 76 refer to the following advertisement.

Last month South Africa, this month Australia! Glorious Hair Care Corporation invites you to learn more about how our range of products can help protect and nourish your hair. On Tuesday, June 13, our team of expert stylists and colorists will show you how our shampoos, conditioners and lotions can leave your hair looking healthy and shiny. The team will be making particular use of our Lemon Gold One Gel, designed to let you easily control your hair during your busy day. Four lucky audience members will also be selected for a free hair styling session. The show starts at 11:00 A.M. at the Sydney Grand Hotel Ballroom, so be sure to arrive early to secure a seat. <u>Seats will be given on a first come, first served basis.</u> For more information visit us online at www.glorioushair.au. Next month we're holding this same event in New Zealand!

## 放送文の訳

問題 74-76 は次の広告に関するものです。

先月は南アフリカ，今月はオーストラリア！ Glorious ヘアケア社は皆さんにぜひ，当社のさまざまな製品がいかにあなたの髪を保護し栄養を与えてくれるかについてより知っていただきたいと思っています。6月13日の火曜日に当社の熟練美容師とカラーリストのチームが当社のシャンプーやコンディショナー，ローションがいかにあなたの髪を健康的にし輝かせてくれるかをお見せします。チームは特に，忙しい毎日でも簡単に髪をコントロールできるように作られた Lemon Gold One Gel を使用します。さらに，無料のヘアスタイリングセッションに幸運な4人のお客様が選ばれます。ショーは Sydney Grand ホテルのボールルームで午前11時に始まりますので，座席を確保するために必ず早めにお越しください。<u>座席は先着順に割り当てさせていただきます。</u>さらなる情報はオンラインで www.glorioushair.au をご覧ください。来月，当社は同様のイベントをニュージーランドで開きます！

## Vocabulary

- nourish [nˈəːrɪʃ] 動 〜に栄養を与える
- stylist [stáɪlɪst] 名 美容師
- colorist [kʌ́lərɪst] 名 カラーリスト
- shiny [ʃáɪni] 形 輝く
- make use of 〜 〜を使用[利用]する
- ballroom [bɔ́ːlrù(ː)m] 名 ダンスホール
- be sure to do 必ず〜する
- secure [sɪkjúər] 動 〜を確保する

## 設問

**74**
What is the advertisement mainly about?
(A) A product demonstration
(B) A travel opportunity
(C) A local competition
(D) A sales campaign

### 設問の訳
主に何についての広告ですか。
(A) 商品の実演
(B) 旅行の機会
(C) 地元のコンテスト
(D) 販売キャンペーン

### 正解と解説
**正解 (A)**
広告の主旨に関する問題。熟練美容師とカラーリストが商品を使って，その良さを伝えるために実演をすると述べているので，正解は (A) A product demonstration。「実演」を飛躍させて，(D) を選ばないように注意。

**75**
What feature of Lemon Gold One Gel is mentioned?
(A) Size
(B) Popularity
(C) Usefulness
(D) Price

### 設問の訳
Lemon Gold One Gel のどんな特徴が述べられていますか。
(A) サイズ
(B) 人気
(C) 実用性
(D) 価格

### 正解と解説
**正解 (C)**
中盤に，〜 designed to let you easily control your hair during your busy day「忙しい毎日でも簡単に髪をコントロールできるように作られた」とある。つまり，使い勝手が良いということなので，正解は (C) Usefulness「実用性」。

**76**
What does the speaker imply when he says, "Seats will be given on a first come, first served basis"?
(A) There are no more seats left.
(B) People should come to the place early.
(C) The show will start earlier than planned.
(D) A light meal will be given during the show.

### 設問の訳
話し手が "Seats will be given on a first come, first served basis" と言う際，何を示唆していますか。
(A) 座席はもう残っていない。
(B) 人々は早めにその場所に来るべきだ。
(C) ショーが予定より早く始まる。
(D) ショーの間に軽食が出される。

### 正解と解説
**正解 (B)**
on a first come, first served basis は「先着順で，早い者勝ちで」という広告や宣伝における決まり文句。この表現を知らなくても，直前の be sure to arrive early to secure a seat から，(B) が正解だと判断できるだろう。(D) の given のような，下線部に含まれる語句を繰り返し用いた選択肢に注意しよう。

## 放送文

Questions 77 through 79 refer to the following news report.

Now for today's business news. Astar Pharmaceuticals Corporation has agreed to buy its smaller Hong Kong rival San Yin for 65 million pounds. The deal is still subject to shareholder approval but has the potential to create the United Kingdom's third biggest drug company. Astar's CEO Daniel Rice said the deal was good news for both firms, and would help cut distribution costs by as much as 36 percent—as well as provide potential entry into the mainland China market. Under Rice's direction, Astar has pursued an aggressive M&A policy over the past four years. Last summer it purchased the 900 Drug Corporation and in January this year acquired Crocus Pharmaceuticals. Shares of Astar rose by 2.75 percent at the release of this news, while San Yin was up 1.27 percent by market close.

## 放送文の訳

問題 77-79 は次のニュース報道に関するものです。

次は今日のビジネスニュースです。Astar 製薬社が自社よりも小規模な香港のライバル会社，San Yin を 6,500 万ポンドで買収することで合意しました。この取引はこれから株主の承認を得なければなりませんが，これにより英国で 3 番目に大きな製薬会社が誕生することになるでしょう。Astar の最高経営責任者 Daniel Rice は，この取引は双方の会社にとって朗報であり，36％もの流通コストの削減につながり，加えて中国本土市場への参入を可能にするものだと語りました。Rice の指示の下，Astar は過去 4 年にわたって積極的な合併・買収政策を遂行してきました。昨年の夏，900 薬品社を買収し，今年の 1 月には Crocus 製薬を獲得しました。このニュースが報道されると Astar の株は 2.75 ％上昇し，一方 San Yin は 1.27 ％終値で上昇しました。

### Vocabulary

- deal [diːl] 名 取引，協定
- be subject to ～ ～を条件とする，～に従うものとする
- shareholder [ʃéərhòuldər] 名 株主
- approval [əprúːvəl] 名 承認
- potential [pəténʃəl] 形 可能性
- distribution [dìstribjúːʃən] 名 流通
- entry into ～ ～への参入
- pursue [pərsúː] 動 ～を遂行する
- aggressive [əgrésiv] 形 積極的な，攻撃的な
- M&A (= merger and acquisition) 名 (企業の)合併と買収
- by market close 引けまでに

---

### 77

What is the report mainly about?

(A) An upcoming takeover
(B) An appointment of a new CEO
(C) An upturn in consumer spending
(D) New markets in China

**設問の訳**
主に何についての報道ですか。
(A) これから起こる買収
(B) 新しい最高経営責任者の任命
(C) 消費者支出の上昇
(D) 中国の新市場

**正解 (A)**

冒頭で，Astar Pharmaceuticals Corporation has agreed to buy its smaller Hong Kong rival San Yin for 65 million pounds. とあり，「企業買収」の話であるとわかるので，正解は (A)。このように，ニュース報道ではふつう冒頭でトピックが述べられるので，聞き逃さないようにしたい。

takeover [téikòuvər] 買収
upturn [ʌ́ptə̀ːrn] 上昇

---

### 78

What will the companies achieve as a result of the deal?
(A) Higher revenue
(B) Better products
(C) Reduced costs
(D) Improved technologies

**設問の訳**
両社は取引の結果，何を成し遂げますか。
(A) より高い収益
(B) より良い製品
(C) コストの削減
(D) 技術改良

**正解 (C)**

質問文の the companies とは，Astar 製薬社と San Yin のことで，the deal はこの 2 社の合併のこと。合併のメリットについて，中盤に the deal ～ would help cut distribution costs by as much as 36 percent とあり，流通コストを削減できることがわかるので，正解は (C) Reduced costs。

---

### 79

According to the report, what has been Mr. Rice's policy at Astar Pharmaceuticals?
(A) Increasing size
(B) Upgrading services
(C) Raising share prices
(D) Production in mainland China

**設問の訳**
報道によると，Astar 製薬での Rice 氏の方針は何ですか。
(A) 規模を大きくすること
(B) サービスを向上させること
(C) 株価を上げること
(D) 中国本土での生産

**正解 (A)**

後半の Under Rice's direction, Astar has pursued an aggressive M&A policy over the past four years. と次の具体的な事例から，Rice 氏は積極的な M&A により会社の規模をどんどん大きくしてきたとわかるので，正解は (A)。(D) は合併により今後期待され得ることなので，正解にはならない。

raise [reiz] ～を引き上げる
share price 株価

## 放送文

Questions 80 through 82 refer to the following telephone message.

Hello, this is Olivia Ross. I'm calling about the Deluxe AZ700 MP3 Player delivered from your store a week ago. The volume mechanism on the device doesn't appear to be working. I can barely hear music on it, no matter which direction I turn the dial. I've read the user manual thoroughly but I don't understand why this is happening. I know this product comes with a 12-month warranty and I'd like to bring it in to a customer service center and have someone take a look at it if at all possible. I think it needs to be replaced. This is the second message I've left, so I'd really appreciate it if someone could get back to me as soon as possible. Thanks.

## 放送文の訳

問題 80-82 は次の電話のメッセージに関するものです。

もしもし，Olivia Ross です。1 週間前にそちらの店から届いた Deluxe AZ700 MP3 プレイヤーについて電話しています。この機器のボリューム部分が機能していないようです。どの方向にダイヤルを回しても，音楽がほとんど聞こえません。隅々まで取扱説明書を読みましたが，どうしてこんなことが起きているのかわかりません。この製品には 12 か月の保証がついていると理解しておりますので，カスタマーサービスセンターに持ち込み，できたらどなたかに見てほしいと思っています。交換する必要があると思います。メッセージを残すのはこれで 2 回目ですので，どなたかができるだけ早くご連絡くださるとありがたいのですが。よろしくお願いします。

### Vocabulary
- ☐ mechanism [mékənìzəm] 图 仕組み；機械
- ☐ device [diváis] 图 装置
- ☐ appear to do 〜するように思われる
- ☐ work [wəːrk] 動 機能する，作動する
- ☐ barely [béərli] 副 ほとんど〜ない
- ☐ direction [dirékʃən] 图 方向
- ☐ I'd (really) appreciate it if 〜 〜していただけるならありがたいです
- ☐ get back to 〜 〜に折り返し連絡する

## 設問 / 設問の訳 / 正解と解説

### 80
What does the speaker imply when she says, "I can barely hear music on it, no matter which direction I turn the dial"?
(A) There is something wrong with the volume dial.
(B) The directions are too complicated for her.
(C) She cannot find the dial to turn.
(D) She wants to know what music is on.

話し手が "I can barely hear music on it, no matter which direction I turn the dial" と言う際，何を示唆していますか。
(A) 音量のダイヤルに何か問題がある。
(B) 彼女には指示が複雑すぎる。
(C) 彼女は回すべきダイヤルを見つけられない。
(D) 彼女は何の音楽がかかっているか知りたい。

**正解 (A)**

barely は「ほとんど〜ない」，〈no matter which ＋ 名詞＋ SV〉は「どの(名詞)を[に]SV しても」という意味。女性は購入した MP3 プレイヤーについて電話をしており，直前の The volume mechanism on the device doesn't appear to be working. からも，(A) が正解とわかる。

### 81
What does the speaker want to do?

(A) Find a manual
(B) Extend a warranty
(C) Locate a repair shop
(D) Receive a new product

話し手は何をしたいのですか。

(A) マニュアルを見つける
(B) 保証を延長する
(C) 修理店を見つける
(D) 新しい製品を受け取る

**正解 (D)**

終盤で，I think it needs to be replaced.「交換する必要があると思う」と述べている。よって正解は，その言い換えである (D) Receive a new product。

locate [lóukeit]（〜の場所）を探す

### 82
What does the speaker say about herself?
(A) She has had the same problem before.
(B) She has made partial repairs.
(C) She has called previously.
(D) She has received a replacement.

話し手は自分自身について何と言っていますか。
(A) 以前に同じ問題を抱えた。
(B) 部分的な修理をした。
(C) 以前に電話した。
(D) 代替品を受け取った。

**正解 (C)**

女性は This is the second message I've left と，これが 2 回目に残すメッセージであることを述べている。つまり，以前にも同じ用件で 1 度電話していることがわかるので，正解は (C)。

partial [páːrʃəl] 部分的な
previously [príːviəsli] 以前に
replacement [ripléismənt] 代替品

## 放送文

Questions 83 through 85 refer to the following talk.

Welcome to the Warsaw City Opera House. As you already know from your sponsorship invitation, the Opera House is one of the oldest in Poland, dating back to the 18th century. However, it is now in need of serious renovation, particularly since its roof is leaking. We have received donations of 2.1 million euros from all over the region, but I'm afraid we still need more. We have therefore chosen this evening to launch a Restoration Fund with the aim of raising 2.3 million more euros. Campaign chairman Lech Havelcek will be joining us soon to explain some of the privileges that sponsorship of the theater carries, such as invitation-only shows. After that, we hope you'll join us for a Champagne Reception in the main lobby. Afterwards, there will be a short performance by classical singer Melanie Farcheau of France, accompanied by Canada's Geoffrey Regan on piano.

## 放送文の訳

問題 83-85 は次の話に関するものです。

ワルシャワシティ・オペラハウスへようこそ。後援のご依頼状で既にご存じの通り、オペラハウスはポーランドで最も古いものの1つで、18世紀までさかのぼります。しかしながら、特に屋根からの雨漏りのため、今では本格的な修理が必要な状態にあります。地域の至る所から210万ユーロの寄付を頂戴しましたが、残念ながらお金はまだ必要です。それゆえに、あと230万ユーロを調達する目的で修復基金を立ち上げるべく今晩を選んだのです。キャンペーン議長 Lech Havelcek が、劇場の後援をしていただくと受けられる、招待者限定のショーといった特典のいくつかについてまもなくご説明いたします。その後でメインロビーでのシャンパン・レセプションにご参加くださいますようお願いいたします。その後、カナダの Geoffrey Regan のピアノ伴奏で、フランスのクラシック歌手 Melanie Farcheau によるミニ公演がございます。

### Vocabulary
- sponsorship [spánsərʃip] 图 後援
- date back to ~ ~にさかのぼる
- in need of ~ ~を必要として
- serious [síəriəs] 形 本格的な
- renovation [rènəvéiʃən] 图 修理
- leak [li:k] 動 (水などが)漏れる
- donation [dounéiʃən] 图 寄付
- with the aim of ~ ~を目的として
- privilege [prívəlidʒ] 图 特権；特典
- accompany [əkʌ́mpəni] 動 ~の伴奏をする

## 83

**設問**
What is the main purpose of the talk?

(A) To announce a schedule
(B) To perform a new opera
(C) To outline a goal
(D) To discuss problems

**設問の訳**
この話の主な目的は何ですか。

(A) スケジュールを知らせること
(B) 新しいオペラを上演すること
(C) 目標の概略を述べること
(D) 問題を話し合うこと

**正解 (C)**

放送文全体を聞いて答える問題。特に、We have therefore chosen this evening to launch a Restoration Fund with the aim of raising 2.3 million more euros. で、さらなる資金の調達とその目標額を述べていることから、正解は (C) To outline a goal。

outline [áutlàin] ~の概略を述べる

## 84

**設問**
According to the speaker, how many euros have been donated so far?
(A) 2.0 million
(B) 2.1 million
(C) 2.2 million
(D) 2.3 million

**設問の訳**
話し手によると、これまで何ユーロが寄付されましたか。
(A) 200万
(B) 210万
(C) 220万
(D) 230万

**正解 (B)**

中盤で、We have received donations of 2.1 million euros from all over the region とあり、これまで 2.1 million euros 集まったことがわかるので、正解は (B)。2.3 million は、さらなる目標額なので (D) は不適切。

## 85

**設問**
What is an advantage of being a sponsor?
(A) Music previews
(B) Backstage passes
(C) Free champagne
(D) Exclusive events

**設問の訳**
後援者になることの利点は何ですか。
(A) 音楽のプレ公演
(B) 楽屋への入場許可証
(C) 無料のシャンパン
(D) 限定イベント

**正解 (D)**

後援者になることにより、特典として invitation-only shows「招待者限定のショー」が見られると述べている。その言い換えである (D) Exclusive events「限定イベント」が正解。

preview [prí:vjù:] 試演；予告編
exclusive [iksklú:siv] 独占的な、排他的な

## 放送文

Questions 86 through 88 refer to the following talk.

Thank you for joining us in the boardroom this afternoon. I'd like to take this opportunity to introduce you all to Richard Kashumbe, senior executive in charge of marketing at Moise and Moise Marketing Company. He'll be joining us from April 1 as our new Director of Communications. Some of you may recognize Richard from the cover of *Business World Magazine*. He is a recent winner of that magazine's Marketing Person of the Year Award. He's also been praised in several other media outlets, such as the *European IT Journal* and *Fast Business Daily*. So we're excited to have Richard run our new multimedia marketing and advertising campaigns for Africa and the Middle East. After this informal "meet and greet" session—please help yourself to refreshments—Richard will be making a short presentation and answering your questions before meeting the business press later this afternoon.

## 放送文の訳

問題 86-88 は次の話に関するものです。

本日の午後の役員会議にご出席いただきありがとうございます。この機会に、皆さんに Moise and Moise マーケティング社でマーケティングを担当しているシニア・エグゼクティブの Richard Kashumbe をご紹介したいと思います。彼は4月1日から新しい渉外部長としてわが社に加わります。皆さんの中には「ビジネスワールドマガジン」の表紙で Richard に見覚えがある人もいるかもしれません。彼はその雑誌で最近、今年のマーケティングパーソン賞を受賞しました。彼はまた「ヨーロピアン IT ジャーナル」や「ファーストビジネスデイリー」といった他のいくつかの報道機関でも称賛されています。ですから、我々は Richard にアフリカおよび中東向けの新しいマルチメディアマーケティングおよび宣伝キャンペーンを指揮してもらうことに期待を寄せています。この非公式の「ごあいさつ」の会の後で…軽食はどうぞご自由にお取りくださいね、のちほど行われる今日の午後のビジネス報道関係者との会見の前に、Richard が短いプレゼンテーションをして、皆さんの質問にお答えします。

### Vocabulary
- boardroom [bɔ́ːrdrùː(ː)m] 役員室
- in charge of ~ ~を担当して
- recent [ríːsənt] 最近の
- media outlet 報道機関
- run [rʌn] ~を指揮する；~を取り仕切る
- help *oneself* to ~ ~を自由に取って食べる

---

### 86
Who most likely are the listeners?

(A) Corporate staff
(B) Business journalists
(C) Media analysts
(D) Market regulators

**設問の訳**
聞き手は誰だと考えられますか。

(A) 会社のスタッフ
(B) ビジネスジャーナリスト
(C) メディアアナリスト
(D) 市場規制者

**正解 (A)**
放送文全体から推測する。序盤で He'll be joining us from April 1 as our new Director of Communications. と述べ、会社の役員たちに Richard Kashumbe が4月から入社することを伝えるとともに、後半は聞き手と懇親の場を持とうとしていることがわかるので、(A) Corporate staff「会社のスタッフ」が正解。

regulator [régjəlèitər] 規制者，監督官

### 87
What is Richard Kashumbe's current occupation?
(A) Marketing manager
(B) Film director
(C) Communication expert
(D) Journalist

**設問の訳**
Richard Kashumbe の現在の職は何ですか。

(A) マーケティングマネージャー
(B) 映画監督
(C) コミュニケーションの専門家
(D) ジャーナリスト

**正解 (A)**
序盤に Richard Kashumbe, senior executive in charge of marketing at Moise and Moise Marketing Company とあり、現在は Moise and Moise マーケティング社のマーケティング担当のシニア・エグゼクティブとわかるので、その言い換えの (A) Marketing manager が正解。

### 88
What will happen next?

(A) Refreshments will be served.
(B) A different speaker will talk.
(C) A press conference will begin.
(D) Questions will be taken.

**設問の訳**
次に何が起こりますか。

(A) 軽食が出される。
(B) 別の話し手が話す。
(C) 記者会見が始まる。
(D) 質問が受け付けられる。

**正解 (B)**
終盤に Richard will be making a short presentation ~ とあり、話し手に代わり Richard が話し始めることがわかるので、正解は (B)。誤答はいずれも起こっていること、もしくは Richard の話の後に起こることなので、しっかりと聞き取って順序を取り違えないこと。

press conference 記者会見

## 放送文

Questions 89 through 91 refer to the following announcement.

Good morning shoppers and welcome to Victoria Supermarket. Those of you new to Victoria Supermarket may not know about our Special One Dollar Aisle. Everything in Aisle 3, just inside our main store entrance, costs just one dollar. <u>Yes, you heard right</u>. Not three, not two, but one dollar. And you'll be amazed at what's on offer there including leading brands! From household goods such as Sharply Floor Cleaner to tasty treats the whole family loves like Crowley's Potato Chips. Why not check it out today? This offer cannot be combined with other discounts, and items purchased in Aisle 3 do not earn Victoria Card purchase points. Cash or credit welcomed.

## 放送文の訳

問題 89-91 は次のアナウンスに関するものです。

お買い物中の皆さま, おはようございます。Victoria スーパーマーケットへようこそお越しくださいました。Victoria スーパーマーケットへ初めていらっしゃった方は, 当スーパーの特別 1 ドル通路のことをご存じないかもしれません。店の正面入り口のすぐ内側にある 3 番通路にあるすべてのものが, たった 1 ドルなのです。<u>そうです, お聞き間違いではありませんよ</u>。3 ドルでもなく 2 ドルでもなく, 1 ドルなのです。加えて, 一流ブランドの商品が含まれたご提供の品々に驚かれることでしょう。Sharply フロア・クリーナーといった家庭用品から Crowley's ポテトチップスのようにご家族全員が大好きなおいしいお菓子まで。本日ご自分の目でお確かめになりませんか。このご提供は他の割引とは組み合わせできず, 3 番通路でご購入いただきました商品には Victoria カードの購入ポイントはつきません。現金でもクレジットカードでもご利用いただけます。

### Vocabulary
- shopper [ʃápər] 名 買い物客
- aisle [aɪl] 名 通路
- be amazed at ～ ～に驚く
- leading brand 一流ブランド品
- household goods 家庭用品
- tasty [téɪsti] 形 おいしい
- treat [triːt] 名 お菓子; ごちそう
- check out ～ ～を自分の目で確かめる
- combine A with B A と B を組み合わせる

---

### 89

**設問:** Why does the woman say, "Yes, you heard right"?
(A) To agree with an opinion
(B) To emphasize what she says
(C) To ask for permission
(D) To show her gratitude

**設問の訳:** なぜ女性は "Yes, you heard right" と言っていますか。
(A) ある意見に同意するため
(B) 自分の言うことを強調するため
(C) 許可を求めるため
(D) 感謝の意を示すため

**正解 (B)**

right は「正しく, 間違いなく」という副詞。you heard right は「あなたが聞いたことは正しいですよ, 私が言ったことは間違いではないですよ」という意味で, 直前で言ったことに念を押しているのである。よって, (B) が正解。

emphasize [émfəsàɪz] ～を強調する
permission [pə(ː)rmíʃən] 許可
gratitude [grǽtətjùːd] 感謝の意

---

### 90

**設問:** What is true of the goods in Aisle 3?
(A) They are from major companies.
(B) They are unique to Victoria Supermarket.
(C) They are all edible.
(D) They are sold only in the morning.

**設問の訳:** 3 番通路の商品について言えることは何ですか。
(A) 大手企業の商品である。
(B) Victoria スーパーマーケットに特有のものである。
(C) すべて食べられる。
(D) 午前中だけ売られている。

**正解 (A)**

放送文中盤の And you'll be amazed at what's on offer there including leading brands! から, 一流ブランド商品が含まれているとわかるので, その言い換えである (A) They are from major companies. が正解。このスーパーに特有なのはセールイベントであって商品ではないので, (B) を正解と勘違いしないこと。

major [méɪdʒər] 主要な; 大きな
edible [édəbl] 食べられる

---

### 91

**設問:** What are customers using Aisle 3 unable to do?
(A) Pay by credit cards
(B) Buy leading brands
(C) Receive shopping points
(D) Shop in other aisles

**設問の訳:** 3 番通路を利用する客は何ができないのですか。
(A) クレジットカードで支払う
(B) 一流ブランドの商品を買う
(C) 買い物のポイントをもらう
(D) 他の通路で買い物をする

**正解 (C)**

～ and items purchased in Aisle 3 do not earn Victoria Card purchase points「3 番通路で購入した商品には Victoria カードポイントはつかない」とあるので, 正解は (C) Receive shopping points。

## 放送文

Questions 92 through 94 refer to the following broadcast.

And for today's business news. In a surprise move, the board of directors of Chow Ling Manufacturing Corporation has appointed Jason Yu Chief Executive Officer. Mr. Yu had been the company's Chief Financial Officer for the last 18 months. He will replace Michael Liggins, who is retiring. Bob Heller, the company's Business Development head, was widely expected to succeed Mr. Liggins, when he moved from rival Homestead Production in Toronto 2 years ago. Observers have reported he is now unlikely to stay with Chow Ling. Those same observers expect Mr. Yu to move quickly to reduce staff by investing in labor-saving technologies. In a statement, the new CEO said he looked forward to outdoing the record profits in the last fiscal year earned through several successful products.

## 放送文の訳

問題 92-94 は次の放送に関するものです。

続いて本日のビジネスニュースです。驚くべき動きですが，Chow Ling 製造会社の取締役会は，最高経営責任者に Jason Yu を任命しました。Yu 氏はこの 18 か月間，同社の最高財務責任者でした。彼は退職する Michael Liggins の後任となります。同社の事業開発部長の Bob Heller が，2年前にトロントにあるライバル社の Homestead プロダクションから移ったとき，Liggins 氏の跡を継ぐというのがおおかたの見方でした。評論家は，彼はもはや Chow Ling のもとにとどまらないだろうと伝えています。また彼らは，Yu 氏が省力化技術に投資することで人員削減を早急に進めるだろうと予想しています。声明で新 CEO は，いくつかの大当たりした製品を通して上げた昨会計年度の収益記録を上回ることを期待していると語りました。

## Vocabulary

- ☐ appoint [əpɔ́int] 動 ～を任命する
- ☐ replace [ripléis] 動 ～の後任となる
- ☐ retire [ritáiər] 動 （一定の年限が来て）退職[引退]する
- ☐ succeed [səksí:d] 動 ～の跡を継ぐ
- ☐ observer [əbzə́:rvər] 名 評論家
- ☐ be unlikely to do ～しそうにない
- ☐ invest in ～ ～に投資する
- ☐ labor-saving [léibərsèiviŋ] 形 省力化の
- ☐ look forward to ～ing ～するのを楽しみに待つ
- ☐ outdo [autdú:] 動 ～をしのぐ
- ☐ fiscal year 会計年度

### 92

What is the broadcast mainly about?

(A) Financial results
(B) Leadership changes
(C) Brand development
(D) Market trends

**設問の訳**

この放送は主に何に関するものですか。

(A) 決算報告
(B) 指導者の交代
(C) ブランドの開発
(D) 市場動向

**正解 (B)**

放送文全体の流れから正解を選ぶ。最高経営責任者に Jason Yu が任命され，退職する Michael Liggins の後任となることを述べている。よって，(B) が正解。

### 93

What is Bob Heller expected to do next?

(A) Leave the company
(B) Hire a rival
(C) Transfer to Toronto
(D) Oversee investments

**設問の訳**

Bob Heller は次に何をすると予想されますか。

(A) 会社を去る
(B) ライバルを雇う
(C) トロントに転勤する
(D) 投資を監督する

**正解 (A)**

中盤に，～ he is now unlikely to stay with Chow Ling とある。he は Bob Heller のことで，彼は会社を辞めると予想されているので，正解は (A)。

oversee [òuvərsí:] ～を監督する，監視する

### 94

What has Jason Yu said he will do?

(A) Increase net income
(B) Raise staffing levels
(C) Lower manufacturing costs
(D) Launch new products

**設問の訳**

Jason Yu は何をすると言いましたか。

(A) 純利益を増やす
(B) 社員の業務レベルを高める
(C) 製造コストを下げる
(D) 新製品を売り出す

**正解 (A)**

最終文から正解がわかる。the new CEO said he looked forward to outdoing the record profits ～とある。the new CEO とは Jason Yu のことなので，正解は (A) Increase net income「純利益を増やす」。

net income 純利益
launch [lɔ:ntʃ] （新製品）を売り出す

| 放送文 | 放送文の訳 |
|---|---|
| Questions 95 through 97 refer to the following telephone message and request form.<br><br>Hi Mike, it's Arleen in Sales. Thanks for setting up Room 4 for tomorrow's meeting. The number of chairs is just right. However, I have a favor to ask: Could you move the projector screen to the other side of the room? If it's by the windows, the afternoon sun makes it hard to see, even with the curtains drawn. The weather is supposed to be cloudless tomorrow. You may have to adjust the projector a little, but aside from the screen, the setup is fine. If you could call me when you get back from lunch to confirm, that would be great. | 問題 95-97 は次の電話のメッセージと依頼書に関するものです。<br><br>こんにちは，Mike。販売部の Arleen です。明日の会議用に会議室4を準備してくれてありがとう。椅子の数はちょうどいいです。ただ，1つお願いがあるのですが，プロジェクタースクリーンを部屋の反対側に移動させてくれますか。窓際だと，カーテンを閉めても午後の日差しで見えにくくなります。明日は雲のない天気になるようなので。プロジェクターを少し調節しなければならないかもしれませんが，スクリーン以外で設置に問題はありません。昼食から戻ったら確認の電話をもらえると助かります。 |

**Johnson Corp.**
Maintenance Request Form
Submitted by: Royce Brown
Supervisor: Michael Halvorsen
Location: Meeting Room 4
Room Setup
- 70 chairs, 7 rows of 10
- Set up projector screen on west side of room

Johnson 社
整備依頼書
提出者： Royce Brown
管理者： Michael Halvorsen
場所： 会議室4
室内設置
- 椅子70脚，10脚7列
- プロジェクタースクリーンを部屋の西側に設置

## Vocabulary
- have a favor to ask 頼みたいことがある
- draw a curtain カーテンを引く[閉める]
- cloudless [kláudlɪs] 形 雲のない，晴天の
- adjust [ədʒʌ́st] 動 ～を調整する
- aside from ～ ～を除いては

| 設問 | 設問の訳 | 正解と解説 |
|---|---|---|
| **95**<br>Why is the woman calling?<br><br>(A) To cancel an order<br>(B) To amend a request<br>(C) To make an appointment<br>(D) To schedule a meeting | 女性はなぜ電話をかけていますか。<br><br>(A) 注文をキャンセルするため<br>(B) 依頼を訂正するため<br>(C) 会う約束をするため<br>(D) 会議を予定するため | **正解 (B)**<br>女性は明日の会議の部屋の準備について話している。I have a favor to ask と言って，聞き手である Mike にセッティングの変更を依頼しているので，(B) が正解。<br><br>amend [əménd] ～を修正する |
| **96**<br>Look at the graphic. What does the woman want Mike to do before the meeting?<br>(A) Put the screen on the east side of the room<br>(B) Move some tables to the other room<br>(C) Reduce the number of chairs<br>(D) Change the type of projector | 図を見てください。女性は会議の前に Mike に何をしてほしいと思っていますか。<br><br>(A) スクリーンを部屋の東側に置く<br>(B) テーブルをいくつかもう1つの部屋に移動させる<br>(C) 椅子の数を減らす<br>(D) プロジェクターの種類を変える | **正解 (A)**<br>相手に頼みたいことは Could you ～? などの依頼表現がヒントになることが多い。女性は Could you move the projector screen to the other side of the room? と言って，プロジェクタースクリーンを「部屋の反対側」に動かすよう頼んでいる。request form を見ると，Set up projector screen on west side of room とある。つまり，一度西側に設置したスクリーンを東側に移動したいことがわかるので，(A) が正解。 |
| **97**<br>When will Mike most likely return the call?<br>(A) This morning<br>(B) This afternoon<br>(C) Tomorrow morning<br>(D) Tomorrow afternoon | Mike はいつ折り返し電話をすると考えられますか。<br>(A) 今日の午前<br>(B) 今日の午後<br>(C) 明日の午前<br>(D) 明日の午後 | **正解 (B)**<br>この後の連絡手段などの情報はたいてい放送文の最後の方にヒントがある。ここでは最後の If you could call me when you get back from lunch to confirm, ～を聞き取る。「昼食から戻ったら」→「今日の午後」と考えられるので，(B) が正解。 |

| 放送文 | 放送文の訳 |
|---|---|
| Questions 98 through 100 refer to the following excerpt from a meeting and chart.<br><br>Here are the latest data from our Sales Department, showing our four top-selling products over the last quarter. As you can see, smartphones accounted for more than half our revenue. I see an opportunity to further expand our line of smartphones, but at the same time, Marketing is putting together a campaign for our new Xenon Z27 copier, the fastest and cheapest on the market. If the campaign is well executed, I project we'll be able to double sales in that field. I'll speak with Accounting after this meeting to find out how much we can allot to the campaign, and I will report what they say at our next meeting. | 問題98-100は次の会議の一部と図表に関するものです。<br><br>こちらは当社販売部からの最新データで，前の四半期を通して最もよく売れた4つの製品を示しています。ご覧の通り，スマートフォンが当社収益の半分以上を占めました。当社のスマートフォンのラインアップを一層拡大する好機だと思いますが，同時に，市場で最速・最廉価である当社の新製品Xenon Z27 コピー機のキャンペーンをマーケティング部が企画しています。このキャンペーンがうまくいけば，この分野の売り上げを倍にすることができると見込んでいます。この会議の後に経理部と話して，キャンペーンにどれほど充てられるか調べ，次の会議で彼らの話を報告します。 |

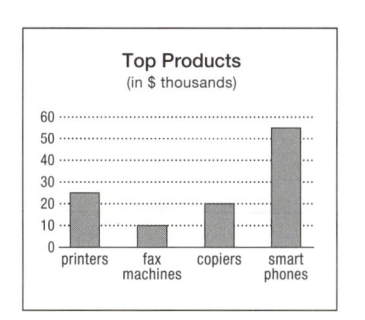

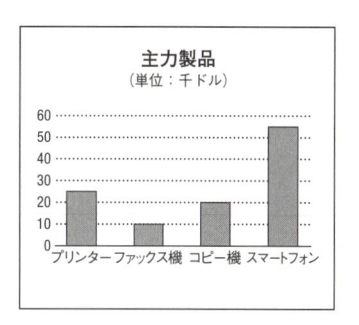

**Top Products** (in $ thousands) — printers, fax machines, copiers, smart phones

**主力製品** (単位：千ドル) — プリンター，ファックス機，コピー機，スマートフォン

## Vocabulary

- account for ～　～の割合を占める
- revenue [révənjùː]　収益
- put together ～　～をまとめる，企画する
- execute [éksəkjùːt]　～を実行する，達成する
- double [dʌ́bl]　～を倍にする
- allot A to B　AをBに充当する

| 設問 | 設問の訳 | 正解と解説 |
|---|---|---|
| **98**<br>Where most likely does the man work?<br><br>(A) At a printing company<br>(B) At an office supply retailer<br>(C) At a research firm<br>(D) At a telecommunications center | 男性はどこで働いていると考えられますか。<br><br>(A) 印刷会社<br>(B) 事務用品の小売業者<br>(C) 調査会社<br>(D) 電気通信センター | **正解 (B)**<br>場面は会議中で，男性はグラフのデータをもとに，自社製品の販売状況やキャンペーンなどについて話している。グラフにある printers や fax machines といった製品からも，(B) が正解とわかる。 |
| **99**<br>Look at the graphic. What figure does the man predict as a result of the campaign?<br>(A) $20,000<br>(B) $30,000<br>(C) $40,000<br>(D) $50,000 | 図を見てください。キャンペーンの結果として男性が予測する数値はどれだけですか。<br><br>(A) 20,000 ドル<br>(B) 30,000 ドル<br>(C) 40,000 ドル<br>(D) 50,000 ドル | **正解 (C)**<br>男性の予測に集中して聞くと，～ I project we'll be able to double sales in that field と言っている。project は「～と見積もる」，double は「～を2倍にする」の意味。この that field は，前の内容からマーケティング部がキャンペーンの対象としている copier のこと。グラフを見ると，コピー機の数値は $20,000 なので，男性の予測はその2倍の $40,000 である。 |
| **100**<br>What will the man do after the meeting?<br>(A) Help with a campaign<br>(B) Put together a report<br>(C) Make a presentation<br>(D) Consult with a department | 男性は会議の後に何をしますか。<br><br>(A) キャンペーンを手伝う<br>(B) 報告書をまとめる<br>(C) プレゼンテーションを行う<br>(D) ある部署と話し合う | **正解 (D)**<br>放送文最後の I'll speak with Accounting after this meeting ～ より，(D) が正解。speak with を consult with に，Accounting を a department と言い換えている。話し手のこれからの行動や意志は will がポイントとなることが多い。ただし，発話では普通 I'll と短縮形を用いるので，発音に慣れておくとよい。 |

# PART 5

## 問題文と訳

### 101
Heart Life Corporation's new medicine will be distributed in pharmacies after ------- over a period of 18 months certifies that it is safe.

(A) test
(B) testing
(C) tested
(D) have tested

Heart Life 社の新薬は，18 か月にわたる試験により安全であると証明された後，薬局に頒布される。

### 102
The entire downtown business area was filled ------- 12 hours with shoppers enjoying holiday discounts.

(A) as
(B) in
(C) on
(D) for

中心部のビジネス地域全体が，12 時間休日割引を楽しむ買い物客でいっぱいだった。

### 103
Analysts report that shopping online for groceries has ------- changed the entire supermarket experience.

(A) dramatically
(B) accusingly
(C) impenetrably
(D) combatively

分析専門家は，食料雑貨類をオンラインで購入することがスーパーマーケットでの買い物の仕方すべてを劇的に変えてきたと報告している。

### 104
Chinese retailer Zin Mart predicted no ------- in profits for the year, despite a slowdown in consumer spending.

(A) deteriorate
(B) deteriorated
(C) deteriorating
(D) deterioration

中国の小売店である Zin Mart は，消費者支出の減速にもかかわらず，その年の収益の悪化はないと予想した。

### 105
In case this event is canceled, ticket holders will each ------- the full face value of their purchase.

(A) entitle
(B) receive
(C) remove
(D) object

このイベントが中止された場合には，チケット所有者はそれぞれ，購入した満額を受け取る。

## 正解と解説

### 正解 (B)
空所の直前にある after は接続詞で，節内は空所から months までが主語で，動詞は certifies である。よって，主語として「18 か月にわたって試験をすることは」となるよう動名詞の (B) testing を入れるのが適切。 【動名詞】

distribute [distríbju(:)t] ～を分配する
pharmacy [fáːrməsi] （調剤）薬局
certify [sə́ːrtəfài] ～を証明する

### 正解 (D)
be filled with ～「～でいっぱいである」に ------- 12 hours が入っている構造。12 hours は時間（長さ）を表しているので，前置詞 for で「～間」がふさわしい。 【前置詞】

shopper [ʃɑ́pər] 買い物客

### 正解 (A)
空所の前後に has と changed があり，changed を修飾する副詞としてふさわしいのは (A) の dramatically「劇的に」である。 【語彙】

analyst [ǽnəlist] 分析専門家；解説者
groceries [gróusəriz] 食料雑貨類
entire [intáiər] 全体の
accusingly [əkjúːziŋli] 非難するように
impenetrably [impénətrəbli] 負けないほどに
combatively [kəmbǽtivli] 闘争的に

### 正解 (D)
動詞は predicted で，その目的語が〈no ＋名詞〉である。文意より，(D) deterioration「悪化」が正解。 【品詞】

retailer [ríːteilər] 小売業者，小売店
predict [pridíkt] ～を予想する
despite [dispáit] ～にもかかわらず
slowdown [slóudàun] 停滞，低迷
consumer spending 消費者支出
deteriorate [ditíəriərèit] ～を悪化させる

### 正解 (B)
空所には the full face value of their purchase を目的語とする動詞が入る。最も文意に合うのは，イベントが中止された場合は購入した満額を「受け取る」という (B) receive。直前の each は副詞で，頻度を表す副詞のように，be 動詞・助動詞の後または一般動詞の前に置く。(A) entitle は「～に資格を与える」という意味では，entitle O to do の形を取る。 【語彙】

remove [rimúːv] ～を取り除く
object [əbdʒékt] 反対する

| 問題文と訳 | 正解と解説 |
|---|---|

## 106

Trascki Automobile Company has gone from strength ------- strength since entering the North American market.

(A) on
(B) in
(C) and
(D) to

Trascki 自動車会社は北米市場に参入して以来，ますます強力になった。

**正解 (D)**

go from strength to strength で「ますます強力になる」の意味。このイディオムを完成させるために (D) to が正解。 **イディオム**

automobile [ɔ́ːtəmoʊbíːl] 自動車

---

## 107

Millions of consumers are rushing to buy the game software, leaving storeowners ------- to meet demand.

(A) conflicting
(B) contesting
(C) targeting
(D) struggling

何百万もの消費者がそのゲームソフトを購入しようと殺到しており，商店主たちは需要に応えようと苦戦している。

**正解 (D)**

leave O C「O を C のままにしておく」で C が現在分詞の構造。多数の消費者がゲームを購入しようと店に押しかけ，商店主がその需要に応えることに「苦労している」と考えるのが自然。正解は (D) で，struggle to do で「～するのに苦労する」という意味。 **語彙**

conflict [kənflíkt] 衝突する
contest [kəntést] ～を争う
target [tɑ́ːrgit] ～を目標にする

---

## 108

The ------- merit of Mr. Rysbecki's financial model comes from its ability to predict demand for the company's products.

(A) relative
(B) relation
(C) relate
(D) relatively

Rysbecki さんの財政モデルの相対的な長所は，会社の製品の需要を予測する能力に由来する。

**正解 (A)**

空所の後には名詞 merit があるので，これを修飾する形容詞の (A) relative「相対的な」が正解。 **品詞**

relation [riléiʃən] 関係
relate [riléit] ～を関係づける
relatively [rélətivli] 比較的に

---

## 109

Mr. Kim said he would prefer ------- in the Seoul office rather than transfer to the smaller branch in Incheon.

(A) remains
(B) to remain
(C) remained
(D) had remained

Kim さんは，インチョンの小さな支店に転勤するよりもむしろソウルのオフィスにとどまりたいと言った。

**正解 (B)**

prefer A rather than B で「B よりもむしろ A を好む」という意味。A と B には名詞相当句がくるので，to 不定詞の (B) が正解。prefer to do で「（むしろ）～をすることを好む」という意味。この文で B に当たる部分は (to) transfer である。 **不定詞**

transfer [trǽnsfɔːr] 転勤する
remain [riméin] とどまる

---

## 110

CEO Gawande of IndoOne Tech was known for his honest and ------- approach to business negotiations.

(A) opening
(B) openly
(C) open
(D) opened

IndoOne Tech の最高経営責任者 Gawande は，ビジネス交渉への正直で率直な取り組み方で知られていた。

**正解 (C)**

his honest and ------- approach で 1 つの名詞句である。honest は形容詞なので，and で結ばれた空所にも形容詞がふさわしい。よって，正解は (C) open。(A), (D) も形容詞的に使われるが，ここでは文意に合わない。 **品詞**

negotiation [nigòuʃiéiʃən] 交渉

| 問題文と訳 | 正解と解説 |
|---|---|

## 111

The client ------- us make several revisions to the advertising campaign literature, such as putting the logo in a more prominent position.

(A) had
(B) did
(C) permitted
(D) got

その顧客は、宣伝キャンペーンの印刷物に、もっと目立つ位置にロゴを入れるといったようないくつかの修正を我々にさせた。

**正解 (A)**

使役動詞の用法を問う問題。文意からも〈have+目的語（人）+動詞の原形〉「（人）に～させる」がふさわしいので、(A) が正解。(D) の got も使役で使われるが、〈get+目的語+to *do*〉の形となる。　　　　　　　　　使役

revision [rivíʒən] 修正
literature [lítərətʃùər] 印刷物
prominent [prάmənənt] 目立った
permit [pə(:)rmít] ～を許可する

## 112

Harris Corporation acted ------- in recruiting the very best personnel for all of its divisions.

(A) assertion
(B) asserting
(C) asserts
(D) assertively

Harris 社は、全部署のためにまさに最適な人材を採用することにおいて積極的に行動した。

**正解 (D)**

動詞 acted を後ろから修飾するのは副詞である。よって、(D) assertively「積極的に」が正解。　　　　　　　　　品詞

personnel [pə̀:rsənél] 人材、人員
assertion [əsə́:rʃən] 断言；主張
assert [əsə́:rt] ～と断言する；～を強く主張する

## 113

Green World Foods emerged as the most ------- brand in a survey, with 93% of respondents feeling positive about the company.

(A) imported
(B) trusted
(C) reviewed
(D) assumed

Green World 食品は、その会社について肯定的に感じている回答者が 93％で、調査で最も信頼できるブランドとして浮上した。

**正解 (B)**

分詞の前置修飾を問う問題。調査の回答者が「肯定的に感じている」という文意から、「最も信頼できるブランド」がふさわしい。よって、(B) trusted が正解。　　　　　　　　　語彙

emerge [imə́:rdʒ] 現れる、浮上する
survey [sə(:)rvéi] 調査
respondent [rispάndənt] 回答者
review [rivjú:] ～を再検討する
assume [əsú:m] ～と仮定する

## 114

The emergence of satellite TV is generating a crucial ------- that even local entertainment companies can market globally.

(A) understands
(B) understandably
(C) understanding
(D) understandable

衛星テレビの出現は、地方のエンターテイメント会社でさえ全世界的に売り込むことができるという重要な理解を生み出しつつある。

**正解 (C)**

空所の直前に冠詞 a がついた形容詞 crucial「重要な、決定的な」があるので、空所には名詞がふさわしい。よって、(C) understanding「理解」が正解。空所直後の that は同格である。　　　　　　　　　品詞

emergence [imə́:rdʒəns] 出現
generate [dʒénərèit] ～を生む
globally [glóubəli] 全世界的に
understandably [ʌ̀ndərstǽndəbli] はっきりと
understandable [ʌ̀ndərstǽndəbl] 理解できる

## 115

The board of directors at Dragon Robotics Co. reacted ------- to the idea of merging with a rival corporation.

(A) positively
(B) positive
(C) positiveness
(D) positivity

Dragon Robotics 社の取締役会は、ライバル社との合併の考えに前向きに反応した。

**正解 (A)**

react to ～で「～に反応する」という意味。動詞 reacted を修飾する副詞の (A) positively「前向きに」が正解。　　　　　　　　　品詞

board of directors 取締役会
positiveness [pάzətivnis] 明白なこと
positivity [pὰzətíviti] 積極性

| 問題文と訳 | 正解と解説 |
|---|---|

## 116

Professor Shah's expertise in industrial engineering earned him an ------- reputation in his field.

(A) insurable
(B) unwarranted
(C) unintentional
(D) enviable

Shah 教授の産業エンジニアリングにおける専門知識は，その分野で人がうらやむような評判を彼にもたらした。

**正解 (D)**

an と reputation の間に入る形容詞を選ぶ問題。どのような reputation「評判」をもたらしたかを考えると，(D) の enviable「人がうらやむような」が最適。 語彙

expertise [èkspərtíːz] 専門知識
insurable [inʃúərəbl] 保険がかけられる
unwarranted [ʌnwɔ́ːrəntid] 保証されていない
unintentional [ʌninténʃənəl] 故意でない

## 117

Director Khan said the senior managers of the company had made a number of ------- comments regarding its reorganization.

(A) construction
(B) constructive
(C) construct
(D) constructively

Khan 部長は，会社のシニアマネージャーたちが会社の再編についていくつか建設的な意見を述べたと言った。

**正解 (B)**

空所の直前に a number of ～「いくつかの～」があるので，名詞を選びたくなるが，空所の直後に名詞 comments があるので，名詞を修飾する形容詞を選ぶ必要がある。よって，形容詞 (B) constructive「建設的な」が正解。 品詞

regarding [rigáːrdiŋ] ～に関して
reorganization [riːɔ̀ːrgənəzéiʃən] 再編
constructively [kənstrʌ́ktivli] 建設的に

## 118

The expansion of Titan Corporation's factories in Indonesia ------- as part of its goal of increasing output from its facilities in the region.

(A) will see
(B) is seeing
(C) was seen
(D) being seen

Titan 社のインドネシアの工場の拡張は，その地域の施設の生産高を増やすという目標の一部と見なされた。

**正解 (C)**

空所の前までが文の主語で，空所には述語動詞が入る。文意より「拡張は～と見なされた」という受動態がふさわしいので，(C) was seen が正解。 受動態

expansion [ikspǽnʃən] 拡張
output [áutpùt] 生産高
region [ríːdʒən] 地域

## 119

Global Footwear Inc. is ------- larger than its domestic rivals, which gives it a much larger marketing budget.

(A) consecutively
(B) considerably
(C) consequently
(D) confusingly

Global フットウェア社は国内のライバル社よりもずっと大きく，そのことが同社にはるかに大きなマーケティング予算を与えている。

**正解 (B)**

空所の直後の larger than ～という比較級を強めて修飾する表現としては，(B) considerably「かなり，ずっと」がふさわしい。 語彙

domestic [dəméstik] 国内の
budget [bʌ́dʒit] 予算
consecutively [kənsékjətivli] 連続して
consequently [kánsəkwèntli] その結果として
confusingly [kənfjúːziŋli] 困惑させて

## 120

Following months of -------, Joshua Technologies publicly announced its takeover of Carpon Digital Design for £375.5 million.

(A) education
(B) speculation
(C) performance
(D) regulation

数か月におよぶ憶測の末，Joshua テクノロジーズは Carpon デジタルデザインを 3 億 7,550 万ポンドで買収することを公に発表した。

**正解 (B)**

長い間買収が「憶測」されていたと考えるのが自然なので，(B) speculation「推論，憶測」が正解にふさわしい。 語彙

following [fɑ́louiŋ] ～の後で
takeover [téikòuvər] 買収
performance [pərfɔ́ːrməns] 業績
regulation [règjəléiʃən] 規制

| 問題文と訳 | 正解と解説 |
|---|---|

## 121

Lopez Telecom Co. won a contract to build a telecommunication network in Eastern Europe, ------- in a 14% rise in profits.

(A) result
(B) to result
(C) resulting
(D) will result

Lopez テレコム社は，東欧でテレコミュニケーションネットワークを構築する契約を結び，その結果収益が14％増加した。

**正解 (C)**

result in ～は「(結果的に)～をもたらす」という意味。カンマの前までで文が完結しているので，分詞構文「～して，その結果…する」が適切。現在分詞の (C) resulting が正解。 〔分詞構文〕

win a contract to do ～する契約を結ぶ

## 122

The success of the Crystal Mountain Resort Hotel ------- by its low vacancy rate of only about 3% almost year-round.

(A) could determine
(B) can be determined
(C) to be determined
(D) is determining

Crystal Mountain リゾートホテルの成功は，ほぼ年間を通してわずか3％ほどという低い空室率によって判断できる。

**正解 (B)**

determine は「～を決定する，判断する」という意味。主語は success で，空所には述語動詞が入る。by「～によって」があることからも，受動態にするのがふさわしい。よって, (B) can be determined が正解。 〔受動態〕

vacancy rate 空室率
year-round [jìəɾráund] 年間を通じて

## 123

One of the main strengths of Ms. Chou's company lies in ------- ability to uncover previously undeveloped markets.

(A) it
(B) herself
(C) hers
(D) its

Chou さんの会社の主な強みの1つは，それまでまだ開発されていない市場を発見する能力にある。

**正解 (D)**

lie in ～は「(力や本質が)～にある」という意味。空所の直後に名詞 ability があるので，空所には所有格が適切。Ms. Chou's company の所有格を表す (D) its が正解。 〔代名詞〕

uncover [ʌnkʌ́vəɾ] ～を発見する
previously [príːviəsli] 以前に

## 124

Attendees at the One Globe Financial Seminar will have a chance to learn ------- corporations should carefully manage their internal cash reserves at all times.

(A) they
(B) why
(C) them
(D) what

One Globe 金融セミナーの出席者は，なぜ企業が常に内部の現金準備を注意深く管理しなければならないのかを学ぶ機会を持てるだろう。

**正解 (B)**

空所の前後に節があることから，主語となる (A) they，2つの節をつなぐことのできない (C) them は除外する。関係代名詞 (D) what の場合は，空所の後に主語または目的語が欠けた不完全な節が続くはずである。ここでは〈主語＋動詞＋目的語〉がそろっているので，関係副詞 (B) why が正解。 〔関係副詞〕

attendee [ətèndíː] 参加者
manage [mǽnidʒ] ～を管理する
internal [intə́ːrnl] 内部の

## 125

Organic foods at Happy Face Restaurants are becoming ------- popular, as people realize the benefits of making healthy food choices.

(A) increasing
(B) increase
(C) increasingly
(D) increment

Happy Face レストランのオーガニック食品は，人々が健康的な食品を選択することの良さを実感するにつれ，ますます人気が高まっている。

**正解 (C)**

become popular で「人気になる」の意味。副詞の (C) increasingly「ますます」が becoming を修飾して，「ますます～になっている」という意味になる。 〔品詞〕

realize [ríː(ː)əlàiz] (実感として)～がよくわかる
benefit [bénəfit] 利益，恩恵
increment [ínkrəmənt] 増加

| 問題文と訳 | 正解と解説 |
|---|---|

## 126

Although White Sky Airlines has lost some of its market share in recent years, it is ------- than its rivals.

(A) establishing
(B) establishes
(C) more established
(D) most established

White Sky 航空は，近年市場シェアをいくらか失ったが，いまだにライバル社よりも安定している。

**正解 (C)**

空所の直後に than があるので，比較級の (C) more established が正解。選択肢と空所直後の than を見ただけで即答できる問題である。　　　　比較

established [istǽbliʃt] 確立した

## 127

The *Dancing Baby* doll created a great ------- among consumers, and sold in very large numbers upon its initial release.

(A) sensation
(B) compensation
(C) determination
(D) promotion

*Dancing Baby* 人形は消費者の間で大きな評判となり，最初の発売で大量に売れた。

**正解 (A)**

and 以下の「最初の発売で大量に売れた」という文脈から，create a sensation で「センセーションを巻き起こす，評判となる」が正解にふさわしい。　　語彙

initial [iníʃəl] 最初の
release [rilíːs] 発売
compensation [kàmpənséiʃən] 補償（金）
determination [ditə̀ːrmənéiʃən] 決心
promotion [prəmóuʃən] 販売促進

## 128

The communications department ------- the company's media coverage, both at home and abroad.

(A) monitors
(B) renovates
(C) contacts
(D) invests

コミュニケーション部は国内と海外の両方で，会社に対するマスコミ報道を監視する。

**正解 (A)**

「マスコミ報道を監視する」が最も文意に合うので，正解は (A) monitors。　　語彙

media coverage マスコミ報道
renovate [rénəvèit] 〜を刷新する

## 129

PetCare1.com is a corporation ------- has been able to tap into the multibillion dollar pet market by shipping a variety of dog and cat-related products directly to owners.

(A) who
(B) whose
(C) which
(D) what

PetCare1.com は，さまざまな犬と猫関連の製品を直接飼い主に送ることによって，数十億ドルものペット市場に進出を果たし得た会社である。

**正解 (C)**

適切な関係代名詞を選ぶ問題。直前の a corporation は先行詞で，後には has been という動詞が続いている。「〜ペット市場に進出を果たし得た会社」という文意から，関係代名詞主格の (C) which が正解。who は先行詞が「人」のときに用いる。whose は後に名詞が続く。what は先行詞を含むので名詞の後には来ない。　　関係代名詞

tap into 〜　〜に進出する
multibillion [mʌ̀ltəbíljən] 数十億の

## 130

Caris Coffee has ------- its commitment to donate 5% of its annual profits to charities in Eastern Kenya.

(A) confirmed
(B) contributed
(C) contacted
(D) concerned

Caris コーヒーは，東ケニアでの慈善事業に年収益の5%を寄付するという方針を固めた。

**正解 (A)**

commitment「約束」を「確認した，表明した」とするのが最も文意に合うので，正解は (A) confirmed。　　語彙

donate [dóuneit] 〜を寄付する
annual [ǽnjuəl] 毎年の
contribute [kəntríbju(ː)t] 貢献する
concern [kənsə́ːrn] 〜に関係する

107

# PART 6

## 問題文

Questions 131-134 refer to the following e-mail.

---

To: Francesco Milletti
From: Masoud Akbar
Date: 31 August
Subject: Replacement request

Dear Mr. Milletti,

I received your e-mail yesterday. In it, you ------- the shipment of the construction materials from Milan. I have pasted information from that e-mail below.
              131.

　　　　Steel beams ･････････････････200
　　　　Wood beams･･････････････････175
　　　　Concrete mix ･････････････････500 kilograms
　　　　Glass Panes ･･････････････････600
　　　　Tools ････････････････････････34 pieces

We have checked the shipment, and most of the goods that arrived are fine. There is one issue, however: ------- the number of glass panes noted above totaled what we had ordered, there were
         132.
variances in quality. Some of the panes were quite thick, for example, while others were thin. -------. We would therefore like to have 100 replacement panes ------- to us.
133.                                                                                    134.

If you are able to do this before 7 September, that would be ideal, as that would mean minimum disruption to our construction schedule. Please let me know when we can expect the replacement units.

Regards,
Masoud Akbar

---

131. (A) confirmed
　　　(B) negotiated
　　　(C) permitted
　　　(D) accepted

132. (A) yet
　　　(B) despite
　　　(C) unless
　　　(D) although

133. (A) We really like these high-quality products.
　　　(B) We really need all the items to be of a similar quality.
　　　(C) These panes are normally either too thick or thin.
　　　(D) There are no complaints whatsoever about the price.

134. (A) send
　　　(B) sent
　　　(C) sending
　　　(D) to send

## 正解と解説

### 131
**正解 (A)**

語彙の問題。空所の次の文に，相手からもらった「Eメールの情報を貼り付ける」とあり，その詳細が列記されている。よって，空所には「建材の発送を確認した」という意味になるよう (A) confirmed を入れるのが適切。

negotiate [nigóuʃièit]（交渉で）～を取り決める

### 132
**正解 (D)**

従位接続詞を問う問題。had ordered の後のカンマの前と後ろでは，相反する内容になっていることに注意。空所の後に主語と動詞が続いているので，譲歩を表す従位接続詞 (D) although が正解。(A) yet にも逆接の意味があるが，従位接続詞ではないし文頭で用いることもない。(B) despite にも逆接の意味があるが，前置詞なので後に文を続けることはできない。

### 133
**正解 (B)**

文挿入問題。メールの書き手は問題点について，2つ前の文で品質にばらつきがあったことを挙げ，届いた窓ガラスに厚いものと薄いものがあったと具体的に伝えている。空所の後では交換品を求めているので，空所に入る内容として適切なのは (B)。(B) の items は panes のこと。
(A)「私たちはこの高品質の製品がとても気に入っています」
(B)「私たちは全商品がほぼ同質であることを切望しています」
(C)「これらの窓ガラスは通常，厚すぎるか薄すぎるかです」
(D)「値段について全く不満はありません」

whatsoever [hwὰtsouévər]（no を伴った名詞の後に置いて）全く（～ない）

### 134
**正解 (B)**

使役動詞を問う問題。〈have + O + 過去分詞〉「O を～してもらう」の構造。would like to have ~ sent to us で「私たちに～を送ってもらいたい」という意味になる。

## 問題文の訳

問題 131-134 は次の E メールに関するものです。

宛先：Francesco Milletti
送信者：Masoud Akbar
日付：8 月 31 日
件名：交換の依頼

Milletti 様
昨日あなたの E メールを受け取りました。その中で，あなたはミラノからの建材の発送を確認されました。以下にその E メールからの情報を貼り付けます。

　　　鉄骨材･･････････････････200
　　　木のはり････････････････175
　　　コンクリートミックス････500 キログラム
　　　窓ガラス････････････････600
　　　工具････････････････････34 個

発送物を確認したところ，届いた品物のほとんどは問題ありませんでした。しかし，1 つ問題があります。上述の窓ガラスの数は，合計すると私たちが注文した数になりましたが，品質にばらつきがありました。例えば，かなり厚い窓ガラスもありましたが，その一方で薄いものもありました。私たちは全商品がほぼ同質であることを切望しています。したがいまして，交換品として窓ガラスを 100 枚送っていただきたいのです。
もし発送が 9 月 7 日までに可能であれば，私たちの建設スケジュールへの混乱が最小限となりますので，それが理想的です。交換品がいつ届くと考えていいかお知らせください。

敬具
Masoud Akbar

## Vocabulary

- shipment [ʃípmənt] 発送（物）
- issue [íʃuː] 問題
- variance [vέəriəns] 相違
- quality [kwάləti] 品質
- therefore [ðέərfɔ̀ːr] それゆえ
- replacement [ripléismənt] 代わりのもの
- ideal [aidíːəl] 理想的な
- minimum [mínəməm] 最低限の
- disruption [disrʌ́pʃən] 混乱

## 問題文

Questions 135-138 refer to the following letter.

---

Ajit Rahman
22 Ackley Road
Nashville, TN
December 3

Dear Mr. Rahman,

Please find a recent summary of the ------- on your account below.
                                          **135.**
    Amount in account at start of period:  $500,000
    Withdrawal, November 13 ................ $6,000
    Deposit, November 15 .................... $5,320
    Withdrawal, November 30 ................ $4,200
    Ending Balance: ............................. $495,120

We'd also like to remind you that ------- for overdraft protection is highly recommended. Such
                                    **136.**
protection guards you against fees which would otherwise be incurred.

You are currently eligible for up to $5,000 in overdraft protection. Many of our customers feel
that this provides them with -------, as they know they will not be penalized if they write checks for
                              **137.**
amounts temporarily not in their accounts. -------.
                                            **138.**

Sincerely,

Renee Zuiller
Account Manager
r.zuiller@d-bank.com

---

**135.** (A) upgrades
    (B) purchases
    (C) transactions
    (D) investments

**136.** (A) applies
    (B) applicable
    (C) applications
    (D) applying

**137.** (A) secure
    (B) secured
    (C) more security
    (D) more securely

**138.** (A) Please e-mail me if you are interested in this program.
    (B) Please let me know if this is possible at your earliest convenience.
    (C) If you have any recommendations, I would like to hear them.
    (D) I look forward to receiving your next report soon.

## 問題文の訳

問題 135-138 は次の手紙に関するものです。

Ajit Rahman
Ackley 街 22
テネシー州ナッシュビル
12月3日

Rahman 様
以下，お客様の口座取引について最近の概要をご参照ください。
    開始時の口座総額：…………50万ドル
    11月13日　引き出し………6,000ドル
    11月15日　預金……………5,320ドル
    11月30日　引き出し………4,200ドル
    最終残高：………………49万5,120ドル

また，ぜひとも当座借越の防止を申請されることをお勧めします。このような防止策は，申請されていなければ発生してしまう料金からお客様を守ってくれます。

お客様には現在5,000ドルまで当座借越の資格があります。一時的に口座にない額の小切手を書いたとしてもペナルティを課されることはないとわかっているので，当行のお客様の多くはこれによってより安心感が得られると感じています。もしこのプログラムにご興味をお持ちでしたら，メールをください。

敬具
Renee Zuiller
経理マネージャー
r.zuiller@d-bank.com

## 正解と解説

### 135

**正解 (C)**

語彙の問題。「以下，お客様の口座の～をご参照ください」とあり，下に口座の取引明細が並んでいる。よって，(C) transactions「取引」が正解にふさわしい。

upgrade [ʌ́pgrèid] 性能向上，改良
purchase [pə́ːrtʃəs] 購入
investment [invésᵗmənt] 投資

### 136

**正解 (D)**

品詞の問題。remind (人) that SV「(人)に～ということを気づかせる」の構造で，that 以下は ------- for overdraft protection が主語で，is が動詞である。apply for ～は「～を申請する」という意味で，空所には主語となるように名詞 (相当語句) がふさわしい。「申請することが勧められる」という意味で，動名詞の (D) applying が正解。(C) の applications は可算名詞「申請用紙」の複数形で，動詞の is と合わない。

### 137

**正解 (C)**

provide A with B で「A に B を与える」という意味。them は Many of our customers を指し，空所に当たる B には名詞 (相当語句) が入る。よって，(C) more security が正解。当座借越のプログラムに申請すると，申請する前と比較して安全性が高いという話なので，比較級が文脈に合う。

### 138

**正解 (A)**

文挿入問題で，文章の締めとしてふさわしい文を選ぶパターン。手紙の目的は顧客の銀行口座の取引の概要を伝えることで，最後の段落は銀行が提供する overdraft「当座借越」の限度額とそのプログラムの説明。よって，文章の締めとしてはプログラムへの興味を喚起する (A) がふさわしい。
(A)「もしこのプログラムにご興味をお持ちでしたら，メールをください」
(B)「これが可能かどうかなるべく早くお知らせください」
(C)「何かお勧めがございましたら，お伺いしたく思います」
(D)「近々，次のレポートをいただくのを楽しみにお待ちします」

## Vocabulary

- withdrawal [wiðdrɔ́ːəl] 图 (預金などの) 引き出し
- deposit [dipázit] 图 預金
- remind [rimáind] 動 ～に気づかせる
- be eligible for ～ ～に対して資格がある
- penalize [píːnəlàiz] 動 ～にペナルティを課す
- temporarily [tèmpərérili] 副 一時的に

## 問題文

Questions 139-142 refer to the following notice.

---

The management at Lysell Corporation ------- staff to take care of their bodies as well as their careers.
　　　　　　　　　　　　　　　　　　　　139.

Apart from our company fitness center and health plan, we have recently launched a Healthy Living campaign, ------- by the Human Resources Department. -------. More precisely, the campaign
　　　　　　　　　　　　140.　　　　　　　　　　　　　　　　　　　　141.
is designed to get our staff to exercise, eat right, and watch their weight. Already, 210 employees have signed up for it.

Elisabeth Choi from the Human Resources Department, who leads the campaign, recommended the staff could get in ------- in various ways, such as cycling to work instead of driving, or taking the
　　　　　　　　　　　　　142.
stairs instead of the elevators.

---

139. (A) encouraging
 (B) encouragement
 (C) encouragingly
 (D) encourages

140. (A) contacted
 (B) converted
 (C) developed
 (D) declared

141. (A) However, the campaign has been running quite smoothly.
 (B) The aim of the campaign is to help our staff improve their well-being.
 (C) The communication plan would boost the campaign's impact.
 (D) Therefore, we would appreciate your contribution to this cause.

142. (A) position
 (B) place
 (C) touch
 (D) shape

## 問題文の訳

問題 139-142 は次の通知に関するものです。

Lysell 社の経営陣は，社員にキャリアと同じくらい体を大事にするよう勧めています。

フィットネスセンターと医療保険の他に，わが社は最近，人事部によって開発された健康生活キャンペーンに着手しました。このキャンペーンの目的は社員の健康増進を助けることです。さらに正確に言えば，キャンペーンはわが社の社員に運動してもらい，正しい食生活をしてもらい，体重に注意してもらうように作られています。すでに，210 人の社員が参加の申し込みをしました。

人事部の Elisabeth Choi は，キャンペーンを指揮しているのですが，車の代わりに自転車で通勤したり，エレベーターの代わりに階段を使ったりするなど，さまざまな方法で社員は体調を整えることができると勧めていました。

## 正解と解説

### 139

**正解 (D)**

品詞の問題。空所の前に名詞句（文の主語），後に目的語があるので，空所には述語動詞がふさわしい。よって，正解は (D)。〈encourage ＋人＋ to do〉で「人に〜するよう勧める」の意味である。

### 140

**正解 (C)**

語彙の問題。直前の a Healthy Living campaign を後ろから修飾するのにふさわしい意味の単語を選ぶ。空所の後には by the Human Resources Department があるので，(C) を入れて「人事部によって開発された」とするのが自然である。

convert [kənvə́ːrt] 〜を変換する

### 141

**正解 (B)**

文挿入問題。前の部分は Lysell 社が健康生活キャンペーンを始めたという内容。後の部分は More precisely「さらに正確に言えば」以下に空所の文の具体的な内容が続くことがわかる。よって，(B) を入れると文脈が通る。exercise, eat right, and watch their weight は (B) の well-being「健康」の具体的な内容である。
(A)「しかし，このキャンペーンはとても順調に進んでいます」
(B)「このキャンペーンの目的は社員の健康増進を助けることです」
(C)「このコミュニケーション計画はキャンペーンの影響力を高めるでしょう」
(D)「したがって，わが社はこの目的に対する皆様の貢献に感謝します」

boost [buːst] 〜を強化する，増加させる
contribution [kɑ̀ntrəbjúːʃən] 貢献

### 142

**正解 (D)**

健康生活キャンペーンにおいて Elisabeth Choi が社員に何を勧めているかを考える。various ways「さまざまな方法」の具体例が書かれた such as 以下の内容からも，get in shape「体を鍛える，体調を整える」が文脈に合う。

## Vocabulary

- take care of 〜　〜を大事にする
- health plan 医療保険
- recently [ríːsəntli] 副 最近
- launch [lɔːntʃ] 動 〜に着手する
- precisely [prisáisli] 副 正確に
- various [véəriəs] 形 さまざまな

## 問題文

Questions 143-146 refer to the following e-mail.

---

From: David Martin, Operations Director
To: Luiz Rodriguez, Carmel Falls Manager
Subject: Georgetown Branch Opening
Date: Monday, May 5

Luiz,

As you know, the Georgetown Branch of PizzaMan Inc. is due to open this fall. As a result, we now need to ------- staff in the local area.
         **143.**

The Carmel Falls Branch is only 10 miles away, so we would like to offer some of your staff the opportunity to join ------- there. We feel that their previous experience of working for PizzaMan
           **144.**
could be extremely important in ------- the new branch a success.
             **145.**

Please let your employees know about this great new career option as soon as possible. -------.
                                                        **146.**

Sincerely,

David Martin

---

143. (A) reorganize
    (B) recruit
    (C) outsource
    (D) survey

144. (A) theirs
    (B) us
    (C) our
    (D) their

145. (A) causing
    (B) going
    (C) letting
    (D) making

146. (A) We will give priority to those who have been with us the longest.
    (B) We look forward to serving you at our new Carmel Falls branch.
    (C) This is the very first time we have treated you like this.
    (D) All staff members should report to work on time each day.

## 問題文の訳

問題 143-146 は次の E メールに関するものです。

送信者：オペレーション部ディレクター David Martin
宛先：Carmel Falls 店マネージャー Luiz Rodriguez
件名：Georgetown 店の開業
日付：5月5日月曜日

Luiz,

知っての通り、PizzaMan 社 Georgetown 店がこの秋に開店する予定です。その結果、今、現地でスタッフを採用する必要があります。

Carmel Falls 店はたった 10 マイル離れているだけなので、あなたの店のスタッフの何人かに私たちに加わる機会を与えたいのです。彼らの PizzaMan での以前の勤務経験が、新店舗を成功させることにおいてきわめて重要になり得ると感じています。

できるだけ早くこの素晴らしい新キャリアの選択肢について従業員に知らせてください。一番長くわが社で働いてきた人たちに優先権を与えます。

敬具
David Martin

## 正解と解説

### 143
**正解 (B)**

語彙の問題。文章が新店舗のオープンの話題から始まっており、空所の直後には staff がある。したがって、スタッフを「採用する」と考えるのが自然。よって、(B) が正解。後に続く文で系列店のスタッフを異動させることを述べているので、(C) outsource「外部委託する」は不適切。

reorganize [riːˈɔːrɡənàiz] ～を再編成する
survey [səˈːrvéi] ～を調査する

### 144
**正解 (B)**

人称代名詞の格を問う問題。動詞 join の目的語となり得るのは目的格の (B) のみ。「私たちはあなたの店のスタッフの何人かに私たちに加わる機会を与えたい」という文脈。offer A B で「A に B を提供する」の意味。

### 145
**正解 (D)**

空所に入る動詞に対して the new branch が O で、a success が C。「新店舗を成功させる」という文意にするためには make O C「O を C にする」がふさわしい。let も SVOC の形をとるが C に名詞は来ない。

### 146
**正解 (A)**

文挿入問題。直前の内容を補足する (A) が正解。priority「優先権」とは、前文の this great new career option「この素晴らしい新キャリアの選択肢（＝新店舗で働くチャンス）」を手に入れる権利のことである。
(A)「一番長くわが社で働いてきた人たちに優先権を与えます」
(B)「新しい Carmel Falls 店のご利用をお待ちしております」
(C)「私たちがこのようにあなたに対応したのは全く初めてのことです」
(D)「全スタッフが毎日定刻に出勤するべきです」

report to work 職場に出勤する

## Vocabulary

☐ previous [príːviəs] 形 以前の
☐ extremely [ikstríːmli] 副 非常に

# PART 7

| 問題文 | 問題文の訳 |
|---|---|

Questions 147-148 refer to the following ticket.

---

**ADMIT ONE ADULT**
## Summer of Strings
*An evening of classical music with the Singapore National Symphony Orchestra*

- Kwan Teok Hall
- Doors Open: 7:30 P.M.
- Performance First Half: 8:15 P.M.
- Intermission: 10:00 P.M.
- Performance Second Half: 10:30 P.M.

No cameras, videos or other recording devices allowed. No admittance after 10 minutes before the show starts. Please turn off all phones prior to entering. Except in the event of a performance cancellation, all ticket sales are final.

---

問題 147-148 は次のチケットに関するものです。

大人 1 人の入場を認めます
弦楽器の夏

シンガポール国立交響楽団による
クラシック音楽の夕べ

Kwan Teok ホール
開場：午後 7 時 30 分
公演第 1 部：午後 8 時 15 分
休憩：午後 10 時
公演第 2 部：午後 10 時 30 分

カメラ，ビデオ，その他の録音装置の持ち込みは認められません。公演開始 10 分前以降のご入場はご遠慮ください。すべての携帯電話はご入場前に電源をお切りください。公演中止の場合を除いて，チケットの払い戻しはいたしません。

## Vocabulary

- □ string [striŋ] 图 (複数形で)弦楽器
- □ performance [pərfɔ́ːrməns] 图 公演
- □ intermission [ìntərmíʃən] 图 休憩時間；幕間
- □ device [diváis] 图 装置
- □ turn off ～ ～(の電源)を切る
- □ prior to ～ ～より前に
- □ in the event of ～ ～の場合には
- □ cancellation [kæ̀nsəléiʃən] 图 取り消し，キャンセル

| 設問 | 設問の訳 | 正解と解説 |
|---|---|---|

### 147
When is the latest that ticketed guests may enter to see the performance?

(A) 7:30 P.M.
(B) 8:05 P.M.
(C) 8:15 P.M.
(D) 10:00 P.M.

チケットを発券された客が公演を見るために入場してよい一番遅い時間はいつですか。

(A) 午後 7 時 30 分
(B) 午後 8 時 5 分
(C) 午後 8 時 15 分
(D) 午後 10 時

**正解 (B)**

公演第 1 部が 8 時 15 分に始まり，No admittance after 10 minutes before the show starts. とある。つまり，最終入場は公演の 10 分前までであることがわかるので，正解は (B) 8:05 P.M. である。

ticketed [tíkitid] チケットを持った

### 148
What is stated on the ticket?

(A) Seating may be unreserved.
(B) Refunds are not usually available.
(C) No cancellations are allowed.
(D) Performance dates are limited.

チケットに述べられていることは何ですか。

(A) 座席は予約されていないかもしれない。
(B) 通常，返金はできない。
(C) キャンセルは認められない。
(D) 公演日は限られている。

**正解 (B)**

Except in the event of a performance cancellation, all ticket sales are final. とあり，公演中止の場合を除いては，チケットの払い戻しは通常は不可とわかる。よって，正解は (B) Refunds are not usually available. である。

unreserved [ʌ̀nrizə́ːrvd] 予約されていない

| 問題文 | 問題文の訳 |
|---|---|

Questions 149-150 refer to the following text message chain.

**Geordie Jacobsen**     May 8, 9:15 A.M.
Hi April, sorry to bother you. I know you're on your way to a client's office. Just curious, do you know if Accounting finished compiling last week's sales figures yet?

**April Meeker**     May 8, 9:18 A.M.
Yes. Sandra told me. They sent the file to her. I'll text her and have her send it to you by e-mail.

**Geordie Jacobsen**     May 8, 9:19 A.M.
Great. I was thinking we could include that data in our presentation tomorrow. Newest is best, right?

**April Meeker**     May 8, 9:21 A.M.
I agree, but ask Accounting first whether it's OK. They have to make the call on that one.

**Geordie Jacobsen**     May 8, 9:22 A.M.
OK. I'll do that now. I'll message you what they say.

**April Meeker**     May 8, 9:23 A.M.
Great!

問題 149-150 は次のテキストメッセージのやり取りに関するものです。

Geordie Jacobsen　5月8日，午前9時15分
やあ，April。邪魔して悪いね。お客様の事務所に向かっていることは知っているんだけど。ちょっと尋ねるけど，経理部が先週の売上高をまとめ終わったか知ってる？

April Meeker　5月8日，午前9時18分
ええ，Sandra が教えてくれたわ。経理部は彼女にファイルを送ったの。彼女にテキストメッセージを送って，あなたにファイルを E メールで送ってもらうわ。

Geordie Jacobsen　5月8日，午前9時19分
よかった。そのデータを明日のプレゼンテーションに入れられないかと思って。最新であるにこしたことないだろ？

April Meeker　5月8日，午前9時21分
賛成だけど，先に経理部にいいか尋ねてね。それは彼らが決めることだから。

Geordie Jacobsen　5月8日，午前9時22分
わかった。今からそうするよ。彼らの返事をテキストメッセージで君に伝えるから。

April Meeker　5月8日，午前9時23分
助かるわ。

## Vocabulary
- curious [kjúəriəs] 形 好奇心をそそる
- compile [kəmpáil] 動 ～を収集[編集]する
- make the call 重要な決断を下す

| 設問 | 設問の訳 | 正解と解説 |
|---|---|---|

### 149
What is Ms. Meeker doing now?

(A) Gathering some data
(B) Preparing for a presentation
(C) Writing an e-mail to Accounting
(D) Going to a client's office

Meeker さんは何をしているところですか。

(A) データを収集している
(B) プレゼンテーションの準備をしている
(C) 経理部宛ての E メールを書いている
(D) 顧客のオフィスに向かっている

**正解 (D)**

冒頭の Jacobsen さんの you're on your way to a client's office から，Meeker さんは今顧客のオフィスに向かっているところだとわかるので，(D) が正解。on one's way to ～ は「～へ行く途中で」。新形式の「テキストメッセージ（携帯電話メール）のやり取り」は，直接会って話す，E メールを送る，電話で話す，などが難しい状況にあると考えられる。よって，2人が今どこでどんな状況でテキストを打っているかをイメージすることが重要。

### 150
At 9:21 A.M., what does Ms. Meeker most likely mean when she writes, "They have to make the call on that one"?

(A) Accounting has to give permission to use data.
(B) Accounting has to give a presentation.
(C) She has to make a phone call to Accounting.
(D) She has to forward the data to Mr. Jacobsen.

午前9時21分に，Meeker さんが書いている "They have to make the call on that one" は，何を意味していると考えられますか。

(A) 経理部がデータを使用する許可を出さなければならない。
(B) 経理部がプレゼンテーションを行わなければならない。
(C) 彼女は経理部に電話をかけなければならない。
(D) 彼女は Jacobsen さんにデータを転送しなければならない。

**正解 (A)**

They は Accounting のことで，that one は「売上高の最新データを明日のプレゼンで使うこと」。make the call は「重要な決断を下す」という意味で，この文を適切に言い換えた (A) が正解。「電話をかける」と取り違えて (C) を選ばないように。

give permission 許可を出す
make a phone call 電話をかける
forward A to B　A を B に転送する

| 問題文 | 問題文の訳 |
|---|---|

Questions 151-152 refer to the following information.

### Annual Pan-Pacific Telecom Association Meeting

Macau Lotus Hotel
Pandora Room
July 7

The Association is pleased to announce that during this year's meeting, a keynote lecture will be given by Mr. Sun Liu Fan, widely regarded as the world's leading authority on global telecommunications. His research has led to the development of new insights on emerging advances in the industry. This has enabled both corporations and government regulators to maximize the benefits of this dynamic field.

Following the release of his latest book, *A World Connected*, Mr. Sun will share his most recent findings on telecommunications in emerging markets.

All those wishing to attend the lecture can get more information at www.panpacifictelecomassoc.net/lectures/.

*Fees for attending the annual meeting are not inclusive of the lecture. Those should be covered in advance through the online address noted above.

---

問題 151-152 は次の情報に関するものです。

汎太平洋電気通信協会年次総会

Macau Lotus ホテル
Pandora Room
7月7日

当協会は，今年度の総会中，世界的な電気通信において世界一の権威と広く認められている，Sun Liu Fan 氏による基調講演が行われますことを謹んでお知らせいたします。氏の研究は，業界で出現している進歩に新たな洞察の展開をもたらしました。このことは，企業と政府規制機関の双方に，この絶えず変化する分野の利益を最大限に活用することを可能にさせました。

最新の著書『つながった世界』の出版に続いて，Sun 氏は，新興市場における電気通信に関する彼の最新の発見を伝えてくださいます。

講演に参加されたい方は，www.panpacifictelecomassoc.net/lectures/ で詳しい情報を得られます。

* 年次総会の参加料には講演は含まれていません。上記のオンラインアドレスを通じて，事前に別途お支払いいただくことになっています。

## Vocabulary

- [ ] Pan-Pacific [pæ̀npəsífik] 形 汎太平洋の    [ ] telecom [téləkɑ̀m] 名（telecommunication の略）電気通信（学）
- [ ] association [əsòusiéiʃən] 名 協会；組合    [ ] keynote lecture 基調講演    [ ] leading [líːdiŋ] 形 第一流の    [ ] authority [əθɔ́ːrəti] 名 権威
- [ ] insight [ínsàit] 名 洞察；見識    [ ] emerging [imɔ́ːrdʒiŋ] 形 現れる；新生の    [ ] regulator [régjəlèitər] 名 規制者；管理するもの
- [ ] maximize [mǽksəmàiz] 動 ～を最大限に活用する    [ ] dynamic [dainǽmik] 形 絶えず変化する    [ ] inclusive of ～ ～を含めて

| 設問 | 設問の訳 | 正解と解説 |
|---|---|---|

### 151

According to the information, what is Mr. Sun renowned for?

(A) His regulatory authority over markets
(B) His financial investments into industry
(C) His many years of experience in different corporations
(D) His expertise and research in a specific field

---

この情報によると，Sun さんは何において有名ですか。

(A) 彼の市場を取り締まる権限
(B) 彼の産業への金融投資
(C) さまざまな企業における彼の長年の経験
(D) 特定分野における彼の専門知識と研究

---

**正解 (D)**

第1段落を参照する。Sun さんは global telecommunications の分野を研究している人物で，企業や政府規制機関に貢献していることからも，(D) が正解とわかる。本文の the industry や this dynamic field, (D) の a specific field は telecommunications のことである。

regulatory [régjulətɔ̀ːri] 規定する；取り締まる

### 152

What will attendees who want to hear the lecture have to do?

(A) Join the Association
(B) E-mail Mr. Sun
(C) Pay an extra charge
(D) Download a pass

---

講演を聞きたい出席者は何をしなければなりませんか。

(A) 協会に加盟する
(B) Sun さんに E メールする
(C) 追加料金を払う
(D) 入場券をダウンロードする

---

**正解 (C)**

文章の欄外に Those should be covered in advance through the online address noted above. とあり，総会の参加料に含まれていない講演については事前に別途支払いをしなければならないので，正解は (C)。

extra charge 追加料金

| 問題文 | 問題文の訳 |
|---|---|
| Questions 153-154 refer to the following instructions. | 問題 153-154 は次の使用説明書に関するものです。 |

**The Revlar Microwave Oven User Guide**

**P**osition your oven away from sources of heat or moisture, for optimum efficiency.

**D**o not operate it when empty.

**U**se appropriate, heat-resistant cookware, including knives, forks or spoons, at all times. Keep bowls partially covered while cooking, but never seal them completely.

**Y**ou may see moisture collecting on the inner walls or the door when the oven is in use. This is normal.

**C**ooking time varies according to quantity, as well as the fat or water content of the food. Monitor cooking progress to prevent food from drying out, burning or catching fire.

**F**ood with skins or membranes – like whole apples, potatoes or tomatoes – must be pierced before cooking.

**C**lean the insides of the oven and its door after each use so that it remains perfectly dry. This will prevent corrosion.

---

**問題文の訳**

Revlar 電子レンジ使用者ガイド

最も効率よく使用するために、電子レンジを熱や湿気の出所から離して設置してください。

中が空のまま操作しないでください。

ナイフ、フォークあるいはスプーンを含めて、適切な耐熱性の調理器具を常に使用してください。調理中はボウルを部分的に覆うようにして、完全には密閉しないでください。

電子レンジ使用中に内部の壁や扉に水分が付いているのが見えるかもしれません。これは正常です。

調理時間は、食品の脂肪分や水分含有量だけでなく内容量によって変わります。食品が乾燥したり焦げたり、引火したりするのを防ぐために調理の進行を監視してください。

皮や薄皮のある食品―丸ごとのリンゴ、ジャガイモやトマトのようなもの―は調理の前に穴を開けなければなりません。

完全に乾燥したままにしておくために、使い終わるたびに電子レンジ内部と扉を掃除してください。こうすれば腐食が防げます。

---

## Vocabulary

- microwave oven 電子レンジ
- source [sɔːrs] 名 出所、源
- moisture [mɔ́istʃər] 名 水分；湿気
- optimum [ɑ́ptəməm] 形 最適な
- efficiency [ifíʃənsi] 名 効率性
- appropriate [əpróupriit] 形 適切な
- heat-resistant [híːtrizístənt] 形 耐熱性の
- cookware [kúkwèər] 名 調理器具
- partially [pɑ́ːrʃəli] 副 部分的に
- seal [siːl] 動 ～を密閉する
- vary [véəri] 動 変わる
- catch fire 引火する
- membrane [mémbrein] 名 膜、薄皮
- pierce [piərs] 動 ～に穴を開ける
- corrosion [kəróuʒən] 名 腐食

---

| 設問 | 設問の訳 | 正解と解説 |
|---|---|---|
| **153**<br>What is stated about the cookware?<br>(A) It should be kept away from moisture.<br>(B) It should not be used in an operating oven.<br>(C) It should be able to withstand heat.<br>(D) It should be sealed inside bowls. | 調理器具について述べられていることは何ですか。<br>(A) 湿気から遠ざけておくべきである。<br>(B) 操作中の電子レンジで使うべきではない。<br>(C) 熱に耐えることができるべきである。<br>(D) ボウルの内側に密閉されるべきである。 | **正解 (C)**<br>電子レンジでなく cookware「調理器具」について聞かれていることに注意しよう。(A) は電子レンジに関してのことなので不適切。説明書には Use appropriate, heat-resistant cookware とあり、その言い換えである (C) が正解。(D) は、部分的に覆うべきで密閉してはいけないと文中にあるので不適切。 |
| **154**<br>What is recommended in the instructions?<br>(A) The oven should be operated when empty.<br>(B) The food should be dry before cooking.<br>(C) Airtight containers should be used.<br>(D) Holes should be poked into some food before cooking. | 使用説明書で勧められていることは何ですか。<br>(A) 電子レンジは中が空の状態で操作されるべきである。<br>(B) 食品は調理前に乾燥させておくべきである。<br>(C) 気密性の容器が使われるべきである。<br>(D) 調理の前に食材を刺して穴を開けるべきである。 | **正解 (D)**<br>Food with skins or membranes ～ must be pierced before cooking. とあり、皮のある食品には調理前に穴を開けておくように指示をしているので、その言い換えの (D) が正解である。<br><br>airtight [éərtàit] 気密の<br>poke a hole 穴を開ける |

## 問題文

Questions 155-157 refer to the following e-mail.

---

**\* E-mail \***

**From:** Kim Su-mi, Director, Han Kang Construction Corp.   KOREA
**To:** Fara Suleiman, President, Malaya One Real Estate   MALAYSIA
**Subject:** Consort Building
**Date:** 1 August

---

Dear Ms. Suleiman,

Following our videoconference of 29 July with our architects Franklin & Josephs, we feel it is necessary to visit your office to discuss the ongoing progress of the Consort Building project. We hope 4 August might be acceptable to you.

In your last e-mail, you also mentioned needing our assistance with some of your interior work. As you are aware, our agreement covers only the exterior of the building. Beyond that, we can recommend Maxima Space Co., headquartered in Rome. They have extensive experience with interiors, and have worked with us on buildings like yours in the past. Maxima Vice-president Ron Fascenelli has told me his corporation is quite capable of installing carpeting, furnishings, and handling painting for each of the 273 offices within the office building, in addition to other decorating needs as may be required.

I have taken the liberty of asking Mr. Fascenelli to send you a brochure package about his company by post. You can also learn more about them through their Web site www.maximaspaceitalia.com or simply e-mailing Mr. Fascenelli at ron.f@maximaspace.com.

We hope this helps you in your situation.

Yours sincerely,

Kim Su-mi

---

## 問題文の訳

問題 155-157 は次の E メールに関するものです。

送信者：Kim Su-mi, Han Kang 建設会社部長　韓国
宛先：Fara Suleiman, Malaya One 不動産社長　マレーシア
件名：Consort ビル
日付：8月1日

Suleiman 様

弊社の設計会社, Franklin & Josephs 社との 7月29日のテレビ会議の後で，私たちは Consort ビルのプロジェクトの進行状況を話し合うために御社を訪ねることが必要であると感じております。8月4日が貴殿にとってご都合がよろしければと願います。

貴殿はこの前の E メールで，弊社が内装作業の一部をお手伝いする必要性についても述べられました。ご承知のように，私たちの契約は建物の外装のみを扱うものです。それ以外は，ローマに本部を置いている Maxima Space 社をお勧めできます。彼らは内装に広範囲の経験を持ち，過去に御社のようなビルに関して弊社と一緒に作業をしたこともあります。Maxima 社副社長の Ron Fascenelli は，彼の会社はオフィスビル内の 273 室それぞれの敷物類の設置，備え付け家具，塗装の処理に加えて，ご要望があれば他の装飾に必要なものについても十分対応可能だと語りました。

勝手ながら，同社についてのパンフレットセットを貴殿に郵便でお届けするように Fascenelli 氏に頼みました。彼らのウェブサイト www.maximaspaceitalia.com を通じて，あるいは単に Fascenelli 氏に ron.f@maximaspace.com まで E メールを送ることで，同社についてもっとよく知ることができます。

これがあなたの状況の助けとなりますように。

敬具
Kim Su-mi

---

## Vocabulary

- videoconference [vídioukùnfərəns] 图 テレビ会議
- architect [á:rkətèkt] 图 建築技師
- ongoing [ángòuiŋ] 形 進行している
- interior [intíəriər] 图 内装
- agreement [əgrí:mənt] 图 契約
- exterior [ikstíəriər] 图 外装
- beyond that その他は
- (be) headquartered in ～　～に本部を置いている
- extensive [iksténsiv] 形 広範囲にわたる
- be capable of ～　～する能力がある；～ができる
- install [instɔ́:l] 動 ～を据え付ける
- furnishing [fə́:rniʃiŋ] 图 （複数形で）備え付け家具
- take the liberty of ～　勝手ながら～する
- by post 郵便で

| 設問 | 設問の訳 | 正解と解説 |
|---|---|---|
| **155**<br>What is the purpose of Ms. Kim's upcoming meeting with Ms. Suleiman?<br>(A) To meet construction architects<br>(B) To propose an additional project outlines<br>(C) To provide updates on construction work<br>(D) To inspect building specifications | Kim さんの Suleiman さんとの次のミーティングの目的は何ですか。<br>(A) 建築技師に会うこと<br>(B) 別のプロジェクトの概略を提案すること<br>(C) 建設工事の最新情報を提供すること<br>(D) 建物の設計書を詳しく調べること | **正解 (C)**<br>第1段落に we feel it is necessary to visit your office to discuss the ongoing progress of the Consort Building project とある。(C) が正解で、本文の the Consort Building project とは次の段落から建設工事 (construction work) のこと。discuss the ongoing progress を (C) では provide updates と言い換えている。<br><br>outline [áutlàin] 概略<br>building specification 建物の設計書 |
| **156**<br>Why does Ms. Kim recommend Maxima Space Co.?<br>(A) They have developed many building exteriors.<br>(B) They dominate the market in Rome.<br>(C) They have done a lot of work in interior projects.<br>(D) They offer the lowest prices. | Kim さんは Maxima Space 社をなぜ勧めているのですか。<br>(A) 彼らは多くの建物の外装を手がけてきた。<br>(B) 彼らはローマの市場を独占している。<br>(C) 彼らは内装のプロジェクトにおいて多くの仕事をしてきた。<br>(D) 彼らは最低価格を申し出ている。 | **正解 (C)**<br>第2段落に They have extensive experience with interiors, and have worked with us on buildings like yours in the past. とあり、Kim さんは過去に Maxima Space 社と仕事を共に行い、内装において彼らが幅広い経験があることを知っているから勧めているのである。よって、正解は (C)。<br><br>dominate [dάmənèit] ～を独占する |
| **157**<br>What does Ms. Suleiman expect to receive soon?<br>(A) An e-mail from the vice-president<br>(B) Some reading material from overseas<br>(C) A phone call regarding construction deadlines<br>(D) A Web site service agreement | Suleiman さんがもうすぐ受け取ると思われるものは何ですか。<br>(A) 副社長からの E メール<br>(B) 海外からの読み物<br>(C) 建設期限に関する電話連絡<br>(D) ウェブサイトサービス契約書 | **正解 (B)**<br>第3段落に I have taken the liberty of asking Mr. Fascenelli to send you a brochure package about his company by post. とあり、Fascenelli さんからパンフレットが入った小包が届くので、正解は (B)。Suleiman さんはマレーシアにいるので、海外からの小包となる。Maxima 社副社長の Fascenelli さんから E メールを送るのではなく、Suleiman さんから E メールを送ることを勧めているので、(A) は不適切。 |

117

Questions 158-160 refer to the following advertisement.

### Come Join the Team at Symington Company
### We Animate the World!

**Symington Company, headquartered in New Zealand, announces openings in its Riga, Latvia office.**

**About us:** We are one of the largest companies in the Asia-Pacific region, known for our cutting-edge animation technologies. Our employees are dedicated, hard-working, and generally long-term. Our compensation packages are in most cases well above industry averages. We were chosen "Best Company to Work For" this year by the business news Web site, 21CTrade.com.

**Our recent moves:** We are now entering the European market. The Riga office is intended to serve as the company's base for the Eastern Europe-Russia region.

We are looking for staff in the following areas:

- Computer Graphics & Animation
- Print Illustration
- Information Technologies
- Management

All applicants must have at least 3 years of experience in their respective fields. Managerial applicants must have at least 4 additional years. Medium fluency in English required; medium or advanced fluency in Russian, German or French is preferred.

Those interested in one of the positions listed above may apply online at www.symingtonanimation.com/jobs/animation/latvia/. Callers to Personnel about this position will be directed back to this site. Faxed résumés will receive no response. Interviews will take place from October 5 to October 12 at our Riga headquarters, and those who are selected for positions will be notified by October 20. Most positions will start October 23.

## Vocabulary

- cutting-edge [kʌ́tiŋédʒ] 形 最先端の
- dedicated [dédəkèitid] 形 献身的な
- long-term [lɔ́:ŋtə̀ːrm] 形 長期の
- compensation package 給与体系
- industry [índəstri] 名 業界；産業
- average [ǽvəridʒ] 名 平均
- be intended to *do* ～することを目的としている
- applicant [ǽpləkənt] 名 応募者
- respective [rispéktiv] 形 それぞれの
- managerial [mæ̀nədʒíəriəl] 形 管理の
- additional [ədíʃnəl] 形 さらなる
- medium [míːdiəm] 形 中位の
- fluency [flúː(ː)ənsi] 名 （言葉の）流暢さ
- résumé [rézumèi] 名 履歴書
- response [rispáns] 名 返答
- take place 行われる
- notify [nóutəfài] 動 ～に通知する

| 設 問 | 設問の訳 | 正解と解説 |
|---|---|---|
| **158**<br>What is indicated about Symington Company?<br>(A) It is well known in the European region.<br>(B) It is respected for its Web site technologies.<br>(C) It is famous for its award-winning products.<br>(D) It is noted for its generosity to its staff. | Symington 社について何が示されていますか。<br>(A) ヨーロッパ地域でよく知られている。<br>(B) ウェブサイト技術で評価を受けている。<br>(C) 賞に輝いた製品で有名である。<br>(D) 社員に対する気前の良さで注目されている。 | **正解 (D)**<br>給与体系がほとんどのケースで業界平均を優に上回ることを述べ、ビジネスニュース・ウェブサイトによって今年の「働くのに一番の会社」に選ばれたとあることから、正解にふさわしいのは、(D) It is noted for its generosity to its staff. である。<br><br>award-winning [əwɔ́:rdwìniŋ] 受賞した<br>generosity [dʒènərásəti] 寛大；気前の良さ |
| **159**<br>How much experience is required for applicants for managerial positions?<br>(A) Three years<br>(B) Four years<br>(C) Five years<br>(D) Seven years | 管理職の応募者はどのくらいの経験が必要とされますか。<br>(A) 3 年<br>(B) 4 年<br>(C) 5 年<br>(D) 7 年 | **正解 (D)**<br>TOEIC 特有の計算問題である。All applicants must have at least 3 years of experience in their respective fields. Managerial applicants must have at least 4 additional years. とあり、管理職希望者は 3 年＋ 4 年＝ 7 年必要なので、正解は (D)。additional を見落とすと、(B) Four years を正解に選んでしまう可能性があるので注意しよう。 |
| **160**<br>When will Symington Corporation inform successful candidates?<br>(A) By October 5<br>(B) By October 12<br>(C) By October 20<br>(D) By October 23 | Symington 社は合格した志願者にいつ知らせますか。<br>(A) 10 月 5 日までに<br>(B) 10 月 12 日までに<br>(C) 10 月 20 日までに<br>(D) 10 月 23 日までに | **正解 (C)**<br>those who are selected for positions will be notified by October 20「それぞれの職に選ばれた人は 10 月 20 日までに通知される」とあるので、正解は (C)。(A) は面接の初日、(B) は面接最終日、(D) は仕事が始まる日なので不適切。 |

Questions 161-163 refer to the following article.

## Accounting for the New Century
## —in the Right Way

If your company commonly has errors in its financial reports, the accounting computer network, not the staff, is usually more to blame. — [1] —. The errors themselves are only a symptom of that underlying problem.

Consulting companies can advise you on which accounting computers to purchase. These computers are able to manage very large amounts of data, and are linked to a central network. — [2] —. Best of all, they commonly have easy-to-follow operation instructions. Consulting companies can offer advice on using these computers and teach staff to increase productivity through them.

These consulting companies also maintain industry-wide benchmarks for your accounting department. — [3] —. Their Ax Blue reports published each year provide an overview of how corporations and corporate departments in over 200 areas stay world-class. Meeting benchmarks like these ensures that your company is rising to the best practices within your industry. — [4] —.

### Vocabulary
- commonly [kάmənli] 副 一般に；よく
- be to blame 責めを負うべきである
- symptom [símptəm] 名 兆候
- underlying [ʌndərláiiŋ] 形 根底にある
- best of all とりわけ
- easy-to-follow [íːzitəfὰlou] 形 わかりやすい
- productivity [prὸudʌktívəti] 名 生産性
- industry-wide [índəstriwàid] 形 業界全体の
- benchmark [béntʃmὰːrk] 名 基準

| 設問 | 設問の訳 | 正解と解説 |
|---|---|---|
| **161**<br>According to the article, why do most accounting errors occur?<br><br>(A) Reports are done too quickly.<br>(B) Companies have insufficient data.<br>(C) Computer systems are inadequate.<br>(D) Supervisors lack management skills. | 記事によると，ほとんどの経理ミスはなぜ起こるのですか。<br><br>(A) 報告が早く行われすぎる。<br>(B) 会社が不十分なデータを持っている。<br>(C) コンピューターシステムが不適切である。<br>(D) 上司に管理能力が欠けている。 | **正解 (C)**<br>the accounting computer network 〜 is usually more to blame「たいてい財務会計コンピューターネットワークの方に大きな責任がある」と述べている。現在のコンピューターネットワークが不適切なためにミスが起こるのだから，正解は (C)。<br><br>insufficient [ìnsəfíʃənt] 不十分な<br>inadequate [inædəkwit] 不適切な |
| **162**<br>How are the Ax Blue reports helpful to corporations?<br><br>(A) They list the largest corporations in each field.<br>(B) They show how to maintain top standards in different sectors.<br>(C) They showcase the best managers at major businesses.<br>(D) They provide an overview of important markets. | Ax Blue レポートは企業に対してどのように役立ちますか。<br><br>(A) 各分野で一番大きな企業を列挙している。<br>(B) さまざまな部門でどのように最高水準を維持するかを示している。<br>(C) 大企業の最も優れた経営者を紹介している。<br>(D) 重要な市場の概要を提供している。 | **正解 (B)**<br>第 3 段落に Their Ax Blue reports 〜 provide an overview of how corporations and corporate departments in over 200 areas stay world-class.「200 を超える分野の企業と経営部門がどのようにして世界レベルでいられるかについて概要を提供している」とあるので，その言い換えである (B) が正解。<br><br>showcase [ʃóukèis] 〜を紹介する<br>major business 大企業 |
| **163**<br>In which of the positions marked [1], [2], [3] and [4] does the following sentence best belong?<br><br>"AxTor Consulting Group is a good example of this."<br><br>(A) [1]<br>(B) [2]<br>(C) [3]<br>(D) [4] | [1], [2], [3], [4] と記載された箇所のうち，次の文が入るのに最もふさわしいのはどれですか。<br><br>「AxTor コンサルティンググループはこの良い例です」<br><br>(A) [1]<br>(B) [2]<br>(C) [3]<br>(D) [4] | **正解 (C)**<br>文を挿入する問題では，this や that などの指示語や his や them などの代名詞が指す内容を見極めることが重要。ここでは AxTor という社名と this の内容から考えて，[3] に入れるのが適切。AxTor Consulting Group は「会社の経理部が業界全体の基準を維持できるようにしてくれるコンサルティング会社」の例であり，後の Their Ax Blue reports 〜ともつながる。 |

Questions 164-167 refer to the following notice.

## BLIGO TRADING SERVICES
### Friday, July 28

Following the senior directors' meeting last week, it has been decided that structural changes at the Bligo Hong Kong branch are necessary. The following measures are to be implemented to make operations more cost-efficient. These changes will be implemented in stages.

**August 1**
All help desk issues will be handled by our Bangalore, India global consumer service center. Help desk facilities in Hong Kong, including both human operators and the automated answering system, will cease.

**August 20**
The human resources department will utilize Web technologies for recruiting, staff management, employee benefits and other staff services to the maximum extent to decrease current costs in the department.

**August 31**
Personnel from the sales and marketing divisions will merge into one group, with expected staffing reductions of 42%.

While it is regrettable that some of these steps will result in job losses for the departments concerned, we are pleased to announce that several new positions have been created in our Mainland China division. Staff who are interested in applying are urged to contact Lisa Vu at lisa.vu@bligo.net for an application form.

| 設問 | 設問の訳 | 正解と解説 |
|---|---|---|
| **164**<br>What is the purpose of the changes being made by Bligo Trading?<br>(A) To improve facilities<br>(B) To reduce operating costs<br>(C) To reward performance<br>(D) To upgrade services | Bligo貿易によって行われる改革の目的は何ですか。<br>(A) 施設を改善すること<br>(B) 運営費を削減すること<br>(C) 業績に報いること<br>(D) サービスを向上させること | **正解 (B)**<br>第1段落に The following measures are to be implemented to make operations more cost-efficient.「事業をもっと費用効率の高いものにするために次の措置が実行される」とあり、その後の文でも具体的なコスト削減策が述べられている。よって、(B) が正解。<br><br>reward [riwɔ́ːrd] ～に報いる |
| **165**<br>What change is being planned for the human resources department?<br>(A) Fewer people will be recruited.<br>(B) Regular work hours will be reduced.<br>(C) Employee benefits will decrease.<br>(D) Online systems will be used. | 人事部でどのような変更が計画されていますか。<br>(A) 採用される人員が減る。<br>(B) 通常の労働時間が削減される。<br>(C) 社員手当が減る。<br>(D) オンラインシステムが使用される。 | **正解 (D)**<br>人事部 (the human resources department) について記載がある August 20 の項目を見ると、コスト削減にウェブ技術を活用すると書かれている。よって、これを言い換えた (D) が正解。<br><br>work hours 労働時間 |
| **166**<br>What will happen on August 31?<br>(A) Sales will be emphasized over marketing.<br>(B) A company merger will occur.<br>(C) Two departments will be combined.<br>(D) The size of a group will be increased. | 8月31日に何が起こりますか。<br>(A) 売り上げがマーケティングよりも重視される。<br>(B) 企業合併が行われる。<br>(C) 2つの部門が統合される。<br>(D) グループの規模が拡大される。 | **正解 (C)**<br>第4段落に Personnel from the sales and marketing divisions will merge into one group, ～とあり、営業部とマーケティング部を統合することがわかるので、正解は (C)。他の会社と合併するわけではないので、(B) は不適切。人員の削減や香港のヘルプデスク施設の閉鎖など規模は縮小しているので、(D) も不適切。<br><br>emphasize A over B B よりも A を重視する |
| **167**<br>The word "concerned" in paragraph 5, line 2, is closest in meaning to<br>(A) worried<br>(B) controlled<br>(C) related<br>(D) detailed | 第5段落・2行目の "concerned" に最も意味が近いのは<br>(A) 心配した<br>(B) 管理された<br>(C) 関係のある<br>(D) 詳細な | **正解 (C)**<br>concerned は「関係している」という意味の形容詞で前の名詞を修飾することがある。これに一番近い意味の語は、(C) related「関係のある」である。<br><br>detailed [díteild] 詳細な |

Questions 168-171 refer to the following online chat discussion.

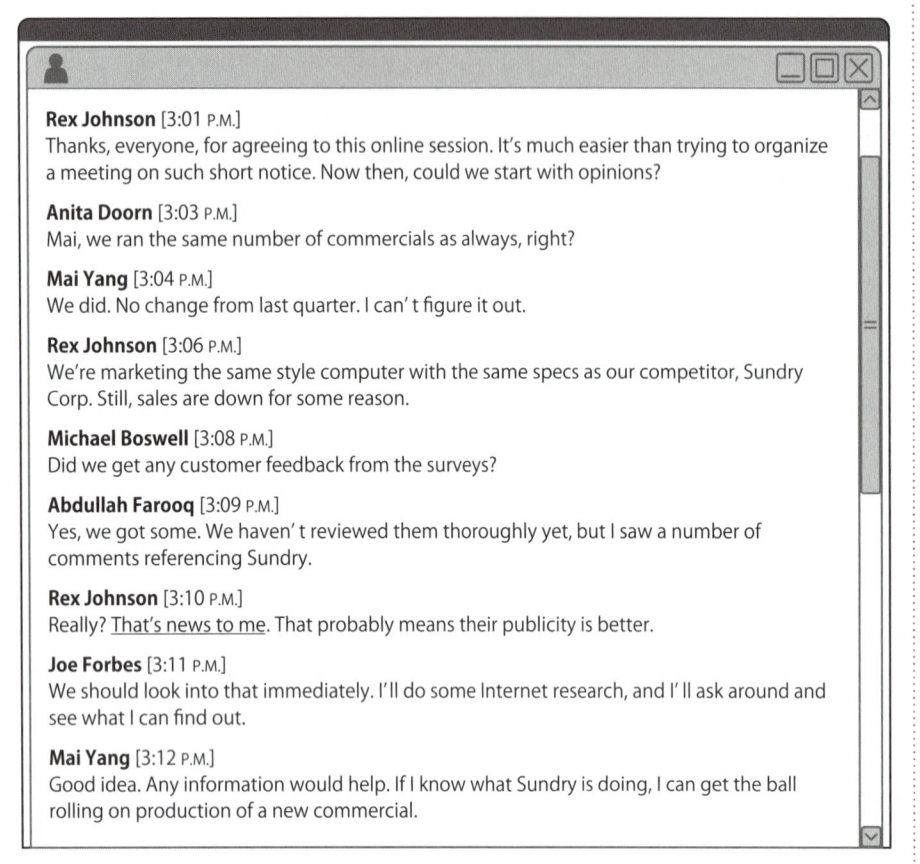

**Rex Johnson** [3:01 P.M.]
Thanks, everyone, for agreeing to this online session. It's much easier than trying to organize a meeting on such short notice. Now then, could we start with opinions?

**Anita Doorn** [3:03 P.M.]
Mai, we ran the same number of commercials as always, right?

**Mai Yang** [3:04 P.M.]
We did. No change from last quarter. I can't figure it out.

**Rex Johnson** [3:06 P.M.]
We're marketing the same style computer with the same specs as our competitor, Sundry Corp. Still, sales are down for some reason.

**Michael Boswell** [3:08 P.M.]
Did we get any customer feedback from the surveys?

**Abdullah Farooq** [3:09 P.M.]
Yes, we got some. We haven't reviewed them thoroughly yet, but I saw a number of comments referencing Sundry.

**Rex Johnson** [3:10 P.M.]
Really? That's news to me. That probably means their publicity is better.

**Joe Forbes** [3:11 P.M.]
We should look into that immediately. I'll do some Internet research, and I'll ask around and see what I can find out.

**Mai Yang** [3:12 P.M.]
Good idea. Any information would help. If I know what Sundry is doing, I can get the ball rolling on production of a new commercial.

## Vocabulary

- the same A as B　B と同じ A
- spec [spek] 名（specification の略，通例複数形で）仕様
- thoroughly [θə́ːrouli] 副 完全に
- reference [réfərəns] 動 〜を引き合いに出す
- publicity [pʌblísəti] 名 広報，宣伝
- look into 〜　〜を調べる
- immediately [imíːdiitli] 副 すぐに
- get the ball rolling （仕事などを）始める

| 設 問 | 設問の訳 | 正解と解説 |
|---|---|---|
| **168**<br>What is the reason for the discussion?<br><br>(A) To discuss a commercial<br>(B) To review sales figures<br>(C) To analyze a customer survey<br>(D) To solicit input from staff | この話し合いの理由は何ですか。<br><br>(A) コマーシャルについて話し合うため<br>(B) 売上高を調べるため<br>(C) 顧客調査を分析するため<br>(D) スタッフから情報を求めるため | **正解 (D)**<br>Johnson さんが Now then, could we start with opinions? と書いた後，それぞれの人物がコマーシャルや売り上げについて意見を出し合っているので，(D) が正解。solicit は「〜を懇願する」，input は「（情報や意見などの）提供」という意味。Johnson さんが sales are down for some reason と言って，その理由を話し合っていることから，(B) は不適切。|
| **169**<br>What most likely is Ms. Yang's job in the company?<br><br>(A) She oversees advertisements.<br>(B) She builds computer applications.<br>(C) She designs Web pages.<br>(D) She manages sales. | Yang さんの社内での仕事は何だと考えられますか。<br><br>(A) 広告を監督している。<br>(B) コンピューターのアプリケーションを作成している。<br>(C) ウェブページをデザインしている。<br>(D) 販売を管理している。 | **正解 (A)**<br>Yang さんの2回の発言を読むと，コマーシャルについて意見を述べているので，advertisement「宣伝・広告」の部門で働いていると推測できる。よって，(A) が正解。<br><br>oversee [òuvərsíː] 〜を監督する<br>application [æ̀pləkéiʃən]（コンピューターの）アプリケーション |
| **170**<br>At 3:10 P.M., what does Mr. Johnson most likely mean when he writes, "That's news to me"?<br><br>(A) He was unaware.<br>(B) He was misinformed.<br>(C) He wants to tell more people.<br>(D) He wants to contact the media. | 午後3時10分に，Johnson さんが書いている "That's news to me" は，何を意味していると考えられますか。<br><br>(A) 知らなかった。<br>(B) 間違った情報を伝えられた。<br>(C) もっと多くの人に教えたい。<br>(D) メディアに接触したい。 | **正解 (A)**<br>この news は「新しい情報，初耳のこと」という意味。That's news to me. は，I'm surprised. のようなニュアンスで使われている。知らなかったことを聞いて驚いているのだから，(A) が正解。<br><br>unaware [ʌ̀nəwέər] 知らない<br>misinform [mìsinfɔ́ːrm] 〜に誤った情報を伝える |
| **171**<br>According to the discussion, what most likely will happen next?<br><br>(A) Customer feedback will be received.<br>(B) Sales will go up.<br>(C) A new commercial will be reviewed.<br>(D) A company will be researched. | 話し合いによると，次に何が起こると考えられますか。<br><br>(A) 顧客フィードバックが受け取られる。<br>(B) 売り上げが上がる。<br>(C) 新しいコマーシャルが見直される。<br>(D) ある会社が調査される。 | **正解 (D)**<br>話し合いの最後の方で，競合他社である Sundry 社の宣伝について調査すると言っている。(D) が正解で，A company は Sundry のこと。|

Questions 172-175 refer to the following information.

## Science-M Contest
### Sponsored by Suvar Corporation
### Islamabad, Pakistan

Are you the next great scientist to come out of Pakistan?

Suvar Corporation is sponsoring a nationwide campaign to find the next generation of young geniuses from our country.

**Top Prize:** A full 4-year scholarship to the university of your choice anywhere within the nation. — [1] —.

**Second Place:** A set of 10 software educational packages from Suvar Corporation.

**Third Place:** Gift certificates for use at department stores in Lahore, Islamabad, Karachi and other major cities.

Here is how you can compete against the best young minds in Pakistan.

To enter the contest, you must be over 12 and under 20.* — [2] —. Entrants may submit any original creation within the following areas:

- Robotics
- Software
- Biotech
- Hardware
- Pharmaceuticals

All submissions must be entirely the work of the entrant, without any assistance from teachers, parents or other adults. — [3] —. If an entrant wishes to work with classmates on a submission, it must then be clearly labeled as teamwork.

The deadline for registering submissions is June 15. — [4] —. Entry inspections by a panel of judges will begin June 18, with a final winner chosen June 21.

*While anyone within this age group can compete, most top prizes in past years have usually gone to those aged between 17 and 19.

| 設問 | 設問の訳 | 正解と解説 |
|---|---|---|
| **172**<br>What is the stated purpose of the Science-M Contest?<br>(A) To find marketable technical products<br>(B) To improve business research capabilities<br>(C) To help fund educational programs<br>(D) To discover talented people | Science-M コンテストの目的として述べられているのは何ですか。<br>(A) 市場性のある工業製品を見つけること<br>(B) ビジネス調査能力を向上させること<br>(C) 教育プログラムに資金を出す援助をすること<br>(D) 才能のある人を見つけ出すこと | **正解 (D)**<br>第2段落に Suvar Corporation is sponsoring a nationwide campaign to find the next generation of young geniuses from our country. とあり、「次世代の若い天才を見つけるため」コンテストを協賛していることがわかるので、正解は (D) To discover talented people。<br><br>marketable [mɑ́ːrkitəbl] 市場性のある<br>capability [kèipəbíləti] 能力<br>talented [tǽləntid] 才能のある |
| **173**<br>Which is NOT listed as a gift for prize winners?<br>(A) Coupons for goods<br>(B) Educational materials<br>(C) Fees for tuition<br>(D) Travel tickets | 受賞者への賞品として記載されていないものはどれですか。<br>(A) 商品クーポン<br>(B) 教材<br>(C) 授業料<br>(D) 旅行チケット | **正解 (D)**<br>Top Prize: A full 4-year scholarship で、まず (C)「授業料」を除外できる。次に Second Place: A set of 10 software educational packages で、(B)「教材」も除外。Third Place: Gift certificates で、(A)「商品クーポン」を除外する。文中に記載されていない (D)「旅行チケット」が正解。<br><br>tuition [tjuːíʃən] 教授；授業料 |
| **174**<br>What rule is mentioned about the contest?<br>(A) Group work must be specified.<br>(B) Adult assistance is encouraged.<br>(C) Registration fees are required.<br>(D) Submissions require teacher approval. | コンテストについてどんなルールが述べられていますか。<br>(A) グループワークは明記されなければならない。<br>(B) 大人の手助けが奨励されている。<br>(C) 登録料が必要である。<br>(D) 提出物には教員の承認が必要である。 | **正解 (A)**<br>分野のリストの下に If an entrant wishes to work with classmates on a submission, it must then be clearly labeled as teamwork. とあり、グループワークは明記されなければならないことがわかるので、正解は (A)。その直前に「大人からのいかなる手助けも借りず、完全に参加者の作品でなければならない」とあるので、(B) は不適切。<br><br>specify [spésəfài] ～を明記する<br>encourage [inkə́ːridʒ] ～を奨励する<br>registration fee 登録料 |
| **175**<br>In which of the positions marked [1], [2], [3] and [4] does the following sentence best belong?<br><br>"While not necessary, a strong background in science is preferred."<br><br>(A) [1]<br>(B) [2]<br>(C) [3]<br>(D) [4] | [1], [2], [3], [4] と記載された箇所のうち、次の文が入るのに最もふさわしいのはどれですか。<br><br>「必須ではありませんが、科学分野においてかなりの経験があることが望ましいです」<br><br>(A) [1]<br>(B) [2]<br>(C) [3]<br>(D) [4] | **正解 (B)**<br>「科学分野においてかなりの経験があることが望ましい」は、コンテストに参加する条件が書かれている箇所にふさわしい内容である。よって、To enter the contest, ～「コンテストに参加するには～」で始まる段落にある [2] に入れるのが最適。<br><br>background [bǽkgràund] 経歴；予備知識 |

## 問題文

Questions 176-180 refer to the following notice and e-mail.

---

June 17

**Project Coordinator**
Orange Tech Co.

Orange Tech is the largest telecom company in our regional markets. Recently, we were awarded a contract for the construction of satellite broadcasting systems throughout the Republic of South Africa.

To cope with this increased workload, we are searching for a reliable project coordinator to assist the operations manager in charge of this task.

Candidates must have a minimum of a BA degree, with a graduate degree preferred. They must have at least three years' experience in the field, and be able to demonstrate excellent interpersonal skills.

Knowledge of the following software applications is required:
- **TX25**
- **InfoScoop**
- **Arcana**
- **IsoFin**

Regular duties will include database management, compilation of weekly reports, installation schedule development, and resolution of any outstanding technical issues.

Please submit credentials by July 9 to Adam De Groot at the following address, adam.degroot@orangetech.za

---

**E-mail**

To: adam.degroot@orangetech.za
From: darren.zimbele@africatel.com
Date: Wednesday, June 20
Subject: Open Position

Attachments: References.doc
CV.doc

Dear Mr. De Groot,

I am writing about your project coordinator position.

I graduated from Keele University, with an MSc in computer engineering two years ago. Since then, I have worked in Kampala Tech Co. as a software analyst, first in their Kimberly and Pretoria branches and now here in Johannesburg. There, I gained extensive experience working with TX25, InfoScoop, Arcana, IsoFin, and many other software packages.

Beyond my technical background, I also get on well with all sorts of people. Even while under the stress of tight work deadlines, I never get angry or frustrated.

I look forward to hearing from you soon.

Sincerely,

Darren Zimbele

---

## Vocabulary

- □ regional [ríːdʒənəl] 形 地域の　□ award a contract 契約を発注する　□ satellite broadcasting system 衛星放送システム
- □ cope with ～ ～に対処する　□ workload [wə́ːrklòud] 名 仕事量　□ reliable [riláiəbl] 形 頼りになる　□ in charge of ～ ～を担当して
- □ candidate [kǽndədèit] 名 志願者　□ interpersonal skill 対人能力　□ duty [djúːti] 名 職務　□ compilation [kàmpəléiʃən] 名 編集
- □ resolution [rèzəlúːʃən] 名 解決　□ outstanding [autstǽndiŋ] 形 未解決の　□ credential [kridénʃəl] 名（通例複数形で）資格証明書；信任状
- □ attachment [ətǽtʃmənt] 名 添付（物）　□ reference [réfərəns] 名 紹介状；人物証明書　□ CV 名（curriculum vitae の略）履歴書
- □ MSc 名 （Master of Science の略）理学修士

| 設問 | 設問の訳 | 正解と解説 |
|---|---|---|
| **176**<br>What will Orange Tech require their new recruit to do?<br>(A) Manage a new project<br>(B) Get a new contract<br>(C) Expand into a new market<br>(D) Acquire a new company | Orange Tech は新入社員に何をするよう求めますか。<br>(A) 新プロジェクトを管理する<br>(B) 新契約を得る<br>(C) 新市場に進出する<br>(D) 新会社を獲得する | **正解 (A)**<br>南アフリカ共和国全体の衛星放送システム構築の契約を手に入れ，増加した仕事量に対処するために社員を雇おうとしているのである。よって，正解は (A)。<br><br>expand into ～　～に進出する<br>acquire [əkwáiər] ～を獲得する |
| **177**<br>In the notice, the word "interpersonal" in paragraph 3, line 3, is closest in meaning to<br>(A) profitable<br>(B) communicative<br>(C) academic<br>(D) linguistic | お知らせの第3段落・3行目の "interpersonal" に最も意味が近いのは<br>(A) 利益になる<br>(B) コミュニケーションの<br>(C) 学術的な<br>(D) 言語の | **正解 (B)**<br>interpersonal には「個人間の」「対人関係の」の意味があり，後に skill が来ることで「対人能力」となる。interpersonal の代わりに communicative を入れると「伝達能力」となり，一番意味が近くなるので正解は (B)。inter- は「相互の」という意味を加える接頭辞である。<br><br>profitable [práfitəbl] 利益になる |
| **178**<br>Where does Mr. Zimbele currently work?<br>(A) Cape Town<br>(B) Kimberly<br>(C) Pretoria<br>(D) Johannesburg | Zimbele さんは現在どこで働いていますか。<br>(A) ケープタウン<br>(B) キンバリー<br>(C) プレトリア<br>(D) ヨハネスブルグ | **正解 (D)**<br>Eメールの第2段落に，I have worked in ～ now here in Johannesburg とあるので，今はヨハネスブルグで働いていることがわかる。よって，正解は (D)。 |
| **179**<br>What can be inferred about Mr. Zimbele from his application?<br>(A) He does not have enough work experience.<br>(B) He does not have the required academic background.<br>(C) He does not have sufficient references.<br>(D) He does not have adequate software skills. | Zimbele さんの応募から彼について何が推測できますか。<br>(A) 彼には十分な職歴がない。<br>(B) 彼には必要とされる学歴がない。<br>(C) 彼には十分な紹介状がない。<br>(D) 彼には適切なソフトウェア技術がない。 | **正解 (A)**<br>両方の文書を見て答える問題。I graduated from Keele University ～ two years ago. とあり，彼の社会経験は2年しかないことがわかる。お知らせによると，求められているのは3年の経験なので，彼には十分な職歴がないことがわかる。よって，正解は (A)。<br><br>sufficient [səfíʃənt] 十分な |
| **180**<br>Why does Mr. Zimbele mention deadlines?<br>(A) To emphasize his attention to details<br>(B) To highlight his computer skills<br>(C) To show his leadership background<br>(D) To demonstrate his patience | なぜ Zimbele さんは締め切りに言及しているのですか。<br>(A) 彼の細部への注意を強調するため<br>(B) コンピューター技能を目立たせるため<br>(C) 彼のリーダーシップの経歴を示すため<br>(D) 彼の忍耐力を実証するため | **正解 (D)**<br>Eメールの第3段落で，Even while under the stress of tight work deadlines, I never get angry or frustrated. と書いてあるが，これは「どんな厳しい状況下でも忍耐力があること」を強調するために持ち出した話だと考えられる。よって，正解は (D)。<br><br>highlight [háilàit] ～を目立たせる<br>demonstrate [démənstrèit] ～を実証する |

Questions 181-185 refer to the following advertisement and e-mail.

# Branson Lawn & Garden Co.
## We make the exterior of every home a lovely one.

- Lawn care
- Garden care
- Bush, tree and hedge trimming
- Special services as required

Deposits accepted but not required.
Handling both commercial and residential projects. Our clients include:
- *XSoft Computer Corporation*
- *Briar City Park*
- *Leviston Apartment Complex*
- *And homes all over the city*

*Voted Number 1 Landscaping Service by City Life Magazine*

Drop by our office at 302 Beckridge Way or contact us at: info@bransononline.com.

You'll be glad you did!

Our Management Team:
**Linda Wu** ———— President
linda.wu@bransononline.com
**Armando Benitez** — Personnel manager
armando.b@bransononline.com
**Mary Listz** ———— Client Project manager
mary.l@bransononline.com
**Frank Cole** ———— Equipment manager
frank.cole@bransononline.com

*On the job seven days a week, through all four seasons. All work done from November 1 through April 1 requires additional fees.

---

**E-mail**

From: michelle017@northtel.com
To: linda.wu@bransononline.com
Date: Monday, May 25
Subject: Your Company

Dear Ms. Wu,

Thank you for taking the time to talk with me on the phone earlier today. After doing so, I think I might be interested in hiring your company for some landscaping projects around my home. Ordinarily, I enjoy taking care of my yard and garden on weekends, but I'm so busy at the office nowadays it's hard for me to devote as much time to it as I used to.

I think that if you carried out the work we discussed for me every fourteen days, I could keep the greenery around my home looking good. So I'd like to start with that sort of schedule. However, weekly visits might be required during spring, when everything grows very fast. If your company also does snow removal, I might also have monthly work for you in winter, or more frequently according to the snowfall.

I understand you will be sending out one of your managers tomorrow who is responsible for customer cost estimates. During that meeting I would like to discuss the service contract, including all labor, equipment and other factors. I would prefer a complete total of that in your estimate, rather than being surprised later by unanticipated prices.

Best regards,

Michelle Walker

| 設問 | 設問の訳 | 正解と解説 |
|---|---|---|
| **181**<br>What is implied about Branson Lawn & Garden Co.?<br>(A) It accepts online payments.<br>(B) It offers big discounts.<br>(C) It has a good reputation.<br>(D) It does interiors as well as exteriors. | Branson 芝生と園芸社について何が示唆されていますか。<br>(A) オンラインによる支払いを受け付けている。<br>(B) 大幅な割引を提供している。<br>(C) 評判が良い。<br>(D) 外装だけでなく内装も行う。 | **正解 (C)**<br>広告の右下に, Voted number 1 Landscaping Service by *City Life Magazine* とあり, 良い評判を得ていることがわかるので, 正解は (C)。 |
| **182**<br>What is stated about Branson Lawn & Garden Co.?<br>(A) It serves only corporate clients.<br>(B) It requires a deposit before beginning work.<br>(C) It limits projects during some seasons.<br>(D) It charges more during certain periods. | Branson 芝生と園芸社についてどのようなことが述べられていますか。<br>(A) 法人顧客だけを取り扱っている。<br>(B) 作業を始める前に手付金を必要とする。<br>(C) ある季節には引き受ける仕事を制限する。<br>(D) 特定の時期にはより多く料金がかかる。 | **正解 (D)**<br>広告の下部に, All work done from November 1 through April 1 requires additional fees. とあり, ある一定の期間は追加料金がかかることがわかるので, 正解は (D)。広告の上部に Handling both commercial and residential projects. とあり, 法人も個人も扱うので (A) は不適切。手付金は必要ないとあるので (B) も不適切。<br>corporate client 法人顧客<br>charge [tʃɑːrdʒ] ~を請求する |
| **183**<br>How often does Ms. Walker want initial service?<br>(A) Every week<br>(B) Every other week<br>(C) Every month<br>(D) Every other month | どのくらいの頻度で Walker さんは最初のサービスを希望していますか。<br>(A) 毎週<br>(B) 2 週間ごと<br>(C) 毎月<br>(D) 2 か月ごと | **正解 (B)**<br>Walker さんが書いた E メールの第 2 段落を参照。every fourteen days「14 日ごと」の作業を希望しているので, その言い換えである (B) Every other week が正解。(A) は春の間, (C) は冬の間に頼むかもしれない頻度である。 |
| **184**<br>Who will Ms. Walker meet tomorrow?<br>(A) Linda Wu<br>(B) Armando Benitez<br>(C) Mary Listz<br>(D) Frank Cole | Walker さんは明日誰に会いますか。<br>(A) Linda Wu<br>(B) Armando Benitez<br>(C) Mary Listz<br>(D) Frank Cole | **正解 (C)**<br>Walker さんは E メールの第 3 段落で one of your managers ~ who is responsible for customer cost estimates「顧客コスト見積もりの責任者であるマネージャー」に会うと書いている。そこで広告を見ると, 経営チーム一覧から顧客プロジェクトマネージャーである Mary Listz のこととわかる。 |
| **185**<br>What is one request made by Ms. Walker?<br>(A) Getting a comprehensive quote<br>(B) Receiving fast performance<br>(C) Confirming top equipment<br>(D) Understanding project details | Walker さんが行った要請の 1 つは何ですか。<br>(A) 包括的な見積もりを得ること<br>(B) 速い作業を受けること<br>(C) 最高の機材を確認すること<br>(D) 仕事の詳細を理解すること | **正解 (A)**<br>Walker さんは E メールの第 3 段落で I would prefer a complete total of that in your estimate, rather than being surprised later by unanticipated prices. と, 後で予想外の価格に驚かないように完全な総額の見積もりが望ましいと言っている。その言い換えである (A) Getting a comprehensive quote が正解。<br>comprehensive [kàmprihénsiv] 包括的な<br>quote [kwout] 見積もり(価格) |

Questions 186-190 refer to the following letter, voucher, and Web page.

October 27

Richard Yeoh
Laxfield Office Supplies Corporation
7861 Clayton Plaza
Denver, CO 98775

Dear Mr. Yeoh,

I was sorry to hear that your stay at our hotel in Portland, Oregon, was less than satisfactory. You should not have had your seminars exposed to the noise from work crews renovating our lobby and main entrance. I understand that at many points your presenters struggled to be heard because of that.

Unfortunately, when taking your reservation for the Premier Gold Room, our receptionist made a mistake by overlooking the fact that it was adjacent to the areas under renovation. As a Sunshine Hotels Card member, you are entitled to nothing less than top-class service.

To make up for your inconvenience in some small way, I hope that you will accept the voucher enclosed.

With very best regards,

*Josef Loos*

Josef Loos
Vice President
Sunshine Hotels, Inc.

---

**Sunshine Hotels Inc.**
Taking care of you 365 days a year!

## Guest Voucher

This voucher entitles the bearer to a 50% discount on our hotels anywhere in the United States or Canada, including our Royal Suite or Deluxe Suite rooms.

Voucher No. A982JQRV08

Expires December 27
Non-transferable, single-use only

Sunshine Hotels Card members receive an additional 10% off. Valid only for online reservations at www.sunshinehotels/vouchers/. Please enter voucher number noted above.

| 問題文 | 問題文の訳 |
|---|---|

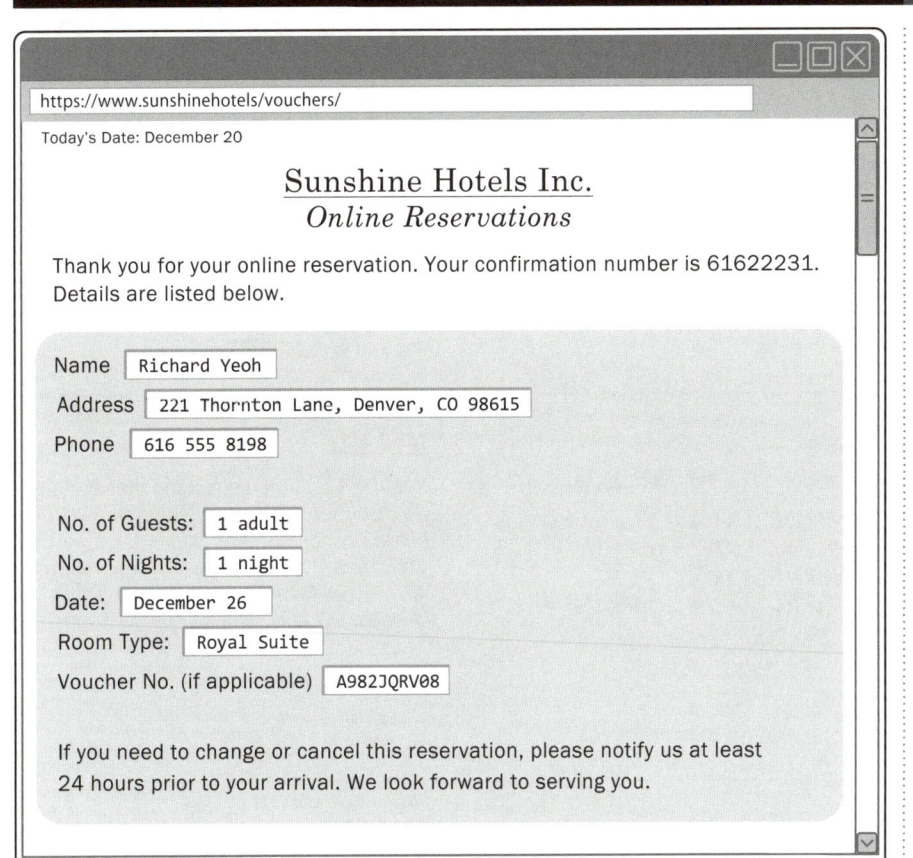

**問題文:**

https://www.sunshinehotels/vouchers/

Today's Date: December 20

### Sunshine Hotels Inc.
*Online Reservations*

Thank you for your online reservation. Your confirmation number is 61622231. Details are listed below.

Name: Richard Yeoh
Address: 221 Thornton Lane, Denver, CO 98615
Phone: 616 555 8198

No. of Guests: 1 adult
No. of Nights: 1 night
Date: December 26
Room Type: Royal Suite
Voucher No. (if applicable): A982JQRV08

If you need to change or cancel this reservation, please notify us at least 24 hours prior to your arrival. We look forward to serving you.

**問題文の訳:**

https://www.sunshinehotels/vouchers/
本日は 12 月 20 日

Sunshine ホテル社
オンライン予約

オンライン予約ありがとうございました。ご予約番号は 61622231 です。ご予約内容は以下の通りです。

お名前 Richard Yeoh
ご住所 221 Thornton Lane, Denver, CO 98615
電話番号 616 555 8198

ご宿泊人数：大人 1 人
ご宿泊日数：1 泊
日付：12 月 26 日
客室タイプ：ロイヤルスイート
割引券番号（適用可能な場合）A982JQRV08

この予約を変更またはキャンセルされる場合は，ご到着の 24 時間前までにご連絡ください。ご利用をお待ち申し上げております。

## Vocabulary

- voucher [váutʃər] 名 割引券, 商品引換券
- satisfactory [sæ̀tisfǽktəri] 形 申し分のない；満足のいく
- (be) exposed to ～ ～にさらされる
- presenter [prizéntər] 名 発表者
- receptionist [risépʃənist] 名 受付
- overlook [òuvərlúk] 動 ～を見落とす
- adjacent to ～ ～に隣接した
- be entitled to ～ ～を受ける資格がある
- nothing less than ～ ～に他ならない
- top-class [tɑ̀pklǽs] 形 最高の
- make up for ～ ～を埋め合わせる
- enclosed [inklóuzd] 形 同封された
- bearer [béərər] 名 持参者
- non-transferable [nɑ̀ntrænsfə́ːrəbl] 形 譲渡不可能な
- valid [vǽlid] 形 有効な
- if applicable 適用可能な場合

| 設問 | 設問の訳 | 正解と解説 |
|---|---|---|

### 186

What is the purpose of the letter?

(A) To confirm a reservation
(B) To explain facilities
(C) To reply to an inquiry
(D) To make an apology

この手紙の目的は何ですか。

(A) 予約を確認すること
(B) 施設を説明すること
(C) 問い合わせに答えること
(D) 謝罪をすること

**正解 (D)**

手紙の冒頭で宿泊客の滞在への不満に対して謝罪し，第3段落で To make up for your inconvenience in some small way, I hope that you will accept the voucher enclosed. と言ってお詫びの割引券を同封しているので，正解は (D)。

make an apology 謝罪する

### 187

What problem occurred at the seminars?

(A) Baggage was not delivered.
(B) Speakers could not be heard.
(C) Locations were changed.
(D) Presentations were rescheduled.

セミナーでどのような問題が起こりましたか。

(A) 荷物が届けられなかった。
(B) 話し手の話が聞こえなかった。
(C) 場所が変更された。
(D) プレゼンテーションの予定が変更された。

**正解 (B)**

手紙の第1段落の I understand that at many points your presenters struggled to be heard because of that. から，セミナーの発表者が騒音で声が届かず苦労したことがわかるので，正解は (B)。presenters を選択肢では speakers と言い換えている。

### 188

In the letter, the word "way" in paragraph 3, line 1, is closest in meaning to

(A) manner
(B) condition
(C) payment
(D) portion

手紙の第3段落・1行目の "way" に最も意味が近いのは

(A) 方法
(B) 状態
(C) 支払い
(D) 部分

**正解 (A)**

in some small way は「ささやかながら」という成句。way にはさまざまな意味があるが，文脈からここでは manner「方法」が最も意味が近い。in some ways「いくつかの点で，ある意味で」などの表現も確認しておくとよい。

### 189

What is the maximum discount available to Mr. Yeoh?

(A) 10%
(B) 50%
(C) 60%
(D) 70%

Yeoh さんが受けられる最大の割引はどれくらいですか。

(A) 10%
(B) 50%
(C) 60%
(D) 70%

**正解 (C)**

割引券を見ると，冒頭の1文から，持参者は50%割引されることがわかる。また，最後の段落から，カード会員はさらに10%割引が受けられる。手紙の第2段落最後の As a Sunshine Hotels Card member, you are entitled to ～から，Yeoh さんはカード会員であることがわかるので，受けられる割引は最大で 50 ＋ 10 ＝ 60% である。

### 190

What is indicated about Mr. Yeoh?

(A) He had seminars at a hotel near his office.
(B) He reserved the wrong room for the seminars.
(C) He will stay at a Sunshine Hotel on December 20.
(D) He was given a voucher valid for two months.

Yeoh さんについて何が示されていますか。

(A) 事務所の近くのホテルでセミナーを開いた。
(B) セミナー用に間違った部屋を予約した。
(C) 12月20日に Sunshine ホテルに宿泊する。
(D) 2か月間有効な割引券をもらった。

**正解 (D)**

手紙の日付 October 27 と，割引券の Expires December 27 から，割引券の有効期間は2か月だとわかるので，(D) が正解。(A) は，手紙のヘッダーから Yeoh さんの事務所はコロラド州（CO）だが，手紙の冒頭からセミナーで利用したホテルはオレゴン州なので，near が不適切。(B) は，Yeoh さんは騒音によって不満を感じたのであって wrong room を予約したとは言えない。(C) は，ウェブページを見ると滞在日が December 26 なので誤答。

Questions 191-195 refer to the following advertisement, form, and e-mail.

# Thorren Industries

## This Week's Top Properties!
### Philadelphia, Pennsylvania

■ *Downtown Office Space in Historic Building—18 Winston St.*
Entire 3rd floor (just under 8,000 sq. feet) in gorgeous historic brownstone, in the heart of downtown. Beautifully restored turn-of-the-century interior, but with all modern amenities including air conditioning and computer facilities.
$13.00/sq. feet/year
**Listing No. 32330**

■ *Modern and Convenient—Portmandieu Mall, 4325 Poplar Way*
Two adjacent showroom properties (about 3,000 sq. feet each) in quiet suburban location, in first-floor-only building. Up-to-date facilities. Just 30 minutes from downtown via expressway, Exit 351.
$13.00/sq. feet/year
**Listing No. 32338**

■ *Spacious Renovated Warehouse—2000 Industrial Drive*
Huge warehouse building, totally renovated. Easy access to the center of town, just 20 minutes by bus. Total 41,000 sq. feet. Landlord willing to subdivide, will rent space according to tenant needs.
$15.00/sq. feet/year
**Listing No. 41323**

For inquiries regarding the above properties, please visit our Web site at www.thorrenind.com/inquiries.

---

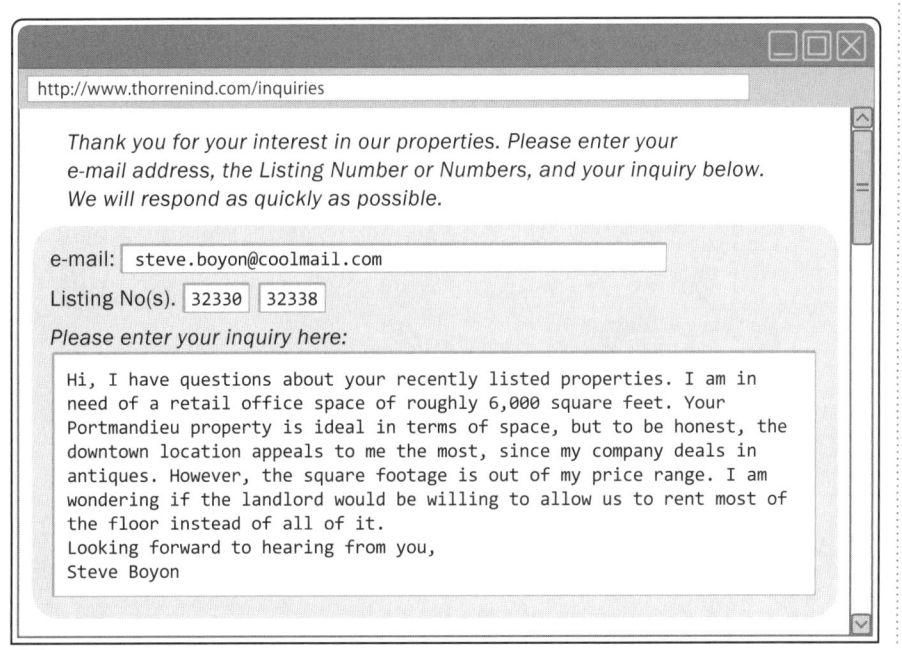

http://www.thorrenind.com/inquiries

*Thank you for your interest in our properties. Please enter your e-mail address, the Listing Number or Numbers, and your inquiry below. We will respond as quickly as possible.*

e-mail: steve.boyon@coolmail.com
Listing No(s). 32330  32338

Please enter your inquiry here:

```
Hi, I have questions about your recently listed properties. I am in
need of a retail office space of roughly 6,000 square feet. Your
Portmandieu property is ideal in terms of space, but to be honest, the
downtown location appeals to me the most, since my company deals in
antiques. However, the square footage is out of my price range. I am
wondering if the landlord would be willing to allow us to rent most of
the floor instead of all of it.
Looking forward to hearing from you,
Steve Boyon
```

## E-mail

**To:** steve.boyon@coolmail.com
**From:** anetta.fasiq@thorrenreal.com
**Date:** May 12
**Subject:** Listing No. 32330

Dear Mr. Boyon,

Thank you for your interest in this property. We have contacted the landlord, Mr. John Fedder. Unfortunately, he has informed us that the property cannot be subdivided. However, he commented that he has spent a lot of time and money having the building restored, and seemed delighted by the nature of your business. He has graciously offered to negotiate a better price per square foot. If this is of interest to you, please contact me via e-mail, or by phone at (612) 555-8181. I will contact him immediately and arrange for you to meet as soon as possible.

Regards,

Anetta Fasiq

---

宛先：steve.boyon@coolmail.com
送信者：anetta.fasiq@thorrenreal.com
日付：5月12日
件名：目録番号 32330

Boyon 様

本物件にご関心をお持ちいただきありがとうございます。家主の John Fedder さんに問い合わせましたが、あいにくこの物件は分割できないとのことです。しかし、建物の改修に非常に時間とお金をかけたとのことで、Boyon 様のご商売の性質に喜んでおられるようでした。彼は平方フィート面積当たりの価格を下げる交渉に快く応じてくれるそうです。もし、これにご興味がございましたら、E メールまたは (612) 555-8181 までお電話で当方にご連絡ください。すぐに彼に連絡を取って、なるべく早くお会いできる手配をいたします。

よろしくお願いします。
Anetta Fasiq

---

### Vocabulary

- □ property [prάpərti] 名不動産物件　□ in the heart of ~　~の中心に　□ restore [ristɔ́ːr] 動~を修復する
- □ amenity [əménəti] 名生活を便利にする設備　□ suburban [səbə́ːrbən] 形郊外の　□ landlord [lǽndlɔ̀ːrd] 名大家, 地主
- □ (be) willing to do　~するのに前向きである　□ subdivide [sʌ̀bdəváid] 動(~を)細かく分ける　□ according to ~　~に準じて
- □ tenant [ténənt] 名賃借人　□ in need of ~　~を必要として　□ roughly [rʌ́fli] 副およそ　□ in terms of ~　~の観点で
- □ appeal to ~　(人)の心に訴える　□ deal in ~　~を扱う　□ graciously [gréiʃəsli] 副寛大に, 快く　□ be of interest 興味深い

| 設問 | 設問の訳 | 正解と解説 |
|---|---|---|
| **191**<br>What most likely does Thorren Industries specialize in?<br>(A) Retail merchandising<br>(B) Real estate<br>(C) Building renovation<br>(D) Construction | Thorren 産業は何を専門にしていると考えられますか。<br>(A) 小売販売業<br>(B) 不動産業<br>(C) 建築リフォーム業<br>(D) 建設業 | **正解 (B)**<br>Thorren 産業は広告（1つ目の文書）を出した会社である。3つの不動産物件を紹介していることから，(B) が正解。<br><br>specialize in ～　～を専門にしている |
| **192**<br>What is the purpose of Mr. Boyon's inquiry?<br>(A) To negotiate a lower price<br>(B) To complete a lease<br>(C) To ask about rental terms<br>(D) To give feedback on a property listing | Boyon さんの問い合わせの目的は何ですか。<br>(A) 価格を下げる交渉をすること<br>(B) 賃貸契約をすること<br>(C) 賃貸条件について尋ねること<br>(D) 物件目録について意見を述べること | **正解 (C)**<br>Boyon さんはフォーム（2つ目の文書）の中で，2つの物件に言及し，後半ではダウンタウンの物件についてフロアを部分的に借りられないかと相談している。よって，(C) が正解。「予算を超えている」とは書いてあるが，価格交渉はしていないので (A) は不適切。<br><br>term [tə:rm]（複数形で）条項，条件 |
| **193**<br>What does Mr. Boyon imply about the property on Poplar Way?<br>(A) The space is ideal.<br>(B) It is too expensive for him.<br>(C) It is not conveniently located.<br>(D) It does not have adequate facilities. | Boyon さんは Poplar 通りの物件について何を示唆していますか。<br>(A) スペースが理想的である。<br>(B) 彼にとって価格が高すぎる。<br>(C) 立地条件が良くない。<br>(D) 適切な設備がない。 | **正解 (A)**<br>Poplar 通りの物件とは，広告にある2つ目の物件のことである。フォームの問い合わせの中で Boyon さんは，Your Portmandieu property is ideal in terms of space と書いていることから，(A) が正解。(B) は広告の1つ目のダウンタウンの物件のことである。立地条件については触れていないので，(C) は不適。 |
| **194**<br>What is implied about Mr. Fedder?<br>(A) He is fond of antiques.<br>(B) He specializes in renovation.<br>(C) He can rent out parts of his property.<br>(D) He has contacted Mr. Boyon. | Fedder さんについて何が示唆されていますか。<br>(A) 骨董品が好きである。<br>(B) 改修が専門である。<br>(C) 持ち物件を部分的に貸し出せる。<br>(D) Boyon さんに連絡を取った。 | **正解 (A)**<br>Eメールの情報から，Mr. Fedder とは，20世紀初頭のインテリアを持つダウンタウン物件の家主で，「the nature of your business に喜んでいる」とある。Boyon さんの商売は，フォームに my company deals in antiques とある。つまり，Fedder さんは骨董品が好きだと推測できるので，(A) が正解。スペースは分割できないと言っているので，(C) は不適切。<br><br>be fond of ～　～が好きである |
| **195**<br>In the e-mail, what does Ms. Fasiq say she can do for Mr. Boyon?<br>(A) Help reduce the rental price<br>(B) Accelerate the rental process<br>(C) Recommend a different property<br>(D) Renovate some facilities | Eメールで，Fasiq さんは Boyon さんのために何ができると言っていますか。<br>(A) 賃貸料を下げる手助けをする<br>(B) 賃貸手続きを早める<br>(C) 別の物件を勧める<br>(D) いくつかの設備を修繕する | **正解 (A)**<br>Eメール中盤の He has graciously offered to negotiate a better price ～から，家主が価格交渉に応じることを伝えている。最後に If this is of interest to you, please contact me ～と言っていることから，(A) が正解と判断できる。<br><br>accelerate [æksélərèit]（進行）を早める，速める |

Questions 196-200 refer to the following draft slide and e-mails.

**X-Cola Consumers: Survey Responses by Age Group** (DRAFT 1)

| Age Group | Number of Responses |
| --- | --- |
| 20-29 | 705 |
| 30-39 | 142 |
| 40-49 | 117 |
| 50+ | 51 |

Hansen Food & Beverage Corporation
X-Cola Market Research Team
Julia Arbenz, Team Leader

Note to Eric: Here's the first draft of the slide for the presentation on Wednesday, for your review. Please e-mail me as soon as possible with any feedback. Thanks! — Julia

---

* E-mail *

**To:** Julia Arbenz <j.arbenz@x-cola.com>
**From:** Eric Bradshaw <eric.b@x-cola.com>
**Date:** January 14, 11:56 A.M.
**Subject:** Consumer data, first draft

Hi Julia,

Thanks for your hard work. At a glance, the data doesn't look that different from last year's. First, it might be good to make the table into a chart. Also, this year, could we add data for consumers between the ages of 13 and 19? In other words, teenagers, but we can label this group "young adults."

The reason I ask is, our senior staff have already proposed diverting more money to ad campaigns for people 30 and over, but personally I'm a little hesitant to concur with that idea.

If you have any survey data on young adults, would you send it to me, as well as your thoughts? I'd appreciate both.

Thanks,

Eric Bradshaw
Marketing Director, Hansen Food & Beverage

## 問題文

**\* E-mail \***

**To:** Eric Bradshaw <eric.b@x-cola.com>
**From:** Julia Arbenz <j.arbenz@x-cola.com>
**Date:** January 14, 1:02 P.M.
**Subject:** Re: Consumer data, first draft

Hi Eric,

I just checked the data you requested. Surprisingly, the number of responses was even lower than the 50+ age group in the survey results I sent in the first draft.

However, that might be because teenagers simply don't bother to return as many surveys as people in older age brackets. So, in actuality, the number of teenage consumers might be greater.

In any event, from a research perspective, I am inclined to side with your opinion. If you would like me to convey that to the senior staff, please let me know. I'll be sending you an updated slide momentarily.

Best wishes,

Julia

## 問題文の訳

宛先：Eric Bradshaw <eric.b@x-cola.com>
送信者：Julia Arbenz <j.arbenz@x-cola.com>
日付：1月14日午後1時2分
件名：Re: 消費者データの第1草案

こんにちは，Eric

あなたに頼まれたデータを今確認しました。驚いたことに，回答数は私が草案1で送った調査結果の50歳以上の層よりさらに低いものでした。

でもそれは，ティーンエイジャーが単に年齢層のより高い人たちほどわざわざアンケートに回答しないせいかもしれません。だから，実際はティーンエイジャーの消費者数はもっと多い可能性があります。

とにかく，調査の立場からは，私はあなたの意見を支持したいと思います。それを上級社員に私から伝えてほしいなら，知らせてください。すぐ改訂したスライドを送ります。

よろしくお願いします。
Julia

## Vocabulary

- □ draft [dræft] 图 草案　□ at a glance 一見したところ　□ in other words 言い換えると，つまり　□ label A B　A を B に分類する
- □ divert money to ～　～に金を回す　□ personally [pə́ːrsnəli] 副 個人的には　□ be hesitant to do　～するのをためらう
- □ concur with ～　～に同意する　□ bracket [brǽkit] 图 同類として区分されるグループ[人々]　□ in actuality 現実に，実際は
- □ perspective [pərspéktiv] 图 見方，視点　□ be inclined to do　～したいと思う　□ side with ～　（議論などで）～の側に付く
- □ convey A to B　A を B に伝える　□ momentarily [mòumənté(ə)rili] 副 すぐに

| 設問 | 設問の訳 | 正解と解説 |
|---|---|---|
| **196**<br>What most likely is Julia's job position?<br>(A) Team assistant<br>(B) Senior manager<br>(C) IT specialist<br>(D) Marketing analyst | Juliaの職位と考えられるのは何ですか。<br>(A) チームの助手<br>(B) シニアマネージャー<br>(C) ITの専門家<br>(D) マーケティングアナリスト | **正解 (D)**<br>Juliaは調査結果のスライドを作成した人物。表の下にある情報から，JuliaはX-Colaの市場調査チームのリーダーである。1通目のEメールからJuliaの上司と思われるEricがマーケティング部長であることや2人のEメールのやり取りの内容などから考えて，Juliaの職位として最も可能性が高いのは(D)である。 |
| **197**<br>What is indicated about the number of teenage consumer responses?<br>(A) It is significantly small.<br>(B) It has increased proportionally.<br>(C) It is the same as last year.<br>(D) It is as was expected. | ティーンエイジャーの消費者の回答数について何が示されていますか。<br>(A) 著しく少ない。<br>(B) 比例的に増加した。<br>(C) 昨年と同じである。<br>(D) 予想されていた通りである。 | **正解 (A)**<br>2通目のEメール冒頭にI just checked the data you requested. とあるが，これは1通目のEメールでEricが依頼した若年層の調査データのこと。これについてJuliaはeven lower than the 50+ age group in the survey results ～と書いている。そこで1つ目の文書のX-Cola消費者の調査結果を見ると，50歳以上の層が51人で最も少なく，ティーンエイジャーの回答数はこれよりさらに少ないということなので，(A)が正解。<br>significantly [signífəkəntli] 著しく，かなり<br>proportionally [prəpɔ́ːrʃnəli] 比例的に |
| **198**<br>What does Julia imply about ad campaign money?<br>(A) It should be spent on ads for younger people.<br>(B) It has already been raised by her team.<br>(C) It is sufficient for more ads to be made.<br>(D) More funding is needed for further research. | 広告キャンペーンのお金についてJuliaはどんなことを示唆していますか。<br>(A) 若者向けの広告に使われるべきである。<br>(B) 彼女のチームによってすでに調達されている。<br>(C) より多くの広告を作るのに十分である。<br>(D) さらなる調査にもっと資金が必要である。 | **正解 (A)**<br>Juliaは2通目のEメールの第3段落でI am inclined to side with your opinion と書いている。Ericの意見とは，1通目のEメールの「30歳以上の人たちに向けた広告キャンペーンにもっとお金を回すという上級社員の提案に同意できない」という意見を指す。2人はティーンエイジャーのデータを利用することで，この提案に反対しようとしていることから，(A)が正解。同意表現のside with ～とconcur with ～もポイントである。 |
| **199**<br>In the second e-mail, the word "brackets" in paragraph 2, line 2, is closest in meaning to<br>(A) lengths<br>(B) ranges<br>(C) differences<br>(D) targets | 2通目のEメールの第2段落・2行目の"brackets"に最も意味が近いのは<br>(A) 長さ<br>(B) 範囲<br>(C) 違い<br>(D) 目標 | **正解 (B)**<br>bracketは名詞で「同類として区分されるグループ[人々]」という意味があるが，この意味を知らなくても，people in older ageに続く名詞を考えると推測がつく。X-Cola消費者の調査結果を見ると20-29や30-39など，年齢に幅があることから，(B) ranges「範囲」が意味として最も近い。調査結果の表や2通目のEメール第1段落にあるage groupのgroupも同意である。 |
| **200**<br>What does Julia say she will do next?<br>(A) Reexamine the data<br>(B) Contact senior staff<br>(C) Call Eric<br>(D) Provide a new slide | Juliaは次に何をすると言っていますか。<br>(A) データを再調査する<br>(B) 上級社員に連絡する<br>(C) Ericに電話する<br>(D) 新しいスライドを提供する | **正解 (D)**<br>Juliaは2通目のEメールの最後でI'll be sending you an updated slide momentarily. と書いていることから，(D)が正解。sendをprovide, an updated slide をa new slideと言い換えている。 |

# MEMO